INDIAN NATIONAL EVOLUTION

INDIAN NATIONAL EVOLUTION

A BRIEF SURVEY OF
THE ORIGIN AND PROGRESS OF
THE INDIAN NATIONAL CONGRESS,
AND THE GROWTH OF INDIAN NATIONALISM

BY
AMVIKA CHARAN MAZUMDAR

GYAN

Published by

GYAN

Gyan Publishing House
5, Ansari Road
Daryaganj, New Delhi-110002
Phone: 011-47034999, 9811692060
E-mail: books@gyanbooks.com

Distribution Network
gyanbooks.com
India, USA, Canada, UK, Australia, France

ISBN: 978-81-212-8252-9 (PB)
First Published, 1915

2nd Impression 2023

Printed at: Gyan Press, Delhi.

INDIAN NATIONAL EVOLUTION
Author: AMVIKA CHARAN MAZUMDAR

INDIAN NATIONAL EVOLUTION

A BRIEF SURVEY OF
THE ORIGIN AND PROGRESS OF
THE INDIAN NATIONAL CONGRESS
AND THE GROWTH OF INDIAN NATIONALISM

BY

AMVIKA CHARAN MAZUMDAR.

SECOND EDITION.

PRICE Rs. Five

G. A. NATESAN & CO.,
MADRAS.

NOTE TO THE SECOND EDITION.

The first edition of this book was brought out in September, 1915. Advantage has been taken by the author of the issue of this second edition to add more incidents in connection with the origin and early stages of the Congress Movement and to bring the book itself up to date *i.e.* down to the last Congress at Lucknow of which the author, the Hon. Mr. Amvica Charan Muzumdar was the President.

The publishers are gratified at the ready welcome accorded by the public to the account of the national movement from the pen of one of the oldest of the congress veterans.

It is hoped that this new and revised edition will meet with equal success.

November, 1917. *The Publishers.*

PREFACE TO THE FIRST EDITION.

Sometime in August 1913 at the instance of some friends I undertook to write a few articles for a magazine on the Rise and Growth of the Indian National Congress, the most important and phenomenal movement in the political history of new India. After only a few pages were written, it was discovered that such a subject could not be properly dealt with in the spare columns of any magazine in the country without taxing its capacity to an unreasonable extent and that for a much longer period than was perhaps consistent with the sustained interests of such a review. The idea was, therefore, abandoned. In January following while turning over some of the materials which I had collected and arranged for the articles, it occurred to me that these might be published in the form of a pamphlet so that they may be of some use to any one who may be disposed to write a well-digested history of this evolutionary movement. That is the origin of the little volume which is now presented to the public. The book was fairly completed by July 1914 when it was partly handed over to Mr. G. A. Natesan of Madras, who kindly undertook to illustrate and publish it. In August the great War broke out and as the book necessarily contained occasional criticisms of Government, it was deemed proper and expedient to defer its publication until the War conditions were fairly settled. Those conditions having passed the doubts and uncertainties, as well as the excitement, of the preliminary stage and taken a definite shape as also a favourable turn, the book is now issued to the public.

My most grateful acknowledgments are due to my esteemed friend and chief, the Hon'ble Mr. Surendranath Banerjea, who not only readily supplied me with whatever information I wanted from him, but also in the midst of his multifarious duties, kindly went through a considerable portion of the manuscript. I am also deeply indebted to my esteemed friends, Mr. D. E. Wacha and Mr. G. Subramania Iyer for a lot of valuable information which they from time to time gave me regarding their respective Presidencies. To Sir William Wedderburn I am no less deeply indebted for the kind permission which he gave me for the free use of his excellent memoirs of Allan Octavian Hume, though I was precluded from using any of his private correspondence. Mr. G. A. Natesan of Madras materially helped me with a number of his valuable publications bearing on the Congress; while to the Education Department of the Government of India I feel deeply obliged for the courtesy and readiness with which they supplied me with the Educational Statement of March, 1914. Mr. Satyananda Bose, the energetic Secretary of the Bengal Provincial Congress Committee, was good enough to supply me with the papers relating to the Surat incident which will be found in an appendix. Lastly, I am highly indebted to my friends Mr. Amrita Chandra Ghosh of the Ripon College, Calcutta, and Mr. Prithwis Chandra Ray, late Editor of the *Indian World*, who kindly undertook to read my proofs when my eyes being affected I was incapacitated from dealing with them myself.

I am perfectly conscious of the many defects which will be noticed in these pages mostly written at intervals of a protracted and distressing illness. These defects may, however, stimulate others to write a more careful and exhaustive book on the subject. If in the meantime these imperfect and desultory notes will attract the attention of my young friends of the rising generation and direct them to a careful study of the Indian Problems and of the Indian Administration, I shall deem my humble labours as amply rewarded.

FARIDPORE,
Sept. 1915. AMVIKA CHARAN MAZUMDAR.

ILLUSTRATIONS.

CONTENTS.

APPENDIX A.

APPENDIX B.

APPENDIX C.

APPENDIX D.

INDEX

THE VENERABLE VETERANS.

HUME DADABHAI WEDDERBURN

W. C. BONNERJEE
PRESIDENT, 1885.

INDIAN NATIONAL EVOLUTION.

CHAPTER I.

INTRODUCTORY.

A FULL and critical account of the origin, progress and development of an epoch-making political event in any country is always a very delicate and difficult task; for, the secret and sometimes silent origin of such a movement, like the many-sided meandering course of a deceptive rivulet at its source, is often shrouded in the mazes of imperfect records and conflicting reports; while the subtle influence of jealousy and spite on the one hand, no less than that of suspicion and distrust on the other, leading to misrepresentations and exaggerations, serves not a little in its onward course to obscure the vision and warp the judgment of contemporary minds. Then the effects of divergent views and colliding interests have also to be reckoned with to no small extent. Even the histories of such great events as the birth of American Independence and the establishment of the French Republic, not to speak of the Great Revolution, have not been altogether free from doubts, difficulties and contradictions. But if the histories of revolutions are sometimes so varying and divergent in their accounts, the history of an evolution must be still more obscure and defective in its narratives. There a much larger area of time and space is covered by the slow and silent trend of gathering events which in their noiseless progress at first naturally attract much less attention and are more tardily recognised than the sensational and dramatic developments of a revolution, and then by the time the tangible results of these events begin to be realised much of the historical accuracy of the process is lost, if not actually sacrificed, to the extravagant demands of either individual or sectional pride and egotism. The history of the Indian National Congress is the history of the origin and development of national life in India, and a bare epitome of that history would involve a critical analysis of the diverse phases of that life in its different bearings and with all its recommendations and its lapses, as well as its successes and its failures during the past thirty years. The object of this book is not, however, to attempt such a venturesome task, nor has the time probably fully arrived for a complete and well-digested history to be written on this great evolutionary movement. Its humble aim is to record a few contemporaneous events and impressions which, in the peculiar shortness of Indian memory on matters historical, are already fast drifting towards the realm of faint traditions, and thus to rescue them from possible oblivion, so that they may be of some use to the future historian. For a correct and adequate appreciation of the movement, it would, however, be necessary to recapitulate, though very briefly, the condition of the country immediately preceding its inauguration, as well as the circumstances which gradually led up to its inception.

The Indian National Congress marks an important epoch in the history of British Rule in India. Apart from the questions of reforms with which it is immediately concerned, it is engaged in a much wider and nobler task for which it has already laid a fairly solid foundation —the task of Nation-building in India after the model of modern Europe. Coming in contact with Western people and Western culture the Indian mind could not fail to expand in the direction of Western ideas and institutions. It is as impossible for one civilization, whether superior or inferior, to come in touch with another civilization without unfolding its own characteristics, as it is impossible for one vessel to throw its search-light upon another without exposing its own broad outlines to the gaze of the latter. A barbarous race may become extinct; but two civilized people coming in close contact are in spite of all their differences and conservatism bound to coalesce and act and react upon each other. The superior may dominate the inferior; but cannot transform it altogether: while the latter, however vigorously it may struggle to maintain its peculiar identity, is bound gradually and even unconsciously to imbibe and assimilate, either for the better or for the worse, some of the properties of the former. The Indian National Congress and the evolution which is slowly working its way through almost every phase of Indian life, are the natural and visible manifestation of such a contact.

CHAPTER II.

THE GENESIS OF POLITICAL MOVEMENT IN INDIA.

Raja Ram Mohan Roy, the recognised progenitor of modern India, was the first apostle of a political creed based upon constitutional agitation in this country. But the political gospel which his versatile genius preached was, under the circumstances of the country very properly subordinated to the prior claims of religious, social and educational reforms, and like all gospels of truth, which have revolutionised human society whether in ancient or modern times, it naturally took time to establish its hold upon the public mind and present any tangible results. His mission to England in 1832 was no doubt a political one; but the remarkable evidence which he gave before a committee of the House of Commons attracted more attention in England than in India, and although that evidence was largely responsible for some of the reforms effected in the Indian administration shortly after his death the Indian public were very little influenced by it at the time. It was not until the fifties of the last century that with the dawning light of Western Education, of which the pioneer Indian Reformer was perhaps the greatest champion of his time, the public mind began to expand and political ideas and activities began to manifest themselves in one form or another in different parts of the country. Since then an association here and an association there sprung up, like a few oases in the desert, some of which no doubt possessed a degree of vitality, but most of which were of ephemeral existence. The British Indian Association in Bengal and the Bombay Association in the Western Presidency were almost simultaneously started about the year 1851, the former under the guidance and inspiration of stalwarts like Mr. Prasanna Kumar Tagore, Dr. Rajendralal Mitra, Mr. Ramgopal Ghosh, Raja Digamvar Mitter, Mr. Pearychand Mitter and Mr. Harish Chandra Mukherjea, the pioneer of independent Indian journalism; while the latter owed its origin to the patriotic labours of Mr. Jugganath Sankersett, who was the first non-official member of the Bombay Legislative Council established in 1863, and of that venerable political Rishi who, thank God, after a strenuous active life extending over half a century, now sits in his quiet retreat at Versova as the patron saint of the Indian political world silently watching and guarding its interests and occasionally cheering it with messages of hope and confidence—Mr. Dadabhai Naoroji.* As the genius of Mr. Kristodas Pal ultimately raised the British Indian Association to a power in Bengal, so the Bombay Association owed not a little of its usefulness to its subsequent acquisition of the services of Sir Mangaldas Nathubhoy and Mr. Naoroji Furdunji who for his stout and fearless advocacy of the popular cause received, like Ramgopal Ghosh and Kristodas Pal in Bengal, the appellation of the "Tribune of the People" in connection with his many fights in the Municipal Corporation of Bombay so graphically described in that excellent book which has

* *Died on June 30, 1917.*

recently been written by Mr. Dinshaw Edulji Wacha on "*The Rise and Growth of Bombay Municipal Government.*"* But while the British Indian Association has vigorously maintained a useful existence for more than half a century, the Bombay Association did not survive more than a decade, and although it was revived in 1870 and galvanized into fresh life by Mr. Naoroji Furdunji in 1873, it shortly became practically extinct in an unequal competition with the East India Association which again in its turn fell into a moribund condition in the early eighties. The Southern Presidency was still more slow in developing its public life; there was an old association called the "Madras Native Association," chiefly worked by some officials, which possessed very little vitality and had practically little or no hold upon the public mind in Madras. Madras was first vivified into life by that able and independent journal, *The Hindu*, which was started in 1878 under the auspices of a galaxy of stars in Southern India composed of Ananda Charlu, Veeraraghavachari, Rangiah Naidu and G. Subramania Iyer (alas! all of whom have now vanished into space). At Poona the *Sarvajanik Sabha* was started towards the middle of the seventies under the management of Rao Bahadur Krishnaji Laxaman Nulkar, Mr. Sitaram Hari Chiplonkar and several other gentlemen of light and leading who gave the first impetus to public activities in the Deccan.

These were practically all the important public bodies in the country between the fifties and the early

* *The Rise and Growth of Bombay Municipal Government.* By D. E. Wacha. G. A. Natesan & Co., Publishers, Madras.

seventies of the last century which, though exercising no inconsiderable influence within their limited spheres of particular activities, were but the general exponents of particular interests and for a long time devoted mainly to occasional criticisms of important administrative or legislative measures affecting their respective provinces. Constructive policy they had none, and seldom if ever they laid down any programme of systematic action for the political advancement of the country. In fact the idea of a united nationality and of national interests; the cultivation of politics in its wider aspects as the fundamental basis of national progress and not merely as a means to temporary administrative make-shifts; the all-embracing patriotic fervour which like the Promethean spark has now made the dead bones in the valley instinct with life; and, above all, the broad vision of political emancipation which has now dawned upon the people and focussed their energies and has directed their operations towards a definite goal and common aspiration, throwing all local and sectional considerations largely into the background—these were still very remote though not altogether foreign to the aims and objects of these Associations. But from this it must not be inferred that it is at all suggested, that these conceptions were the sudden evolution of a single year, or the revelation of a single evangelist who saw them in an apocalypse and proclaimed them to a wondering people at a single session of the Congress in the blessed year of 1885. Great events always cast their shadows before. Prior to 1880 even the semblance of a political status the people had none, while their economic condition was becoming more and more straitened every day. Indian wants and grievances were accumulating with the rapidly changing conditions of the country, education was expanding Indian views and aspirations and Indian thoughts from various causes had been for a long time in a state of ferment vainly seeking for some sort of palliatives for the complicated diseases from which the country had been helplessly suffering in almost every direction. Many were thus the causes at work which contributed towards forcing the educated Indian mind into new channels of thought and action.

CHAPTER III

The Early Friends of India.

It must be gratefully recorded that while India was thus struggling in a sub-conscious state, alternating between hope and despair, painfully alive to her sufferings, yet quite helpless as regards any appropriate and effective remedy, she was not a little comforted by the fact that even among Englishmen, who were held responsible for the situation, there were men who, though they belonged to a particular nationality, were men born for justice and fairness towards suffering humanity. Since the time of Edmund Burke scarcely a voice had been heard in England in favour of the "voiceless millions" of India until John Bright sounded his warning note against the injustice systematically done to this country. In 1847 Bright entered Parliament and he was not long in the House of Commons before his generous impulses turned his attention to India. From 1847 to 1880, amidst his multifarious duties as a British politician and cabinet minister, he worked for India as none had worked before him. In the famous debate on Sir Charles Wood's India Bill of 1853, Mr. Bright entered a vigorous protest against the system of Government established in India and categorically pointed out nearly all the defects of that system some, if not most, of which are still applicable to the present-day arrangement. In his passionate eloquence he called the attention of the House to the extreme inadequacy of Parliamentary control over the administration of India which both sides of the House formally agreed in proclaiming as a "solemn sacred trust", though neither side raised its little finger even to treat it as more than a grazing common. He held that there was no continuity or consistency of any settled policy with regard to India, while everything was allowed to drift, there being no real disposition to grapple with any difficulty; that Indian opinion was unanimous in calling for a constitutional change and in complaining of the delay and expense of the law courts, the inefficiency and low character of the police and the neglect of road-making and irrigation; that the poverty of the people was such as to demonstrate of itself a fundamental error in the system of Government; that the statute authorising the employment of Indians in offices of trust was a dead letter; that the continuance of the system of appointments and promotion by seniority in the covenanted service was a "great bar to a much wider employment of the most intelligent and able men among the native population;" that taxation was clumsy and unscientific and its burden intolerable to a people destitute of mechanical appliances; that the salt-tax was unjust and the revenue from opium precarious; that the revenue was squandered on unnecessary wars; that the Civil Service was overpaid; that there was no security for the competence and character of the collectors whose power was such that each man could make or mar a whole district; that Parliament was unable to grapple fairly with any Indian question; that the people and Parliament of Britain were shut out from all considerations in regard to India, and that "on the whole the Government of India was a Government of secrecy and irresponsibility to a degree that should not be tolerated." In the peroration of this remarkable speech referring to the Indian people John Bright said:—

> "There never was a more docile people, never a more tractable nation. The opportunity is present, and the power is not wanting. Let us abandon the policy of aggression and confine ourselves to a territory ten times the size of France, with a population four times as numerous as that of the United Kingdom. Surely, that is enough to satisfy the most gluttonous appetite for glory and supremacy. Educate the people of India, govern them wisely, and gradually the distinctions of caste will disappear, and they will look upon us rather as benefactors than as conquerors. And if we desire to see Christianity, in some form professed in that country, we shall sooner attain our object by setting the example of a high-toned Christian morality, than by any other means we can employ."

Again in 1858 when the question of the reconstitution of the Government of India came up for discussion in Parliament after the Mutiny, John Bright submitted a scheme of his own for the better Government of India embodying many a liberal principle which have not yet been fully accepted. He contended that

> "The population of India were in a condition of great impoverishment and the taxes were more onerous and oppressive than the taxes of any other country in the world. Nor were the police arrangements, administration of justice, the educational policy and the finances in a satisfactory condition."

And he urged that what was wanted with regard to the administration of India was "a little more daylight, more simplicity and more responsibility." It may not be generally known that, although Lord Derby had a just tribute paid to him for the drafting of the Great Proclamation of 1858, its original inspirer was John Bright. In the celebrated speech to which reference has just been made, he said:

> "If I had the responsibility of administering the affairs of India there are certain things I would do. I would, immediately after the Bill passes, issue a Proclamation in India which should reach every subject of the British Crown in that country and be heard of in the territories of every Indian prince or *rajah*."

Much of what he suggested was actually embodied in the Greart Proclamation and almost in the form and style in which the originator of the idea put it. According to Bright's biographer, the opportunity of "administering the affairs of India" was actually offered to him by Mr. Gladstone in 1868, but unfortunately for India he did not see his way to accept the Indian portfolio, not only because the task was too heavy for his delicate health, but also because he thought that public opinion in England was not sufficiently advanced to allow him to adopt his views with regard to the Government of India. But although he declined to be the Secretary of State for India he never lost sight of India during his active Parliamentary career which extended down to 1886. So great was his genuine sympathy for the Indians, that when on a certain occasion a responsible member in the House of Commons made certain unparliamentary observations with regard to the people of India Mr. Bright indignantly observed :—

> "I would not permit any man in my presence, without rebuke, to indulge in the calumnies and expressions of contempt which I have recently heard poured forth without measure upon the whole population of India."

And in that last great speech, which he made touching India in the House of Commons, he poured forth his genuine love for the Indian people in the following pathetic strain :—

> "All over those vast regions there are countless millions, helpless and defenceless, deprived of their natural leaders and their ancient chiefs, looking with only some small ray of hope to that omnipresent and irresistible power by which they have been subjected. I appeal to you on behalf of that people. I have besought your mercy and your justice for many a year past : and if I speak to you earnestly now it is because the object for which I plead is dear to my heart. Is it not possible to touch a chord in the hearts of Englishmen, to raise them to a sense of the miseries inflicted on that unhappy country by the crimes and the blunders of our rulers here ? If you have steeled your hearts against the natives, if nothing can stir you to sympathy with their miseries, at least have pity upon your own countrymen."

It may be interesting to learn that the great Indian orator, the late Mr. Lal Mohan Ghose, was a political disciple of John Bright and the masterly diction and style which he commanded in his orations he inherited from his great master. The one great lesson which he learnt from John Bright, as he himself once said to the writer of these pages, was to make as few speeches as possible, but always to make those few speeches telling and effective—a lesson which the apt Indian pupil religiously enjoined upon himself with rather too much austerity in his after-life.

Next to John Bright, Henry Fawcett was one of the greatest and truest friends of India in England. He was a trained financier and economist and entering Parliament in 1865, he soon found ample materials to direct his attention to the Government of India which soon earned for him the sobriquet of "Member for India" by his close vigilance and unremitting attention to the Indian finance. Mr. Fawcett always maintained that "the natives of India should be given a fair share in the administration of their own country" and that the ablest among them should be provided with "honourable careers in the public service". In 1868 he accordingly moved a resolution in the House of Commons for holding the Civil Service Examination simultaneously in Calcutta, Bombay and Madras, as well as in London. It was precisely the same resolution which 25 years later Mr. Herbert Paul moved and carried in the House to be only ignominiously consigned ultimately into the dusty upper shelves of the India Office. He bitterly complained of the culpable apathy and indifference of the British Parliament towards the grievances of the Indian people. Twitted in Parliament and not unoften charged outside it with neglecting the interest of his own constituency, Fawcett fought for India single-handed with a resoluteness of purpose, sense of justice and mastery of facts which extorted the admiration of even his worst critics. Addressing his own constituency of Brighton in 1872, he said:—

> "The most trumpery question ever brought before Parliament, a wrangle over the purchase of a picture, excited more interest than the welfare of one hundred and eighty millions of our Indian fellow-subjects. The people of India have no votes, they cannot bring even so much pressure to bear upon Parliament as can be brought by one of our Railway Companies; but with some confidence I believe that I shall not be misinterpreting your wishes if, as your representative, I do whatever can be done by one humble individual to render justice to the defenceless and powerless."

While on another occasion speaking from his place in the House of Commons he boldly said, that all the responsibility resting upon him "as a member of Parliament was as nothing compared with the responsibility of governing 150 millions of distant subjects." In 1870 Fawcett vehemently protested against the orthodox practice of introducing the Indian Budget at the fag end of a session to be silently debated before empty benches. He maintained that India was a poor country and complained that the British public failed to appreciate the dangerously narrow margin upon which the mass of the population lived on the verge of starvation. In 1871 it was at his instance that a Parliamentary Committee was appointed to inquire into the financial administration of India, he himself being elected as its President. All this time India was keenly watching the movements of the one man who was single-handed, fighting her cause against tremendous odds, and in 1872 a huge public meeting in Calcutta voted an address to Fawcett expressing India's deep gratitude towards him and urging him to continue the fight in defence of her dumb and helpless millions which he had voluntarily and so generously expoused. At the general election of 1874, Fawcett, like many other Liberals, lost his seat for Brighton and for the first time in those days, India seemed to have practically risen to the exigencies of the situation. A subscription was at once started in this country and a sum of £750, in two instalments, was remitted to England to enable Fawcett to contest another seat at the earliest opportunity, and soon after, Fawcett was returned member for Hackney. In 1875 Fawcett vigorously opposed Lord Salisbury's well-known ball to the Sultan of Turkey at the expense of India. Fawcett was not satisfied with his specious plea and pointedly asked Lord Salisbury how he could "reconcile it to himself to tax the people of India for an entertainment to the Sultan" in England. It was on this occasion that Fawcett coined that smart expression which has since become so familiar in English phraseology. He described the ball as an act of 'magnificent meanness" which in later years Lord Morley by slight embellishment converted into "magnificent melancholy meanness" on the occasion of the Suakim Expedition. The "magnificent meanness," the first of a series, was committed in spite of Fawcett's spirited protest and was soon followed by the Abyssinian war when the member for India again stood in defence of the dumb Indian tax-payer, and it was owing to his repeated protests that at last the cost of that unrighteous and abortive war was divided between England and India. Fawcett again protested when the Duke of Edinburgh's presents to the Indian princes were also debited to the Indian account, and violently opposed another proposal for display of "magnificent meanness" by debiting the entire expenses of the Prince of Wales' visit to India to the Indian revenues, and as a result of this protest poor India escaped with the payment of £30,000 only, making the *magnificence* of the *meanness* still more visible. In 1877 he denounced Lord Lytton's unjust and indefensible sacrifice of the cotton import duties for the sake of party interest in England and raised, though ineffectually, his loud voice against the unconscionable extravagance of the Delhi Assemblage in the midst of a terrible famine. Lord Lytton's Afghan War also came under the searching examination and scathing criticism of Fawcett who, in 1879, brought forward another motion asking for the appointment of a Select Committee of the House to enquire into the working of the Government of India Act. In 1880 Fawcett had the satisfaction of seeing at the end of a series of extravagance of a dark and dismal administration the dawn of a bright morning ushered by the appointment of the Marquess of Ripon as Viceroy and Governor-General of India.

Last but not least there was Charles Bradlaugh, the poor errand boy, who had by the sheer force of his character raised himself into a power in British politics of the nineteenth century. Born of the people

JOHN BRIGHT.

THE MARQUIS OF RIPON.

HENRY FAWCETT.

CHARLES BRADLAUGH.

his attention and sympathies were naturally directed towards the people. Charles Bradlaugh was however slow in developing his sympathy for India; but having once developed that sympathy he became the staunchest friend of the Indian people. It has been truly said that "slow rises merit when by poverty depressed," and added to that this freedom of conscience proved a serious obstacle from his early career towards his advancement in public life. But even in the midst of the deadly struggle in which he was engaged, with very few friends to back him up and a host of enemies to put him down, in his legitimate way to Parliament, he never ceased to study Indian problems. His prominent attention to India was drawn by the Ilbert Bill agitation of 1883. The man who in his early career had espoused the side of Republican France against Imperial Germany, the man who had enlisted his sympathies for the Italian patriots, Garibaldi and Mazzini and congratulated Signior Castela upon the establishment of a republic in Spain, was not likely to tolerate the grossly selfish and insensate opposition raised against a measure which aimed at nothing more than the removal of an unjustifiable stigma on the Indian judiciary in the administration of their own country. Mr. Bradlaugh's subsequent labours in the cause of India relate to a later period and will be noticed in their proper place.

These three remarkable British statesmen were among the early pioneers of Indian reform in the British political field. Most of their projects no doubt failed, as they were bound to fail in a cold atmosphere of ignorance, apathy and indifference: but they largely succeeded in drawing the attention of the British public to the affairs of India and in impressing them with the idea that there was at least something rotten in the state of Denmark. They also by their example served in a large measure to conciliate Indian feeling and inspire the Indian mind in the seventies and early eighties with the hope that all may still be well. There were many in those days to twit these political philosophers and brand them as visionaries; but the time may not be far distant when they will be fully recognised by all parties concerned as the truest friends of both India and England.

Following in the footsteps of this distinguished triumvirate there were also a few other fair-minded Englishmen who interested themselves in Indian affairs at this early stage. Among these may be mentioned Sir James Caird, Sir William Hunter, Lord Dalhousie, Mr. R. T. Reid, M. P., Mr. Slagg, M. P., Mr. Baxter, M. P., and last but not least that extraordinary Englishwoman who, having passed through different phases in her life and undergone persecutions of no ordinary character, has at last made India her home and her special interest—Mrs. Annie Besant. In 1878 when Benjamin Disraeli was the Premier and Lord Lytton the Viceroy of India, Mrs. Besant, who was then the friend and co-adjutor of Charles Bradlaugh, wrote a little book entitled *England, India and Afghanistan* exposing the misrule in India in such fierce and bitter language that it has been truly observed by a shrewd writer that "if it were published by an Indian at the present time he would likely enough strand himself into difficulties of a highly serious character." Lord Ripon's sympathies for India even after his retirement were too well-known to require any mention. If the utterances of these early friends of India in England failed to render any immediate practical good to India, they at all events served to inspire men of light and leading in this country with the hope and confidence that if they could organize themselves and carefully formulate their grievances, men would not be wanting in England to defend their cause either on the floor of Parliament, or at the bar of public opinion in Great Britain.

In India and among the Anglo-Indian officials, Mr. A. O. Hume was for a long time noted for his strong sympathies for the Indian people. His kind and considerate treatment of the people of Etawah during the dark days of the mutiny endeared his name throughout the Punjab and led the people of the country justly to regard him as a friend and as a rare officer truly worthy of the administration of Clemency Canning. Sir Henry Cotton in Bengal and Sir William Wedderburn in Bombay also developed their love for the Indian people from an early stage of their Indian career, and both of them suffered not a little in the hand of the bureaucracy for their remarkable independence and strong sense of justice and fairness. These three Anglo-Indians were regarded as the most sincere friends of the people and the brightest ornaments of the Indian Civil Service.

CHAPTER IV.

THE INDIAN PRESS.

While the public associations were thus slowly but steadily inoculating the educated community in the country with political thoughts and ideas, and the early friends of India in England persistently, though ineffectually, drawing attention of the British public to Indian affairs, there was yet another and a more powerful agency at work silently moulding and shaping public opinion on a much larger scale throughout the country. The Indian Press, which, like the public Associations, was founded after the Western model, was with the rapid spread of education steadily gaining in strength and rising into power. The early history of that Press does not date back earlier than 1780 when the *Bengal Gazette* was started in Calcutta. From that time to the first decade of the nineteenth century it was practically an English Press conducted in English and managed and edited by Englishmen only. The Indo-English and the Vernacular Press were of much later growth and strange as it may sound, the Vernacular Press preceded its Indo-English comrade. The Vernacular papers were at first few and feeble and not much given to politics. The *Sambad Kaumudi* of Raja Ram Mohan Roy, the pioneer of pure Indian Journalism, sometimes purveyed but rarely criticised the acts of the administration. It was generally devoted to social, religious and educational questions, although it must be conceded that as the Raja was the founder of the Bengali Press he was also the first and foremost advocate of the liberty of the Press in India. From 1799 to 1834 the Press in India was kept under strict censorship and instances were neither few nor far between where European editors sharply criticising the Government were visited with deportation to Europe. In 1835 the Government of Sir Charles Metcalfe restored the freedom of the Press and it was from this time that the Vernacular Press began to make rapid strides and the Indo-English Press gradually came into existence. The *Probhakar* of Iswarchandra Gupta was probably the earliest Vernacular paper in the country, which ventured to tread on political grounds though not without a faltering step and quivering hand. The Gagging Act of Lord Canning, necessitated by the exigencies of the Mutiny in 1858, was in force only for a year and did not much interfere with the normal expansion of the Press. The *Hindu Patriot*, the *Hurkura*, the *Indian Mirror*, the *Amrita Bazar Patrika*, which was at first an Anglo-Vernacular paper, the *Brahmo Public Opinion* which, under the name of *Bengal Public Opinion*, was subsequently incorporated with the *Bengalee*, the *Reis and Rayet*, the *Somprokash*, the *Nababibhakar*, the *Sulabh Samachar*, a pice paper, the *Sanjibani*, the *Sadharani* and latterly the *Hitavadi* and several others in Bengal; the *Rast Goftar*, the *Bombay Samachar*, the *Indu Prakash*, the *Jam-e-Jamshed*, the *Maharatta* and latterly the *Dnyan Prokash* and the *Kesari* in Bombay; the *Hindu*, the *Standard*, the *Swadesha Mitran* and several other papers in Madras, and laterly the *Tribune* in Lahore, the *Herald* in Behar and the *Advocate* in Lucknow became powerful instruments of political education for the people and exercised considerable influence over the public mind up to the eighties of the last century. In spite of all that was said, written or done against it, the growth and development of the Indian Press was almost phenomenal, so that in 1875 there were no less than 478 newspapers in the country the bulk of which were conducted in the vernacular languages and freely circulated broadcast throughout the country. In Bengal particularly quite a number of cheap news sheets, written mostly in the Bengali language, purveying all sorts of informations and criticisms, sometimes ill-informed and sometimes over-balanced, but seldom losing touch with the new spirit, rapidly sprung up, and congregations of dozens of eager, illiterate listeners to a single reader of these papers at a stationery stall or a grocer's shop in the leisurely evening became a common sight. Thus from the petty shop-keeper to the princely merchant and from the simple village folk to the lordly landed aristocracy all were permeated with the spirit of this Press. The Anglo-Indian Press, though now naturally jealous of its formidable rival, was in those days sometimes conducted in a more liberal spirit and contributed not a little to the diffusion of western methods of criticism and the expansion of the political views of the people. It is not contended that a section of this Press was not altogether amenable to the charge so often levelled against it, that it was as inefficient as it was ill-informed and injudicious; but it can hardly be denied that on the whole the much-abused

Indian Press acted not only as a powerful adjunct towards popular education, but might have with a little more sympathetic treatment been easily turned into a useful guide to a more popular administration. John Bright, speaking of the Indian Press of the time, once made the following trenchant observation :—

> "There are two sets of newspapers, those first,—which are published by Englishmen,, and these being the papers of the services, cannot, of course, be in favour of economy. They assail me every time I mention India in a speech, if it is even only in a paragraph, and no doubt they will do the same for what I am saying now. Then there are the native papers; and although there are a great many published in the native languages, still they have not much of what we call political influence. The Government officials look into them to see if they are saying anything unpleasant to the Government—anything that indicates sedition or discontent, but never for the purpose of being influenced by the judgment of the writers and editors. The actual press of the country, which touches the Government is the press of the English; and that press, generally, has been in favour of annexation of more territory, more places, more salaries and ultimately more pensions."

What a mastery of facts relating to India which he had never visited and what a remarkable insight into its internal administration with which he was never connected? It would perhaps be no wonder if Indian youths of the present generation, who know nothing about the situation in the seventies and eighties of the last century, were to regard the above observation as only a prophetic pronouncement of the present-day condition of the Indian Press clothed only in the language of the past. Lord Lytton, like Lord Wellesley, became nervous and, at the instance of an impatient bureaucracy, gagged the Vernacular Press in 1878. Four years later the Vernacular Press Act was repealed by Lord Ripon as an early instalment of his noble policy of conciliation. The subsequent history of the Indian Press is well-known and though not altogether irrelevant, it seems hardly necessary to pursue it for the purpose of this narrative. Suffice it to say, that with all its defects and lapses, as well as its numerous disadvantages, difficulties and disabilities, the Indian Press has played an important part in the evolution of the national life, and its chequered history is no mean evidence of the sustaining energies of a growing people. It has suffered in the past and is passing through a severe ordeal at the present moment. From the proud position of the Fourth State it has been reduced since 1910 to a humble suppliant before a district officer with the halter tight around its neck, and yet there is no knowing when that halter will be either removed or relaxed to enable it to breathe more freely. But there is no cause for despair. The Indian Press Act of 1910, with its drastic provisions for security, forfeiture and prosecutions without any remedy and the almost arbitrary powers vested in the magistrates, is no doubt a serious menace to the healthy growth of public opinion in the country and has practically paralysed for the moment all honest and independent criticism ; but all violent measures defeat their own end and the vitality of a national life gathers strength not so much from easy indulgence as through violent repression. Liberty is always nurtured on the lap of Persecution and " action and reaction " is the law of Progress in all living organisms.

CHAPTER V.

The Gathering Clouds.

Those who confidently indulge in lavish criticisms of the present unrest as a sudden and unprecedented development of public agitation in this country would do well to remember; that it is not altogether a new organic change in the body politic, but only a recrudescence of the malady, though somewhat in an aggravated form, from which the country has suffered in the past and is likely to suffer still more for some time at least in future. The Government of the East India Company was largely tainted with corruption, and the trial of Warren Hastings and the judicial murder of Nund Coomar were only typical illustrations of the kind of administration established in this country since the battle of Plassey. The military rising of 1857 was a protest against that scandalous administration, although for the time being religion was the ostensible compelling force. Though the people wisely and loyally dissociated themselves from that protest there are enough evidence on record to show that there was as much discontent among them as there were insecurity, inequality and injustice prevailing in the country. The transfer of the sovereignty of the country from the Company to the Crown in 1858, therefore, led not a few to suppose that a millennium was at last in sight and the change was hailed by the people with a deep sigh of relief; while the great Proclamation simultaneously issued to the princes and the peoples of

India filled the public mind with high hopes of reform and progress. But a few years' experience greatly disappointed them. For, although peace was restored and substantial measures were adopted for the improvement of the administration of justice and three Universities were established in the three Presidencies for the spread of education among the people, the political aspect of the defunct administration remained altogether unchanged, if it did not in some respect become even more retrograde. The Secretary of State for India became a more autocratic and irresponsible substitute for the Court of Directors without, however, a Board of Control to supervise his action; while the control of Parliament which used periodically to enquire into the affairs of India upon the renewal of the Company's charter at the end of every twenty years—a salutary check faithfully exercised since 1773—was practically wholly removed. A whole nation was disarmed and the entire administration was vested in a bureaucracy which with all its recommendations became in its gradual development as imperious in its tone and as unsympathetic in its attitude as it was saturated with the principles and prejudices of autocratic rule. That bureaucracy was no doubt at times and within certain limits, generously disposed to grant patronage and extended favours of a minor description to any native of the country who might successfully court them: but as regards any material advancement and participation in the administration, the entire population were jealously kept at arm's length and the slightest indication on their part of a desire to enter even the border land of its close preserves was resented as an intolerable and dangerous trespass. In fact no better expression than "benevolent despotism" could be coined honestly to denote the form of administration established in the country. The vast mass of the people were suffering from abject poverty and practically living on "one meal a day"; while at recurring intervals of few years they were decimated not by hundreds or thousands, but by hundreds of thousands, through famine and pestilence. The indigenous industries of the country were ruined and the bulk of the population driven to the soil to eke out a precarious subsistence as best as they could and left wholly without any substantial means to keep the wolf out of the door. The people had neither any share nor any voice in the administration which was conveniently allowed to drift according to the current of events and circumstances. The feeble and ineffectual complaints from time to time made either by the public Associations, or by the Press, and the failure of the spasmodic, though perfectly honest, efforts made by Government towards a superficial treatment of these organic deseases caused a deep and widespread commotion among a patient and docile people until a strong tide set in to swell the wave of popular restlessness and discontent. The invidious distinction sharply drawn along the whole line between the ruling race and the ruled, and the repeated instances of glaring and irritating miscarriage of justice in cases between Indians and Europeans—a most deplorable phase, if not a foul blot, still extant—served as a constant reminder to the educated community, which every year received fresh accessions to its strength, weight and importance, that some solution must be found for this highly unsatisfactory, if not intolerable, situation. That situation however reached its climax during the weak and extravagant Viceroyalty of Lord Lytton who in his innate love for the romance came with a light heart to play the role of an administrator in a country fabled for its romances. The military ruled, while a selfish, short-sighted bureaucracy found it convenient to pander to the extravagant tastes and designs of a modern Dupleix without however the consummate powers and abilities of the great French adventurer. The costly and gigantic farce of the Delhi Assemblage was enacted in 1877 while a terrible famine was committing havoc among millions of helpless population in Southern India whose dire effects were severely felt even in Bengal and the Punjab, and which led an intrepid veteran journalist in Calcutta openly to declare that "Nero was fiddling while Rome was burning." The wanton invasion of Cabul, the massacre of Sir Louis Cavagnari, and his staff followed by the Second Afghan War; the large increase of the army under the hallucination of the Russian bugbear; the costly establishment of a "scientific frontier" which afterwards did not stand the test of even a tribal disturbance, the complete disarming of an inoffensive and helpless population, although the Eurasians were left untouched; the gagging of the Vernacular Press as a means to stifle public voice against all these fads, which led another indomitable journalist in Bengal to convert in one night a Vernacular paper into an English journal; the sacrifice of the import cotton duties as a conservative sop to

Lancashire, and the unmerited and undignified rebuff administered by the Viceroy personally to a leading association in the country which had the temertiy to raise its voice against this iniquitious measure and which was deeply resented by the entire Indian Press not altogether unsupported even by a section of the more fair-minded Anglo-Indian journalists, followed in quick, bewildering succession; and at last a reckless bureaucratic Government, as bankrupt in its reputation as in its exchequer, sat trembling upon the crumbling fragments of a "mendacious budget" on one side and the seething and surging discontent of a multitudinous population on the other. The theory of the disappointed place-seekers" and the "microscopic minority" of the educated community was invented to minimise the importance of the growing unrest. The educated community in the minority in every country, but none the less it is everywhere the mouthpiece of the majority and the exponent of the popular voice. History does not perhaps present a single instance where the mass has been actively associated in any evolution, although it has everywhere been largely in evidence in a revolution. Besides, if any evidence were needed to show that the discontent had sunk deep into the mass, enough of such evidence was furnished to an unbiassed mind by the mass-meetings held at Jhingergacha, Salem and other places where the people attended in their thousands to ventilate their grievances though they were unable to formulate any remedy.

It was about this time that the Indian Association was established in July 1876 with the object of organising a system of active political propaganda throughout the country and to rouse the people to a sense of political unity and concerted activity. As the British Indian Association was mostly composed of the landed aristocracy, the Indian Association became the centre of the educated community in Bengal. Its moving spirit was Mr. Surendra Nath Banerjee who had, luckily for himself and for the country, been recently discharged from the Civil Service and whose talents and abilities, but for this incident, would in all probability have remained buried among the dusty shelves of either a Divisional Office or a Secretariat and entirely lost to the country. In the establishment of the Indian Association, Mr. Banerjee was associated with that brilliant star of Eastern Bengal, Mr. Ananda Mohan Bose, and assisted by a band of energetic men among whom the late Mr. Dwaraka Nath Ganguly, Mr. Bama Charan Banerjee, the brother of Mr. Justice Pramada Charan Banerjee and the founder of the Utterparah Hitakari Sabha, Mr. Bhairab Chandra Banerjee, cousin of Mr. W.C. Bonnerjee, and Mr. Jogendra Chandra Vidyabhushana who was one of the early pioneers of practical social reform and a remarkably independent member of the subordinate Judicial and Executive Service, are worthy of particular mention. The first president of the Association was that eminent jurist, the author of the *Vyadastha Darpan*. Mr. Shama Charan Sarkar who was shortly afterwards succeeded by the illustrious savant and linguist, the Rev. Dr. K.M. Banerjee. The first secretary was Mr. A. M. Bose both on account of his high attainments as well as probably because it was not deemed expedient at the outset to place a "dismissed servant of Government" at the executive head of a newly established political association. That "dismissed servant of Government" has however long outlived that dreaded disqualification which was not only voluntarily removed by a Lieutenant Governor, but acted as no bar to his being twice elected by his countrymen as president of the great National Assembly, four times as their trusted representative in the Bengal Council and at last as a prominent member of the Supreme Legislative Council. The Indian Association was hardly a year old when the Government of Lord Salisbury reduced the age-limit for the Civil Service examination to nineteen years. Strong and emphatic were the protests raised throughout the country and none stronger or more emphatic than that entered by Mr. Dadabhai Naoroji, a host in himself, through the columns of the English Press. The new Association however went upon a somewhat different plan. It at first organised a representative meeting held at the Calcutta Town Hall and armed with its mandate opened a political campaign, the first of its kind throughout the country. Mr. Surendra Nath was chosen as the first missionary to undertake this active political propaganda. He made his first tour in the summer of 1877 all through Northern India from Benares to Rawalpindi. The principal questions raised in this campaign were (1) the raising of the age-limit for the Civil Service examination which a conservative Government had reduced to such an extent as to practically shut out all Indians from admission into that service, and (2) the establishment of Simulaneous Examinations held both in England and in India for the recruitment of the service. Meetings were held and adressed by the rising orator at Benares, Allahabad, Lucknow, Cawnpore, Meerut, Agra, Delhi, Aligarh, Amritsar, Lahore and Rawalpindi, at all of which he was listened to with breathless attention which led Sir Henry Cotton to make pointed reference to this significant incident in his *New India.* At the Aligarh meeting Sir Syed Ahmed himself presided and strongly supported the proposed Simultaneous Examination, though for reasons best known to him, as a member of the Public Service Commission, he afterwards resiled from that position. The great meeting at Lucknow was held in the historic *Burdwari* palace and was attended, as at Aligarh, by a large number of respectable Mussalmans who form such an influential majority in that city. On his return journey Mr. Banerjee stopped at Bankipur and addressed a meeting there. The tour was a grand success and, as remarked by Mr. Nam Joshi of the Poona Sarvajanik Sabha, fully demonstrated that educated India, despite all racial and linguistic differences, could easily be brought upon a common platform on political ground. It will be remembered that Mr. Banerjee also attended the Delhi Assemblage as the representative of the *Hindu Patriot.* Men like Sir Jamsetji Jeejeebhoy, the second baronet of that name, Mr. Viswanath Narain Mandlik, Sir Mangaldas Nathubhoy and Mr. Naoroji Furdoonji with many others from different parts of the country witnessed the brilliant function. It must have struck these men of light and leading, that if the princes and the nobles in the land could be forced to form a pageant for the glorification of an autocratic Viceroy, why could not the people be gathered together to unite themselves to restrain, by constitutional means and methods, the spirit of autocratic rule? Mr. Banerjee personally gave expression to a similar sentiment on a subsequent occasion which will be noticed in its proper place. The idea worked and was freely, though somewhat vaguely, discussed in the Associations, as well as in the Press. The platforms had not up to this time come into such prominent use as now for the discussion of political subjects. Verily good often cometh out of evil, and if the idea of a united India was presented by a spectacular demonstration, the Delhi Assemblage of 1877 was, in spite of its extravagance, truly a blessing in disguise. Mr. Murdoch gives currency to an opinion that "the idea of a Congress was suggested by the great International Exhibition" held in Calcutta in 1884. But the more generally accepted and consistent theory seems to be that it had its inspiration from the Delhi Assemblage of 1877. The Exhibition might have supplied an immediate impulse to put the idea into execution, but if ever there was an object lesson, as contemporary testimony bears out that there was, for the great movement, that lesson could only have been furnished by the Assemblage and not the Exhibition, as the one could appeal only to the passive admiration of the people for the economic and scientific development of the world; while the other was calculated directly to force their attention to the political aspect of it, and as the country secretly resented the useless display, the princes on account of their humiliation and the people for its painful extravagance, it is not unnatural to suppose that it created a general desire to draw some honey out of the sting. Besides, the object-lessons presented by the Assemblage could not be wholly lost upon the mind of a quick and imaginative people. Encouraged by the success of his first tour Mr. Surendra Nath Banerjee undertook a second tour in the following year. In 1878 he travelled through Western and Southern India holding meetings at Bombay, Surat, Ahmedabad, Poona and Madras, and as a result of this campaign an All-India Memorial was presented to the House of Commons on the Civil Service question.

CHAPTER VI.

THE CLOUDS LIFTED.

Whether it was a mere accident, or the part of a settled policy, a progressive and broad-minded statesman of the School of Bentinck and Canning followed a short-sighted and reactionary administrator of the Dalhousie type: Lord Lytton was succeeded by Lord Ripon. He was evidently chosen by the Government of Mr. Galdstone to save the situation, and inspired by a genuine desire for the permanent good of England and India, Lord Ripon came holding the olive branch of peace, progress and conciliation for the people. Landing in Bombay in January 1880 the first words which the noble Marquess uttered were:—" Judge me by my acts and not by my words." And judged he was by his various acts of beneficence and high statesmanship which, in spite of the systematic attempts of successive administrations to stunt, stint and starve, if not actually rescind them, stand to this day as the strongest cement which not only successfully averted at the time the severe shock of a lowering storm, but still holds a discontented yet grateful people reconciled to the unpopular methods of a bureaucratic administration. Few Englishmen in this country probably even now realise and appreciate what and how much they owe to that large-hearted nobleman and far-sighted statesman whom they were not ashamed at the time foolishly to hoot and insult even under the gates of Viceregal palace. Lord Ripon at once put an end to the Afghan War and further development of the Scientific Frontier which with the reckless expenditure of the pageant show at Delhi had drained the public Exchequer to such an extent as to compel the author of these extravagances ultimately to submit to the humiliation of having recourse to a secret loan raised at the metropolis with the help of a plastic lieutenant and through the good offices of a prominent leader of the people who acted as a non-commissioned broker in the transaction. Lord Ripon concluded an honourable treaty with the Ameer which has since proved a much stronger bulwark against Russian invasion than the fortifications in the Khyber and Bolan Passes. Lord Ripon understood that the most effective defence of India lay in the construction of a *rational interior* rather than of a *scientific frontier* broad-based upon the contentment, gratitude and loyal co-operation of a prosperous people, and one of the first acts of his great administration was the repeal of the obnoxious and invidious Vernacular Press Act amidst the rejoicings of a whole nation when not a few of those who had stood at the baptismal front to announce themselves as its godfather eagerly came forward with their "shovelful of earth" to bury the ill-starred measure. Then came the inauguration of Local Self-Government throughout the country, the greatest measure ever inaugurated by any Viceroy either before or after him. It was the first step taken towards the political enfranchisement of the people. In foreshadowing the future of the measure the noble Viceroy courageously observed that "Local Self-Government must precede National Self-Government." With all its drawbacks and difficulties it has initiated the people in the art of local administration and supplied a nucleus and a basis for the recent expansion of the Legislative Councils. It may not be known to many that Lord Ripon also contemplated a tentative reform of the Indian Legislative Councils. But there was yet another measure of his reign which further stimulated the political activities of the people and roused their national self-respect. In evolution the highest successes are often achieved through reverses and the Ilbert Bill turned a signal defeat into a decisive victory. Lord Ripon made a desperate attempt, even at no small personal risk, to remove the racial bar which he found to be one of the foulest blots in the administration of criminal justice in this country. The matter was initiated by a spirited note submitted by Mr. B. L. Gupta to the Government of Sir Ashley Eden in 1882. In the autumn session of 1883 the Hon. Mr. C.P. Ilbert, as Law Member to the Council introduced a Bill which afterwards went by his name with the object of removing the improper disqualification attaching to the Indian Magistracy in the trial of European and American offenders. It was a spark thrown into a powder magazine, and the entire Anglo-Indian community, both official and non-official, at once rose in arms headed by a rebellious Lieutenant-Governor to oppose the innovation, not so much from a real sense of actual danger as through pride and vanity of a ruling race coupled with a feeling of practical immunity which they enjoyed under the existing system. Lord Ripon stood alone having his own Council, including the Commander-in-Chief, divided against him, with only the nominal support of the framer of the Bill and of Major Baring, now Lord Cromer. We have it on the authority of Mr. Buckland that "a conspiracy had been formed by a number of men in Calcutta who had bound themselves in the event of Government adhering to their projected legislation to overpower the sentries at Government House, to put the Viceroy on board a steamer at Chandpal-Ghat and send him to England *via* the Cape." The existence of this conspiracy, it is said, was known to the Lieutenant-Governor of Bengal and also to "the responsible officer" who subsequently gave this information to the author of "Bengal under the Lieutenant-Governors." The Europeans have taught many a lesson to the Indians, but, thank God, they forebore to teach them this one lesson of supreme folly. An Anglo-Indian Defence Association was hurriedly organised and at its instance a wanton and savage attack was made upon the natives of the country by a rising English counsel in Calcutta, which was followed by an equally virulent rejoinder from an eminent Indian member of the same bar, and the estrangement of the two communities was complete. But while the opposition to the Bill was so well organised, the support given to it by the Indian community was certainly very weak and extremely inadequate. The agitation stirred up the public mind only in Bengal and Bombay. An influential public meeting was held in the Bombay Town Hall which voiced Indian public opinion in the Western Presidency and several demonstrations were held in Bengal in support of the measure. But the agitation produced little or no effect in Madras, while the N.W. Provinces and the Punjab were perfectly silent. Practically most of the agitation was confined to violent recriminations in the columns of the Press. Lord Ripon's just and generous attempt practically failed and a *concordat* was arrived at towards the close of the year 1883 upon a bare recognition of the principle in the case of the District Magistrates and the Sessions Judges only. A section of the Bengal public seemed at first irreconcilable to the "Compromise" and it was feared that it was going to "throw native Bengal into a fury" making the position of the great Viceroy still more critical. Bombay discovered the rock ahead and promptly issued a manifesto counselling the country to stand by the much-abused Viceroy. This timely action successfully baulked the Anglo-Indians and their organs of their secret desire to see the Viceroy suffer as much in the hands of the Indians as he had suffered at their own. But though the measure failed, it opened the eyes of the people to two cardinal points in the case. It was recognised that the failure was largely owing to the want of adequate, vigorous and united support throughout the country to counterbalance the spirited and well-organised opposition of the Anglo-Indian community, and it was further felt that if political advancement were to be achieved it could only be by the organisation of a national assembly wholly devoted to wider politics than hitherto pursued in the different provinces independently of each other. The Ilbert Bill agitation thus went a great way towards impressing the Indian races, that in the political world success did not depend so much upon men as on organized efforts and so paved the way to united and concerted action. It also proved an eye-opener to those talented and highly educated Indian gentlemen who having returned from England and adopted English habits and manners had lost nearly all touch with their countrymen and were apparently seeking to form a class by themselves in the vain hope of assimilating themselves as far as practicable with the Anglo-Indian community. Forces were thus at work driving the people from different points of the compass to a common fold and to concentrate their thoughts, ideas and activities to a common focus for the attainment of the political rights and privileges of the people who being under a common rule, it was understood, could have but a common goal and a common destiny. All the time the Indian Press throughout the country was incessantly urging the people to unite under a common standard.

CHAPTER VII.

THE DAWNING LIGHT.

Almost simultaneously with the close of the Ilbert Bill agitation, the new idea, as indicated above, forcibly burst forth into the minds of the people, and Bengal, Bombay and Madras set to work to put their own houses in order and prepare themselves for the coming struggle. In Bengal, a new institution was started in 1884 which, in its constitution, as well as in its aim and object, bore ummistakable testimony to the fact that the old orthodox associations of the previous generation were also caught in the rising tide and had considerably drifted away from their original moorings. The National League was established under the leadership of Sir Joteendra Mohan Tagore, who was then the first citizen in the metropolis and one of the central pillars of the British Indian Association, with the question of representative institutions for India in the forefront of its programme.

But there was yet another movement in Bengal which seems to have anticipated the Congress by two years and in a large measure prepared the ground for the great national assembly. At the instance of the Indian Association a National Conference was held in Calcutta in 1883 with almost the same programme which was subsequently formulated by the first Congress held two years later in Bombay. The Conference was held at the Albert Hall, opposite the old Hindu and

Sanskrit Colleges on the south and the new Presidency College buildings on the west. It is a historic place associated with the Royal family and other memories and a wise and thoughtful government has recently saved it from a threatened destruction. It was an unprecedented gathering attended by a large number of educated men from different parts of Bengal and in which old men like the venerable Ramtanu Lahiri rubbed their shoulders with a much younger generation headed by Messrs. Ananda Mohan Bose and Surendra Nath Banerjee. It was an unique spectacle and the writer of these pages still retains a vivid impression of the immense enthusiasm and earnestness which throughout characterised the three days' session of the Conference and at the end of which everyone present seemed to have received a new light and a novel inspiration. It was in his opening address at this Conference that Mr. Surendra Nath Banerjee referring to the Delhi Assemblage exhorted the audience to unite and organise themselves for the country's cause. It is worthy of note that Mr. Wilfred Blunt and Mr. Seymour Keay, M. P., were present at the Conference. Mr. Seymour Keay spoke at the meeting, while Mr. Blunt has left a pointed notice of this significant movement in his personal memoirs. In the following year, when the great International Exhibition was held in Calcutta, the Conference could not somehow be organised ; but this year Mr. Surendra Nath made his third tour visiting this time Multan and other places in the Punjab where he preached the importance of national unity and the necessity of establishing a national fund for the systematic carrying out of a political propaganda.

In Madras the old "Madras Native Association" which, in the words of Mr. G. Subramania Iyer, dragged on for some years only "a spasmodic life" died a natural death with its last feeble gasp over the Self-Government Resolution of Lord Ripon's Government. But the quiet and steady people of the Southern Presidency at this stage organised a more powerful and energetic political association to keep themselves abreast of the sister presidencies in the coming struggle. The "Madras Mahajana Sabha" was established early in 1884 under the auspices of those thoughtful and sagacious publicmen who had started the *Hindu* in 1878. This new association was invested with a truly popular and representative character and it naturally very soon enlisted the active sympathy and co-operation of almost all the culture and public spirit of the presidency. As the popular Viceroy could not arrange to pay a parting visit to Madras before leaving for England at the close of a most brilliant and beneficent reign, the Mahajana Sabha sent a deputation to Bombay to bid farewell to Lord Ripon whose departure from this country was marked by an outburst of popular demonstration simply unparalleled not only in India but also probably in the history of any other civilised country. Before the deputation started there was also a Provincial Conference held in Madras. Both in the capital city as well as in the districts of the Presidency several active and energetic men came into prominence and began to work harmoniously under the guidance of the *Hindu* and the "Mahajana

Sabha" for public weal. It seems worthy of remark that though Madras was rather slow in developing her public life, she has been most forward in associating herself with the work of the Congress since its establishment. Not only in the first session but in almost all the subsequent sessions of the Congress, she has, despite her distance and other inconveniences, both climatic as well as social, contributed a larger contingent of delegates than any other province, the particular province where each session was held being of course excepted.

A great development also took place at this juncture in the politicial life of Bombay. Every since the collapse of "the old Bombay Association" that great city of light and leading had no popular political organisation to join hands with the sister presidencies in undertaking any common political movement. But from this it is not to be understood that she was altogether a *Sleepy Hollow*. Apparently cold, calculating Bombay was usually immersed in business taking things quite easy under ordinary circumstances, but when the wind blew high she at once put forth all her sails and was seldom found to lag behind any of the provinces in any public movement, although the occasion and its turmoil over, she again relapsed into her ordinary calm. But this was not a condition which was permissible in the coming contest. "Even five years before," wrote a political Rishi in 1885, "the country was wont to set its eyes on Calcutta and take its inspiration more or less from her." "The luminous intellect," he added, "and the spirit of eloquence which the Babu carries about him wherever he goes, as if it were his natural birth-right, gave him a vantage ground over the rest of India." But the new situation demanded all the provinces not only to rally under one common standard, but also to share equal responsibility and to assume equal command. Bombay was equal to both. A public meeting of the citizens of Bombay was convened on the 31st January, 1885, at the Framjee Cowasjee Institute in response to an invitation from that distinguished triumvirate who largely controlled the public life of the Western Presidency, the Hon. Mr. Budruddin Tyabjee, Mr. Pherozeshah Mancherjee Mehta and the Hon. Mr. Kashinath Trimbak Telang. The meeting was presided over by the distinguished Parsi baronet Sir Jamsetjee Jejeebhoy, and the present "Bombay Presidency Association" was ushered into existence under very happy auspices and with imposing ceremony. Mr. Pherozeshah Mehta, the Hon. Mr. K. T. Telang and Mr. Dinshaw Eduljee Wacha were appointed Joint Secretaries, a position which the last named gentleman still holds with no small credit to himself and to the Association.

Another incident, as narrated by Mrs. Annie Besant in her admirable book, *How India Wrought for Freedom* took place about this time. In December 1884 there came a number of delegates from different parts of the country to the Annual Convention of the Theosophical Society at Adyar. After the Convention was over seventeen prominent Indians met in the house of Dewan Bahadur Raghunath Rao in Madras. They were the Hon'ble Mr. S. Subramania Iyer, Mr. P. Rangiah Naidu and Mr. P. Ananda Charlu of Madras, Messrs. Norendra Nath Sen, Surendra Nath Bannerjee, M. Ghosh and Charan Chandra Mitter of Bengal; the Hon'ble Mr. V.N. Mandlik, the Hon'ble Mr. K.T. Telang and Mr. Dadabhai Naoroji of Bombay; Messrs. C. Vijiaranga Mudaliar and Pandurang Gopal of Poona; Sirdar Dayal Singh of the Panjab; Mr. Haris Chandra of Allahabad; Mr. Kaliprosad and Pundit Lakshminarayan of N.W.P., and Mr. Shri Ram of Oudh. These seventeen "good men and true" met and discussed various problems affecting the interest of the country and probably supported the idea of a national movement started at the Calcutta Conference of 1883.

CHAPTER VIII.

THE INAUGURATION AND THE FATHER OF THE CONGRESS.

The country was thus fully prepared both in men as well as materials for the construction of a national organisation. It only required the genius of an expert architect to devise a suitable plan and lay the foundation stone truly and faithfully. That architect was found in Allan Octavian Hume, now known as the "Father of the Indian National Congress." Mr. Hume, who was Secretary to the Government of India in the Home Department in 1870 and then in its newly created Department of Revenue, Agriculture and Commerce from 1871-1879, had closely followed the trend of events particularly during the Viceroyalty of Lord Lytton and anxiously watched the gathering clouds which were slowly but ominously rising above the horizon. The more he watched and studied the situation the more he became convinced that some definite action was called for to counteract the growing unrest. When therefore in 1882 he resigned service Mr. Hume settled at Simla and began to apply his great and almost inexhaustible energies and his intimate knowledge of the people, as well as of the Government, to the task of directing the popular impulse into a channel of constitutional agitation for the common benefit of both. As the worthy son of the founder of the Radical Party in England, Mr. A. O. Hume was essentially democratic in his instincts, but as a shrewd Scotchman he was also fully conscious of the limitations which must be imposed on and the safeguards to be provided against democratic institutions in a country governed like India. The first step he took towards the realisation of his plan was shadowed forth in an open letter dated the 1st March, 1883, which he addressed to the "Graduates of the Calcutta University" as largely representing the educated community in the country. In its deep pathos and fervid eloquence, no less than in its burning zeal and warm sympathy, this remarkable letter reads like St. Paul's epistle to the Romans. For a full and adequate appreciation of this spirited appeal to educated India reference is made to Sir William Wedderburn's excellent memoir of Mr. Hume which has recently been published by T. Fisher Unwin, London. The writer of the present article cannot, however, resist the temptation of quoting the concluding portion of this memorable letter which runs as follows:—

"And if even the leaders of thought are all either such poor creatures, or so selfishly wedded to personal concerns that they dare not strike a blow for their country's sake, then justly and rightly are they kept down and trampled on, for they deserve nothing better. Every nation secures precisely as good a government as it merits. If you, the picked men, the most highly educated of the nation, cannot, scorning personal ease and selfish objects, make a resolute struggle to secure greater freedom for yourselves and your country, a more impartial administration, a larger share in the management of your own affairs, then we, your friends, are wrong and our adversaries right, then are Lord Ripon's noble aspirations for your good fruitless and visionary, then, at present at any rate all hopes of progress are at an end, and India truly neither lacks nor deserves any better government than she enjoys. Only, if this be so, let us hear no more factious, peevish complaints that you are kept in leading strings and treated like children, for you will have proved yourself such. *Men* know how to act. Let there be no more complaints of Englishmen being preferred to you in all important offices, for if you lack that public spirit, that highest form of altruistic devotion that leads men to subordinate private ease to the public weal, that patriotism that has made Englishmen what they are,—then rightly are these preferred to you, rightly and inevitably have they become your rulers. And rulers and task-masters they must continue, let the yoke gall your shoulders never so sorely, until you realise and stand prepared to act upon the eternal truth that self-sacrifice and unselfishness are the only unfailing guides to freedom and happiness."

This passionate appeal did not go forth in vain. Men who had already waked up and were only looking for a *modus operandi* mustered from the different provinces at the trumpet call of a beloved friend and a trusted guide and the "Indian National Union" was formed towards the close of 1884 which, however, like the proverbial crab died immediately after the birth of its issue. A lot of correspondence passed between Calcutta and Bombay, though it is now difficult to trace them accurately with the exception of one addressed by Mr.

Telang to Mr. Surendra Nath Banerjee enquiring about matters connected with the National Conference of 1883. In March 1885 it was decided by the Union to hold a meeting of representatives from all parts of India at the forthcoming Christmas in Poona which was considered the most central and convenient place for the purpose, and in April the following manifesto was issued and circulated throughout the country :—

"A Conference of the Indian National Union will be held at Poona from the 25th to the 31st December, 1885."

"The Conference will be composed of delegates—leading politicians well acquainted with the English language from all parts of Bengal, Bombay and Madras Presidency."

"The direct objects of the Conference will be—(1) to enable all the most earnest labourers in the cause of national progress to become personally known to each other, (2) to discuss and decide upon the political operations to be undertaken during the ensuing year."

"Indirectly this Conference will form the germ of a Native Parliament and, if properly conducted, will constitute in a few years an unanswerable reply to the assertion that India is still wholly unfit for any form of representative institutions. The first Conference will decide whether the next shall be again held at Poona, or whether following the precedent of the British Association, the Conference shall be held year by year at different important centres."

"This year the Conference being in Poona, Mr. Chiplonkar and others of the Sarvajanik Sabha have consented to form a Reception Committee in whose hands will rest the whole of the local arrangements. The Peshwah's Garden near the Parvati Hill will be utilised both as a place of meeting (it contains a fine hall, like the garden, the property of the Sabha) and as a residence for the delegates, each of whom will be there provided with suitable quarters. Much importance is attached to this since, when all thus reside together for a week, far greater opportunities for friendly intercourse will be afforded than if the delegates were (as at the time of the late Bombay demonstrations) scattered about in dozens of private lodging houses all over the town."

"Delegates are expected to find their own way to and from Poona, but from the time they reach the Poona Railway Station until they again leave everything that they can need, carriage accommodation, food, &c., will be provided for them gratuitously."

" The cost thus involved will be defrayed from the Reception Fund which the Poona Association most liberally offers to provide in the first instance, but to which all delegates whose means warrant their incurring this further expense will be at liberty to contribute any sum they please. Any unutilised balance of such donations will be carried forward as a nucleus for next year's Reception Fund."

"It is believed that exclusive of our Poona friends, the Bombay Presidency including Sindh and the Berar will furnish about 20 delegates, Madras and Lower Bengal each about the same number and the N. W. Provinces, Oudh and the Punjab together about half this number."

Mr. Hume was wisely and appropriately placed at the head of the movement and the task of framing an organisation and settling the details naturally devolved on him. A preliminary report was issued to the members of the Union, that "so far as the Union was constituted there was absolute unanimity that unswerving loyalty to the British Crown was the key-note of the institution," and that the Union was also "prepared when necessary to oppose by all constitutional methods all authorities, high or low, here or in England, whose acts or omissions are opposed to those principles of the Government of India as laid down from time to time by the British Parliament and endorsed by the British Sovereign." As has already been stated, Poona, the capital of the Deccan, was selected as the place of the meeting and the historic place of the Peshwas, the *Heerabag* standing on the lake at the foot of the famous Parvati Hill from the windows of whose sacred temple the ill-fated Peshwa Baji Rao witnessed the fatal battle of Khirki, was chosen both for the Conference as well as for the residence of the delegates. Those who attended the eleventh session of the Congress held at Poona in 1895 must have visited this interesting spot. As stated in the manifesto quoted above, the "Poona Sarvajanik Sabha," the most important and influential public body in the Deccan, generously undertook all the necessary arrangements including the feeding of the delegates ; in fact it assumed all the functions of the latter day Reception Committee to the Congress. When all the preliminaries were thus settled, Mr. Hume left for England to consult friends and particularly with the object of guarding the British public against all possible misrepresentation, suspicion and distrust to which the new organisation was naturally exposed. Like the shrewd Scotchman that he was, Mr. Hume cautiously cleared his way in this country also before leaving for England. He saw Lord Dufferin and explained to him the scheme which had been settled. We have it on the authority of Sir William Wedderburn, based upon Mr. Hume's own notes, that "whereas he (Mr. Hume) was himself disposed to begin his reform propaganda on the social side, it was apparently by Lord Dufferin's advice that he took up the work of political organisation as the matter first to be dealt with. Lord Dufferin seems to have told him that "as the head of the Government he had found the greatest difficulty in ascertaining the real wishes of the people, and that for purposes of administration it would be a public benefit if there existed some responsible organisation through which the Government might be kept informed regarding the best Indian public opinion." His Lordship is said to have further observed, that owing to the wide differences in caste, race and religion, social reform in India required local treatment, rather than the guidance of a national organisation. There is a further corroboration of this interesting episode from no less an authority than the late Mr. W. C. Bonnerjee than whom no other Indian perhaps ever enjoyed a closer touch and greater intimacy with Mr. Hume. Writing for the *Indian Politics* issued by that enterprising publisher Mr. G. A. Natesan of Madras in 1898, Mr. Bonnerjee recorded his testimony as follows:—

"It will probably be news to many that the Indian National Congress as it was originally started and as it has since been carried on, is in reality the work of the Marquess of Dufferin and Ava when that nobleman was the Governor-General of India. Mr. A. O. Hume, C. B., had in 1884 conceived the idea that it would be of great advantage to the country if leading Indian politicians could be brought together once a year to discuss social matters and be upon friendly footing with one another. He did not desire that politics should form part of their discussions, for there were recognised political bodies in Calcutta, Bombay, Madras and other parts of the country, and he thought that these bodies might suffer in importance if, when Indian politicians from different parts of the country came together, they discussed politics. His idea further was that the Governor of the Province where the politicians met should be asked to preside over them and that thereby greater cordiality should be established between the official classes and the non-official Indian politicians. Full of these ideas he saw the noble Marquess when he went to Simla early in 1885 after having in December previous assumed the Viceroyalty of India. Lord Dufferin took great interest in the matter and after considering over it for some time sent for Mr. Hume and told him that in his opinion Mr. Hume's project would not be of much use. He said there was no body of persons in this country who performed the functions which Her Majesty's Opposition did in England. The newspapers even if they really represented the views of the people were not reliable, and as the English were necessarily ignorant of what was thought of them and their policy in native circles, it would be very desirable in the interests as well of the rulers as of the ruled that Indian politicians should meet yearly and point out to Government in what respects the administration was defective and how it could be improved; and he added that an assembly such as he proposed should not be presided over by the local

Governor, for in his presence the people might not like to speak out their minds. Mr. Hume was convinced by Lord Dufferin's arguments, and when he placed the two schemes, his own and Lord Dufferin's, before leading politicians in Calcutta, Bombay, Madras and other parts of the country, the latter unanimously accepted Lord Dufferin's scheme and proceeded to give effect to it. Lord Dufferin had made it a condition that his name in connection with the scheme of the Congress should not be divulged so long as he remained in the country and this condition was faithfully maintained, and none but the men consulted by Mr. Hume knew anything about the matter."

And it is an open secret that Mr. W.C. Bonnerjee was one of the men who were associated with Mr. Hume in organising the new movement and who were consulted by Mr. Hume on the subject of this important and interesting interview. Those who at a later period openly charged the Congress as being an unsavoury political organization fraught with dangerous consequences might well have profited by the information, that though the main idea was that of Mr. Hume and his co-adjutors its immediate political aspect was due to the suggestion, though not the actual initiation, of a responsible Viceroy and a statesman of no ordinary distinction who had added a territory of over 150,000 square miles to the British Empire. The subsequent change which apparently took place in the attitude of the great Viceroy and of which so much was at one time made by the critics of the Congress will be noticed in its proper place.

In the meantime encouraged by the success of the first National Conference of 1883, the three leading Associations in Calcutta, the British Indian Association, the Indian Association and the National Mahomedan Association conjointly invited and organised the second

National Conference which met in the spacious hall of the British Indian Association on the 25th, 26th and 27th of December 1885. Nearly all the districts including many of the sub-divisions and even important villages of Bengal were represented at the Conference. Nor did the other provinces go wholly unrepresented. Bombay was represented in the person of the Hon. Rao Saheb Viswanath Mandlik and Behar in the person of His Highness the Maharaja of Darbhanga as the President of the Behar Landholders' Association. Delegates also came from such distant places as Assam, Allahabad Benares and Meerut. Among the distinguished visitors present there were His Excellency the Ambassador of Nepal, Mr. H. J. S. Cotton, I.C.S. and Mr. Ameer Ali. All the representatives of the ancient houses of the Ghosals of Bhukailas, the Singhs of Paikparah, the Mookerjees of Utterparah, and the Tagores, the Mallicks and the Laws, as well as the Marwaris of Calcutta were there; while the intellectual aristocracy of Bengal was fully represented in the persons of Dr. Gooroodas (afterwards Sir Gooroodas) Banerjee, Messrs. Kali Mohan Dass, Mohesh Chandra Choudhury, Peary Mohan Mookerjee, Surendra Nath Banerjee, Kali Charan Banerjee and Dr. Trailokya Nath Mitter. Mr. Ananda Mohan Bose was at this time touring in Assam in connection with the political mission of the Indian Association. There were nearly 200 delegates to the Conference, while the visitors densely crowding the back of the hall, the corridor and all the passages from where a glimpse of the assembly could be secured numbered over a thousand. It was a grand spectacle where the old and the young vied with one another in their enthusiastic zeal and patriotic fervour under a new inspiration. On the first day Rajah Durga Charan Law, the merchant prince of Calcutta presided, on the second day that half-blind astute statistician, Mr. Joykrishan Mukherjee, who was not inaptly called the Indian Fawcett, and on the third and last day Maharaja Narendra Krishna, the heir and successor to the historic Nabakrishna, occupied the chair. The Conference in its three days' labours discussed and passed six resolutions on (1) the Reconstitution of Legislative Councils, (2) the modification of the Arms Act, (3) the retrenchment of public expenditure, (4) the Civil Service Question, (5) the separation of the Judicial from the Executive functions and (6) the Reconstitution of the Police. It will be seen later on that the programme of the Conference was practically the same as that of the first Congress, with this noticeable difference that while the Congress did not, the conference did, take up and thoroughly discuss the important question of the separation of the Judicial and the Executive Functions in the Criminal Administration of the country. It is worthy of remark that Mr. H. J. S. Cotton (now Sir Henry Cotton) who at the time was on active service not only attended the Conference as *Amici curie*, but also took part in its deliberations. Speaking on the important and foremost question of the reform of the Legislative Councils, Mr. Cotton said:—

"Even in India amongst members of my own service and out of it, I do not think many will be found who deny that a change must now take place in the constitution of our Legislative Councils. And I am quite certain that in England all liberal politicians will be found to take this view. The view of Lord Ripon, as he himself told me when discussing it with me last summer, was almost identical with that stated to you by the mover (Mr. S. N. Bannerjee), and there can be no doubt that he would use his powerful influence in England in assisting any proposal which the natives of this country may make in this direction."

The Cottons and the Wedderburns, who have for three generations served India, have always been among her best and truest friends whether here or in England, and Mr. H. J. S. Cotton in speaking of the members of his own service could only speak of the Cottons and the Wedderburns, but not of many others of his service. The conference was a great success, and on the last day on receipt of an information that on the following day the First Indian National Congress was going to meet in Bombay, the whole assembly went into a rapturous acclamation, and a message was despatched from the Conference welcoming the birth of the long expected National Assembly. Both the Conference and the Congress were thus the simultaneous offshoots of the same movement ; but the Bengal leaders wisely and patriotically merged their movement in that of the one inaugurated at Bombay, as it had indeed no necessity for separate existence except to the detriment of the other, or possibly of both.

To return however to the main topic and to Mr. Hume. In England Mr. Hume saw Lord Ripon, Mr. John Bright, M. P., Mr. R. T. Reid, M.P., (now Lord Loreburne who has figured so prominently in connection with the Home Rule agitation in England), Lord Dalhousie, the heir and successor of the renowned Indian Governor-General, Mr. Baxter M.P., Mr. Slagg, M.P., and many other friends of India. He explained to them the critical nature of the situation, the aims and objects of the new organisation, its constitutional character and the dangers which it was intended to forestall. Under the advice of Mr. Reid he saw nearly 150 members of the House of Commons and succeeded in obtaining from them a promise, though not a pledge, that they would pay some attention to Indian affairs, and also made arrangements for the reception and publication of the Union's messages by a section of the Liberal Press. Having fortified himself with these measures and assurances, Mr. Hume returned to India in November when he found all the arrangements complete, but a discussion was going on as regards the name by which the new organisation was to be baptised. Some were for calling it the National Union, some National Conference, while the majority were for christening it as the Congress, though not a few of them were afraid that it might carry a bad odour in certain quarters. At last it was decided that it should be styled as the Indian National Congress. It may be remembered that early in 1885 a deputation was sent to England composed of Mr. Manomohan Ghose of Bengal, Mr. Narayan Ganesh Chandavarkar of Bombay and Mr. Sivalaya Ramaswami Mudaliyar of Madras. They were called Delegates and to distinguish from them it was further decided that the members of the Congress should be called Representatives. It may not be known to many at this distance of time, that it was at first actually proposed to ask Lord Reay to preside at the first Congress. Lord Dufferin was approached on the question, but the Viceroy, while welcoming the proposal "as shewing the desire of the Congress to work in complete harmony with the Government" considered such a step inadvisable as many difficulties might arise both for the people as well as for the Government if a high official were to preside over such an assembly. The proposal was therefore dropped. But nevertheless the first Congress received official sympathy in an unstinted measure.

CHAPTER IX.

THE FIRST SESSION OF THE CONGRESS.

When all the arrangements were thus complete an untoward circumstance happened. Several cases of cholera appeared in Poona and it was considered unsafe and inadvisable to put the representatives coming from long distances and under fatiguing journey to any risk or possible danger. To the infinite disappointment of the good and patriotic people of Poona it was decided to change the venue of the session from Poona to Bombay. It was thus that the beautiful and romantic island city on the Malabar Coast with the Arabian Sea perpetually leaving her feet and the sombre Ghat Mountains mounting guard over her from behind acquired the honour of being the birthplace of the Indian National Congress. The newly established Presidency Association readily supplied the place of the "Sarvajanik Sabha," and the authorities of the Gokul Dass Tejpal Sanskrit College came forward to sanctify and immortalise their institution by lending its grand buildings, as well as its boarding houses, for the meeting and the accommodation of the representatives. The place is situated on the Gowalia Tank Road of the city and any one feeling interested on the subject may yet visit the sacred hall where the brave band of 72 Representatives met and discussed the first programme of the first National Assembly of India.

By the morning of the 27th December the Representatives from different parts and provinces began to arrive and were duly conducted to the Gokul Dass Tejpal College. In the evening some of the leading official and non-official gentlemen came to the College to meet the Representatives. Nearly two hours of the evening were devoted to the reception of the Hon'ble Sir William Wedderburn, the Hon'ble Mr. Justice Jardine, Colonel Phelps, Professor Wordsworth and a large number of other distinguished citizens of Bombay who came to the College to welcome the Representatives and express their sympathy with the work on which they were about to enter. "During the whole day," says the official reporter, "and far into the night of the 27th, informal discussions were carried on between the Representatives and the proceedings of the next three days were settled. The number of Representatives registered was 72, distributed as follows:—Calcutta 3, Bombay 18, Madras 8, Karachi 2, Viramgam 1, Surat 6, Poona 8, Agra 2, Benares 1, Simla 1, Lucknow 3, Allahabad 1, Lahore 1, Amballa 1, Ahmedabad 3, Berhampore (Madras) 1, Masulipatam 1, Chingleput 1, Tanjore 2. Kumbakonum 1, Madura 1,

Tinnevelly 1, Coimbatore 1, Salem 1, Cuddapah 1, Anantapore 1, and Bellary 1. The Bengal contingent was numerically weak owing, as the president said, to a series of misfortunes arising from death, illness and the like, but perhaps chiefly on account of the National Conference which was almost simultaneously holding its second session in Calcutta. Nearly all the prominent men of Bombay and Madras were present, while Bengal was represented by Mr. W. C. Bonnerjee, Mr. Norendra Nath Sen and Mr. Girijabhusan Mukherjee whose premature death was a heavy loss to the Bengal public. That silent and devoted votary of the Congress who never missed a single session of it, although seldom taking any prominent part in its deliberations in any, Mr. Janaki Nath Ghosal, came from Allahabad while Mr. Ramkali Choudhury represented Benares. It seems worthy of note that Mr. Hume although coming from Simla appears to have sat as a representative for Bengal probably as it would seem to make up considerably for the weakness of her numerical strength.

The first meeting of the Congress took place at 12 o'clock noon on Monday the 28th December 1885 in the Great Hall of the Gokuldass Tejpal Sanskrit College where all the Representatives were assembled amidst a distinguished, though somewhat limited, gathering of officials and leading citizens of Bombay. It was a solemn and imposing spectacle where all were animated, both the representatives and the visitors, the officials as well as the non-officials, with intense interest and inspired with noble enthusiasm on the birth of a new epoch. There sat Mr. Woomesh Chandra Bonnerjee, the

Doyen of the Calcutta Bar and the first Indian Standing Counsel in a Chartered High Court, in his tall and graceful figure with broad forhead and beaming eyes calmly awaiting in his firm attitude and sober dignity the great and unique honour which all the provinces were about to confer in his person upon their eldest sister province of Bengal. There was that slim but godly figure shining like a chiselled marble statue, short in stature but colossal in intellectual equipments, whose national turban considerably made up for his height and in whom nature seemed to have wonderfully blended the dwarf and the giant, the Grand Old Man of India,—Mr. Dadabhai Naoroji. There sat that intrepid journalist in his flowing hairs reaching down to his broad shoulders and with the fixed glare of a bull-dog countenance which quailed not even under Viceregal palace, the brave editor of the *Indian Mirror*—Mr. Narendra Nath Sen. There were those two out of that bright constellation of the three rising stars of the Western Presidency, who formed a happy conjunction combining patriotism with sobriety, enthusiasm and moderation of three different races,—Messrs. Kashinath Trimbak Telang and Pherozeshah Mancharjee Mehta, while the position of the third was not unworthily filled by another luminous member of his race, Mr. Rahimatulla Sayani. There sat beside the Grand Old man that well-posted statistician and indefatigable worker who has never flagged in his zeal and devotion during the lifetime of a generation in the service of the Congress,—Mr. Dinshaw Eduljee Wacha. There was that unostentatious, silent worker who was behind almost every public movement in the United

Provinces, but whose modesty seldom pushed him to the forefront in any, although grown grey in the service of his country—Mr. Gangaprasad Varma ; while from the Punjab there was that quaint and caustic critic whose familiar face has seldom been missed in any of the subsequent Congresses,—Lala Murlidhar. There also sat that level-headed, sober yet keen-sighted veteran lawyer, Rangiah Naidu, the respected President of the Mahajana Sabha, supported by that noble band composed of Messrs. Subramania Iyer, Ananda Charlu, Veeraraghavachariar, G. Subramania Iyer and Sabapathi Mudaliar of whom Madras has been ever so justly proud. There came from Poona Krishnaji Luxman Nulkar, the President and Sitaram Hari Chiplonkar, Secretary of the Sarvajanik Sabha, who but for the unfortunate accident already noticed would have had the honour of being the host to the delegates to the first session of the Indian National Congress ; and above all, there sat the "Father of the Congress ;" who had refused a Lieutenant-Governorship to serve a people, beaming with anxious joy and hope at the birth of his own child and inspiring and moving all with the magnetic current of his own ardent soul,—Mr. Allan Octavian Hume. Among the distinguished visitors there were men like Mr. D. S. White, President of the Eurasian Association, Dewan Bahadur Raghunatha Rao, Collector of Madras, the Hon. Mahadev Govinda Ranade, Judge, Small Cause Court, Poona and a member of the Bombay Legislative Council, Lala Baijnath of Agra, Professor Abaji Vishnoo Kattawatha of Ahmedabad, Professor Kadambi Sundararaman of Arcot, Professor R. G. Bhandarkar of the Deccan College and many others who, with two notable exceptions, sat as *Amici Curic* only to listen and advise.

On the motion of Mr. Hume (Bengal), seconded by the Hon. Subramania Iyer (Madras) and supported by the Hon. K. T. Telang (Bombay) Mr. W. C. Bonnerjee was unanimously elected and duly installed as President of the Congress, " the wise and firm hand that took the helm when the good ship was launched." The Reception Committee and its Chairman's address which has now assumed such indordinate proportions, probably beyond its legitimate scope, have been a later development, and consequently the first Congress opened with the inaugural address of the President of the Congress. That speech though condensed and short was fully worthy of the man and worthy of the occasion. Mr. Bonnerjee, who was eminently a practical politican, after graphically describing the representative character of the gathering, laid down the objects of the Congress with great force and sober dignity which drew the unstinted admiration of all sections of the Press. The address concluded with the following pregnant and pithy observation :—

> " She (Great Britain, had given them order, she had given them railways and above all she had given them the inestimable blessing of Western Education. But a great deal still remained to be done. The more progress the people made in education and material prosperity the greater would be the insight into political matters and the keener their desire for political advancement."

He thought their

> " desire to be governed according to the ideas of Government prevalent in Europe was in no way incompatible with their thorough loyalty to the British Government. All that they desired was that the basis of the Government should be widened and that the people should have their proper and legitimate share in it."

The proceedings of the meeting were marked by sobriety, judgment and firmness and the speeches characterised by dignity, independence and deep study of the subjects, which have probably been seldom surpassed in any subsequent session of the Congress. The subjects discussed were :—(1) Enquiry into the working of the Indian Administration by a Royal Commission, (2) the abolition of the Council of the Secretary of State as at present constituted, (3) the reform and expansion of the Imperial and the Local Legislative Councils, including the right of interpellation and the submission of the Budgets to the Councils, (4) the simultaneous Examination for the Civil Service, (5) the reduction of Military Expenditure, (6) the re-imposition of the import cotton duties and extension of the License Tax, together with an Imperial guarantee to the Indian debt and (7) separation of Burma from the Indian Viceroyalty. It was also resolved that the foregoing resolutions of the Congress be forwarded to all the political associations in the country with request to adopt such measures as may be calculated to advance the settlement of the various questions dealt with in those resolutions. It was decided that the next Congress should re-assemble in Calcutta.

Among the official visitors, that intellectual giant of the Deccan, the Hon'ble Mahadev Govinda Ranade, who did not find it impossible for him boldly to attend many a session of the Congress, and whose loftly patriotism combined with honest loyalty always bore him straight, was the only person who could not forbear from addressing the meeting on the second day upon the hotly debated question of the proposed abolition of the Council of the Secretary of State ; while Mr. D. S. White, the President of the Eurasian Association struck a most important note which although somewhat lightly treated at the time has now assumed considerable importance in connection with the labours of the Royal Commission which is now conducting its investigations and particularly in the light of the opinion which has been so forcibly expressed by that staunch friend of India, Sir Henry Cotton, through the columns of the *Contemporary Review* on the question of the reconstitution of the Indian Civil Service.

After the three day's labours the Congress was dissolved with the customary vote of thanks to the president which he more than deserved for "the great tact and judgment with which he had tackled many a knotty point during the debates and for his "very able conduct in the chair." This was followed by "three cheers" for Mr. Hume which the "Father of the Congress" ever since received as an annual tribute at every session of the Congress until his death, and by an outburst of loyal demonstration when Mr. Hume called for "three times three cheers" for Her Majesty the Queen Empress.

Here closes the narrative as regards the origin of the great national movement. Twenty-nine sessions of the Congress, with one lamentable break, have since been held in different centres of British India, the history of which is well preserved in the records of the Congress which may be said to form a most valuable compendium, if not a library, of the modern Indian

DR. DADABHAI NAOROJI
PRESIDENT, 1886, 1893 & 1906.

BUDRUDDIN TYABJEE
PRESIDENT, 1887.

political literature of more than a quarter of a century. It is perhaps not necessary to agree with all or any of the conclusions arrived at in these voluminous records to form a just and adequate estimate of the encyclopedic character of the mine of informations which they contain, the vast amount of thought and reflection on various subjects which they embody and the awakening of self-consciousness among a rising people, as well as the trend of popular ideas and aspirations, which they disclose at a momentous period of transition in a world of rapid changes and transformations. All these materials are there for the future political historian of India. But a brief survey of the various phases through which the Congress has passed, the trials and tribulations it has undergone, the difficulties it has overcome, the success which has so far attended its labours and the prospects it has opened for future progress, may not be altogether out of place and without some interest.

CHAPTER X.

The Career of the Congress.

It was Mr. George Yule who, in his presidential address at the fourth session of the Congress held at Allahabad, said that there are three phases through which all important movements have to pass:—that of "ridicule," "abuse," and "partial concession," which with a slight modification might be termed the stages of Ridicule, Opposition and Surrender. It was truly a prophetic pronouncement which is fully illustrated in the history of the Congress. At first the movement was ridiculed by its critics as a fantastic dream which they confidently hoped would shortly meet the fate of Alnasker's glass-wares. The first stage was, however, quickly got over: for, although Anglo-India at the outset pooh-poohed the idea of a United India, it was shortly disabused of its delusion and impressed with the serious nature of the business to which the educated community had solemnly and deliberately put its hand. But the second stage was a rather prolonged period during which the Congress was engaged in a desperate struggle against calumny and misrepresentation on the one hand and the difficulties of defeat and despair on the other. The stubborn opposition of a powerful bureaucracy, backed by the Anglo-Indian Press and coupled with the growing despondency of the people themselves, made the position of the Congress at times almost critical. The leaders, however, learnt to "labour and to wait" with the fullest confidence in the justice and righteousness of the cause and in the ultimate triumph of British statesmanship until, as a reward for their honest perseverance, the third and the last stage of "partial concession" may fairly be said to have at last dawned upon the country.

Although the Congress was born in Bombay its real baptism took place with all the formal rites and ceremonies in the following year in the metropolis of the

Empire under the high prelacy of the Nestor of India, Mr. Dadabhai Naoroji. In the Calcutta Congress of 1886, a Reception Committee was formed with that illustrious savant and antiquarian, Dr. Rajendralal Mitra, who was then the President of the British Indian Association, as its chairman, and the representatives (henceforth styled delegates) were formally elected either by established associations, or at duly organised public meetings held throughout the country. The representation thus secured was naturally much larger and more thorough than at the first Congress. The number of delegates rose from 72 to 406 and included all that was best in the land whether in point of intellect, wealth or influence. An opening address by the Chairman of the Reception Committee welcoming the delegates was introduced, and for its graceful language, fervid eloquence and patriotic zeal, no less than for its political insight, the spirited address delivered by the learned doctor on the occasion stands to this day as a model for the Reception Committee's address of welcome to the delegates. The Presidential Address of the Grand Old Man, embodying the results of a lifelong study of Indian problems and the direct experience of English politics, was listened to with reverent attention by an assembly of over four thousand educated people. The meeting was at first arranged to be held in the hall of the British Indian Association where the National Conference had been held in December previous; but judging by the number of the registered delegates, as well as the vast number of expected visitors, it was wisely removed to the Calcutta Town Hall with the Hooghly decked with its splendid shipments on one side and the grand *maidan* with the imposing Fort William and the beautiful Eden Gardens on the other. The historic hall was densely packed to its utmost capacity and a small temporary platform had to be improvised for the President in the middle of the southern side of the spacious hall, as he would have been otherwise lost to view amidst the sea of faces around him. The large *dais* which now adorns the eastern end of the hall was not then in existence. The subjects discussed at this session were also more comprehensive and better digested than at the first Congress and included the important question of the separation of Judicial from Executive functions in the administration of criminal justice in the country. As a practical step towards the working of the Congress, Provincial Committees were also established throughout the country. The session marked throughout by unabated enthusiasm and earnestness as well as by animated debates, some of which had to be settled in committees, was a grand success and staggered not a few among the Anglo-Indian Community who had lightly indulged in a belief of the "effervescent character" of the movement. At the close of the session, Lord Dufferin very courteously received a deputation from the Congress headed by the President.

If the Congress of 1885 was little more than an experiment, and the Congress of 1886 marked a period of vigorous adolescence, the Congress of 1887 "bore every appearance of its having become a permanent national institution." The third Congress held in Madras evoked still greater enthusiasm and the number of delegates rose to over 600, of whom fully 250 hailed from outside the Madras Presidency. The bulk of the Bengal delegates, numbering about 80, chartered the B and I Company's *S. S. Nevassa* which, starting from Calcutta and after experiencing a severe gale continuously for three days and three nights in the Bay, at last landed the delegates from Bengal in Madras amid the hearty cheers of a vast and expectant crowd awaiting the distressed vessel on the magnificent beach of which Fort St. George is so justly proud. It was in Madras that for the first time a special pavilion was constructed for the meeting of the Congress, which in Tamil was called *Pandal*, and this term has since been accepted by all the provinces for the pavilion at all successive sessions of the Congress. That veteran statesman who, after a long and distinguished career as the Prime Minister of three of the most important independent principalities of Travancore, Indore and Baroda, each and all of whom owe their advancement in no small measure to his genius, had retired into private life, was drawn from his seclusion in his old age to assume the function of Chairman of the Reception Committee; and the masterly address with which Raja Sir T. Madhava Rao cordially welcomed the delegates may even to this day be read with much profit both by the members of the Congress as well as its critics. Referring to the latter, he said:

"Judged most unsparingly, the worst feature of gatherings of this description might be super-abundance of enthusiasm and youthful impetuosity. But, as a great thinker has said, men learn to run before they learn to walk; they stagger and stumble before they acquire a steady use of their limbs. What is true of individuals is equally true of nations; and it is uncharitable to form a forecast of the future from the failings and weaknesses, if any such *should* exist, incidental to a nascent stage."

Addressing the members of the Congress, he counselled moderation and forbearance. "It is the character of renovated youth," he said, "to be carried away by excessive zeal. Steer clear of such shoals and quicksands. Discuss without prejudice; judge without bias; and submit your proposals with the diffidence that must necessarily mark suggestions that are tentative in their character." The President of the Congress this time was the Honourable Mr. Budruddin Tyabji, at that time a distinguished member of the Bombay Bar and the first and foremost Mahomedan who if he failed actually to attend the first Congress yet heartily supported the movement from its very inception. It was at this session that a constitution was also sought to be provided for the institution. A committee was formed which drafted a set of tentative rules, and an attempt to adopt these rules was repeated from year to year without any decision being arrived at until it was overtaken by a catastrophe twenty years later. But for the vacillation and indecision of the leaders, who had been repeatedly warned of the dangers to which such a huge organisation was naturally exposed in the absence of fixed rules and regulations defining its constitution and laying down a procedure for its working, that catastrophe might possibly have easily been avoided.

For a closer touch among the delegates some sort of social entertainments were contrived from the beginning of the Congress. In Bombay, the Representatives besides being housed at one and the same place were taken to a visit of the celebrated cave temples at Elephanta. In Calcutta, although the large number of delegates did not admit of their being accommodated in one and the same house, a magnificent steamer party was organised by Mr. Moheschandra Choudhury, a leading vakil of the Calcutta High Court and a prominent member of the Congress, in which several prominent officials, including the Hon'ble Mr. Justice, afterwards Sir. Chunder-Madhav Ghose joined ; and pleasant entertainments were combined with serious business as some of the matters referred to a Committee of the Congress were discussed and settled on board the vessel as it glided along the Hooghly, decked with hundreds of flags, amidst the playing of bands on the flats on either side and the cheerings of thousands of spectators who lined all the way up along the shores. At Madras, it was understood that Lord Connemara was personally desirous of attending the Congress ; but Lord Dufferin thought it would be preferable for the Governor to receive the delegates. Lord Connemara accordingly first attended the magnificent reception given by Mr. Eardley Norton and on the following day, himself received the delegates at Government House in a manner befitting his exalted position and fully worthy of the occasion. It was a brilliant function in which His Excellency freely mixed and conversed with the delegates and gave unmistakable evidence of his sympathies with the movement. Sumptuous refreshments were also provided for the delegates and the Governor's own band was in attendance.

But here the curtain dropped over official sympathies for the Congress and the fourth session at Allahabad witnessed a complete change in the official attitude towards the movement. The Anglo-Indian community and their organs had from the beginning ridiculed the idea of a United India and although the Indian Civil Service made no secret of its dislike for the movement it was precluded from manifesting any open hostility to it owing to the sympathies evinced by the heads of the administrations. It is a significant fact that the first and the third Congresses were held within Presidency Governments and although the second was held within the territories of a Lieutenant-Governor, it was held in the capital of the Empire where his presence was completely overshadowed by the higher personality and influence of the Viceroy. Thus it was not until the Congress removed its seat to within an independent Lieutenant-Governorship that the official circle found a free scope to vent its antipathy towards the new movement. A few perfectly harmless leaflets, such as "the Old Man's Hope," written by Mr. Hume, a catechism in Tamil written by Mr. Veeraraghava Chariar and a parable in the form of a dialogue between one Moulvie Fariduddin and Rambuksh, circulated among the people for attracting public attention to the movement, were regarded in official circles as savouring of the practice of the Anti-Corn Law League in England; and the Reception Committee of the Fourth Congress headed by that enthusiastic congressman and recognised leader of public opinion in the United Provinces, Pundit Ajudhya Nath, experienced considerable difficulty in procuring a suitable site for, the *Pandal.* They were driven from pillar to post both by the civil and the military authorities until that patriotic nobleman of Behar who was a Gothic pillar of the Congress, Maharajah Sir Luchmeswar Singh Bahadur of Dhurbunga, came to the rescue. He hastily purchased Lowther Castle just opposite Government House and at once placed it at the disposal of the Reception Committee saying, that the first use to which the newly acquired property was to be dedicated was the service of the motherland. Sir Auckland Colvin left Government House and went out on tour shortly before the sitting of the Congress. The interest and enthusiasm of the people however rose in proportion to the opposition which they received, and Pundit Ajudhya Nath with his characteristic genial good-humour bulletined from day to day the large number of delegates who were pouring in by almost every train into the city. There were two prominent men at this time who rose to greater prominence by their opposition to the Congress: one was Sir Syed Ahmed Khan of Aligarh and the other Rajah Siva Prasad of Benares. Rajah Siva Prasad, apparently bent upon attracting pointed attention of the authorities by openly denouncing the Congress, managed to secure a representation from the Benares division, which however was strongly repudiated by the other delegates from that division as a fraud, and personally attended the Congress. His fellow-delegates from Benares though submitting to the decision of the Congress authorities declining for several reasons to exclude him from the meeting, had to be partially reconciled by allowing him a seat outside the delegates' enclosure and far away from their block. It may be noted here that the practice of arranging the delegates in groups or blocks according to provinces was started at this session and Rajah Siva Prasad though admitted as a delegate had to be provided with a separate seat close under the presidential platform. The Rajah though appearing in the garb of a delegate took advantage of his position to pronounce, like Balaam, an anathema on the movement which so much exasperated the vast assembly that at the end of the day's proceeding he had to be sent to his quarters under a strong escort supplied by the Reception Committee. All the leading men of all the provinces were present at this session which besides being held at the most central city in India also carried with it the additional attraction of a sacred place of great antiquity and the just pride of a spot where the Great Proclamation of the "White Queen" was announced to her Indian subjects in 1858. The Presidential Address of Mr. Yule, who as the recognised leader of the European mercantile community in Calcutta was a tower of strength to the Congress and whose association with the movement was a powerful vindication of its legitimate character, was a masterly document unsurpassed by any in the annals of the Congress either in manly dignity, sober judgment, or fearless independence. The vigorous correspondence which followed between Sir Auckland Colvin and Mr. Hume, the former attacking and the latter defending the Congress is well-known to the public and need not be re-capitulated here. The Anglo-Indian Press, which had from the beginning showed no sympathy, active or passive, towards the movement, now began to manifest symptoms of open suspicion and distrust of it. The *Pioneer* led the cry against the Congress and the whole *Jingo* Press yelled out in a responsive chorus denouncing the movement and its methods as resembling Irish Fenianism and strongly savouring of a lurking seditious organisation devoid of representative character and substance. It was, however, a significant feature of the situation that the supreme head of the administration, the Viceroy, imbued with the spirit of the British constitution and accustomed to the methods and practices of public agitation at Home, never winced, and although surrounded by bureaucratic influences that supreme authority was generally found to regard the movement as perfectly constitutional. It is perhaps as true of the moral as of the physical world that the higher one mounts, the purer becomes the atmosphere. Lord Dufferin who courteously received the delegates to the Second Congress openly said that the proposal for the separation of the Judicial from the Executive functions was a "counsel of perfection" to which he was ready to subscribe, though on a subsequent occasion the same strong Viceroy appears to have succumbed to his stronger environment and characterised the Congress party as a "microscopic minority" and their ultimate ambition as a "big jump into the unknown." He apparently forgot his early conversations with Mr. Hume and his own share in the business, though it must be said to the credit of the leading congressmen who were in the known that they could hardly be persuaded even under extreme provocation to abuse the confidence reposed in them. The after-dinner speech of Lord Dufferin was however promptly met by a most caustic rejoinder from Mr. Eardley Norton, whose "open letter" to His Lordship was received with the utmost gratification throughout the country and created a sensation in the official circle. The whole Indian Press joined in the protest in some cases even bordering on disrespect to the high authority from whom the unfortunate observations emanated, as it formed also the subject of not a few severe though well-restrained comments at the next session of the Congress. But there was yet another and a more powerful man possessed of "a frame of adamant and a soul of fire" who stood to defend the Congress and its propaganda against these light-hearted strictures. Charles Bradlaugh's attention was drawn by a report in the *Times* to Lord Dufferin's speech delivered at the St. Andrew's Dinner in Calcutta on November 30, 1888, and the "Member for India" in a great speech made at Newcastle at once replied to Lord Dufferin's criticisms with such driving force and convincing arguments as made the latter unreservedly to climb down, if not actually come down on his knees, before his powerful antagonist. Lord Dufferin forthwith wrote to Mr. Bradlaugh explaining himself. In his letter Lord Dufferin assured Mr. Bradlaugh :

"That he had not misrepresented the Congress, that he neither directly nor by implication suggested that the Congress was seditious, that he always spoke of the Congress in terms of sympathy and respect, and treated its members with great personal civility, that he was always in favour of Civil Service Reform, so that Indians might obtain more appointments in it, as proved by his appointment of the Indian Civil Service Commission and that he himself was in favour of such a reform of the Provincial Councils in India as he (Mr. Bradlaugh) appeared to advocate."

Then after his retirement from the Viceroyalty of India at Lord Dufferin's special request an interview was arranged and held in London between the two, in which Lord Dufferin further explained himself; while in writing to Mr. Bradlaugh after his appointment as Ambassador in Rome, Lord Dufferin said:—

"I think our efforts should be applied rather to the decentralisation of our Indian Administration than to its greater unification, and I made considerable efforts in India to promote and expand this principle. In any event, I am sure the discussion which you will have provoked will prove very useful, and I am very glad that the conduct of it should be in the hands of a prudent, wise and responsible person like yourself, instead of having been laid hold of by some adventurous *franc tireier* whose only object might possibly have been to let off a few fire-works for his own glorification."

As regards his "big jump into the unknown," he had no doubt his defence as well as his explanation; but if the conqueror of Burma had been living to-day, he would certainly have had the gratification to find how grievously mistaken he and his advisers were and that in spite of his and their warning at least an initial step towards the "big jump" has been taken without the Government either in England or in India being any the worse for it.

The most brilliant session during the first period of the Congress was however that of 1889, commonly known as the "Bradlaugh Session," held in Bombay under the presidency of Sir William Wedderburn. The number of Delegates who attended the session was 1889 a figure strangely coinciding with the year, and it has been the highest on the record up to this day. It was a historic session which attracted an unusual number of people, including even officials in disguise, to see and hear the great commoner, the hero of a hundred fights on the floor of the House of Commons and one of the early friends of India in the pre-Congress period, who by his unswerving conviction and dauntless courage, as well as by his sympathies for poor suffering humanity, had created a name known throughout the civilized world and which was almost a household word among the educated community in India.

Although the question of the Congress-constitution was repeatedly postponed from year to year, an important rule was passed at the fifth session of the Congress by which the number of representatives returnable from each Congress circle was limited to five per million of its total population. This salutary provision was found necessary party to avoid disproportionate representation of the various provinces and partly to check the enormous size to which the assembly was growing; but this rule seems never to have been strictly observed except at two or three sessions of the Congress.

Speaking of the Congres of 1889 it is impossible to avoid a passing reference to an important debate which took place at this session on the Bill which the "member for India" himself had drafted for introduction in the House of Commons for the reform of the Indian Councils. One of the objects of Mr. Bradlaugh's coming out to India was, as he himself, said, personally to ascertain the views of the Indians on the spot as regards the provisions of his Bill, and he had the pleasure of listening to a full dressed debate on the subject. How that Bill was superseded by a tinkering measure of Lord Cross and the cherished hopes of the Indian Nationalists deferred for another decade is well-known to congressmen. But if a kind Providence had spared Charles Bradlaugh for another ten years he would have had the satisfaction of seeing that his own Bill was accepted as the substantial basis for the reform and expansion of the Legislative Councils in India at the hands of a future Secretary of State. At the conclusion of the proceedings of the session an address was presented to Mr. Bradlaugh from the Congress, and quite a pile of addresses in silver and gold caskets as well as other presents from different parts of the country were laid covering the large presidential table, which could only be taken as read. Mr. Bradlaugh then delivered an address which in its earnestness, sincerity, as well as fervid eloquence, made a deep impression on the minds of the audience, which comprised also a section of the European population of Bombay. In his deep, resonant voice, which held the vast assembly spell-bound, the great friend and champion of India said :—"For whom should I work if not for the people? Born of the people, trusted by the people, I will die of the people." Here was a man who was a fearless advocate of truth and justice, who "never dreamed, though right *were* worsted, wrong *could* triumph;" and when shall England and India have such another!

The next Session of the Congress held under the leadership of Sir Pherozeshah Mehta in 1890 in the city of Calcutta was distinguished no less for its splendid organization than for its enthusiasm. It thoroughly exposed the secret antipathy of the bureaucracy and at the same time established its own claim and position as a legitimate representative institution. The amusing incident which drew this important declaration from the Government of India is quite illustrative of the temper and attitude which the Civil Service has throughout maintained towards the national movement. On the eve of the sixth session of the Congress in Calcutta the public were surprised by a notice which appeared in the various Anglo-Indian newspapers in the metropolis which ran as follows :—

"THE CONGRESS."

"The Bengal Government, having learnt that tickets of admission to the visitors' enclosure in the Congress Pavilion have been sent to various Government officers residing in Calcutta, has issued a circular to all secretaries and heads of department subordinate to it pointing out, that under orders of Government of India the presence of Government officials even as visitors as such meetings is not advisable, and that their taking part in the proceedings of any such meetings is absolutely prohibited."

And this was followed by a characteristic reply from Belvidere to the Secretary to the Congress Reception Committee, who had with respectful compliments sent some cards for the use of His Honour the Lieutenant-Governor and his household :—

"BELVIDERE, *25th December, 1890.*

"DEAR SIR,

"In returning herewith the seven cards of admission to the visitors' enclosure of the Congress pavilion which were kindly sent by you to my address yesterday afternoon, I am desired to say that the Lieutenant-Governor and the members of his household could not possibly avail themselves of these tickets, since the orders of the Government of India *definitely prohibit the presence* of Government officials at such meetings."

This communication, which was read by the Anglo-Indian Press as a highly gratifying snub administered to the Congress, was over the signature of Mr. P. C. Lyon who was then the Private Secretary to Sir Charles Elliot and who in his subsequent distinguished career found much ampler and freer scope for associating his name with circulars and manifestoes which, though no longer extent, have acquired a historic fame. This strange correspondence formed the subject of a heated discussion in the Congress in course of which that level-headed typical Scotchman, Mr. George Yule, described it as the production of "some Dogberry clothed in a little brief authority" and characterized it as "a piece of gross insolence" offered to a body of men who were perhaps in no way inferior to any official in the land either in their "honesty of purpose," or "devotion to the Queen." Mr. Yule visibly waxed red when he said from his place in the tribune, "any instructions, therefore, which carry on their face, as these instructions do in my judgment, an insinuation that we are unworthy to be visited by Government officials, I resent as an insult and I retort that in all the qualities of manhood we are as good as they." A reference was made to H. E. the Viceroy who at once declared that the Belvidere interpretation of the order of Government of India was based upon a clear misapprehension, that in the opinion of Government the

Congress Movement was "*perfectly legitimate in itself,*" that the "*Government of India recognise that the Congress Movement is regarded as representing in India what in Europe would be called the more advanced Liberal Party, as distinguished from the great body of Conservative opinion which exists side by side with it,*" and that *the real attitude of the Government was one of perfect* "*neutrality in their relation to both parties.*" The Private Secretary to Lord Lansdowne while clearly indicating that it was only *participation* in its proceedings from which Government officials were necessarily debarred concluded this important letter, addressed to the General Secretary to the Congress, with the following observation :—

> "In reference to a specific question which you addressed to His Excellency, I am to say, that the orders apply only to those who are actually, at the time being, Government Servants but not to pensioners and others who have quitted the service of the Government for good."

A pointed reference to this passing incident has been deemed necessary not only to exemplify the secret disposition of the Indian bureaucracy towards popular institutions, but also to remove, if possible, the lurking suspicion which, having regard to that disposition, yet prevails in certain quarters and particularly among a class of Indian officials, that the Government is really ill-disposed towards the Congress and that it is not safe for pensioners or even retained Government advocates to express any sympathy for the Congress movement. It cannot, however, be denied that athough the Supreme Government has been generally quite frank and intelligible in the exposition of its views about the Congress, the ideas of the subordinate administrations in their practical application have seldom been free from a distinct bias against it; and those who had from an early stage of the Congress looked through the rose-tinted official spectacles and could never discern the rock ahead regarded the movement with positive jealousy and suspicion, and ever since the fourth Congress at Allahabad a systematic campaign was kept up not only to discredit the organization, but also to calumiuate it before the British public. The bureaucracy as a whole was like Narcissus of old so enchanted with the loveliness of its own shadow that it had neither the leisure nor the inclination to contemplate beauty in others: while those placed high in offices resented all suggestions at improvements as a direct reflection against them.

It was at this session of 1890 that a decision was arrived at for holding a session of the Congress in London in 1892. Owing, however, to the impending general election in 1891 the proposal was subsequently postponed and never afterwards revived owing to a difference of opinion as regards the relative advantages and disadvantages of such a venturesome step. In 1892 Sir Charles Elliott's notorious Jury Notification was published and the whole country was convulsed by the threatened abrogation of a valued, vested right. Bengal naturally led a violent agitation; but the country was no longer a congeries of disintegrated peoples and the Congress at once took up the question in right earnest. A Jury Commission was appointed and in the end not only was the obnoxious notification withdrawn, but a distinct advance was secured towards a further, though limited, extension of that system.

Another brilliant session of the Congress was that held in 1893 in the historic capital of the Punjab. Mr. Dadabhai Naoroji, M. P., who recently returned to Parliament by the British constituency of Central Finsbury was the first Indian that sat in the British House of Commons, was again unanimously elected as President of the Congress this year. The tremendous ovation which he received from the warm-hearted and chivalrous people of the land of the Five Rivers resembled more the triumphal entry of a conquering hero than a customary ceremonial demonstration: and a conquering hero it was who had not only opened the gate of the Mother of Parliaments to the Indian people; but also came out triumphant with the famous Resolution of the House of Commons of the 2nd June on the important question of the Simultaneous Examinations for the Indian Civil Services. Mr. Dadabhai also brought with him the welcome messages of good will and sympathy not only from his own constituency, but also from the Irish Labour and Radical members of the House, who through their accredited mouthpiece, Mr. Davitt, charged him on the eve of his departure from England,—"Don't *forget to tell your colleagues at the Congress that every one of Ireland's Home Rule members in Parliament is at your back in the cause of the Indian People.*" A session of the Congress held under such happy auspices and under the leadership of such a man was bound to be a most unqualified success both in form as well as in substance. It was at this session that the question of the Medical Service, of which the late lamented Dr. Bahadurji of Bombay was such a staunch advocate, received the earliest attention of the national assembly, and the important question of the Separation of Judicial and Executive functions assumed a practical shape in the appointment of a Committee of the Congress to formulate definite schemes for the proposed reform. But perhaps the highest interest evoked at this session was embodied in the protests which the Congress entered against the closing of the Indian mints to private coinage of silver, whereby the people were subjected to a further indirect taxation and some of the most important trades and industries in the country seriously disorganized and injured, as also against a system of State-regulated immorality practised in the Indian cantonments which had been dragged into light by a Purity Society in England specially under the indefatigable exertions of Mrs. Josephine Butler, whose thrilling revelations were at first stoutly repudiated by Lord Roberts, then the Commander-in-Chief in India, but were ultimately fully confirmed by a Departmental Committee appointed by the Secretary of State to independently investigate into the matter. It must be said to the credit of Lord Roberts that when the odious charge was proved beyond question, the gallant soldier voluntarily came forward to offer his unqualified apology to Mrs. Butler and her colleagues among whom were included two American ladies who were also members of the Society and had taken a prominent part in the shameful disclosures which, in the words of Mr. D. E. Wacha who with his characteristic force of facts and figures moved the resolution, at last "unmasked the organized official hypocrisy of those in India who had so long successfully misled the British public."

The Madras Congress of 1894 under the presidency of Mr. Alfred Webb, M.P., was marked by considerable excitement over the questions of two fresh imposts proposed to be laid on the already overburdened Indian taxpayer: one was called a countervailing excise duty on Indian cotton manufactures evidently introduced under pressure from Lancashire; while the other was the levy of an arbitrary penalty in the shape of costs of punitive police forces quartered in disturbed areas under an amendment of the Indian Police Act of 1861. The excise duty has done its best to cripple the infant textile industries of Bombay, while the police-penalty has ever since fallen heavily on the guilty and the innocent alike and is most sorely resented by a suffering people as being due solely to the incompetency of the ordinary police to preserve peace and order in the country. It is felt and regarded by the people as one of those avenging thunderbolts, too common in India, which are visited on the Indian peasant when Jupiter himself is in the wrong.

Another most successful session of the Congress was that held at Poona in 1895. Having lost her first opportunity the capital of the Deccan had to wait for ten long years to secure her turn in the yearly expanding cycle of the gigantic movement. Mr. Surendranath Banerjee, whose name was a signal for popular enthusiasm, was the President at this session and the remarkable address which he delivered *extempore* for over two hours and a half was a masterpiece of eloquence combining facts with rhetoric. The country was at this time threatened with another reactionary measure of far-reaching consequences to the national movement. The legal practitioners formed the bulk of the independent educated community, who led public opinion and guarded popular rights and privileges in the country. Being directly under the authority of the High Courts they were comparatively free from the nightmare of local official influence, and in 1894 a Bill was introduced in the Supreme Legislative Council, at the instance of a bureaucracy which was never shown to devise means for striking at the root of the rising spirit, to amend the Legal Practitioners' Act of 1879, by which the provincial legal practitioners were sought to be completely subordinated to the District Judges and the Revenue Commissioners. Bengal again led the opposition which the other provinces soon joined, and the Congress of 1895 entered a vigorous protest of the united country against this mischievous measure. The High Courts generally and the High Court at Fort William in particular here supported the people and as in the case of the Jury Notification so in the case of the Legal Practitioner's Bill a threatened danger was turned into a signal success. The legal practitioners were not only saved from the clutches of the bureaucracy; but the dignity of their position was further enhanced by the repeal of the degrading provisions in the existing law as regards imprisonment in certain cases of professional misconduct. In 1897 the people were rudely apprised of the existence of three rusty but deadly weapons in the armoury of Government to summarily dispose of the liberty of a British subject. The Sirdars Natu brothers were deported by the Bombay Government under Bombay Regulation XXV of 1827 without a trial and without their offence being made public, and the Congress of the years entered a vigorous protest against the use of an obsolete Regulation which was expressly intended to meet the circumstances of a time when British power was hardly established in the country and was positively threatened with internal commotions of no ordinary magnitude. The Congress also urged for the repeal of the three cognate measures for the three Presidencies which, like the three Gorgon Sisters, had but one eye and one object to terrorize the people—the Bengal Regulation III of 1818, the Madras Regulation II of 1819 and the Bombay Regulation XXV of 1827. Unfortunately however a nervous bureaucracy was unwilling to part with even the most indefensible of the offensive weapons in its possession, and neither the religious nor the social reformer, nor the educationist, nor the political demagogue has since escaped their ruthless operation; while the barbarous measures are still suspended like the proverbial sword of Damocles over the heads of a devoted people living in British territories. It was in this year also that the initial step was taken towards widening the scope of the law of sedition by amending Section 121-A of the Indian Penal Code against the pledge of the expert political juggler, Sir James Fitz

James Stephen, and the first foundation laid for the suppression of liberty of speech and freedom of the Press. The Congress at once raised its voice against this dangerous innovation in the law of the land, but that voice went altogether unheeded in the rising temper of the bureaucracy with what result is now well-known to the country. The Congress of 1901 under the presidency of Mr. D. E. Wacha was remarkable for the interest it evoked in the question of immigration in Assam and the "melancholy meanness" to which the Government of India had submitted in postponing the very small relief which Sir Henry Cotton had fought so hard to grant to the indentured labourers in the tea-gardens. It was at this Congress also that, with a view to meet the deficit of the expenses of the Congress organ *India* and of the British Committee in England, the "delegation fee" was raised from Rs. 10 to Rs. 20 with effect from 1902. This increase was to no small extent responsible for thinner attendance of delegates at some of the subsequent Congresses and continued to be a source of bitter complaint until the Bankipur Congress of 1912, when it was remitted to its former incidence.

The Bombay Congress of 1904 under the presidency of Sir Henry Cotton and the Benares Congress of 1905 under the leadership of the Hon'ble Mr. Gopal Krishna Gokhale were also among the remarkable sessions of the National Assembly. The former dealt with the reactionary policy of Lord Curzon's administration as evidenced by the Indian Universities Bill, the Bengal Partition Scheme and the Official Secrets

Bill ; while the latter witnessed the first manifestation of the new spirit evoked by the recently established Swadeshi movement consequent upon the Partition of Bengal, which will be separately dealt with later on.

It has been already observed that whatever the attitude of the Anglo-Indian bureaucracy was that supreme head of the administration had throughout maintained an attitude of perfect neutrality between that bureaucracy and the people as represented by the Congress. It was, however, reserved only for Lord Curzon to thoroughly identify himself with the bureaucracy and to treat the Indian National Congress, as indeed everything Indian, with positive discourtesy. He refused to receive a deputation which proposed to wait upon His Excellency under the leadership of Sir Henry Cotton with the resolutions of the Bombay Congress of 1904. The refusal though meanly discourteous was not altogether unexpected. The Congress of 1904 had not only entered its protests against the officialization of the Universities and the newly hatched scheme of the Partition of Bengal, two of the most cherished fads of the Indian Kaiser, whose chief enemy according to the *Times* was his own tongue next to his manners ; but it was this time presided over by a man whose pro-Indian tendencies had been long known to the bureaucracy, a man whose stern opposition to any scheme of dismemberment of a province, which he was proud to call the land of his adoption for which he earned the sobriquet of the "White Babu" from the demoralized members of his own service, was pronounced as long ago as 1896 and whom the "Superior Person" had not only treacherously thrown to the wolves for his benevolent efforts to add an *eight anna* silver piece to the hard lot of legalized slavery in the tea gardens of Assam, but had actually removed out of his way by effectually barring him from the Satrapy of Bengal even at the risk of sacrificing another valuable life, and above all a man, whose immense popularity in the country could by no means have been pleasing to the proud Viceroy, was perhaps not the man whom his Magnificence could have consistently with his high dignity and higher insolence admitted to his august presence. Sir Henry Cotton, however, presided at a huge anti-partition demonstration held at the Calcutta Town Hall and then went to Assam the closing scene of his distinguished official career in India. Such was the demoralisation of the bureaucracy that there too he had to encounter a worthy lieutenant of a worthy general. His successor Mr. J. B. (afterwards Sir Bamfylde) Fuller treated him with such gross discourtesy as was utterly repugnant to the ordinary rules of hospitality in Eastern countries, and people were not wanting who actually gave expression to a supposition that the Chief Commissioner acted either under inspiration, or through intution. But Sir Henry had his ample compensation in the unique hearty reception which the people of Assam gave him on the occasion to the infinite chagrin and mortification of the future hammering *Lat*, who to avenge a supposed insult thus offered by the people completed the triumph of his magnificent meanness by ordering the removal of a silent portrait which a grateful people had presented to the Gowhati College whose name however he was unable to efface. In 1902 when Sir Henry Cotton left Assam he received such an ovation as had never been accorded to any administrator of that planter-ridden province, and so great was his popularity in Bengal that a whole district town came with a farewell address to receive him at a railway terminus on the sandy banks of the Ganges where he first touched the soil of Bengal on his return journey, while the warm reception given to him in the metropolis of the empire was second only to that of the Marquis of Ripon in 1884. The people had, under the inspiration of the Congress, learnt to rise above the frown of official displeasure, learnt to respect themselves and learnt to honour those to whom honour was justly due.

But perhaps the most brilliant session of the Congress held since the Bradlaugh Congress of 1889 and undoubtedly the most stormy session that came to a successful termination was that held in Calcutta in 1906 under the third and last presidency of Mr. Dadabhai Naoroji. It was at this session that the long pent-up resentment of the people at the apathy and indifference of the Government towards popular demands, intensified by an avowed policy of reaction and retrogression along the whole line, burst forth into a blaze and the Congress was for the first time threatened with a split which only the strong and revered personality of Dadabhai averted for the time being. In this Congress the four famous resolutions were passed which embodied the spirit of the time and afterwards became at least the ostensible cause of a most regrettable schism in the Congrees camp.* It was at this Congress that Mr. Dadabhai in his Presidential Address used that historic expression *swaraj*, which was subsequently used as a watchword by a section of the Nationalist Party leading ultimately to an ugly development of the new situation. These will be noticed in detail later on.

Such is the short summary of the strenuous career of the national movement during the first twenty-two years of its life. All the twenty-two sessions were marked by unflagging zeal and earnestness and by a spirit of self-sacrifice which alone could have kept the fire burning in the midst of the frosty atmosphere by which its path had been throughout surrounded. The abortive session of 1907 opened a new chapter in the history of the movement which with its subsequent career is reserved for separate treatment. If only a few of the sessions have been selected for special reference in this report it is simply with a view to direct the attention of the young student of Indian politics to those landmarks which may serve as a useful guide to a careful study of some of the important stages through which the Congress has passed in its evolution of the national life. Among the various subjects, embracing nearly all the political issues, material to the development of that life, which have received the attention of the Congress during this period, the reform and expansion of the Legislative Councils the separation of Judicial and Executive functions, simultaneous examinations for the Indian Civil services, the reduction of Military Expenditure and a fair adjustment of account between the Indian and the British Exchequers, the larger employment of the children of the soil in the Public Services and the maintenance of strict economy in the most costly, if not the most extravagant, administration in the world, the reform of the Executive Councils of the Governor-General and of the Secretary of State by the admission of qualified natives of India into them, the position of Indians in the Colonies of Great Britian, the expansion and improvement of Education in all its branches, and the economic development of the country as a means to prevent periodical visitations of famine, and a fair reduction of the heaviest of taxations upon the poorest of people in the world have been the most important and common to all the Congresses, although new facts have been adduced and fresh lights thrown on almost each of these questions at every succeeding session. The many-sided activities of the movement, together with the vast amount of thought it has given to nearly all the grievances of the people, the means which the collective wisdom and patriotism of the country have been able to formulate for their remedy and above all the path which it has so clearly and definitely laid out for the ultimate attainment of the salvation of the country, will be found writ large in the pages of the Congress records and it will be for the future historian to critically analyse and sift them for the student of Indian politics.

The history of the Constitution of the Congress of which so much has been made in latter years may also be briefly noticed here. It was at the third Congress held at Madras in 1887 that a Committee was appointed to frame a set of rules for the guidance of the

Congress. The Committee submitted a set of well-devised rules which the Congress from year to year put off for the consideration of each succeeding session. In fact some of the leading members, pointing to the unwritten constitution of some of the most advanced representative institutions in the world, vehemently opposed the formulation of a hard-and-fast constitution for the Congress. In 1898 the matter being closely pressed, the Congress passed a resolution asking the "Standing Congress Committees" appointed by the Second Congress in 1886 to form "Central Committees" in their respective provinces and appointed another Committee to consider the Draft Constitution circulated by the Reception Committee of Madras. In the following year when the policy of procrastination could be carried no further, the Congress at last passed eleven good rules defining the object of the Congress, though somewhat loosely expressed, as being the "promotion by constitutional means of the interests and the well being of the people of the Indian Empire." The other rules provided for the establishment of a Committee styled "The Indian Congress Committee," afterwards known as the "All-India Congress Committee" and the appointment of "Provincial Congress Committees" at the capitals of the different Provinces. It was at this Congress also that the nomination of the Congress President as well as the drafting of the Resolutions were formally made over to the Indian Congress Committee. The maintenance of the British Committee in England was also made obligatory on the part of the Congress. Then there was a lull until 1906 when the rules were further extended and revised. This time the Standing Congress Committee was fully organised by a fair re-distribution of its members among the various provinces, the rule for the selection of the President made still more circumscribed and the decision of the Standing Congress Committee on the nomination of the President-Elect made final to avoid an ugly discussion on the subject at any session of the Congress a tendency which had manifested itself at some of the preceding Congresses. For several years past some difficulty had been experienced in forming a properly representative Subjects Committee and one of the rules now framed not only limited the number of members for the Subjects Committee, but also distributed the number fairly among the different provinces. The Congress broke down in 1907 and the next step taken by the Congress was the comprehensive and codified regulations provided by the Allahabad Convention of 1908. Mr. Hume was the General Secretary of the Congress from its very beginning. It was several times proposed to install him once in the Presidential Chair; but the "Father of the Congress" could never be persuaded to exchange the sword for the crown and so he continued to be its Secretary till his death in July 1912. In 1890-91 Pundit Ajudhyànath and in 1893 Mr. Ananda Charlu acted as Joint General Secretaries. Mr. Hume left India in 1894, and Mr. D. E. Wacha was appointed Joint General Secretary to act for him in India from 1895, Mr. Gokhale being appointed Additional Secretary from 1903. Since 1912 Mr. D. E. Wacha and Mr. G. K. Gokhale were Joint Secretaries.

Mr. Wacha still holds his appointment, but Mr. Gokhale was succeeded by Mr. Daji Abaji Khare in 1908. The birthplace of the Congress has long maintained the executive leadership of the organisation ; but it has recently been transferred to Madras. In 1889 Messrs. W. C. Bonnerjee, Pherozeshah Mehta and Ananda Charlu were appointed Standing Counsel of the Congress to advise the Secretary in all matters of importance, an arrangement which afterwards ceased to be necessary under the subsequent Constitution of the Congress. In point of organising spirit evoked by the Congress, Bombay again heads the list among all the major provinces. While it has been so far possible for Bengal and Madras to hold their turn of the Congress Sessions only in the two capital cities, and for the United Provinces in three places, Bombay has held the Congress at five different centres within the Presidency with equal zeal and enthusiasm.

Upon a careful examination of this eventful career of the Congress movement, it will appear that its one object has been the upbuilding of an Indian National life and to that end it has throughout laboured to generate forces for the fusion of a heterogeneous population into a homogeneous mass and then to direct its weight and impetus to operate against the stubborn resistance of an impregnable bureaucracy as strong in its organization as it is conservative in its instincts and traditions. The various questions, to which the Congress has drawn attention, are all supplementary to that one great object, and although they are apparently independent of one another, they form as it were close links in a chain which drawn like a cordon converges to a common point encircling a common centre. It is some times argued that the Congress might have done better by concentrating its attention only to a few important points instead of dissipating its energies over an immense area. But it is as often overlooked that such a selection is only possible where the contending forces are fairly matched, and both sides command a base for their respective operations. Here the entire ground being in the effective occupation of one party, the other side was bound to deliver an attack everywhere to gain a footing somewhere. The work of the Congress at the outset was more of new creation than of normal development. It had to produce men as well as materials and to devise plans for the execution of its uphill work. There was not a single ground upon which the people could stand on their legs. Every avenue in political life was closed against them, while the people themselves were disintegrated congeries without any clear perception of the various disabilites under which they laboured and without any *locus standi* anywhere in the administration of the country to press for their solution. They were practically Utilanders in their own native land. Besides, where a body suffers from serious complications of a number of acute maladies, it is difficult to prescribe or rely upon a single specific as a panacea for all the complaints. The Congress was therefore, fully justified, at all events in its initial stage, to draw attention of both the people as well as the Government to all the grievances from which the country suffered, and which were its avowed object to remedy by constitutional means and methods.

CHAPTER XI.

THE SURAT IMBROGLIO AND THE ALLAHABAD CONVENTION.

Twenty Sessions of the Congress were held in perfect peace and patience supported only by an unswerving confidence of the people in the strong sense of British justice and the ultimate triumph of British statesmanship of which it was confidently affirmed that if it had blundered in many places, had failed nowhere at the end, although within this sufficiently long period the only concession of note obtained was a half-hearted measure of nominal reform of the Indian Councils under a Parliamentary Statute of 1892 which the Government of India took precious good care still further to restrict in its application as an experiment. It was a reform to which the Congress had attached the greatest importance from the very beginning and for which it had made no small sacrifices both here as well as in England. In 1890 Charles Bradlaugh on behalf of the Congress at last introduced in the Commons a Bill for this reform and the Government of the day, true to its conservative instinct and tradition, seeing that a change was inevitable adroitly wrested away the proposed legislation from the hand of a private radical member and introduced a Bill of its own which was a perfect counterfeit, both in form as well as substance. In vain Mr. Gladstone expressed the hope that in its practical operation it might carry some value with the people and Lord Cross' so-called reform measure fell flat upon the country. As regards the other complaints of the Congress and the people not even a courteous reply was vouchsafed to any of them. A feeling was thus gradually gaining ground in the country, in spite of the robust optimism of its leaders, that the Government with all its commissions and committees, as well as its elaborate minutes, despatches and resolutions, was not disposed to make any real concessions to the people: that its settled policy was to keep the people under perpetual tutelage and govern the country by its annual pyrotechnic displays of honours and titles and by occasionally throwing, when absolutely necessary, a morsel here and a morsel there to the children of the soil in the public services and above all by steadfastly clinging to the pestilental doctrine of *divide-et-empira*. The feeling was perhaps somewhat exaggerated and not fully justified; but there it was among a considerable section of the people who sincerely believed that the authorities were, as a whole, strongly opposed to the slightest modification of the vested rights and privileges of the bureaucracy upon whose inviolable strength the safety of the Empire was supposed to be based and that as such they were fully prepared to treat Indian public opinion as voiced by the Congress, as well as the Press, with perfect indifference if not with absolute disregard and contempt. Men were not indeed wanting even in high places who decisively snapped their fingers at the suggestion of driving discontent underground. The regrettable feeling became further intensified during the weak Viceroyalty of Lord Elgin, when the bureaucracy attained its highest ascendancy and secured a complete mastery over the administration. When King Log was succeeded by King Stock the position of the Congress became still more critical. No Viceroy ever came out to India with brighter prospects of success and left it with greater unpopularity than Lord Curzon. The retrograde policy which he so vigorously and unreservedly initiated in all directions culminated in a series of unpopular measures which successively marked the unfortunately extended period of his Viceroyalty. The Official Secrets Act, the Indian Universities Act and last of all the Partition of Bengal followed in quick succession and the wave of popular discontent began to surge from one end of the country to the other. He was reported to have actually proposed the appointment of a permanent Viceroy for India, and whether he had an eye on himself or not it was a most fortunate circumstance both for India as well as England that such an extravagant proposal was not entertainable under the British constitution. The effects of the Congress during this period were almost paralysed, and the bulk of the people nearly lost all confidence in its propaganda.

Towards the end of 1905 the Liberals came into power with Mr. John Morley as Secretary of State for India. The people who had the utmost confidence in Mr. Morley's liberalism fondly hoped that with the change of government a change would also be perceived in the policy of the Indian administration. In this they were painfully deceived, and a section of the Nationalist party, as represented in the Congress, feeling themselves tired of what they called the "mendicant policy" of the movement wanted to divert it on new lines. This the sober leaders, backed by an overwhelming majority in the Congress and the country, stoutly resisted and the result was that the people were divided into two camps, the Moderates and the Extremists—terms invented by the official organs since 1904, but which are used in these pages in no offensive sense. The êarliest symptom of this difference appeared at the Benares Congress of 1905, and the first open rupture manifested itself in the Calcutta Congress of 1906 when a small body of these Extremists finding themselves unable to have their own way rushed out of the Pandal leaving, however, no perceptible void in the densely packed assembly of over sitxeen hundred delegates and five times as many visitors. It was no doubt true that the whole country had grown dissatisfied with the stolid indifference and immobility of the Government and that an overwhelming majority of the educated community had taken deep offence at the constant flouting of public opinion and the deliberate substitution of a policy of reaction in almost every branch of the administration. Moderates and Extremists alike and with equal emphasis protested against the attitude of the Government and with equal firmness deprecated an ignominious begging spirit and urged the people to take their stand more upon justice than upon generosity and upon their own just rights more than upon concessions of Government. There was however this difference, that while the majority of the Nationalist party knew what they were about, the minority hardly knew their own mind and in a spirit of exasperation lost their balance. At this memorable session held under the third and the last distinguished presidency of the Grand Old Man of India, the Congress unanimously passed four important resolutions which bore unmistakable evidence of the spirit of the times, confining itself however within the strict limits of constitutional agitation and in keeping with its original constitution as well as its past traditions. These were Self-Government on the Colonial lines, National Education, Swadeshi and Boycott of foreign goods. The first had been the avowed object of the Congress almost from the very beginning. It was now laid down with precision and firmness as the ultimate goal of the National Assembly. The secoud resolution was felt as necessitated by the officialization of the Universities and the threatened curtailment of Education under the policy inaugurated by Lord Curzon ; the third was deemed imperatively necessary for the protection and encouragement of the dying industries of the country ; while the fourth and the last was intended as a protest against the systematic flouting of public opinion in the country, as also to draw the attention of the British public and Parliament to the grievances of the Indian people. The first resolution was announced by the Extremist press as the *Swaraj* resolution though the dubious word *Swaraj* was to be found nowhere in the resolution itself, and was used only once by the President in his inaugural address, of course, in a perfectly legitimate sense. The separatists evidently smarted under a sense of wrong and throughout the year that followed kept up an agitation through the columns of their papers as well as upon the platforms decrying the Congress and preaching the "utter futility" of the Congress propaganda; although what other propagandum there was to present to the country, they were able neither to formulate nor to indicate. Theirs was apparently a work of destruction and not of construction.

The next Congress was to have been held at Nagpur, but some serious local differences arising, the All-India Congress Committee had to change the venue of the session from Nagpur to Surat which was the rival candidate for the honour at the previous session of the Congress. Early in November 1907 a rumour was circulated by some mischievous or designing people that the Twenty-Third Session of the Congress would have nothing to do with the four new resolutions of the preceding session and this *canard* was persistently kept up till the 24th and 25th December when all the delegates to the Twenty-Third Indian National Congress arrived at Surat, although no one, when asked, was able precisely to refer to the source of his information. It was evidently like the proverbial story of the ghost whom every one had heard of, but none had seen. The Extremists under the leadership of that remarkable man, Mr. Bal Gangadhar Tilak, encamped themselves at a place three miles distant from the Congress camps, and many were the rumours afloat that something serious was going to happen at this session of the Congress. The baseless accusation about the exclusion of the four resolutions was again repeated; but it was at once refuted not only by the verbal assurances of the responsible authorities of the Congress, but also by the subsequent production of an agenda paper containing those resolutions. The oppositionists then laid hold on the question of presidentship and urged that Lala Lajpat Roy and not Dr. Rashbehary Ghose should have been nominated as president-elect. The patriotic Lala however cut the Gordian knot by publicly declining to stand as candidate for the presidential chair. Upon this another person was mentioned as a probable candidate for the post. It seemed rather difficult to ascertain what really the motive was in all these manœuvres; but people were not wanting in the Congress camps who actually believed that the speech of Dr. Ghose, the president-elect, had somehow leaked out and that the extreme section of the Congress party having discovered that there were certain caustic observations regarding them and their ideals in that speech they were determined at all hazards to prevent that speech from being delivered at the Congress. However that may be, the Congress met on the 26th December at about 2-30 p.m., on account of the sudden death of a Sindhi delegate, in the grand pavilion constructed by the Reception Committee in the old historic French Garden, which had been converted into a pretty little town for the occasion. Full 1,200 delegates and over 5,000 visitors were assembled in the Pandal. Every face was beaming with enthusiasm and as every prominent man passed on to the *dais* he was lustily cheered. At last the president-elect entered the hall in a procession and he received such a tremendous ovation that the last shred of doubt and suspicion about the success of the session seemed at once to have vanished from the hall. No sooner calm was restored a whisper was however heard going round a very limited block that all was not well and that an untoward incident was brewing somewhere; but not a few among the robust optimists confidently hoped that the lowering cloud would instantly pass away and the session prove a brilliant success. The rest of the painful and humiliating episode may, however, be narrated, for merely historical purposes, in the words of an impartial observer. The following telegraphic report, under date the 26th December, from the special correspondent of the *Statesman*, appeared in that paper and was reproduced in the *Pioneer* of the 30th idem:—

The twenty-third National Congress met on Thursday afternoon in the grand pandal at Surat at a place known as the French Garden. The pandal is a large square with seating capacity for over 7,000, and the whole place was filled to its utmost capacity. Long before the President-elect, the Hon. Dr. Ghose, arrived the delegates and spectators had taken up every available seat and some of the busy Extremist leaders took occasion to harangue their followers. Mr. Khare, an Extremist leader of Nasik, intimated to a group of Mahratta Extremists that the Congress should be asked to include the resolutions on boycott, swaraj, and national education in the year's programme and if this was not considered favourably, Mr. Tilak was to oppose the motion formally voting Dr. Ghose to the presidential chair. This announcement was received with approval and applause by the Poona Extremists, and also elicited approbation from the feeble ranks of the Madras Extremists. There were appeals made to the excitable spectators by irresponsible and mischievous preachers in the pandal, with the result that for over an hour before the President's arrival, the scene was one of excitement among the Extremists and intense anxiety among the Moderates.

Meanwhile the leading Congressmen from several parts as they arrived were received with ovations. Lala Lajpat Rai's arrival was the occasion for the greatest enthusiasm, demonstrated in a most unmistakable manner. He was conducted to the platform and took his seat between Dr. Rutherford and Mr. Surendra Nath Banerjee. Sardar Ajit Singh also received some demonstrations. The long platform at the western end of the hall was occupied by a distinguished gathering of the principal Congressmen and visitors. There were among those present at the Congress, leaders like Sir Pherozeshah Mehta, the Hon. Mr. Gokhale, Sir Balchandra Krishna; merchant princes like the Hon. Vithaldass Damodar Thakersey, Lalubhai Samal Dass, Ibrahim Adamji Peerbhai from Bombay; patriots like Surendra Nath Banerjee and Bhupendra Nath Basu from Calcutta; and Punjab leaders like Lal Harkisen Lal and Lajpat Rai from Lahore, and the Hon'ble Krishnasami Iyer and Govindaraghava Iyer, N. Subha Rao and others from Madras; also Extremist leaders, Messrs. Tilak and Khaparde.

Dr. Ghose arrived, accompanied by Sir Pherozeshah Mehta and other members of the Congress executive, and was welcomed with loud and prolonged cheering, not unmingled with stray shouting of "Shame" from some of the Extremists.

As soon as Dr. Ghose took his seat the Chairman of the Reception Committee (Mr. Thribhuvandas Malvi), delivered his address of welcome to the delegates, in the course of which he referred to the great historic antecedents of Surat and its subsequent downfall as a commerical centre, and in consequence, the rise of Bombay. He also dealt with the good work which the Congress had done in the past in the cause of the country, and hoped that it would continue its policy of moderation, loyalty, firmness and unity.

This statement roused the fire of the Extremists, who hissed and cried "No, no" and otherwise attempted to interrupt him whenever they heard him preach moderation.

When he sat down Dewan Bahadur Ambalal Sakar Lal Desai proposed that Dr. Ghose do take the presidential chair, in a short speech in which he extolled his patriotic services, and he, too, was again interrupted by cries of "No, no" from the Extremists.

Then Mr. Surendranath Banerjee rose to address the assembly. It was hoped that he would be able to command the audience with his powerful voice and compelling eloquence; but the moment he uttered the first word the Extremists were determined to give him no chance. The greatest disturbance proceeded from the front rows of the Madras and Deccan blocks of delegates which were nearest the platform, and the rowdy section among the Extremists made a determined effort to obstruct the proceedings. They called loudly for Mr. Tilak and Lajpat Rai, and would have none of Mr. Banerjee; but the Moderates urged him to go on and he made repeated attempts to make himself heard, but scarcely a word could be heard above the noisy clamour of the Extremists. They were only about 30, the majority of these coming from Madras. At this stage the Chairman of the Reception Committee stood up and warned the Extremists that, if they kept up like that, the sitting would be impossible, and he would be compelled to suspend the Congress. Even he was not heard.

Mr. Banerjee made another futile attempt and was obliged finally to retire, giving rise to great shouts of triumph on the part of the disturbers.

Meanwhile some parleying went on among the leaders and a movement in the direction of Messrs. Tilak and Khaparde was noticed with a view to persuade them to intervene. This attempt was unsuccessful. Either they did not intervene, or only did so in an equivocal manner, so that their following could not understand them. Meanwhile the Bengalis in particular, and the audience in general, resented the insult offered to the great Bengali leader and orator, and would not hear any one in preference to him. The rowdies, however, continued their noisy demonstration and the Chairman was compelled to declare the Congress suspended for the day, and the leaders retired. But for long afterwards the Extremists held possession of the pandal, men of both parties crying "Shame" against each other.

It is obvious that the disturbance during the afternoon was the result of a deliberately pre-concerted plan of action on the part of the Extremist leaders. These seeing that they and their party were in a hopeless minority were determined not to take defeat on the industrial resolutions before the Congress and so resolved to make the situation impossible at the outset and wreck the Congress. The ostensible pretext of the Extremists in support of their conduct is the alleged omission of the Congress authorities to include resolutions on boycott, swaraj, and national education, which turns out to be absolutely unfounded. A statement denying the rumours set afloat by scheming Extremist leaders was circulated over the signature of the Secretary, but apparently they were spoiling for a split, and they have succeeded in creating an impasse.

Telegraphing on the 27th the same correspondent added :—

"Since last night a manifesto has been issued over the signatures of about twenty leading Congressmen of all parts of the country appealing to the delegates. The manifesto is signed for each province by the respective leaders and runs as follows :—

"Babu Surendra Nath Banerjee, who was to second the proposition moved by Dewan Bahadur Amba Lal Sakar Lal Desai, for the election of Dr. Ghose as President of the Congress has been prevented from speaking against the established practice of the Congress and violation of old traditions. The session of Congress has had to be suspended for the day. If similar obstruction continues it might be necessary to close the session of Congress, a situation which is humiliating for all delegates and an event which will bring disgrace to the country. It is requested that all delegates to the Congress of all shades of opinion will express their differences in a proper constitutional manner and it is hoped that all will use their influence towards this end."

The Congress assembled at 1 p. m., a large number of visitors and delegates were present. The proceedings began where they were left yesterday by voting Dr. Ghose to the Presidential chair. This was supported and declared carried. Dr. Ghose stood up, but before his address began Mr. Tilak went up on the platform. The audience would not hear him and cried "Shame." Great confusion then ensued. Mr. Tilak would not leave the platform despite pressing requests from eminent men, including Dr. Rutherford. Dr. Ghose then proceeded with his address whereupon Mr. Tilak appealed to his followers, who were considerably excited and rushed up to the platform and attacked every one with sticks with which they were armed. The ladies were removed in safety. Confusion still reigns supreme. The police came in and made arrests. The Magistrate of Surat on the afternoon of the 27th, telegraphed to the Government of India that, "Indian National Congress meeting to-day became disorderly blows being exchanged. The President called on the police to clear the house and the grounds which was done. Order now restored. No arrests. No one reported seriously hurt. No further hurt anticipated." As a matter of fact some arrests were made, but the Reception Committee declining to proceed the prisoners were at once released by the police.

The following official statement was issued on the 28th Friday evening by the Hon. Dr. Rash Behari Ghose, President, Mr. Tribhuvandas N. Malvi, Chairman of the Reception Committee, and Mr. D. E. Wacha and Mr. G. K. Gokhale, Joint General Secretaries of the Indian National Congress:—

"The twenty-third Indian National Congress assembled yesterday in the Pavilion erected for it by the Reception Committee at Surat at 2-30 P.M. Over sixteen hundred delegates were present. The proceedings began with an address from the Chairman of Reception Committee. After the reading of the address was over Diwan Bahadur Ambalal Sakerlal proposed that the Hon. Dr. Rash Behari Ghose having been nominated by the Reception Committee for the office of President under the rules adopted at the last session of the Congress, he should take the Presidential chair. As soon as the Dewan Bahadur uttered Dr. Ghose's name, some voices were heard in the body of the hall shouting "No, no" and the shouting was kept up for some time. The proposer, however, somehow managed to struggle through his speech; and the Chairman then called upon Babu Surendranath Banerjee to second the proposition. As soon, however, as he began his speech —before he had finished even in his first sentence—a small section of the delegates began an uproar from their seats with the object of preventing Mr. Banerjee from speaking. The Chairman repeatedly appealed for order, but no heed was paid. Every time Mr. Banerjee attempted to go on with his speech he was met by disorderly shouts. It was clear that rowdyism had been determined upon to bring the proceedings to a standstill, and the whole demonstrations seemed to have been pre-arranged. Finding it impossible to enforce order, the Chairman warned the House that unless the uproar subsided at once, he would be obliged to suspend the sitting of the Congress. The hostile demonstration, however, continued and the Chairman at last suspended the sitting for the day.

The Congress again met to-day at 1 P.M., due notice of the meeting having been sent round. As the President-elect was being escorted in procession through the Hall to the platform, an overwhelming majority of the delegates present greeted him with a most enthusiastic welcome, thereby showing how thoroughly they disapproved the organised disorder of yesterday. As this procession was entering the Pandal a small slip of paper written in pencil and bearing Mr. B. G. Tilak's signature was put by a volunteer into the hands of Mr. Malvi, the Chairman of the Reception Committee. It was a notice to the Chairman that after Mr. Banerjee's speech, seconding the proposition about the President was concluded, Mr. Tilak wanted to move "an amendment for an adjournment of the Congress." The Chairman considered a notice of adjournment at that stage to be irregular and out of order. The proceedings were then resumed at the point at which thay had been interrupted yesterday, and Mr. Surendranath Banerjee was called upon to conclude his speech. Mr Banerjee having done this, the Chairman called upon Pandit Motilal Nehru of Allahabad to support the motion. The Pandit supported it in a brief speech and then the Chairman put the motion to the vote. An overwhelming majority of the delegates signified their assent by crying "All, all" and a small minority shouted "No, no." The Chairman thereupon declared the motion carried and the Hon. Dr. Ghose was installed in the Presidential chair amidst loud and prolonged applause. While the applause was going on, and as Dr. Ghose rose to begin his address, Mr. Tilak came upon the platform and stood in front of the President. He urged that as he had given notice of an "amendment to the Presidential election," he should be permitted to move his amendment.

Thereupon, it was pointed out to him by Mr. Malvi, the Chairman of the Reception Committee that his notice was not for "an amendment to the Presidential election," but it was for "an adjournment of the Congress;" which notice he had considered to be irregular and out of order at that stage; and that the President having been duly installed in the chair no amendment about his election could be then moved. Mr. Tilak then turned to the President and began arguing with him. Dr. Ghose in his turn, stated how matters stood and ruled that this request to move an amendment about the election could not be entertained. Mr. Tilak thereupon said, "I will not submit to this. I will now appeal from the President to the delegates." In the meantime an uproar had already been commenced by some of his followers, and the President who tried to read his address could not be heard even by those who were seated next to him. Mr. Tilak with his back to the President, kept shouting that he insisted on moving his amendment and he would not allow the proceedings to go on. The President repeatedly appealed to him to be satisfied with his protest and to resume his seat. Mr. Tilak kept on shouting frantically, exclaiming that he would not go back to his seat unless he was " bodily removed." This persistent defiance of the authority of the chair provoked a hostile demonstration against Mr. Tilak himself and for some time, nothing but loud cries of "Shame, shame" could be heard in the Pandal. It had been noticed, that when Mr. Tilak was making his way to the platform some of his followers were also trying to force themselves through the volunteers to the platform with sticks in their hands. All attempts on the President's part either to proceed with the reading of his address or to persuade Mr. Tilak to resume his seat having failed, and a general movement among Mr. Tilak's followers to rush the platform with sticks in their hands being noticed, the President, for the last time, called upon Mr. Tilak to withdraw and formally announced to the assembly that he had ruled and he still ruled Mr. Tilak out of order and he called upon him to resume his seat. Mr. Tilak refused to obey and at this time a shoe hurled from the body of the Hall, struck both Sir Pherozeshah Mehta and Mr. Surendranath Banerjee who were sitting side by side. Chairs were also hurled towards the platform and it was seen that Mr. Tilak's followers who were brandishing their sticks wildly were trying to rush the platform which other delegates were endeavouring to prevent. It should be stated here that some of the delegates were so exasperated by Mr. Tilak's conduct that they repeatedly asked for permission to eject him bodily from the hall; but this permission was steadily refused. The President, finding that the disorder went on growing and that he had no other course open to him, declared the session of the 23rd Indian National Congress suspended *sine die*. After the lady-delegates present on the platform had been escorted to the tents outside, the other delegates began with difficulty to disperse, but the disorder, having grown wilder, the Police eventually came in and ordered the Hall to be cleared."

The heavy Deccan shoe which hit Sir Pherozeshah Mehta and Mr. Surendranath Banerjee may be still in the possession of the latter and if its fellow could be found it might well have been preserved by the former also, and both might have left them either as a trophy or as a memento from their countrymen for their lifelong services to the country. On the evening of the 26th the bulk of the Bengal delegates issued a manifesto protesting against the proceedings of the day and the insult so gratuitously offered to Mr. Banerjee; while the leading delegates from all the provinces belonging to the moderate camp issued an appeal to all the delegates imploring them to use their influence to effect a settlement and avert a catastrophe. But all was in vain; the Congress was broken up. Statements and counter-statements were subsequently issued by both sides each presenting its own view of the case, for a better understanding and fair judgment on the merits of which all these papers are published in an appendix.

On the evening of the 27th after the Congress was suspended *sine die*, the leading delegates met and discussed the situation, and on the 28th nearly 900 of the delegates in the presence of a large number of visitors, who had been greatly excited over the disorderly proceedings of the previous day, again met in the Congress pavilion and adopted a manifesto calling upon the country to subscribe to an article and revive the Congress under convention. A committee was formed to frame a well-defined constitution for the Congress and it was decided that this committee should meet at Allahabad in April next. After this a few speeches were made by some of the prominent speakers present for the satisfaction of the Surat people and with a view to alleviate to some extent the grievous disappointment and mortification of the Reception Committee who had worked so hard and incurred so much expense for the session; but no business of the Congress was or could be transacted and the meeting dispersed in solemn silence as on a mournful occasion.

Thus ended the Twenty-Third Session of the Indian National Congress which had promised to be one of the most brilliant sessions of the National Assembly. The Anglo-Indian Press of the time while generally deploring the incident could ill-disguise its secret satisfaction at the threatened collapse of the national movement. One paper used the incident as a most powerful argument, as it thought, for its invincible contention, that the Indians were unfit for representative institutions and that if the Indian Legislative Councils were made elective they would soon be converted into so many bear-gardens, conveniently forgetting of course that even graver incidents not infrequently occurred in the British House of Commons and French Chamber of Deputies, although these two were the highest exponents of democratic evolution in modern European civilization. The great Liberal organ of the *London Daily News*, however, with its charcteristic firmness and frankness observed that it "hoped that the fiasco at Surat may do good, and that the failure of the Moderates was due to the slow pace and grudging scope of British reforms," and it urged the "adoption of a policy of restoring faith in British wisdom and justice." In closing this lamentable incident it should however be remarked, whether it is very material or not, that there seemed to have arisen considerable *bona-fide* misapprehension either on the one side or the other as regards the actual purport of Mr. Tilak's missing slip to the Chairman of the Reception Committee, and that however deplorable the action of the rowdies was and however mistaken Mr. Tilak may have been in assuming the attitude which he ultimately did assume on the platform, it is hardly conceivable that a man of Bal Gangadhar Tilak's position and patriotism could have knowingly and willingly associated himself with any plan of action calculated to wreck the Congress. Whatever may have been his actual share in the business Mr. Tilak has since paid heavier penalties for his courage of conviction and undergone severer trials and tribulations for his rare freedom of thought and expression, and it is very much to be hoped that his services to the country will not be lost for ever.

THE CONVENTION AND AFTER.

Agreeably to decision arrived at Surat, over a hundred delegates from the different provinces met at Allahabad in April 1908, and at two long sittings held in the Town-Hall of that city on the 18th and 19th April, discussed and settled a constitution for the Congress and passed a set of rules and regulations for its management. The object as set forth in the constitution was commonly known as the inviolable creed of the Indian National Congress to which every member was required unconditionally to subscribe before he could take his seat in the assembly. It may be here remarked that the Bengal delegates, numbering no less than 38, supported by a few delegates from the other provinces, strongly urged that the Rules and Regulations so passed by the Convention Committee should be submitted to a whole house of the Congress at the next session. The proposal, however, did not recommend itself to the majority of the Committee.

The first Congress under the Convention was held at Madras in December 1908 with Dr. Rash Behary Ghose as its president and under the happy auspices of Lord Morley's Reform scheme. How sad it is to contemplate that if these reforms had been inaugurated one year earlier the deplorable split among the Nationalists, nor the yet more deplorable consequences which have since flowed from it, might have happened. Born at Bombay and buried at Surat, the Congress attained its resurrection at Madras, purged and purified through years of persecutions, trials and tribulations, it rose from its grave in triumph vindicating the truth of its gospel and restoring public hope and confidence in the ultimate success of its mission. It was a red-letter day in the history of the country when after twenty-two years of patient and persistent knocking, the barred gate was at last opened unto the people. Though attended only by the conventionists, the Session of 1908 was a most enthusiastic one, at which nearly all the veterans of the Congress were present. The masterly address of the learned president enlivened by his forensic skill and flashes of caustic good humour, no less than by its manly dignity and incisive arguments, presented a most graphic account of the origin aud character of the prevailing unrest which at the time engrossed the attention of the Government and the public. The Madras Congress of 1908 was recorded as the 23rd Congress, the people having like Alexander Selkirk in crossing the burning Equator lost a day in their political almanac. Although the Bengal proposal was rejected by the Convention Committee, the Rules and Regulations passed by it were formally laid on the table of the Congress of 1908 and duly adopted at the Calcutta Congress of 1911, whereupon Mr. A. Rasul, than whom a more ardent lover of his country's cause was scarcely to be found on either side of the Nationalist party, with a few others rejoined the Congress. These Rules and Regulations with certain amendments were again, submitted to and re-affirmed by the Bankipore Congress of 1912; but the rest of the separatists have still held out although upon what reasonable ground it is difficult to appreciate.*

In 1909 Lord Morley's reform of the Legislative Councils came into operation and the Hon'ble Mr. S. P. Sinha was appointed as the first Indian member of the Viceroy's Executive Council and the Right Honourable Mr. Ameer Ali as a member of the Privy Council; but the Congress while fully appreciating these liberal measures of reform had the misfortune to enter its emphatic protest against the Council Regulations which in a large measure neutralized the effects of these wholesome changes. In the following year

* The Nationalists have since joined the Congress.

Sir William Wedderburn, who came out for a second time as President of the Congress, made a vigorous effort for a *rapprochement* between the Mahomedans and the other communities so fully represented in the Congress, and long and earnest were the debates which took place in Committees on the Council Regulations in course of which prominent Mahomedan leaders frankly admitted the unfair and disintegrating tendencies of the regulations and the anomalous distinctions introduced by them in the composition of the Councils. The Congress of 1911 witnessed a complete change in the political atmosphere of the country. The King personally appeared on the scene, modified the Partition of Bengal and sounded the watchword of hope and contentment throughout the country. The long-deferred policy of conciliation was at last substituted for the policy of repression which had been tried for seven long years and found wanting. With the dawn of the fresh bright morning, the great Mahomedan community also awoke to a consciousness of their situation, and in 1912 the Moslem League under the guidance of that distinguished and patriotic Mahomedan leader, Sir Ibrahim Rahimtullah, openly accepted the Congress ideal and the Congress programme for the realization of the inter-dependent, inter-woven, and inseparable destinies of the diverse communities owing allegiance to a common Mother-land. The Congress this year was appropriately held under the guidance of another patriotic Mahomedan leader in the new Province of Behar, where the Hindus and Mahomedans had lived for generations in perfect peace, amity and concord, and it laid the foundation for the re-union of the two great communities which was materially advanced twelve months later in the rising capital of Guzerat under the presidency of Nawab Syed Mahomed of Madras.

Upon a careful examination of the political situation of the country during the last six or seven years it will appear that the Surat incident marks a turning point in the history of the Indian National Congress. It has given a definite shape and form to that movement and marked out a well-defined course of action for the Indian Nationalist. It has also dispelled some of the crudest and most fantastic misconceptions with which its aims and objects were shrouded at the hands of its critics ever since its birth. If it has to some extent thinned the ranks of the Nationalists, it has, on the other hand, strengthened the movement by laying its foundation upon a sure concrete basis and by investing it with the unassailable character of a constitutional organization completely divested of all wild fancies and feverish excitements of impatient idealism. Every great movement has its ups and downs, its successes as well as sit reverses. All evolutions in human society are marked by a 'continuous struggle between divergent currents of thought and action, and a virile people ought only to gain and not lose by occasional differences of opinion in its rank, when such differences are inspired not by any sordid motive, but by a common impulse towards its general advancement. In England the political field is held by a number of factions arrayed in hostile camps and representing different shades of opinion and interest. These divergent forces at times seem to shatter the constitution, but in reality they serve only to strengthen it. The Tories and the Whigs, the Liberals and the Conservatives, the Radicals and the Unionists, and the Labourites and the Socialists are all but the diverse manifestations of two grand evolutionary forces tending towards the maintenance of an equilibrium which is so essential to the growth and preservation of the entire system. If one of these two main opposing forces were to be either destroyed or removed, the other would fly off at a tangent leading either to anarchy or despotism. No honest differences of opinion in politics can, therefore, be either unwelcome or undesirable, provided they are all constructive and not destructive in their tendencies and are sincerely prompted by a healthy patriotic impulse for the common good of the community. If the separatists at Surat had, instead of attempting to wreck the Congress, started a counter organization with a definite policy and programme, they might well have established their position either as progressives or conservatives in Indian politics; and if even after the regrettable incident they had openly and earnestly placed a legitimate scheme before the country instead of sulkily retiring to their tents and dissociating themselves from all practical politics, they would not have been charged with committing "political suicide," and they could have in all probability gained and not lost by their opposition. Healthy opposition is the highest stimulant of political life, and if both parties to a question can honestly carry on their propaganda beyond the range of mere destructive criticism, the direct result of such contests can only tend towards the invigoration of both and the ultimate attainment of their common object.

Upon the Reform of the Councils the force of reactionary policy was supposed to have spent itself, and it was confidently hoped, that the tide would now roll back removing one by one some, if not all, of the ugly stains which that policy had engraved on the administration as well as on the national character, healing the wounds it had inflicted upon the public mind and restoring peace and confidence in the future administration of the country. But here again the people were doomed to considerable disappointment. Lord Morley's reform was no doubt a substantial measure of improvement, though by an irony of fate the Rules and Regulations framed by the Government in this country considerably neutralized its effects and largely frustrated its objects by providing watertight compartments for the Councils, unfair distribution of seats, differential treatment of classes and communities tending towards a disintegration of the national units and by placing the educated community which had fought for the reform under considerable disadvantage. People were, therefore, not wanting who openly indulged in the belief, that when the long discussion over the reform of the Councils was nearing its conclusion and a change in the constitution could no longer be deferred, the bureaucracy at first attempted to divert it by certain fantastic proposals for the establishment of Advisory Councils of Nobles and Princes to the practical exclusion of the People; but when this idea of creating an irresponsible House of Lords without a representative House of

Commons for the Indian administration was stoutly opposed by the people and a Liberal Government was found ill-disposed to repeat a blunder in India which they were bent upon rectifying in the constitution at Home, that bureaucracy apparently summoned all the resources of its ingenuity to devise means for the maintenance of its own threatened prestige, for accentuating racial differences by dangling the bait of communal representation before certain classes and above all for avenging themselves upon those who were primarily responsible for these disagreeable changes of far-reaching consequences. There was no doubt the other side of the shield; but in their positive distrust the people were ill-disposed to turn to it. Lord Minto succeeded to a legacy of serious troubles left him by his predecessor, and though his administration was marked by a series of repressive and retrograde measures, it must be admitted that he had to deal with a situation of enormous difficulties for which he was hardly responsible, except for the extreme remedies with which he was ill-advised to combat it. The violent dismemberment of Bengal and the other reactionary measures of Lord Curzon still rankled in the heart of the people who were goaded to desperation under the relentless operation of a number of repressive laws, recklessly driving discontent underground, when the hydra-headed monster of anarchism at last reared its grim head in a country where its existence was wholly unknown and unsuspected. The hammering lieutenant, whom the real author of this ugly development had left in charge of the new province and whose unhappy allusion to his "two wives" disgusted the Hindus and Mahomedans alike, went on with fad after fad until Lord Minto was compelled to take him up in hand and send him away bag and baggage to England. But even Lord Minto ultimately succumbed to the irresistible influence of the bureaucracy and in an evil hour lent his sanction to the forging of the most indiscriminate and drastic measures for the treatment of the situation. Conciliation was regarded as a sign of weakness although the fear of being regarded as weak was perhaps a much greater weakness, and the situation without being in the least improved began to grow from bad to worse. During this period the Congress was driven to a position very nearly between the devil and the deep sea. On the one hand there were the forces of disorder which very much weakened its position and hampered its work, while on the other an unrelenting bureaucracy found ample opportunities of attacking it with redoubled violence and fury. The Congress, however, went on urging its demands with calmness and moderation laying particular stress on the adoption of a policy of conciliation. While strongly denouncing lawlessness, it clearly pointed out that conciliation and not repression was the true remedy for the situation. But the Government turned a deaf ear to its advice and went on forging one after another a series of repressive measures muzzling the press, closing the platforms and placing even the colleges and schools under surveillance. In an apparent display of its undisputed power and strength the Government betrayed in no small degree the nervousness from which it suffered. The plainest suggestions for peace were regarded with suspicion and the most friendly warnings were mistaken for covert threats. In 1910 the vexed question of Separation of Judicial and Executive functions, which was at the root of most of the troubles, was taken up for decision and it was indeed understood that a despatch was also sent to the Secretary of State with definite proposals on the subject. But again a nervous bureaucracy stood in the way and taking advantage of the alleged disturbed state of the country succeeded in shelving the measure in the India Office. All measures of progress were stopped, the spirit of repression was rampant and even the genius of British justice seemed for a time to stand in a state of suspended animation. The advent of a strong Chief Justice for the High Court of Judicature at Fort William in Bengal at this juncture was the only redeeming feature of the desperate situation. If Lord Morley has established his claim to the lasting gratitude of India by his reform of the Indian Legislative Councils, he will also be long remembered for his most judicious appointment of Sir Lawrence Jenkins at the head of the highest tribunal in the most disturbed province at this critical time. The chartered High Courts in India form the only palladium for the protection of the rights and liberties of the Indian people and constitute the sole counterpoise to an absolute, autocratic rule in the country. But even the High Courts, being only the expounders and not the framers of the law, were hardly able to maintain the balance in a position where the Legislature was practically a machinery in the hands of the executive to decree and register the fiats of a bureaucratic administration. Thus matters went on from bad to worse until 1911 when the King, who in a single previous visit to this country appeared to have studied the people far more accurately than his responsible officers during the long tenure of their service, at last personally appeared on the scene and with the single stroke of a policy of conciliation, for which the Congress had so long vainly pleaded, dispelled all the figments of sedition and disloyalty and restored peace and order, pouring oil upon troubled waters and reviving faith and confidence in British justice.

Henceforth the Congress found itself upon a much firmer ground and in a more secure position. The royal message of good-will and confidence which the Congress of 1911 received in return for its loyal welcome to His Majesty set as it were a royal sanction to its perfectly legitimate character and constitution; while the outburst of stupendous ovations which spontaneously greeted the royal progress throughout the country at once hushed the insensate cry of sedition into silence. Fortunately also there was a strong and far-sighted statesman at the head of the Indian Government at this time. Lord Hardinge, who was primarily responsible for the modification of the Partition of Benal, firmly took the bull by its horns and impressed upon the bureaucracy that despite its long legend of infallibility and inviolable prestige, its orthodox practices and tactics of mutual admiration and whitewashing must have a limit prescribed to them. The firmness with which he was understood to have handled the local authorities in connection with a serious riot in course of which the metropolis of the Empire was disgracefully allowed for three days to be in the hands of an organized mob before the eyes of the ambassadors of the civilized world, and which was supposed to have compelled another bureaucrat to retire before his time, and the bold magnanimity and keensighted statesmanship with which he rectified the bunglings of an incompetent Executive in a most regrettable dispute over a mosque in defence of which half-a-dozen unarmed people lost their lives, clearly marked him as the strongest of Viceroys who had come to rule India in recent years; while the extraordinary fortitude with which he bore a most dastardly attempt on his own life, which under another Viceroy since Lord Ripon would undoubtedly have set in motion the most drastic of punitive measures, and the calm and self-sacrificing spirit with which he faced the situation without budging an inch from the declared policy of trust and confidence in the people, filled the country with a thrill of gratitude and admiration unparalleled in the history of British rule in India since the dark days of the Mutiny of 1857.

In higher politics Lord Hardinge's famous despatch of August 1911 contained the first recognition of the ultimate aim of the Congress and foreshadowed the future destiny of India in the evolution of her national existence. As a preliminary step towards ths solution of that problem, Lord Hardinge took up the thorny question of the position of Indians in the colonies of Great Britain. The question had engaged the attention of the Congress ever since 1894 when delegates from Natal and other South African colonies first joined the national assembly and explained the barbarous treatment accorded to the

Indian settlers in South Africa. The Government of England, although it referred to the Indian question as one of the grounds justifying the Boer War, again relapsed into its normal apathy and indifference when that war was ended and the Union Government established. The Indians in South Africa were not only not allowed the ordinary rights of citizenship, but were actually treated as helots burdened with disabilities and penalties of the most outrageous description, while the colonists themselves were free to emigrate to India and enjoy all the rights of British citizenship in this country. The question was at last brought to a head by a resolution moved by Mr. Gokhale in the Supreme Council and which was accepted by the Government of Lord Hardinge restricting Indian Emigration to South Africa. But the Union Government, in its utter disregard for all consideration of justice and fairness, went on forging the most humiliating and exasperating conditions against the Indian settlers whose services they could not dispense with, but whose personal rights and liberties they would neither recognize nor respect beyond those of hewers of wood and drawers of water. One brave Indian like Hampden at last rose against this selfish confederacy of burghers whom a conquering nation had in its generosity granted an autonomus Government over a territory four times the size of their original country. Mr. Mohandas Karamchand Gandhi, assisted by a band of noble-minded Englishmen among whom Mr. Polak was the most noted, organized a fierce passive resistance in course of which hundreds of men and women with dauntless courage suffered incarceration rather than submit to the indignities of legalised slavery in which even the sacred ties of marriage rights were not respected. In this struggle Lord Hardinge, as the responsible protector of the Indian people, threw the whole weight of his authority with the resisters and by his firmness, no less than by his tactful intervention, in the face of not a little hostile criticism even in England, at last succeeded towards the beginning of 1914 in bringing the question of the South African imbroglio to a temporary solution and thus paving the way to a final adjustment of the Indian question in all the British colonies on the basis of perfect reciprocity. It undoubtedly marks an important landmark in the evolution of Indian National Life.

CHAPTER XII.

THE WORK IN ENGLAND.

It has already been stated that early in 1885 Mr. Hume visited England and in consultation with Mr. Reid, Mr. John Bright and other parliamentary friends of India arranged for a Congress propaganda in England. The first step towards the establishment of a Congress organisation in England was taken by Mr. Dadabhai Naoroji who volunteered to act as a Congress agent before the British public. But nothing important was done until 1888 when Mr. W. C. Bonnerjee and Mr. Eardley Norton joined Mr. Dadabhai and succeeded in enlisting the sympathies of the great labour leader, Mr. Charles Bradlaugh, who with the consent of his constituency of Northampton openly assumed the title of " Member for India." A British Committee of the Indian National Congress was established in July, 1889, and it was confirmed by the Congress of that year held at Bombay which voted Rs. 45,000 for its maintenance. Now the chief difficulty in the successful working of the Committee lay in the Council of the Secretary of State which, composed mainly of the veterans of the Indian Civil Service, always presented a roseate view of Indian affairs in the House of Commons and thus prevented the British Committee from obtaining a fair hearing either in the House or from the British public. This led to the organisation of an Indian Parliamentary Committee in 1893 chiefly through the exertions of Sir William Wedderburn and Mr. W. S. Caine both of whom were members of Parliament at the time. The apathy and indifference of the authorities in India who had not evinced the slightest inclination within a period of nine years towards meeting even in a small degree the crying demands of the people, or for removing any of their long-standing grievances, fully convinced the leaders of the movement that there was no hope of success in India unless pressure could be brought to bear upon the Indian Government by the British public and the British Parliament. Mr. Hume accordingly finally left India in 1894 and threw himself heart and soul into the working of the British Committee of the Congress and the India Parliamentary Committee in the House of Commons. Towards the close of the session no less than 154 members of the House joined the Indian

Parliamentary Committee and for a time the star of India seemed to be in the ascendant. The result was at once manifest. With the support of this formidable array of members, among whom were included men like Messrs. Jacob Bright, W.S. Caine, John Ellis, W. A. Hunter, Swift MacNeil, Herbert Paul, C. E. Schwann, Herbert Roberts, R. T. Reid, Samuel Smith, Sir Wilfred Lawson, Sir William Wedderburn and many other friends of India, the British Committee of the Congress was able in 1894 to address Sir Henry Fowler, then Secretary of State for India, pressing for a searching enquiry into Mr. Westland's Budgets under the weak Viceroyalty of Lord Elgin. This led to the famous debate in Parliament which resulted in Mr. Dadabhai Naoroji's motion for a Parliamentary Enquiry and eventually obliged Sir Henry Fowler to appoint a Royal Commission, known as the Welby Commission on Indian Expenditure. Then for nearly nine years the Conservatives were in power and the Indian Parliamentary Party gradually thinned away. At the General Election of 1906, the Liberals again came into power and Sir William Wedderburn, who has been the most steadfast moving spirit of the Congress movement in England, lost no time in resuscitating the Indian Parliamentary Committee under the leadership of Mr. Leonard (afterwards Lord) Courtney. Nearly 200 members of the House joined the Committee, and among the new members there were distinguished men and sincere friends of India like Sir Henry Cotton, Sir Charles Dike, Dr. Rutherford, Mr. Ramsay Macdonald and many others. The invaluable services which they rendered particularly at a most trying and troublous situation are all recorded in the Parliamentary proceedings of the period and are well-known to the Indian public. Though the Liberals are still in power, the Indian Parliamentary Party gradually became very much weakened by the retirement from the House of devoted and ardent workers like Sir Henry Cotton, Sir William Wedderburn and Mr. Dadabhai Naoroji, and by the death of powerful friends like Charles Bradlaugh, W. S. Caine, Schwann, John Bright, Sir Charles Dike and Lord Ripon, and has now practically ceased to exist.

In England no reform, whether social, economic or political, can be achieved without the aid of the Press which has thus come to be recognised, along with the two Houses of Parliament, the Church and the Sovereign, as the Fifth Power of the State. In the earlier stages of the Congrees the British public were found densely ignorant of the real state of things in India, while the natural pride, so common even in individuals, which makes people loath to believe in their own shortcomings, often prevented even enlightened Englishmen from easily crediting any story of injustice or wrong perpetrated by their accredited agents ten thousand miles away and who were besides invariably supported by the minister in charge with a council mostly composed of retired Anglo-Indian fossils whom it may be no disrespect te describe as King Arthur's Knights of the Round Table. An incident fully illustrating this ignorance, apathy and indifference of the ordinary British public was not long ago quoted in an English paper. Two average Englishmen, says the paper, were one day travelling in a railway carriage. It was the day following the death of Lord Northbrook, late Viceroy and Governor-General of India. One of them looking through the news columns of the paper in his hand quietly asked, "Who is this feller Lord Northbrook that snipped off yesterday?" "Who knows," replied his equally indifferent companion, "may be some relation of Lord Cromer." Whether Lord Northbrook was a relation of Lord Cromer, or Lord Cromer was a relation of Lord Northbrook, the pathetic humour of this simple incident was quite characteristic of the prevailing temper and attitude of the British public in general towards Indian affairs. To acquaint that public, who are the virtual makers of the House of Commons and of the Ministers of the Crown, with the actual state and condition of Indian administration was the first and foremost duty of the national party in this country. It was early recognised that the battle of India must be fought, if it has to be fought, on British soil, and in that fight the British Press must be our ally to guide and direct the operations if not actually to deliver the frontal attack. The journal *India* was accordingly started by the British Committee in 1890 for a correct and faithful statement of India's complaints and with a view to popularise Indian thoughts and aspirations in England, as also to interest the British public generally on Indian questions. It was at first conducted by Mr. William Digby and is now edited by Mr. H. E. A. Cotton, that worthy son of a worthy father who ever since his return home has been closely following in the footsteps of his illustrious parents in watching and serving the interests of India. The Cottons have for three generations steadfastly served India and loved her devotedly, as only few Englishmen have done, through good report and evil report and often at no small personal sacrifice. It is a great pity that so few people in this country have even now fully realised the importance and necessity of maintaining the British Committee and the journal *India* in an efficient condition. True it is that a lot of money has been spent upon them and there may or may not be any just ground for the disappointment felt in some quarters at the present working of these agencies. But it was clearly understood at the very outset that it was an uphill work and the country must be prepared to make enormous sacrifices both in money as well as in patience for it. Then it would be quite unfair to deny that both the Committee and the paper have advanced the Congress cause a good deal in England. It must be gratefully acknowledged that all the prominent men in the British political field and a large number of influential men outside Parliament now know more and discuss more seriously about the Indian polity, and India is no longer that *Terra Incognita*, that region of romance and "barbaric gold," which it used to be even fifty years ago; nor is England so profoundly apathetic to-day towards the Indian administration as she was even twenty years before. India has now become an important factor in the policy of the Imperial Government, and she looms very much larger in the eyes of British statesmen on either side of both the Houses. Indian grievances, which sometimes fail to attract the attention even of the local administrations, do now go seldom unnoticed in the House of Commons. An act of oppression in a tea-garden, a gross insult offered to an Indian gentleman in a railway carriage, the mal-practices of the police and the bunglings of the Executive, though these scarcely find a remedy, now all find their way into Parliament, and indirectly exercise a chastening influence upon the Indian administration. The questions of the separation of Judicial from Executive functions, of simultaneous examinations for the Civil Services, of the expansion of the Councils and of the admission of the children of the soil into the administration of the country, as well as the other reforms formulated by the Congress, are now all nearly as familiar to the enlightened British public as they are in this country. India now finds greater notice in the British Press and there is now a marked disposition on the part at least of the thinking portion of the British public to know more of the country which really constitutes the British Empire. All this has been the work of the British Committee and its organ *India*.

After years of stress and storm the tide seems to have at last set in for India, and it would be not only deplorable, but simply disastrous, if Indians should at this opportune moment give up their oars and cry out in despair, that they have worked at them hard and long and can now work no more. If they give up now the agencies which have been established at such immense sacrifice, they simply lose the money they have spent as well as the opportunities which they have created. Even in ordinary life no substantial business can be carried on without suitable and properly equipped agencies at all important centres and particularly without necessary advertisements and reliable quotations of its principal market. There may be occasional lapses and failures of such agencies; but no prudent man can dispense with them unless he means to close his business and go into voluntary liquidation. The Moslem League is quite a recent case in point. If it had not its London Branch, the Mahomedan community in India could hardly have made one-tenth of the progress it has made during the last few years. If the British Committee of the Congress is no longer as active as it used to be at one time, the true remedy lies not in either abolishing or starving it, but in improving or, if necessary, in reconstructing it and galvanising it into fresh life again. These remedial measures may not be altogether free from practical difficulties; but they have to be boldly faced, discussed and solved if the labours of a generation are not to be thrown away in a fit of vexation or distemper.

People are not wanting who, in their earnest desire to hurry up, simply retard progress. With them the work of the Congress in England though a foreign agency is practically at an end and other means should be devised to give it a fresh start. It is vaguely urged that we must stand on our own legs. Standing on one's own legs is undoubtedly a counsel of perfection, provided it is not used as a pretext for sitting altogether idle. Besides, until the legs are sufficiently strong it would not do to throw away the crutch because it fails to help us in running. Noble things are better said than done, and nothing seems easier than to talk of putting in "fresh blood" in a long-standing public institution; but it ought to be remembered, that true blood, whether fresh or old, is always thicker than water and that there can hardly be enough of superfluous blood to be gratuitously spared for us in an alien country and by an alien people ten thousand miles away. The idea of placing the management of the British Committee and of the paper *India* in "Indian hands" may be refreshing; but let us first arrange for the *hands* and then there will be enough time for arranging the *management*. There was not perhaps an abler or more generous "Indian hand" than Mr. W. C. Bonnerjee practically settled in England, or one who has more freely spent his blood as well as his purse in the Congress cause, and yet he did not feel himself equal to the task of directly managing either branch of the agency. As to the suggestion made in certain strange quarters for managing the Committee or editing the paper *India* either from Calcutta or Bombay—well, that is an idea which does not strike very forcibly the average Indian intellect however tempting to its ambition it may be. If the British Committee were to be discarded like an opera house that fails to produce fresh sensations every night, or the organ *India* either discontinued or supplanted by a "live paper" because it has yet failed to fit up an Argonautic expedition in search of the "golden fleece," it is very much to be doubted if the Indian Nationalist will ever achieve any more progress than present the same texture every day and count his time like the faithful Penelope unraveling by night what is woven by day. The work of destruction is always much easier than the process of construction and the people are not wanting who in the name of the one contribute simply to the other. It is want of proper nourishment more than any organic disease that often causes anæmic condition in a system. The Congress agencies seem to be all right. Give them sufficient food and exercise, or to be more explicit, put sufficient money into their pockets, and the necessary *blood* will come of itself.

DEPUTATIONS TO ENGLAND.

Another means adopted by the Congress for popularising its propaganda in England and acquainting the British public with the wants and wishes of the Indian people was by sending from time to time deputations of competent men to England. The earliest of such deputations, since the time of Rajah Rammohan Roy, was that sent under the auspices of the Indian National Union in 1885. It was composed of three of the ablest public men of the time, *viz* :—Mr. Monomohan Ghose of Bengal, Mr. Ganesh Narayan Chandavarkar of Bombay and Mr. Sivalaya Ramaswami Mudaliar of Madras. They formed as it were the advance guard of the Congress mission. The first Deputation formally appointed by the Congress was in 1889 and it was composed of Mr. George Yule, Mr. A. O. Hume, Mr. J. Adam, Mr. Eardley Norton, Mr. Pherozeshah Mehta, Mr. Surendranath Banerjee, Mr. Monomohan Ghose, Mr. Sharfuddin, Mr. R. N. Mudholkar and Mr. W. C. Bonnerjee. The work done by this deputation was simply invaluable; for while Messrs. Bonnerjee and Norton succeeded in thoroughly establishing the Congress agency, Mr. Surendranath Banerjee made a profound impression upon the mind of the British public by his able and eloquent exposition of the Congress propaganda. It was on this occasion that Mr. Hume saw Mr. Gladstone and urged him to support Mr. Bradlaugh's India Bill, when the great Commoner was reported to have said, "I wish your father were present to-day." Mr. Bradlaugh's Bill forced the Government to introduce a Bill of their own and the historic speech which Mr. Gladstone made on the occasion of the passing of that Bill is well-known to the public. He asked the Government to construe that half-hearted measure in a liberal spirit and clearly foreshadowed the real reforms that were demanded and which sixteen years later were carried out by his friend and biographer. The next deputation appointed by the Congress was in 1890 and it was composed of Messrs. George Yule, Pherozeshah Mehta, W. C. Bonnerjee, John Adam, Monomohan Ghose, A. O. Hume, Kalicharan Banerjee, Dadabhai Naoroji and D. A. Khare. It should be gratefully recorded that Mr. W. C. Bonnerjee and Mr. Dadabhai Naoroji, both of whom practically settled themselves in England in the service of the country, were among the strongest pillars of the movement, as they were among its original founders, and neither grudged their time, energies or money in the sacred cause to which they had consecrated their lives. In 1889 Mr. D. E. Watcha, Mr. G. K. Gokhale and Mr. Surendranath Banerjee were deputed to give evidence before the Royal Commission on Expenditure and the remarkable evidence which they gave not only fully justified the confidence reposed in them, but also vindicated the character and weight of the political organization started in India. The next Congress deputation in 1904 consisted of Mr. G. K. Gokhale and Mr. Lajpat Rai. Mr. Gokhale was again sent in the following year and on both the occasions he made such an impression as to mark him as one of the foremost politicians in India. For careful study, lucid marshalling of facts and incisive arguments, no less than for his unassuming manners and devotion to duty, Mr. Gokhale stands out a most prominent figure in the Indian political world. If Mr. Surendranath Banerjee towers head and shoulder over his colleagues in his stupendous energies and matchless eloquence, Mr. Gokhale* also appears to be unsurpassed in his mastery of facts and close reasoning for which Sir Guy Fleetwood Wilson went so far as to compare him with Mr. Gladstone. But through a strange irony of fate, for which India is not at all responsible, neither of these trusted leaders of the people has yet been found worthy of a place in the bureaucratic administration of the country. The last deputation sent by the Congress was that authorised by the Karachi Congress of 1913. It was composed of Mr. Bhupendra Nath Basu (Bengal), Mr. Sarma (Madras), Messrs. M. A. Jinnah and N. M. Samarth (Bombay), Messrs.

* Since these pages were sent to the press Mr. Gokhale has been cut off in the prime of his life, and both the Government and the country have now come equally to mourn the irreparable loss.

S. Sinha and Mazhar-ul Haque (United Provinces and Behar) and Lala Lajpat Rai (Punjab). In one sense it was a most unfavourable time for an Indian deputation, as the British public were almost distracted over the Irish Home Rule Bill introduced in Parliament and which obliged the King to make an extraordinary step of summoning a conference of all the leading politicians in the country to avert a civil war with which it was threatened; while on the other hand it was a most momentous occasion for India when Lord Crewe introduced in the Upper House a Bill to amend the constitution of the India Council in Whitehall. The extremely unsatisfactory composition of that Council was fully discussed by the first Congress in 1885 which passed a resolution for its absolution in the form in which it stood at the time. Lord Morley, along with his Reform Scheme, considerably liberalized the constitution of the India Council by an informal admission of two Indian members into its composition. Lord Crewe proposed to go a step further by giving a statutory sanction to the Indian element of the Council and by providing a system of nomination for this element out of a panel of forty to be elected by the various Legislative Councils in India. It was of course not a measure of perfection, while its proposal for instituting a departmental system of administration by the Council was certainly open to grave objection. But the Bill contained germs of great potentialities and if passed through the Lords might have undergone further improvements in the Commons, and there is an overwhelming body of opinion in this country that there was a great tactical blunder committed in allowing Lord

Curzon and others of his school to be able to lay hold on Indian opinion, of whatever character or complexion, as an additional weapon of attack in their opposition to the proposed legislation. It is to be deeply regretted that in this, as in not a few other cases, India has inadvertently played into the hands of her shrewd adversaries. It is, however, no use crying over split milk. Attempts should now be made to have a Bill introduced in the Commons at an early opportunity to deal with the question. If one thing has been made clearer than another by the failure of Lord Crewe's Bill it is the fact, that there should be some Indian representative in England to work in conjunction with the British Committee, to stimulate British sympathy and to take time by the forelock at every opportunity to further the interests of India at the seat of real power. Such were the works which were at one time done by Messrs. Dadabhai Naoroji and W. C. Bonnerjee and means should be devised to install at least one such Indian representative in London.

CHAPTER XIII.

THE CONGRESS: A NATIONAL MOVEMENT.

For a long time the claim the Congress to be styled a national movement was strenuously, if not quite sericusly, disputed by its critics. Some derisively called it a "Bengalee Congress," although the Bengalees had clearly no more hand in it, either in its inception or in its development, than the Parsis, the Maharattas, or the Madrasis, and the Bengalees would have been simply proud to accept the doubtful compliment paid to them if only it were the barest truth others, professing to be a little more catholic dubbed it as a "Hindu Congress," as if the Hindus were altogether a negligible factor in the country and that such a disqualification was sufficient for its disparagement in the estimation of the public and to discredit its weight and importance with the authorities: while the more adroit among these critics denounced it as an organization of the "Educated Minority" in the country, as though it were an established fact, that the recognized political associations in all other civilized countries were, as a rule, composed of their illiterate majority and that where such an element failed an organization, however strong in its moral, intellectual or material equipment, must stand forfeited of all claims to be recognized as a national institution. The truth, however, seems to be, that early exiled from the healthy public life of their own native land, trained in all the ways of a dominant race in a subject country and nurtured in the traditionary legends of their racial superiority, the Anglo-Indian community naturally received a rude shock at the first appearance of the new spirit and taxed all the resources of their ingenuity to nip it in the bud. These captious critics, to whom history apparently furnished no logic of facts, had the catching expression of "microscopic minority" coined for them by a high authority, while they themselves were not slow to invent a few more smart phrases to discredit the movement in this country and prejudice public opinion in England. No abuse was deemed too strong and no criticism too severe for the condemnation of the new movement whose aims and objects were regarded not only as a threatened invasion of their prescriptive rights and privileges rendered indefeasible by long enjoyment, but also as a serious disturbance of the established order of things permanently sanctioned by custom, usage and tradition of the country. "Dreaming idealists," "impotent sedition-mongers," "self-constituted delegates," "disappointed place-seekers," "pretentious body of irresponsible agitators," and many other elegant phrases of the same description were among the weapons offensive and defensive forged by these critics to dispose of the members of the Congress and to discredit the movement. But if the movement was really as nothing, it is rather difficult to appreciate why so much powder and shot were simply wasted for destroying such a tiny gnat and why such severe attention was paid to a handful of political somnambulists. It was, however, not found possible to sustain these reckless charges for a long time, as quite a different verdict was pronounced at an early stage both here as well as in England establishing the claim of the Congress to represent the enlightened views of the Indian public without distinction of caste or creed, colour or race. It may be perfectly true, that all the communities in the country have not equally distinguished themselves on the Congress platform; but it can hardly be denied that the better minds of every community have been throughout in perfect agreement with its aims and objects and have never dissented from its programme.

It has already been pointed out, that so far back as 1890, when the Congress was but five years old, the Government of Lord Lansdowne recognised that the Congress was regarded as representing the advanced Liberal Party in India as distinguished from the powerful body of conservative opinion ruling the country. Since then Lord Morley, Mr. Justin McCarthy, Sir William Hunter, Sir Charles Dilke, Lord Randolph Churchill, Mr. Herbert (now Lord) Gladstone, Sir Richard Garth and many other distinguished and responsible authorities have from time to time admitted the character of the Congress as a national assembly fairly representative of the Indian people. Speaking in 1890 Sir Charles Dilke said :—

> "Argument upon the matter is to be desired, but not invectives, and there is so much reason to think that the Congress movement really represents the cultivated intelligence of the country that those who ridicule it do harm to the imperial interests of Great Britain, bitterly wounding and alienating men who are justified in what they do, who do it in reasonable and cautious form and who ought to be conciliated by being met half-way."

There is the testimony of Mr. Herbert Gladstone who said that :

> "The national movement in India, which has taken a purely constitutional and loyal form and which expresses through the Congress the legitimate hopes and requirements of the people, is one with which I sincerely sympathise. I should consider it a high honour in however small a degree to be associated with it."

Sir William Hunter, than whom there is hardly a more experienced Indian authority, observed :

> "The Indian National Congress is essentially the child of British rule, the product of our schools and universities. We had created and fostered the aspirations which animated the Congress, and it would be both childish and unwise to refuse now to those aspirations both our sympathy and respectful consideration."

Lord Morley, speaking from his place in the House of Commons as the responsible minister for India, said:—

"I do not say that I agree with all that the Congress desires; but speaking broadly of what I conceive to be at the bottom of the Congress I do not see why any one who takes a cool and steady view of Indian Government should be frightened."

The Right Hon. Sir Richard Garth, *Kt.*, Chief Justice of Bengal, writing in 1895, said:—

"It seems to me that so far from being in any way objectionable, the Congress affords an open, honest and loyal means of making the views and wishes of the most intelligent section of the Indian people known to the Government."

And, above all, His Imperial Majesty George V, was himself pleased to accord his recognition to the Congress by accepting its message of welcome and thanking it for its loyal devotion to the Throne on the occasion of his auspicious visit to India in 1911. It seems unnecessary to multiply further evidence in support of the official as well as the popular verdict in favour of the claim and character of the Congress as a representative institution. It may simply be added for the satisfaction of those who may still continue to be at heart dissatisfied with that verdict, on the ostensible ground of the mass of the population not being in evidence on the Congress platform, that the "microscopic minority" in every country, whether in the East or in the West, have always represented the telescopic majority, and that nowhere have the inarticulate mass of a people spoken except through the mouth of the educated few. Then as regards the old, orthodox and favourite argument of the Anglo-Indian community based upon the assumed differences between the classes and the masses it were

PRESIDENT, 1889 & 1910.

GEORGE YULE
PRESIDENT, 1888.

SIR P.M. MEHTA
PRESIDENT, 1890.

well to remember, that even in the seventies of the century that has just closed over us John Bright had to complain that the Parliament of Great Britain was not after all a "transparent mirror of public opinion" and that the Labour party in that Parliament representing the masses of England is only of very recent growth and as yet furnishes but a wholly inadequate representation of its immense working population. It may be no mere disputatious argument to advance, that if the Mother of Parliaments, which in its origin was no more than an assembly of a handful of "wise men," and which even in its later developments was composed of a hereditary aristocracy and a few hundred chosen representatives drawn only from the ranks of advanced enlightened communities could have constitutionally governed for centuries the destinies of the greatest empire in the world, it would hardly be decent to put forward any pretext based upon a question of class interest to dispute the representative character of an advisory political organization without any legal origin or statutory constitution. Nobody contends that the Congress is a "transparent mirror of public opinion" in India; but if it is not so transparent as the Parliament of Great Britain, or the Chamber of the French Republic, is it really very much more opaque than the Duma of Russia, or even the Reichstag of Germany, as far as reflection of public opinion is concerned? If there has been no objection to the National League representing the cause of Ireland for more than half-a-century, with one of its four divisions in open arms against it, the title of the Indian

National Congress, with only one of its many communities partially standing aside as neutral and passively watching the fight, may not be deemed so extravagant as to form a point in a serious discussion on such general issues as are involved in this great movement. The Congress is not even thirty years old, and if within this short period it has established its claim to be the mouthpiece of the teeming millions of India even in some respects and has never done anything to forfeit their tacit confidence, then nobody need fairly grudge its just and legitimate aspiration to be called a National Assembly.

It is certainly not the essential condition of a national institution that every member or even every community of the nation should be actively associated with it; for if it were so, even the most thoroughly representative of Parliaments would cease to be a national institution. An institution is quite national if it possesses in the main a representative character, embodies the national spirit and is guided by aims and objects of national advancement. It may sometimes fail to be a transparent mirror of public opinion particularly where such opinion is in such a nebulous condition as to be unable to cast a distinct reflection even on the most powerful camera; but it is always expected faithfully to reflect an interest which once it is presented in proper shade and light, at once catches the attention of the public and attracts the national sympathies and energies towards its attainment. In this way national organizations have everywhere preceded national awakening in its widest sense, and sometimes a single individual gifted with extraordinary vision has revolutionized an entire national life. Nations are not born but made, and the highest evolution of national, like individual, life is attained through a slow and laborious process of organized efforts. Judged by the above test the claim of the Congress to be recognized as a national assembly could hardly be disputed by any but the most perverse critics. If Mr. Disraeli, Lord Hartington, Mr. Joseph Chamberlain, Mr. Balfour and other millionaires could represent the labouring classes of England, because a percentage of them were able to exercise their forced votes in their favour, then surely men like Dadabhai Naoroji, W. C. Bonnerjee, Pherozeshah Mehta, Surendranath Banerjee, Rash Behary Ghose, Kashinath Trimbak Telang, Budruddin Tyabjee, Gopal Krishna Gokhale, Abdul Rasul, Ananda Charlu, Krishnaswami Iyer, Sirdar Dyal Singh, Lajpat Rai, Madan Mohan Malaviya, Muzur-ul-Haque, Hasan Imam and many others, men all born of the people, might well have been depended on to voice forth more faithfully the wants and wishes of the voiceless millions of India than the editors of the *Pioneer*, the *Civil and Military Gazette*, the *Englishman*, the *Statesman* and other birds of passage of nearly the same feather, whatever their pretensions may be in the position which they occupy in the administration of the country.

Among the Indians themselves the Parsis as a community were no doubt for a short time wavering in their attitude; but the great personality of Mr. Dadabhai Naoroji and the firm attitude of men like Sir Pherozeshah Mehta and Mr. Dinshaw Edulji Wacha settled the question, and that important community bodily cast in their lot with the national movement. The Eurasian community, having its stronghold in Madras, did not fail to realise its true position during the Ilbert Bill controversy and having wisely stood aloof, at least in the Southern Presidency, from that controversy it heartily joined the new movement under the leadership of Messrs. W. S. White, and W. S. Gantz; while Captain Banon from the Punjab. Mr. Howard, the President of the Anglo-Indian and Eurasian Association at Allahabad, Captain Hearsay from Dehra-Dun, Mr. Crowley of the firm of Messrs. Crowley & Co., and Mr. George Yule from Bengal with many other Europeans and Eurasians of note from time to time joined and strengthened the rank and file of the organisation.

An artificial and mischievous manœuvre was engineered by a section of the Anglo-Indian Press which with the active support of a shortsighted bureaucracy doted on the mean policy of *Divide-et-impera* and captured the great but backward Mahomedan community who were taught the unworthy tactics of lying in wait for the other communities to draw the chestnuts out of the fire, so that they might comfortably mounch them without burning their fingers in the fire of official displeasure. At the first Congress in 1885 Mr. Rahimtullah Sayani was the only Mahomedan present, and the Anglo-Indian Press of the time complacently remarked that even he did not take any active part in its deliberations. But it would appear from the subsequent presidential addresses of both Mr. Budruddin Tyabji and Mr. Rahimtullah Sayani that they were heart and soul with the movement from the very beginning. In the Second Congress the number of Mussalman Delegates was 33, while at Madras in 1887 their number rose to 81. At the fourth Congress at Allahabad the Mahomedan Delegates numbered 221 out of a total of 1,248 Delegates. Thus the interest of that great community in the national movement, in spite of the syren song of the Anglo Indian press, was steadily and rapidly increasing. But since the Allahabad Congress, when the attitude of the authorities become more pronounced, the Mahomedans began to secede, and their "approved loyalty", which some silly persons on the other side irreverently called "oilty", was turned into a "valuable asset" by certain designing people.

It is no doubt true, that in the fifth session of the Congress held at Bombay the number, though not the percentage, of Mahomedan Delegates rose higher than at the preceding session at Allahabad. There were 254 Mahomedans out of a total of 1,889 Delegates. But it should be remembered that it was a historic session commonly known as the "Bradlaugh Congress" which, as has been already pointed out, attracted an unusually large number of people, including even officials in secret to see and hear the great champion of democracy, and that a large majority of these Mahomedan Delegates attended from the Bombay Presidency where the Mahomedan community, though numerically smaller, has been until very recently ever more progressive than in the rest of India. It is however worthy of notice that two of the Mahomedan Delegates at this very Congress, one hailing from the Punjab and the other from the United Provinces made no secret of their racial opposition to the Congress proposal as regards the reform of the Legislative Councils. Besides, the remarkable dearth of Mahomedan Delegates at all subsequent sessions of the Congress, until the last sessions held at Karachi, conclusively proved that the official reporter of 1889 was quite premature in his forecast of growing Mahomedan interest in the national movement. It is doubtless true that advanced Mussalmans like Mr. Abdul Rasul in Bengal and Mr. Comuruddin Tyabji in Bombay not to speak of stalwarts like Messrs. Budruddin Tyabji and Rahimtullah Sayani, never swerved from their allegiance to the national cause ; but the bulk of the Moslem community were led astray and successfully kept back for a long time from joining the movement. Several unfortunate incidents also contributed towards widening the breach between the two main communities in the country, while their separation from a common platform served not a little to make the relation between them more and more strained under the continuous fanning of the Anglo-Indian community who scarcely made any secret of their policy of playing one against the other. But the game has happily been almost played out. The intelligent Islamic community, with the rapid growth of education, are gradually awaking to a consciousness of the ignominious position into which they have been led and are steadily pressing forward to take their legitimate place by the side of the other communities, fighting shoulder to shoulder for the attainment of their common destiny.

The Moslem League, whatever the object of its founders and the attitude of some of its early members may have been, has, in the dispensation of an inscrutable providence, done for the Mahomedans what the Congress had done much earlier for the other communities in the country. It has slowly imbued them with the broad vision of national interests and inoculated them with ideas of common rights and responsibilities, when at the last Session of the League they openly embraced the common political faith so long preached by the Congress. If men like Mazur-ul-Haque, Hassan Imam, Wazir Hussain, Ibrahim Rahimatullah, Jinnah, Mahomedali and last but not least the present Agah Khan could have appeared in the Eighties and joined hands with Messrs. Budruddin Tyabji, Rahimatullah Sayani and Abdul Rasul the history of the Indian National Congress might now have been written in an altogether different style. But it must be said to the credit of the Mahomedan community, that although for a long time they kept themselves aloof from the Congress, they never could be persuaded to start any active movement to counteract its progress. The fictitious counter-agitation was kept up only by the selfish Anglo-Indian press at the instance of a narrow and nervous bureaucracy in the ostensible name of the Mahomedan community, and there is sufficient reason to believe that intelligent Mahomedans were not wanting who saw through the bluff and thoroughly understood in whose interest the agitation was really engineered, though from prudential considerations they were unable openly to denounce it. The great sage of Aligarh, who during his lifetime was the recognized leader of the community, did not fail frankly to acknowledge that the Hindus and the Mussalmans in India "were like the two eyes of a fair maiden" and that "it was impossible to injure the one without affecting the other," and, he might well have added, without disfiguring the maiden altogether. It is worthy of remark, that the Congress from an early stage took care to safeguard the interests of all minorities and with a view to remove all possible misapprehension from the minds of the Mussalmans distinctly provided, that when any community in the Congress being in the minority should appear to be even nearly unanimous in opposing any motion such motion shall be dropped. Besides, it is an incontrovertible fact that the Congress has up to this time never passed a single resolution advocating the interests of any particular community, or of the classes against those of the masses. On the contrary it has throughout recognized that the future destiny of the country largely, if not solely, depended upon the harmonious co-operation of all the communities and the amelioration of the condition of its huge working and agricultural population, and has as such persistently urged for educational facilities for the backward communities in the country. Education is the only leaven that can leaven the whole lump, and the Congress has never failed to realize that as education advances the apparently heterogeneous elements in the country are bound to coalesce and solidify into a homogeneous mass.

In the meantime, however, in the midst of the perennial controversy that raged between a jealous, bureaucracy and a distrustful public and in spite of the opposition, calumny and misrepresentation which never ceased to dog its footsteps, the movement went on gaining strength both in volume and intensity every year. In its majestic march it swept away all obstacles presented by differences of creed and caste, of language as well as of customs, habits and manners, and the process of unification went on apace rounding off those local and racial angularities which stood in its course and bearing down those treacherous shoals and bars which the opposition fondly hoped would wreck it one day. It has passed through many trials and tribulations and tided over many dangers and difficulties which lay in its way. Many were the "candid friends" who in season and out of season ráised their warning voice against what they deemed its "mad career"; but the collective wisdom of a renovated people under the guidance of a higher inspiration has gone on working in the sacred cause with stout heart and sincere devotion. The acuteness of the opposition has now nearly died out; while with the falsification of the ominous prophecies of the "birds of evil presage" their shrieks are heard growing fainter and fainter as the day of the inevitable seems to be approaching. It is no less an authority than Sir William Hunter who has borne his ungrudging testimony to the fact that "the Indian National Congress has outlived the early period of misrepresentation; it has shewn that it belongs to no single section of the population"; while it may be fairly remarked, that Hindus, Mussalmans, Parsis and Christians, all have been proud of the honour of occupying the presidential chair of the Congress as the highest distinction in the gift of the country and its people.

It is however still argued, that although the Congress may be a national assembly it can never hope to attain its chimerical object in view—the establishment of an Indian nationality; for there are said to be four essential conditions for the constitution of a nation, in that there must be a common race, common government, common tongue and a common religion, and that India being a congeries of people lacking in all these essential elements can never hope to evolve a nationality out of a Babel of confusion into which she has been hopelessly plunged by centuries of revolutions and changes unparalleled in the history of the world. These are all plausible arguments no doubt;—but not one of them will probably stand the test of careful examination in the light of modern political evolution of the world. The race question, strictly speaking, is more or less of a larger or smaller formula of ethnological classification. The modern Indians are broadly divided into two races, the Hindus and Mussalmans, the former having larger and sharper sub-divisions than the latter; but both descended from a common *Aryan* stock, more agnatic in their relation to each other than most of the European peoples. The Hindu anthropology indeed traces them to one common descent within the legendary period of ancient history. However that may be, the question is, does this difference in races constitute a permanent bar to their so uniting as to constitute a political unit or nation? Without going far back into antiquity it may be confidently asked, is there any nation of modern times which is not composed of distinct and different racial units which have been welded together by forces other than those of mere ethnology? The Picts and the Scots, the Angles and the Saxons, the Celts and the Welsh are all incorporated in the great British nation, although they one and all still retain distinctive racial characteristics of their own to no small extent. In Germany the Teutons and the Slavs, the Prussians, the Bavarians and the Silicians and in that curious Dual-Monarchy of Austria-Hungary the Germans, the Magyars or Hungarians, Czechs, Poles, Slavs, Serbs, Croats and Roumanians are all distinct racial units consolidated into a national federation of no ordinary solidarity and strength. So it is idle to contend that racial differences in India can by themselves stand as an insuperable difficulty in the way of the Hindus and Mussalmans, with an intermediate link of the Parsis between them, coalescing and forming a political unit. The process has already started and it is only a question of time when they will become completely fused into a consolidated national organization.

As regards religion, it must be admitted, that although in the early stages of social evolution and even down to the end of the middle ages religious faiths constituted the strongest cement of national unity, a mighty change has taken place in modern times all over the world. With increased facilities of communication, both through land and water, and ever increasing expansion of trade and commerce a rapid diffusion of people throughout the world has taken place converting every civilised country into a congeries of people, each with distinct habits, manners and religious beliefs. The ancient territorial distributions on the basis of religious ties have all been broken up and with the advancement of science and development of materialism a nation has received the connotation more of a political organization than of a religious confederacy. Freedom of conscience and religious toleration have revolutionized every country and every society, and different and even divergent faiths no longer count against the forces of a national evolution. Even education has been secularized throughout the world, and the spirit of Martin Luther's reform, which first effected in Europe a permanent divorce of Education from Religion has permeated the entire civilization of the world and considerably weakened, if not completely shattered, the influence of the church and clergy of every creed in moulding and shaping the destinies of nations. A nation therefore is now more a political unit than a religious organization. The differences between the *Saivas* and *Vaishnavas* and *Saktas*, or for the matter of that between the Hindus and the Buddhists, the Jains and the Sikhs are not more marked than those between the Catholics and the Protestants, the Methodists and the Greek Church. Then are there not Unitarians and Positivists, Free-thinkers and Non-conformists side by side with members of the Orthodox Churches in every country in Europe and America forming integral parts of one, indivisible nation? No man now cares more about the religious convictions of his neighbour than of his private character. It is now the public life of a people, as reflected in public interest and public opinion, combined with a singleness of purpose and unity of aims and objects which constitutes the national spirit. It is not at all suggested that other moral and spiritual qualities do not go far to exalt the individual as well as the nation; but these higher attributes are not among the inseparable accidents of national life.

Common government and common language no doubt form the basis of a national organisation, the one furnishing articulate expression of common interests and common sentiments and the other translating them into action. In India the English language has become the *lingua franca* of the educated community whose number is daily increasing and whose ideas, thoughts and actions are purveyed to the rest of the population through the medium of a number of allied dialects all derived from a common source, and it is no more difficult for the people of the different provinces to understand each other than it is for the mass of the Irish, Scotch and Welshman to understand the Englishman. A common script for all the Indian languages would undoubtedly facilitate, as it has facilitated in the case of Europe, the study of the various dialects in this country; but even if that is not possible the difficulty may be solved by introducing some of these languages in an interprovincial curriculum of the departments or universities at certain stage of the educational system of the different provinces. The Bengalee, the Hindustani, the Mahrattee and the Telugu are the most important among the spoken and written languages in the country and if these are taught in our schools or colleges of all the provinces the linguistic connection between the different races may be satisfactorily established.

As regards government, the Indian peoples occupy a still more favourable position. For the evolution of a national life it is absolutely necessary that the entire population of a geographical unit, whatever differences there may be in their racial, linguistic or religious composition, should be under one and the same rule. Where this condition fails there is disintegration even among people belonging to the same race, speaking the same language and professing the same faith, and each integral section under a separate rule forms a distinct nation. As has already been said, a nation in the modern acceptance of the term is now a political unit formed out of community of interest, community of laws and community of rights and responsibilities. These are all created and conserved under the guidance and inspiration of a force which is generated by a common rule whether it be monarchical, democratic or republican in its character. There was a time when the Bengalees, the Punjabis and the Mahrattas formed distinct nations, as the Prussians, the Bavarians and the Silicians on the one hand and the Bohemians, the Magyars, the Czechs and the Slavs on the other did at one and no distant time. But being brought under the same rule, subject to the same laws and invested with the same rights and responsibilities, emanating from the same fountainhead, the Bengalee, the Panjabi and the Mahratta are now but different factors of one and the same political unit or nation. Thus the Parsi or the Mahomedan in India no longer owes any temporal allegiance to the Shah of Persia or the Sultan of Turkey, nor do they belong to the Persian or Turkish nation. They are both incorporated in the body of the vast Indian Nation. The Government is the cement of a national organization and without such a cement even the most advanced countries in the world would fall to pieces like a house of cards. It is quite true, that under the existing conditions it is simply impossible for India to aim at sovereign independence and yet maintain its nationalism; for no sooner such an attempt is made it must stand split up into its racial factors, the cement would be gone and the vast fabric of its national organization tumble down entirely broken up. There may be then a Bengalee, or a Punjabi, or a Mahratta State, but no longer an United-India, or an Indian Nation. For the higher evolution of such a nationality the Indian National Congress from the very beginning set up an ideal on the permanent basis of a great confederacy under a common rule such as was furnished by the paramount authority of Great Britain. The Congress certainly aims at freedom; but not at separation. On the contrary it is the freedom of the different members of a body which while they are perfectly free to discharge their respective functions independently are at the same time dependent upon one another for their vital existence as a whole, and which in their mutual relation imply no subjection, but enjoin equality and interdependence. It is in this conception that lies the true inwardness of Indian nationalism and it is this ideal which constitutes the just claim of the

Indian National Congress to be styled a national movement. Lord Hardinge's famous despatch of the 25th August 1911 gives a correct expression to the spirit of that movement and clearly indicates the only legitimate development of a permanent British rule in India. However much British diplomacy may turn and twist the plain terms of that important document to wriggle out of an inevitable situation, it is bound to work out its peaceful solution at first in the formation of a confederacy of autonomous units within the country and at the consummation in the evolution of a larger, stronger and prouder unit, self-contained, self-adjusted, self-reliant, and standing side by side and co-operating with the other self-governing limits of the Empire. Such a conception must no doubt take time to materialize itself; but it is by no means a fantastic dream. Besides, the world bas always dreamt before its waking and evolved its sternest realities out of its wildest dreams. But even without indulging in dreams it is permissible to read the signs of time which in its onward and irresistible march is visibly arraying the moral forces of humanity for a thorough revision and re-adjustment of the destinies of the world from which India alone cannot be excluded. If the Philippinos in the Pacific, the Poles in Central Europe, and even the Negroes of Liberia bave succeeded in evolving their destinies as self-governing people, the claim of India for an equal partnership in the federation of the British Empire may be neither so extravagant, nor so remote and visionary as to be altogether beyond the range of practical politics.

ALFRED WEBB
PRESIDENT, 1894.

RAI BAHADUR P. ANANDA CHARLU
PRESIDENT, 1891.

R. M. SAYANI
PRESIDENT, 1896.

HON. BABU SURENDRANATH BANERJEA
PRESIDENT, 1895 & 1902.

CHAPTER XIV.

THE SUCCESS OF THE CONGRESS.

Unification

Human nature, says Hobbes, is a strange admixture of contrarieties. It is always dissatisfied with the present, and while the eternal law of progress incessantly impels it to court the future, it seems never tired of its lamentations for the "good old days" which it has deliberately changed and which never can return. If such inconsistency is only an aberration of human nature in general, it is the marked characteristic of the Indian temperament. To the Present it can hardly be reconciled until it has vanished into the Past, while its feeble attraction for the Future looses all its force even as it makes a new approach to the living Present. While the robust living nations of the world, believing as they do in its perpetual evolution, generally look to the past only to receive inspiration for the future, old decaying people like the Indians, whose only pride is in their past, regard the moral progress of that world as having long passed its meridian and as now being on its descending node. They have no faith in the world's resurrection until its annihilation and as such very little confidence in its future. Centuries of revolutions and changes have made them sceptical of the justice and conscience of a materialistic world, while the teachings of a mystic philosophy, which represents that world as a delusion, furnish them sufficient consolation for patient submission to "the slings and arrows of an outrageous fortune." Like hopeless bankrupts they fondly dote upon the legends of their vanished glories and while bitterly complaining of the present they are more inclined to suffer the evils which they know than fly to others which they know not. Their loyalty and devotion to time-honoured institutions and established order of things make them generally averse to a change and naturally dispose them to drift. Their contact with Western culture has however gradually changed the angle of their vision and from the dreamland of their mystic philosophy they are slowly awakening to the realities of a living world. The Congress working on Western ideas and ideals has been largely instrumental in breaking down this inertia and in infusing a spirit of useful activity in the national character. It has dissipated the wildest fancies of a people who, in their philosophical contempt for this life, seemed to have acquired more intimate knowledge of the unknown than of the known, more of the next world than of this. It has inspired them with a living consciousness which has diverted their mind from the dead past to the living present and fixed their attention on the coming future with hope and confidence. But though the consciousness has come, the latent poison in the system seems not to have entirely lost its deleterious effects. In the Indian temperament a moral aversion to fight and a habitual love of repose act in the first place as a deterrent to the assumption of an aggressive attitude for the assertion of any right, and when force of circumstances constrains it to take the defensive, or to seek for a change, that temperament cannot keep up a long and sustained struggle and naturally demands a speedy solution. One score and eight years are nothing in the life of a nation, and yet within this short period there are not few people who seem to have become tired of the fight. It is besides a strange feature of the situation, that those who have rendered the least active service are the most sceptical of success and in their inert pessimism despondently, if not derisively, ask what has the Congress done for a quarter of a century? But a little reflection would show that the Indian National Congress has done more for India in twenty-five years than what the National League with all its superior advantages did in about fifty years for Ireland.

Next to the national consciousness which it has awakened the first and foremost work done by the Congress is the unification of the various and diverse races inhabiting this vast country. It has moulded a vast heterogeneous population into a homogeneous whole. If the Congress had done nothing else, this one achievement alone would have justified its existence for twenty-five years. A generation ago the stalwart and turbulant Punjabi, the intelligent and sensitive Bengalee, the orthodox and exclusive Madrassi, the ardent and astute Maharatta, the anglicised Parsi and the cold, calculating Guzerati, were perfect strangers to one other, and if they happened to meet anywhere they learnt only to despise each other. Their hereditary tradition was one of mutual distrust, while their past history was marked only by internecine feuds, pillage and bloodshed. But what are they to-day? They are now all united by a strong and indissoluble tie of brotherhood, overriding all distinctions of caste and creed, and inspired by mutual appreciation and common fellowship. Hatred has given place to love and callousness to sympathy. In the prophetic words of Dr. Rajendralala Mitter "the scattered units of the race have coalesced and come together." The "geographical expression" has become a political entity and the "congeries of people" have come to form a nation. The descendants of the Burgis are now among the fastest friends of the Bengalees and many a young man now in the Gangetic delta wonder why there ever was such a thing as the Maharatta Ditch, or how the sweet lullaby with which the Bengalee baby is composed to sleep was ever invented by the matrons of an earlier generation.* A magnetic current has been established from North to South and from East to West and a common pulsation now vibrates throughout the land. A Land Alienation Bill or a Colonization Bill in the Punjab, a revision of Land Settlement in Bombay or Madras, a territorial redistribution in Bengal and a mosque dispute in the United Provinces—now all strike the national chord and the whole country resounds in unison, and whatever administrative measure injuriously effects one

---

* As the Germans are nick-named by the French as *Boches*, so the Maharattas who used to carry on depredations in Bengal and levy the *chouth* were called *Burgis* by the Bengalees. The doggerel to which reference is made may be rendered as follows:—"My baby sleeps; the neighbours have gone to rest; but the *Burgis* have come; the locusts have destroyed the crop, and whence shall I pay the *chouth*?" The *Burgi* at one time was the *Bona* of India.

province is now sorely felt and automatically resented by the other provinces. India is no longer a menagerie of wild and discordent elements and its peoples can now hardly be used as game-cocks to one another. They are now imbued with a national spirit and are daily growing in solidarity and compactness. The Congress has thus laid the first concrete foundation for the colossal work of nation-building and the establishment of an united Indian federation under the ægis of the British Crown.

DEVELOPMENT OF NATIONAL CHARACTER.

During the last thirty years the national character and characteristics have also undergone a remarkable change. As under the breath of the new spirit the popular mind has expanded and narrow communal sentiments have broadened into wider visions and conceptions, so the national character has also acquired a corresponding hue of healthy tone and complexion. Ideas of self-respect, self-reliance and self-sacrifice, though not yet fully developed, are quite manifest in almost every grade of society and in nearly every phase of life; while greater love of truth, courage and straightforwardness, sometimes bordering even on impertinence, are among the notable traits in the character of the educated young men in the country. The sense of humiliating dependence even in domestic relation is fast dying out, while in some places even the time-honoured corporate character of the family, the special feature of Indian social organisation, has become so much loosened as to be almost threatened with a collapse. Individualism is the most marked characteristic of the educated community and whether young or old they are all animated by a manly desire to think and act for themselves, although this tendency is too often carried to extravagant excess, on the one hand through blind, indiscreet attempts to enforce implicit obedience, and on the other hand from inordinate conceit and impatience of control. It is in fact in this development of their character, even more than in their higher conceptions of future hopes and aspirations, that the educated community as a whole have come into direct contact and conflict with the notions and traditions of an orthodox bureaucracy which, unable to divest itself of its long-standing prejudices, starts at every change and suspects every fresh development to be a malignant growth. A claim for better treatment, a tendency to resent gratuitous insults and resist forced exactions of homage, so long enjoyed as *abwabs* by a dominant race, and above all a demand for justice and fairness are the natural outcome of the education which the people have received and the new consciousness to which they have awakened. Whether in official or public life there is no longer in the country that heavy atmosphere of cringing servility which provoked Lord Macaulay's highly coloured picture of the Indian character towards the middle of the last century, and if the noble lord had been living to-day he might well have been surprised to find, that while the people themselves have so largely shaken off the moral weaknesses with which they were so lavishly charged, there are those among his own countrymen who secretly regret the change and would fain perpetuate in this country the spirit which he so strongly and eloquently condemned. It may be said with pardonable pride that in uprightness and integrity, in honesty of purpose and devotion to duty, in fortitude and patience no less than in their intelligence and aptitude for work, Indians in the inferior ranks of the public services, to which their lot is generally confined, fully hold their own against Europeans who are sometimes very much their artificial superiors in position, authority and influence; while as regards the larger body of the educated public it may be no exaggeration to say, that with all their defects and shortcomings, they are on the whole now a manlier race imbued with higher ideas of public duties and responsibilities in the discharge of which their own patriotic impulse supplies the only motive power and for the fulfilment of which they neither claim nor expect a higher reward than the appreciation of their countrymen and the approbation of their own conscience. Whether it be a disastrous flood or a decimating famine, an awful outbreak of pestilence or an overwhelming pressure of a vast religious concourse, everywhere they are ready bravely to face the situation and make the necessary sacrifices. Even in anarchism, the ugliest development of the present situation, which is regarded in this country not simply as a social crime but as a mortal sin, there is a spirit of wreckless courage which, if directed in proper channels, might have proved a valuable asset towards a higher development of the national life, and many a young man like Kanayelal Dutt might have under better guidance and with proper opportunities died as martyrs, rather than as murderers, in the service of their King and their country.* It is not at all suggested that this national character is above reproach, or has become even properly developed. On the contrary it still suffers from many a serious defect which severe training and systematic discipline alone can eradicate. It lacks that vigour and tenacity, patience and perseverance, and above all that stiffness and elasticity which constitute the backbone of a people and make human nature proof against reverses and despair. People still want that confidence in themselves and trust in others which respectively form the asset and credit of the corporate life of a nation. However unpalatable and humiliating the confession may be, if we are only true to ourselves, it must be frankly recognized that one of the darkest spots and weakest points in our national character is jealousy. Many years ago in course of a private conversation, a European friend, who subsequently rose to the position of Commissioner of a division, asked the writer of these pages,—What was the distinguishing feature between the Indian and European character which made merit rise so slow in India and so fast in Europe? The writer began by referring to the superior intelligence, sagacity and industry of the European; but before he could proceed further his friend interrupted him saying, that he was mistaken and going in a wrong line, as the real explanation lay in another and in quite a different direction.

* The present European war has opened such an opportunity. Indeed the French who are nothing if not original in everything have formed regiments of their "criminal heroes" who are giving good account of their desperate character and a similar experiment in this country might prove equally successful.

The average European, he said, was not more intelligent than the average Indian, while as regards industry he had always found to his surprise that the ill-paid Indian ministerial officers worked more assiduously and with greater devotion than any European officer could be expected to work under similar conditions. The real answer to his question according to him was to be found in the national trait and not in any individual characteristic of the two races. "In a Western country," he said, "when a man shows signs of any extraordinary talent in any direction the whole community rushes in to push him up; but in India the general tendency is to pull him down." Although there are other material differences in the circumstances of the two races and much may be said against a generalization of this kind, it seems impossible to deny that there is considerable force in this observation. The Indian character has no doubt attained, as has already been observed, a higher level in many directions; but it can hardly be denied that even now public men have more detracters than admirers and that appreciation of public services, which is the most potent incentive to public action, is yet very feeble and inactive in this country. If we are really anxious to elevate ourselves in the scale of nations we must not deceive ourselves by putting the flattering unction to our soul. True patriotism does not consist either in blind, idolatrous veneration of a dead past, or in subtle ingenuity to extract metaphysical secrets out of metaphorical aphorisms for the gratification of vanity and egotism. A thoughtful writer has somewhere observed, that "there are natures which can extract poison from everything sweet," and it will be found upon close examination, that a spirit of captious criticism wanting in due appreciation of merit, whether in a friend or an adversary, is a mental disease which in its chronic stage works as a slow poison to the understanding as well as to other mental faculties and in the end terminates fatally to the moral nature also. There are always two sides to a question, and a cultivated mind ought carefully to weigh the *pros* and *cons* before pronouncing judgment on it. A well-regulated, disciplined character is the first requisite of a national development. As license is not liberty, so arrogance is not independence. Leadership is not a privilege but a responsibility, and one must learn to follow before he can aspire to lead a community where everybody is ready to command and none to obey must be either a Babel, or a Bedlam, or a Billingsgate.

SOCIAL AND INDUSTRIAL PROGRESS.

Next in order of importance is perhaps the inauguration of social reform and industrial development to both of which the Congress has so largely contributed. It will be remembered that at the outset many were the "candid friends" who advised the movement to be directed towards social and industrial reforms rather than towards premature political activities. The members of the Congress, however, neither overlooked nor underestimated the importance of these reforms, as they were perfectly conscious that in the process of an evolution all the three were handmaids to one another, although it was equally clear to them that with all the diversities of manners, customs, habits and even laws and religions of the various races inhabiting such a vast continent, it was not possible directly to bring all the people together except upon a political platform. As the three reforms were inter-dependent, moving on a common axle, they understood that if a force could be imparted to one of the wheels the other two also would automatically move with it. It is a well-known fact, that it was largely the members and the supporters of the Congress who individually and in their respective spheres of influence started social and industrial movements which gradually spread throughout the country, the Congress itself being the centre from which the forces emanated in different directions. The Social Conference started in 1888 and the Industrial Conference inaugurated in 1904 were two important bodies, which, like two satellites revolving each on its own axis, have moved round the Congress in its annual course and contributed not a little towards social and economic advancement of the country. The Hon'ble Mahadev Govinda Ranade on the social and the Hon'ble Rao Bahadur R. N. Mudholkar on the industrial side are two of the outstanding figures of the Congress whose services to the cause of these reforms must be acknowledged with gratitude and respect. The Congress as a huge deliberative body cannot, as a matter of course, concern itself with the details of these reforms which depend upon different conditions in different provinces, but it cannot fairly be denied, that it has always acted as the pivot of all the public movements and the mainspring of all the activities which are now at work in all directions and throughout the countrv Whether it be the question of sea-voyage or of the "depressed classes," whether it is the cause of marriage reform or scientific education, the actual working bodies may and must be different; but the motive impetus generated and manifested in all these directions may easily be traced to one common source—the spirit of national consciousness evoked by the Congress. It has roused a slumbering people from the lethargy of ages and vivified them into new life. The Indians have drifted too long; but they are no longer disposed to drift. Conferences, associations and organizations have become the order of the day, and whether it be literary or historical researches, or scientific studies, or the resuscitation of decaying arts and industries, or the solution of knotty social problems, everywhere there is the manifestation of a new spirit. The restlessness and commotion which are observable almost in every walk of life, the zeal and earnestness which characterise the activities of almost all classes and communities for bettering their status and prospects in life and the high ideals which animate the people, are all symptoms of a mighty evolution that is noiselessly working its way. In the ferment of this evolution some objectionable things here and there have no doubt come to the surface, but this was unavoidable. It is impossible to extract the crystal without bringing the impurities of sugar on the surface in the boiling cauldron. The Congress no doubt is primarily a political organisation; but its social and economic aspects cannot also be disputed Mr. Hume in his celebrated reply to Sir Auckland Colvin clearly enunciated the real aim and object of the movement. They were, he said, at that early stage of the institution, "the regeneration of India on all lines, spiritual, moral, social, industrial and political." "The main body of the Congress," he added, "was directed to national and political objects upon which the whole country was able to stand on a common ground." But, as was pointed out, "the social requirements varied according to race, caste and creed, so that they had to be dealt by separate organizations suited to each province or community." Thus while the actual working machineries were different, the electric installation which supplied the motive power for all of them was one and the same, which led Sir William Wedderburn to point out that as a matter of fact "the workers for political progress were the most active friends of social reform," and, he might well have added, that they were also among the early pioneers of the industrial movement and the founders of not a few of the small industries which made such marked progress during the last few years. Some of these enterprises have no doubt suffered a serious collapse; but these occasional lapses are almost incidental to a nascent stage. Children stagger and stumble before they acquire a steady use of their limbs. Want of training and absence of sound knowledge and experience and possibly some lack of moral strength also are at the root f these failures which, however deplorable in themselves, afford no just ground either for alarm or despair. The South Sea Bubble in England and the Panama enterprise in France were far greater disasters; but both the British and the French people have long outlived these misadventures. A spirit of enterprise once created cannot die; but fanned by its own wings Phœnix-like it is bound to rise out of its own ashes.

The much-abused Swadeshi movement has a history of its own. Bombay was earlier in the field of industrial development with modern appliances and machineries; but Bengal and Madras had an indigenous textile industry on a more extensive scale which was practically extinct under foreign competition. The situation was everywhere viewed with grave anxiety, though nowhere, except in the Western Presidency, any active effort was made to grapple with it until a cry for the revival of the indigenous industries was raised in Bengal where the immortal patriotic song of Mr. Mon Mohan Bose, the founder of the now defunct Swadeshi Mela, is still heard with thrilling interest. The necessity for preferential treatment of indigenous article was vigorously pressed at some of the earlier Provincial Conferences in Bengal, notably at Burdwan in 1894, and also on several other occasions where ardent Congressmen drew prominent attention to the growing poverty and helplessness of the people for want of sufficient encouragement of indigenous industries. A formal proposal for preferential treatment of home-made products was for the first time submitted to the Subjects-Committee of the Congress held at Ahmedabad in 1902; but owing to a divergence of opinion it failed to pass through the Committee. In 1905, the people of Bengal exasperated by a violent disruption of the province adopted a general boycott of all foreign articles. On the 7th of August, a huge and unprecedented demonstration was held at the Calcutta Town Hall in which at a modest calculation over thirty thousand people took part in three different sections, two in the upper and lower floors of the historic hall and the other and by far the largest section in the spacious open *maidan* in front. So intense was the feeling that the spirit of the movement marched like wild fire and the contagion spread in no time from Lahore to Tuticorin and from Assam to Guzerat. It was generally based upon economic grounds; but it cannot be denied that the movement had its origin in Bengal as a protest against the Partition. The Congress, while not countenancing the boycott, gave formal sanction to the *Swadeshi* in 1906 and enjoined the people to give preference to indigenous articles "wherever practicable and even at a sacrifice." With all its lapses and indiscretions, which are almost inseparable from all movements which have their origin in tremendous popular excitement the Swadeshi movement must be admitted to have given a great impetus to the development of indigenous industries in this country. That development may not yet have been very remarkable; but it is doubtless gratifying that it has revived the weaving industry and directed the energies of the people into new channels of activity. For soap and scent, shoes and trunk, nib and ink, socks and vests, pottery and cutlery, as well as various kinds of woollen and silken stuff, the country can now well afford to stand, though not in the best style, substantially on its own leg; while the Bengal Chemical and Pharmaceutical Works started under the initiative and guidance of that eminent Indian scientist, Dr. P.C. Roy. have elicited the unstinted admiration of even those who are disposed to draw a sharp distinction between true and false *Swadeshi*.

Above all the patriotic labours of Mr. Jamsetji Nesservanji Tata have created an epoch in the industrial regeneration of India. Bombay received her early initiation in Industrialism from the American Civil War of 1861-65 when her attention was drawn to her opportunities in cotton trade. Although Bombay has never ceased to complain about the arbitrary and exacting system of her land settlement under the operation of which the fruits of the agricultural labours are periodically shorn off like the proverbial sheep to meet the demands of the State, she may yet find sufficient consolation in the thought that the industrial activities and enterprises of her people may be due in no small measure to the depressing conditions imposed in their case upon agricultural pursuits which appear to have so largely absorbed the comparatively indolent population of the permanently settled provinces; while her own people driven from the fields to the factories have found ample compensation for the precarious doles of nature in the larger bounties of arts and industries. The first cotton mill in Bombay was started in 1855 by Cowasji Nanabhoy Davar who was followed by a noble band of equally enterprising industrialist among whom the names of Roychand Premchand, Sir Jamsetji Jejeebhoy and Sir Dinshaw Manekji Petit are known throughout the country. But the greatest and brightest of this galaxy of stars who ushered in the industrial renaissance of modern India was perhaps Jamsetji Nasservanji Tata. Full of patriotic ideas and sentiments Mr. Tata established in 1886 a new cotton mill which he appropriately styled the "Swadeshi Mills." But the greatest work of Mr. Tata which will ever enshrine his name in the grateful memory of his countrymen is the Scientific Research Institute for which he made a princely donation of 30 *lakhs* of rupees and which planned and matured during his lifetime was subsequently established, with the help and co-operation of the Government of India and of Mysore, by his worthy son Sir Dorab Tata at Bangalore within the territories of the latter. Mr. Tata's Vulcan Steel and Iron Factory recently established at Sakchi within the territories of another Indian prince, the Maharajah of Morbhunj in Orissa and his Electric Installation at Bombay for utilizing the waters of the Western Ghauts, are colossal projects which bear testimony not only to his extraordinary genius and enterprise, but also to the vigour and robustness of the industrial renaissance which has dawned upon the country with the first awakening of its national consciousness. Truly has the biographer of Mr. Tata remarked that he "was a Swadeshi of Swadeshists long before Swadeshism was boomed in Bengal."

The Co-operative Movement, which has made such rapid strides during the last few years throughout the country and particularly in Bengal, is another evidence of the spirit of self-help which has come to animate the national character and of the aptitude which the people have acquired for the management for their own affairs. It is indeed a matter of as much regret as of gratification that in all this healthy developments the people had so little to count upon the active help and co-operation of the State and so largely to depend upon their own resources. With the notable exception of the Tata Iron Works there appears to be no industrial project in which the Government has as yet either taken the initiative or generously extended a substantially helping hand. Whether for training men in scientific and industrial education in foreign countries, or in starting new industries at home, the people have had practically to depend upon their unaided efforts and their extremely limited resources; while the examples of Japan and China in the East and of the Philippines in the West have served only to tantalize and mortify a people proverbially the poorest in the modern civilized world. The patriotic efforts of Messrs. Norendra Nath Sen, Jogendra Chandra Ghose in Bengal and J. N. Tata in Bombay for giving technical education to our young men were movements in the right direction; but for want of adequate support and encouragement they practically collapsed after a short but very useful career of existence. It may be remembered, that even in the seventies and eighties of the last century it was almost a fashion in certain quarters to twit the people with their universal hankering after services under the State which it was truly impossible for any Government to satisfy; but now that the people have realized their mistake and turned their attention to industrial and other developments, men in authority are not wanting to remind them that "India is essentially an agricultural country," and that as such their hands should be directed to the plough and not to the steam-engine: while a responsible member of the Supreme Government, being recently driven almost to a corner on the question of State aid to some of the crippled industries in the country, plainly said, that India need not care about her industrial development when there was England to supply all her requirements. What a frank confession and a bitter disappointment! If England could have supplied all the wants of India it would not have been possible for Germany to swamp her market. Besides, where is the Ordinance of Nature which has made this classification among mankind and provided that some people must not learn to govern themselves, but be content with being well-governed, and that some countries must extract only raw materials from Mother Earth leaving others to convert them into more valuable finished articles? Providence certainly has nowhere prescribed these conditions and sanctioned this division of labour. True it is that all people are not at all times equally trained and equally competent to participate in the blessings of arts and sciences; but it should be the highest aim of a benevolent Government, whether foreign or indigenous, to foster and stimulate as far as lies in its power the energies and activities of the people committed to its care in every right direction for the advancement and amelioration of their economic condition. Even free and resourceful countries like Germany and Japan have had to count upon state bounties and subsidies for their economic development, and India cannot fairly be expected to work out her salvation through more enquiries, reports and exhibitions.

The present European war has opened a vast field for the expansion and development of Indian industries. The extensive trades of Germany and Austria have been driven out of the Indian market and if prompt measures could be taken to replace them by indigenous productions, the economic problem of the country might be easily solved and at the same time the position of Government materially strengthened. But the Government seems hardly to realize the importance of this opportunity which has arisen as a unique good coming out of a dire evil. The Congress at its last session as well as the Indian public, earnestly pressed the question on the attention of Government, nor has the European mercantile community altogether failed to express its views on the subject. Mr. Ledgard, as Chairman of the Upper India Chamber of Commerce, is reported to have pressed at its last annual meeting "the importance of vigorous preparations for stepping into Germany's shoes in the matter of trade" and regretted that the "Government had not been able to give any indication of a policy of assistance towards industrial enterprise that might enable the country to take advantage of the situation." It may, however, be hoped that it is not yet too late to indicate that policy, so that the precious opportunity may not be entirely lost.

Local Self-Government and Reform of Judicial Administration.

The efforts of the Congress towards the expansion of Local Self-Government and the reform of the Judicial

Administration have not, however, met with any encouraging success. Nearly thirty years have elapsed since Lord Ripon introduced the principle of Self-Government in the administration of the local affairs of the people in the ardent hope that it might prove the stepping-stone towards their attainment of National Self-Government in the higher administration of the country. But within this period the institution has not advanced one step forward and it is still held in the same leading string with which it was started, though it seems doubtful if in certain directions its tether has not been even appreciably shortened. The number of the municipal corporations, which are properly speaking the really self-governing bodies in the country, has undergone no perceptible increase, while their powers and privileges have clearly not been enhanced, although in not a few cases they have been ruthlessly curtailed. As regards the larger bodies of District and Local Boards, these have been practically converted into a department of the District Administration directly under the District Officer, and it certainly looks strange that not a single District has been found within the life-time of a generation fit to be entrusted with a non-official Chairman for this institution. Times without number has the Congress pressed for a provisional experiment which the law expressly provides, and at least one Commissioner of an important division in Bengal strongly recommended such a trial. But a consideration of the official prestige of the District Officer, who must be provided octopus-like as it were with a number of tentacles to enable him to maintain his position and dignity, has apparently overridden all claims of justice and fairness, and perhaps it would be no exaggeration to say that the Local Self-Government Acts of the different provinces are, to all intents and purposes, a misnomer and the institutions themselves have become fossilized without any possibility of growth of development, though they may of course be liable to further decay. There can be no reasonable complaint against legitimate control. But if the Government has a responsibility in supervising the workings of these popular institutions, it is also not without its corresponding obligation to foster, develop and improve them. Control without co-operation is only another name for obstruction. It is in the air, that it is in the contemplation of Government also to officialize the Co-operative Credit Societies which the people have evolved and worked out partially to relieve their economic pressure. It is to be hoped that a powerful government will not lay itself open to the charge of assuming the sponsorship of institutions in whose baptism it had little or no hand, and however justly responsible it may feel for safeguarding the honesty and integrity of these institutions, it may be fully expected that nothing will be done either to stunt their growth, or to alienate popular sympathies and confidence from them.

As regards the reform of the Judicial Administration, the first principle enunciated by the Congress is practically admitted, and it is no longer disputed that the administration stands in need of revision; but here also, as in the case of Local Self-Government, the morbid bugbear of official prestige stands in the way. The Decentralization Commission simply evaded the question; but the present Public Service Commission will have to decide it either one way or the other. Various palliatives have been suggested by those who are no longer able to defend the existing system, but are at the same time unwilling to part with it. But these are mere makeshifts which can only defer and not solve the question. The question has considerably matured itself and the Congress will have to start a fresh campaign in the light of the Royal Commission's pronouncements to drive the discussion to a satisfactory conclusion.

PARLIAMENTARY ENQUIRIES.

As has already been observed, the last Parliamentary enquiry into Indian affairs was made in 1854, and ever since the transfer of the rule to the Crown in 1858 both Parliament as well as the Government, whether Liberal or Conservative, were alike indifferent to the Indian administration which was complacently left into the hands of a close bureaucracy. The very first Congress of 1885 vigorously protested against this indifference and pressed for a Royal Commission to enquire into the Indian administration. In 1897 the Welby Commission was appointed, and since then there have been the Decentralisation Commission in 1902 and the Chamberlain Commission and the Islington Commission which are now carrying on their investigations. The Government of India also instituted the Education Commission of 1882 and the Police Commission of 1902. The results of these Commissions may not have so far come up to the fullest expectations of the people and may have in some cases proved even disappointing to them. But they bear undoubted testimony to the growing interest felt both in England, as well as in this country, in the increasingly important and complicated administration of India. It is in the nature of all bureaucratic rules to accord a readier acceptance to retrograde suggestions than to progressive recommendations; but the Indian Nationalist need not despair. However cautious or dilatory the Government may be giving effect to the various wholesome recommendations of these Commissions, it can never hope to set them aside. There they are among the permanent archives of the Government laying down policies and principles which may be carried forward, but upon which it would be difficult, if not absolutely impossible, to go back. Stern, necessary changes may be deferred, but cannot be averted when they are pressed by the irresistible force of time and circumstance.

PUBLIC MEN AND PUBLIC SPIRIT.

The vitality of a nation is gauged by its power of producing capable men at all critical stages of its life. Mazzini and Garibaldi in Italy, Thiers and Gambetta in France, Yungshi-kai and Sun-Yet-Sen in China, Enver Bey and Izzat Pasha in Turkey,—all have proved, that though passing through the severest ordeal of their national existence, neither the Italians nor the French, neither the Chinese nor the Turks were among the dead nations of the world. The Indian National Congress, though dealing with a subject race, labouring under enormous difficulties and disabilities, has produced a class of self-sacrificing, self-reliant, resourceful, robust and patriotic men some of whom, at all events, under more favourable circumstances might well have taken their places by the side of some of the foremost men in European politics. Their lot might have forbidden them from commanding the applause of the political world and consigned them to the strictures and captious criticisms of an orthodox and inflated bureaucracy; but there are men among them who, if their Sovereign had commanded, might have formed a cabinet or held a portfolio. The most obdurate of pessimists will probably admit and the most cynical of critics acknowledge, that with all their shortcomings these men are not altogether unworthy products of the modern Indian renaissance which has dawned under the ægis of the British rule. They have at all events conclusively proved that most of the Indian races still possess sufficient vitality and moral stamina to aspire to a place in the comity of civilised nations in the world. The public men whom the Congress has produced and the spirit of self-help which it has evoked are perhaps among the most valuable working capital of the country.

The nineteen eminent Indians who have so far adorned the presidential chair of the Congress will, no doubt, go down to posterity as among the pioneers of Indian nation-builders. They are all men who have made their mark in Indian History. But besides these, the Congress has produced a galaxy of men of whom any country might be justly proud. Dr. Rajendra Lala

Mitra, Rajah Peary Mohan Mukherjee, Sir Romesh Chander Mitter, Sir Goorudas Banerjee, Mr. Monomohan Ghose, Mr. Norendra Nath Sen, Mr. (now Mr. Justice) Ashutosh Choudhury, Mr. Baikunta Nath Sen, Dr. Rabindra Nath Tagore, Mr. A. Rasul, Mr. Motilal Ghose, Mr. Kalicharan Bannerjee and Mr. Bhupendra Nath Basu * in Bengal; Maharajah Sir Luchmeswar Singh, Mr. (now Mr. Justice) Hasan Imam, Mr. Dip Narain Singh, Mr. Guruprasad Sen, and Mr. Mazar-ul-Haque in Behar; Pundit Ajudhya Nath, Pundit Biswambhar Nath, Dr. Sunderlal, Mr. Ganga Prasad Varma and Raja Rampal Singh in the United Provinces; Sirdar Dayal Singh Mejhatia, Lala Lajpat Rai and Mr. Mahomed Ali in the Punjab; Mr. M.G. Ranade, Mr. K. T. Telang, Mr. Daji Abaji Khare, Mr. Luxman Nulkar, Mr. Hari Chiplankar, Mr. Bal Gangadhar Tilak, Sir Ibrahim Rahimtullah, Dr. Bhandarkar, Mr. Setalvad and Mr. Mahomedali Jinnah in Bombay; and Mr. Krishnaswami Iyer, Mr. G. Subramania Iyer, Mr. Veeraraghava Achari, Mr. Ramaswami Mudaliar, Sir Subramaniya Iyer and Mr. Veejararaghava Achari in Madras,—all rank among the shining lights of this period. Many of these distinguished men would ere long have taken their places in the illustrious roll of the Congress Presidents but for premature death which seems to be the prevailing curse of India. The public services of some of these men have also been recognised by the Government, while all of them occupy a high position in the estimation of their countrymen as their trusted guides and leaders.

* Since elected President of the Madras Congress of 1914.

THE PUBLIC SERVICES.

From the very beginning the Congress has persistently urged the larger admission of the children of the soil into the public services of the country, and a mere glance through the pages of the Civil Lists will at once show what substantial advancement the country has made in this direction. Even up to the Sixties of the last century the average people were under the impression, that the Principal Sudder Ameen on the one side and the Deputy Collector on the other were the highest appointments open to the children of the soil and the idea of a native of India sitting as a Sessions Judge or as a District Officer appeared only as a dream. The first Indian Civilian who was a Bengali was not appointed to his own province; while the distinguished triumvirate, also Bengalis, who followed in the next decade, received an ovation upon their return in 1871 which is now seldom accorded to the Governor of a province. Whole Calcutta went to the Seven Tanks Gardens in the Belgachia Villa to witness as it were an exhibition of a curious specimen of speaking lions brought from Europe; while no less a sober person than the venerable Dr. K. M. Banerjee in his patriotic pride and exultation cried out at a public meeting that the event was the "second great battle of Plassey fought on British soil." Many a "battle of Plassey" of the same description have since been fought and won without attracting much attention. Compare the earlier picture of the public services with the present and there will be no difficulty in realising the actual measure of the inwardness of that robust optimism which possess the minds of the veterans of the Congress as regards the future prospects of the people in the administration of the country. Even so late as the Eighties of the last century none dared seriously entertain the faintest hope of seeing Indians on the Council of the Secretary of State, or in the Executive Councils of the Governments in this country, or even in a Provincial Board of Revenue. Yet all these are now accomplished facts. The Indians have now fully established their claims from the chartered High Courts and the Executive Governments downwards to almost every branch of the Civil administration, and the question now is only one of percentage, regard being had to alleged efficiency of the services and exigencies of the State. There is still a sharp distinction drawn between what are called the Imperial and the Provincial Services in the general administration, as well as in the Education, Medical and almost all other departments of the State; but this is a shallow, artificial devise to keep up a monopoly which cannot, however, be long maintained, and a systematic vigorous campaign is all that is necessary to break down this racial and colour-fencing which still bars the people's entrance into the inner sanctuary of the administration. But as the irritating and invidious distinction cannot be defended on any rational principle and as breaches have been effected at certain points, the surrender of the strongholds of a close, selfish bureaucracy can only be a question of time. Attempts may be made, as are not infrequently made, to repair these breaches, but the ultimate fall of these citadels is inevitable. It is, however, a matter of great regret, if not of surprise, that men are not wanting even among people of this country who having themselves risen high in the rung of the public services as the result of persistent public agitation should be among those who denounce such agitation lest further agitation might interfere with their future prospects. There is a grim humour about such an attitude which is not unlike that of a belated railway passenger who, before he reaches his station, eagerly wishes that the train might be a little late; but as soon as he has comfortably secured his own berth begins to grow impatient that it should be any more late in starting. Apparently with a view to cover their own selfishness these good people confidently assert, that public agitation has stopped the right of public meeting and necessitated the Press Law. But can these critics picture even in their own mind a public meeting without some sort of agitation behind it? Or, can they conceive of any use of the valued right of the freedom of public meeting and of speech if it were to be divorced from agitation either for the removal of existing grievances, or for the acquisition of fresh rights? Public meetings cannot be always confined to singing *requiem* to an ex-judge or a retired magistrate however brilliant his career may have been, nor does the salvation of the country wholly depend upon the success of a few subservient officers who seem to have learnt the art of "kicking the ladder behind" almost to gymnastic perfection. As for the new Press Act, or the other repressive measures which the Government has latterly introduced, it is the grossest ignorance that can attribute these to public agitation which the British constitution not only allows, but also encourages. Even the authors of these reactionary measures did not attribute them to public agitation, but to some other condition too well-known to require any particular reference. It is healthy agitation that invigorates public life in every civilised country; and it is a well-recognised fact that it is opposing forces which, in their resultánt action, keep up the vitality of a system, and serve to maintain and strengthen it. Those who are afraid of agitation and enamoured of the calm repose of an easy-going, smooth, indolent life ought to remember that the stagnant water of a pool, though transparent and tempting to the naked eye, is always full of noxious germs and injurious to the system: while the muddy water of the running stream is not only wholesome to drink, but is also fertilising to the ground which it inundates.

THE YOUNG MEN VOLUNTEERS.

Another achievement of which the Congress may justly be proud is the healthy and vigorous impetus which it has given to the development of moral courage and discipline of the Indian youths. The system of "Volunteers," which was first introduced in connection with the Second Congress held in 1886 and was more fully organised in Madras in the following year, was a very useful institution for the training of our young men not only for the immediate object with which it was started, but also for preparing them to become proper and efficient citizen-soldiers for the battle of life. These "Volunteers" no doubt came to carry a bad odour with the authorities at a subsequent stage and in connection with a situation for which no one perhaps deplored more deeply or suffered more grievously than the Congressmen; but the Indian public have never been able to divest themselves of the belief that the "Congress Volunteers" were really more sinned against than sinning and that they had a bad name given to them only to justify their being afterwards hanged for it. If their open and occasional services to the Congress really could have anything to do with the secret, abominable practices of a disreputable gang of fanatics, why, then, the drilling and the gymnastic exercises in the schools and even the laboratories in the colleges, for which the Government itself so amply and generously provided, might with equal, if not greater, propriety have been held responsible for these untoward and disgraceful developments. It seems to have been well remarked by a shrewd Frenchman that "when John Bull begins to suspect he generally begins at the wrong end." This suspicion has no doubt succeeded in a large measure in segregating the youths of the country, not sparing even young men in colleges, from the sphere of all political activities; but no reasonable explanation is forthcoming as to how beardless boys are strangely developing criminal instincts and dispositions being practically confined within what may not be improperly called as insecure goals under a strict politico-educational surveillance. In a laudable anxiety to protect the boys the schools have been practically converted into plague camps where, completely cut off from the bracing atmosphere of healthy public influence, these unsuspecting and impressionable innocents fall easy prey to the insidious, pestilential spirits which are abroad and which, working in secret, find ample opportunity to penetrate into the closest recesses to misguide these immature lads under grossest misrepresentations and allure them to their ultimate ruin. It seems extremely doubtful if the moral nature of man can be entirely governed by physical laws and regulations. Stunt that nature in its normal development in one direction, it will burst out in a malignant growth in another. Besides, there are to be found a few black sheep in almost every flock to poison the rest. Thus schools may be barricaded and students segregated and circularized; but there seems to be no island of Juan Fernandez where a resourceful mind may not devise means for its occupation and ultimately escape out of it. It seems a grievous mistake to exclude impressionable young minds altogether from the chastening influence of public opinion and try to turn useful citizens out of cloisters and dormatories. The public is a great monitor and a force, and if it sometimes misleads, it oftener exercises a healthy influence in shaping and moulding social life. Whatever that may be, the Congress Volunteers practically discharged from the Congress service have found scope for more active occupation in other and more useful directions. Mr. Gokhale's "*Servants of India*" in Bombay and Mr. Krishna Kumar Mitra's "*Irregulars*" in Bengal are highly useful bodies whose invaluable services in time of distress and difficulty have not failed sometimes to elicit the unstinted approbation and admiration of even responsible officers of Government. They may not yet be recognized as occasional, useful adjuncts to the administration; but they are undoubtedly a most valuable help to the public on many a pressing occasion. On the whole these institutions are a training academy for the Indian youths which have made them ever so manly, so enduring, so courageous, so resourceful and so self-sacrificing in their life and conduct.

THE EXPANSION OF THE LEGISLATIVE COUNCILS.

Among the many minor reforms effected at the instance of the Congress may be mentioned the increase in the taxable minimum for the Income Tax; the raising of the age-limit for the Civil Service Examination; a further extension of Trial by Jury though on a very limited scale; a partial redress of forest grievances; the re-imposition of the import duties on cotton, though with a countervailing excise duty on the indigenous products which practically operates as a protection to British manufactures, and the repeal of the English duty on Silver plates, for all of which the Congress carried on a persistent agitation both in this country as well as in England. But by far the greatest political achievement of the Congress is perhaps the reform and expansion of the Legislative Councils and the appointment of Executive Councils for the major provinces in which at least one Indian member has found a place. All the provinces and administrations, whether under Lieutenant-Governors or Chief Commissioners, are provided with local

Legislative Councils of their own. The number of members for the Councils has been increased and the area of representation considerably widened. The right of interpellation with the power of putting supplementary questions and the right of moving resolutions and introducing Bills, are all important privileges secured, the value of which cannot be under-estimated. The Congress strenuously fought for these reforms ever since 1885, and it is these substantial privileges, which were partially conceded in 1892 and more fully granted in 1910, that have led many an alarmist to cry 'halt' and to urge that the Congress having achieved its main object has no just ground for its further existence. To the Indian Nationalist, however, it is only the thin end of the wedge, and if ever there was a time to strike vigorously that time has now arrived. The Congress has never made any secret of its ultimate goal, and while that goal is yet faintly looming in the dim, distant future, it cannot afford to rest on its oars, nor regard its mission as even partially fulfilled. If the attainment of national Self-Government within the Empire is its aim, if India is to throw off the yoke of a Dependency and acquire the status of a Dominion, then it must be admitted that the Congress has only just entered on a career of useful existence and that these reforms mark only the beginning and not the end of its arduous task. It is no doubt a matter of rejoicing that a breach has at last been effected in the outer ramparts of a benevolent Despotism; but if the inner citadel be the real objective it would be simply foolish to pass the live-long day in only dancing and revelling over that breach. Besides, what are the reforms that have really been effected? Without being guilty of want of proper appreciation it seems quite permissible to point out that these reforms are mere faint adumbrations of a rough political sketch, the full representation of which in its true colours has yet to be evolved. It is only the shadow and not the real substance which has been thrown on the screen. The representation granted is still very inadequate and the electorates highly defective; the majority is still with the Government and where it has been conceded to the people it is simply nominal and illusory. The representatives of the people have yet no control over the finances and the resolutions which they are privileged to move, and upon which they are entitled also to divide the councils, too often prove to be the proverbial Dead-Sea Apple that crumbles to the touch. They have yet no binding force and cannot influence the policy of Government. As regards the substantial modification introduced in the composition of the Executive Councils of both the Imperial and the Provincial Governments it has to be noticed, that public opinion does not count for anything and popular representatives of unquestioned ability, judgment and independence, who fought for the reform, are carefully excluded from the list. Men like Sir Pherozeshah Mehta, Mr. G. K. Gokhale,* Mr. Surendra Nath Banerjee and Dr. Rash Behary Ghose have no place in these

* Alas! Mr. Gokhale is no more! Since these pages were sent to the press the saintly politician has passed away leaving a void in this ill-fated country which is not likely to be soon filled up.

Councils, and the people cannot be very much blamed if they still labour under the impression that the bureaucracy are ill-disposed to admit their equals and that there is still a marked tendency to take away with one hand what is given with the other. The voice of the people thus still continues to be practically the same cry in the wilderness that it used to be before, with this difference that, that voice has found a channel for its articulation and cannot now be stifled. People are not therefore wanting who honestly think, that the present Councils are at best counterfeit representations of representative institutions as understood in the British constitution. They certainly bear a striking family resemblance to not a few of the mimic reforms which have found their way in this country and among which mention may be made of the system of trial with the aid of assessors with which a renowned political juggler, more than thirty years ago, hoodwinked the people of this country as being a fair substitute for Trial by Jury. From this, however, it must not be inferred that these reforms are altogether discounted. In fact they are neither such shams as some hyper-critics among us would represent them to be; nor are they the very quintessence of British statesmanship as Sir Valentine Chirol and others of his school would have us believe. They undoubtedly mark a distinct advance in Indian politics and constitute a substantial instalment of political enfranchisement of the people. If they have done nothing else, these reforms must be admitted to have furnished the people with powerful weapons for clearing the ground before them, while they are not yet out of the wood. Lord Morley's imagination may not be able to pierce through the prevailing gloom to catch the faintest glimpse of India's future destiny; but all the same he may have been the unconscious instrument in the hand of an inscrutible Providence to work out her salvation, and it may be the proud privilege of the future historian to reckon him as the Simon de Montfort of an Indian Parliament. The Congress from the very outset pressed either for the abolition or for the reform of the Council of the Secretary of State. Although no statutory reform has yet been introduced, the appointment of two Indians to this Council has gone a great way towards a fair recognition of the principle of representation in this Council so persistently advocated by the Congress; while the recent attempt of Lord Crewe for the reform of this Council was an augury of considerable importance towards a satisfactory solution of the question, though unfortunately that attempt has proved abortive at least for the present.

Such is the brief survey of the work done by the Congress during the last twenty-eight years of its existence. With all its lapses and shortcomings, it must be fairly conceded even by its worst critics, that this is no mean record of its achievements; while its friends will readily admit that the Congress has worked out almost a revolution in the country unprecedented in the history of a subject people under an alien rule. Apart from its political aspects the Congress has been the fountain-head and mainspring of not a few of the activities which have manifested themselves in various directions.

during the last quarter of a century and inspired the people with ideas of a nobler, manlier and healtheir life.

THE NATIVE STATES—AN OBJECT LESSON.

It may not be in the recollection of many at this distance of time, that at one of the early stages of the Congress a question was actually raised and discussed in the Press as to whether the sphere of the movement should not be extended to the independent Native States. It was, however, wisely decided that the subjects of these States should be left to themselves and the work of the Congress confined to British India only. But the blessed contagion did not take much time in crossing the frontiers and spreading far beyond the British territories when the echo of the Congress was also heard in some of these independent principalities, although it was there the Princes rather than the People who took time by the forelock and adopted the initiative in advanced administration. The enlightened rulers of Baroda, Mysore and Travancore have set an example even to the paramount power, the significance of which cannot be lost upon the minds of the more advanced British subjects. Much has been said and written on the supposed differences between the East and the West and where logic has failed, fallacies have been invoked to support the contention that India is constitutionally unfit for the advanced institutions of the West and that no attempt can therefore be made to cultivate them even in a hot-house in this country. But these Indian Princes have, among other things, conclusively proved that representative institutions are not altogether foreign to Indian instincts and that there need be no nervousness about either the introduction of free and compulsory education among the masses, or in the separation of the judicial and the executive functions of a State. What a sad commentary this to the vacillating policy of a mighty, distrustful bureaucracy!

CHAPTER XV.

THE PARTITION OF BENGAL.

There are certain paradoxes which the accumulated experience and the collective wisdom of ages have accepted as established truths all over the world, and "good cometh out of evil" is one of them. Of all the blessings in disguise, which ever fell to the lot of the Indian people, the Partition of Bengal by Lord Curzon was perhaps one of the most remarkable in the history of British rule in India. If the Ilbert Bill agitation first opened the eyes of the Indian people to the utter helplessness of their position and forced their attention to the real source of their national weakness, in the Partition of Bengal and its sequel they received the first open challenge for a trial of the moral strength which they had steadily developed during the past twenty years under the guidance and discipline of the national organization. The Congress has made the dry bones in the vally instinct with life and breathed a new spirit into them under the spell of which the "scattered units of the race" had coalesced and come to realize that in national evolution unity was the main cement and that in the race of life firmness, determination and perseverance were the only passports to success. Little perhaps did the vigorous author of this violent measure and his advisers calculate, that although hammering was one of the orthodox methods of effecting division and disintegration, it served sometimes also to beat soft metals into solid, hard lumps. They were also probably unaware of the real extent to which the Congress had worked towards infusing fresh vitality in the people, in unifying them for common action and in stiffening their backs against reverses. It was apparently overlooked that the India of 1903 was no longer the India of 1883, and that within a single decade the force of a new spirit had completely transformed the caterpillar into the butterfly. New ideas had burst upon the eyes of the people and new ideals had taken possession of the public mind. In the new cult preached by the Congress the people had received a higher revelation under the inspiration of which they had renounced individualism and embraced nationalism as their common article of faith. Twenty years had wrought a great transformation, if not a complete revolution, in the country, and a people who in 1883 scarcely knew how to organize themselves even in support of the Government were now fully prepared to oppose that Government in defence of their just rights and were certainly not disposed to take lying down any outrage upon the cherished ideas and sentiments of a growing nationality. The history of the ill-starred measure of the

Partition of Bengal and the various phases through which it passed may not strictly appertain to this narrative; but a brief survey of its origin, the part played in it by the Congress and the influence it exercised on the national character may not be deemed irrelevant and out of place.

Although the project of dividing an indivisible people was entirely his own, the idea of territorial redistribution of Bengal did not originate with Lord Curzon. The proposal to dismember the largest and premier province of the Empire sprang from a very small beginning. In 1874 the two districts of Cachar and Sylhet, which formed part of Bengal, were for administrative convenience transferred to Assam. There was hardly any public opinion at the time and the severance of two frontier districts did not attract much public attention. In 1891 a small conference between the Lieutenant-Governor of Bengal, the Chief Commissioners of Burma and Assam and a few military authorities was held to consider measures for the greater protection of the North-Eastern frontier. It was then proposed to transfer the Lushai Hills as a further addition to Assam coupled with a recommendation that the Chittagong Division might also go with them. In 1896 Sir William Ward, who was then the Chief Commissioner of Assam, submitted an elaborate scheme for the transfer of the Chittagong Division and expressed, in a general way, a hope that the two districts of Dacca and Mymensingh also might eventually be given to Assam. It was precisely the old story of the camel and the tent-keeper. Fortunately, however, just at this time Sir Henry Cotton succeeded Sir William Ward and the broad-minded administrator, who could never be persuaded to sacrifice the interest of justice and fairness to an aggrandisement of his own power and authority, lost no time in nipping the project in the bud. With his intimate knowledge of Bengal and the Bengalees, with whose legitimate aims and aspirations he always sympathised, Sir Henry Cotton opposed the scheme of his predecessor and condemned the idea of severing the Chittagong Division and the two important districts of Dacca and Mymensingh and thereby emasculating a rising people. The result was that only the Lushai Hills, which were mainly inhabited by a number of wild tribes, were made over to Assam and the question of the transfer of the Chittagong Division and the two trans-Gangetic districts of Bengal was entirely dropped.

Then came the vigorous administration of Lord Curzon who was nothing if not original in everything. Full of the idea that the past administration of India was a series of blunders he was reported to have come with "twelve problems" in his pocket with which he was resolved to overhaul every branch of that administration and recast it in a new mould. In course of this Herculean adventure a series of reactionary measures were passed which naturally produced widespread alarm in the country. The first ordinary period of his Viceroyalty, though not quite sensational, sufficiently disclosed the original bent of his mind. In 1899 when he assumed charge of his exalted office he began his policy of *efficiency* by reducing the elected members of the Calcutta Corporation to half their original number and practically vesting the administration in a General Committee in spite of strong protests on the part of the electors. This was followed by his honest denunciation of a British battalion in Rangoon, some privates of which were believed to have outraged a native woman to death, but could not be detected owing to a conspiracy of silence among the members of the battalion. This gave umbrage to a section of the Anglo-Indian community with whom the honour and life of a *native* woman were apparently not of much consequence when compared with the position and prestige of the British soldier in India. In the following year Lord Curzon increased his unpopularity among the same class of Anglo-Indians by punishing the 9th Lancers because at Sialkot two other privates were charged with having beaten a *native* cook to death for having refused to procure a *native* woman for them and who likewise remained undetected. In the same year Lord Curzon carved out the North-West Frontier Province, and the last year of his administration of this period was signalized by a costly Durbar at Delhi which bore striking resemblance to the Imperial Assemblage of 1877 in that it followed upon another terrible famine which decimated the Central Provinces in 1900-1. Unfortunately for India, as well as for his own reputation, Lord Curzon obtained an extension to his Viceroyalty and it was within this extended period that were crowded almost all the violent, reactionary measures with which his *efficient* administration is so largely associated. In all these measures the Indian public saw nothing but a deliberate reversal of the generous policy which, laid down by the Proclamation of 1858, had been the recognized guide of successive administrations and which if not uniformly observed in practice had never been openly violated in principle. Lord Curzon began by laying the axe at the root of Local Self-Government and emasculating the premier corporation of the metropolis of the Empire. Then the officialization of the Universities, the curtailment of high education, the abolition of open competitive tests for the Provincial Civil Services, the penalization of the civil official secrets followed in succession, and nowhere were these retrograde measures more keenly resented, or more sharply criticized, than in Bengal which the official barometer always pronounced to be the centre of political disturbances in the country. Lord Curzon determined to break this centre to facilitate the progress of his policy. He turned up the old records which had been consigned to the upper shelves of his Secretariat and ransacked them to reopen the question of the territorial readjustment of Bengal, and on the 3rd December 1903 there appeared the famous Resolution of the Government of India over the signature of Mr. now Sir., Herbert Risley, then Secretary to the Home Department, announcing the intention of Government to revive the question of the transfer of the entire Chittagong Division and the two districts of Dacca and Mymensingh to Assam. Without any complaint from the local Government, without any suggestion from any quarter and without a warning, Lord Curzon proceeded to relieve the Government of Bengal of its heavy burden, and his proposal fell like a bomb-shell among the people. But the people though surprised were not staggered and the very announcement of this Resolution was the signal for an outburst of opposition throughout the Province which, in its magnitude, volume and intensity was simply unprecedented in the history of public agitation in this country. It stirred the public mind in Bengal to its very depth, and the rich and the poor, the prince and the peasant, the educated and the uneducated all rose as one man to oppose the violent dismemberment of their ancient province, and with it the dissipation of their cherished hopes of forming a united nation. From December 1903 to October 1905 over 2.000 public meetings attended by 500 to 50,000 people were held in the two parts of Bengal at which Hindus and Mahomedans with equal zeal and earnestness joined in the protest. The late Nawab Sir Salimullah of Dacca at an early stage of the agitation was reported to have denounced the scheme as a "beastly arrangement," though at a later period he seceded from the opposition for reasons well-known to the public.

As the agitation began to increase Lord Curzon grew more and more nervous; while public criticisms both in the press as well as on the platforms gradually made him more and more relentless. In February 1905 Lord Curzon made his famous speech at the Convocation of the Calcutta University in which he would not tread, as he said, on the "dusty fields" of education; but read a homily on the difference between Eastern and Western ethics and wantonly charged the oriental character with want of veracity. He had evidently drawn his inspiration from Macaulay, but had failed to study the character of the people who had long outgrown Macaulay's over-drawn picture. The *Amrita Bazaar Patrika* at once met this sweeping denunciation with an equally scathing retort. An ugly incident from an account of his lordship's early travels in the Far East was unearthed out of its forgotten pages with which he was rudely reminded of the trite old saying, that it was unwise for one who lived in a glass house to pelt stones at others. This was followed by a huge demonstration at the Calcutta Town Hall where on the 11th March 1905 the people of Bengal met to protest against the utterances and proceedings of the Viceroy which had irritated the people beyond all measure of endurance. The meeting was presided over by Dr. Rash Behary Ghose who, deeply immersed in his professional business, had so long held himself aloof from all political discussions in the country and whom the sheer necessities of the situation forced to throw himself into the vortex of the agitation. The meeting after reviewing the entire administration of Lord Curzon passed a Resolution condemning all his retrograde proceedings culminating in the proposal for the disruption of an advanced province and of an extremely sensitive people passionately attached to their country. This was the first time when the people met openly to pass a vote of censure upon a Viceroy. This was, of course, too much for an equally sensitive Viceroy to tolerate and, descending from the proud pedestal of a Viceroy, Lord Curzon assumed the rôle of a political agitator which he had so strongly condemned in his convocation speech. Fully resolved to crush this new spirit by dividing the people against themselves, Lord Curzon proceeded to East Bengal and there at large meetings of Mahomedans, specially convened for the purpose, explained to them that his object in partitioning Bengal was not only to relieve the Bengal administration, but also to create a Mahomedan province, where Islam would be predominant and its followers in the ascendancy, and that with this view he had decided to include the two remaining districts of the Dacca Division in his scheme. The Mussalmans of East Bengal headed by Nawab Salimullah of Dacca saw their opportunity and took the bait. Henceforth the Mahomedans of Eastern Bengal forgetting the broader question of national advancement and ignoring the interests of their own community in Western Bengal deserted the national cause and gradually began to secede from the anti-partition agitation. It is, however, only fair to admit that the most cultured and advanced among the Mussalmans did not flinch and speaking at the Congress of 1906. Nawabzada Khajah Atikullah, the brother of Nawab Salimullah openly said, "I may tell you at once that it is not correct that the Mussalmans of Eastern Bengal are in favour of the Partition of Bengal. The real fact is that it is only a few leading Mahomedans who for their own purposes supported the measure." The Central Mahomedan Association in Calcutta, in submitting its opinion to the Government through its Secretary, the late Nawab Ameer Hossain, C.I.E., observed :—" My Committee are of opinion that no portion of the Bengali-speaking race should be separated from Bengal without the clearest necessity for such separation, and they think in the present case such necessity does not exist."

The agitation, however, went on in course of which hundreds of memorials wery submitted to Government as well as to the Secretary of State, one of which was submitted over the signature of 70,000 people of Eastern Bengal. But the Government maintained an attitude of mysterious silence until July, 1905, when a Government notification suddenly announced that the Secretary of State had sanctioned the Partition with effect from the 16th October 1905 and that the new Province was also to include the six districts of Northern Bengal. The people of Bengal would not however yield and took courage from despair. The idea of protecting indigenous industries had been long before the country, and now the people in different places began to discuss the question of eschewing British articles, when that devoted and unostentatious worker, Mr. Krishna Kumar Mitra, openly advocated a general boycott in the columns of his well-known paper the *Sanjibani*. About a dozen of the leaders in Bengal met to discuss the situation at the Indian Association and after solemn deliberation resolved to boycott all foreign goods as a protest against this act of flagrant injustice. And on the 7th August was held the memorable meeting which inaugurated the Swadeshi Movement. Such was the intensity of feeling created and such the stubbornness acquired by the national character, that on the fatal day of 16th October the

HON. SIR DINSHAW EDULJI WACHA
PRESIDENT, 1901.

HON. SIR C. SANKARAN NAIR
PRESIDENT, 1897.

ROMESH CHUNDER DUTT
PRESIDENT, 1899.

SIR N. G. CHANDAVARKAR
PRESIDENT, 1900.

scene in Bengal became one of wild demonstrations unparalleled in the history of the country. As on the day of the execution of Maharajah Nund Coomar the people of Calcutta rushed to the banks of the Ganges and bathed themselves in its sacred water as an expiation of the sin they had committed in witnessing for the first time a judicial murder in the land, so from the early morning of the 16th October, 1905, corresponding to the 30th Aswin 1312 of the Bengalee Era, the people in their hundreds and thousands in every city, town and village marched in solemn processions bare-footed and bare-bodied chanting, as dirges, national songs and repaired to the nearest channel or stream and after performing their ablution tied the *Rakhi*, the silken band of unity and fraternity, round one another's wrists when amid the deafening cries of *Bandemataram* took the solemn vow in the name of God and Motherland, that united they stood and no earthly power should divide them, and that so long as the Partition was not undone they would eschew as far as practicable all foreign articles. They fasted the whole day during which all shops were closed and business and amusements stopped, while many were the towns which even according to official reporters wore the appearance of the city of the dead. Men, women and children all joined in the demonstration. So intense and widespread was the outburst of this unprecedented upheaval of the popular sentiment that the authorities had to take, in many places, particularly in the several districts, extraordinary measures in anticipation of breach of the peace. But the leaders had strictly resolved upon passive resistance and constitutional agitation and everything passed off without any hitch anywhere. In their utter dislike of the Partition the people nicknamed the new Province as Ebassam and to accentuate their solidarity paradoxically designated the two severed Provinces as United Bengal. For seven long years the people persistently carried on the struggle and every year with renewed vigour and energy observed the 7th August as the day of national rejoicing and the 16th October as the day of national mourning.

Thus the Partition of Bengal was forcibly carried out in the teeth of a most frantic opposition, and although Lord Curzon appeared to have been fully justified in his bold assertion that, as far as the British public were concerned, the opposition would end in a blank volley of "a few angry speeches" on the floor of Parliament, he was entirely mistaken in his calculations that the last words on the subject would be heard in the House and that the people would after a short struggle quietly submit to the inevitable accepting his decision as a final-settlement of their destiny. As has already been said Lord Curzon was reported to have come to India with "twelve problems" in his pocket: but whatever the other problems were, the three which he had put forward on Local Self-Government, Education and Administration were sufficient to convince the people that he came with a veritable Pandora's Box and let loose all the forces of disorder in the country, Hope alone remaining. Even the Anglo-Indian Press which was ever so loyal to the bureaucracy found itself unable to support his extravagant measures which, in the name of efficiency, aimed at a complete revision, if not a revolution, of the entire system of British rule in India. The *Times of India* remarked :—

"One might well wish that Lord Curzon had not returned to India for the second time, for he could not have chosen a more effective way of wrecking his reputation than he has done."

Another Anglo-Indian paper observed, that :—

"Best of the measures (of Lord Curzon's administration) against which public criticism has lately been directed are designed to check a development which has at once been the conscious aim and the justification of British rule in India, and the worst of them are nothing more nor less than deliberate steps in reaction, opposed in method and in character, to those traditions which underlie what is commonly allowed to be, not only the greatest experiment, but the most remarkable attempt towards the government of an alien people of which the modern world has any record."

The *Englishman*, writing shortly after the Town Hall Meeting of the 7th August, 1905, said :—

"The change which is threatened has been determined upon in the teeth of a practically unanimous public opinion. There is no reason to suppose that this public opinion will become silent or non-existent as soon as the Partition is carried into effect. The situation will therefore be this : An administrative *Coup d' etat* without precedent will have been carried out. The people who will have to live under its results will be dissatisfied and uneasy. Now all governments, even the most despotic, are obliged to rule in the long run in accordance with the wishes of the governed, or at least to refrain from governing in direct opposition to those wishes. The difficulties of the Governor of the new province under the peculiar circumstance of its emergence would, one fears, be extreme, if not insuperable."

The *Statesman* of Calcutta wrote :—

"There never was a time in the history of British India when public feeling and public opinion were so little regarded by the Supreme Government as they are by the present administration. In this matter of the Partition of Bengal the force of public opinion has been remarkable. It could not indeed be otherwise, for in spite of their parade of consulting the 'legitimate interests' of the districts involved in the proposed separation, the Government is well aware that its scheme is a direct attack upon the solidarity and the growing political strength of the Bengali race. * * * The Government may or may not choose to give weight to the outburst of feeling on the subject of the Partition, but it will necessarily recognize the new note of practicability which the present situation has brought into political agitation and it will sooner or later realise, that just as religions thrive on persecution, so there is nothing half so effectual as the systematic disregard of public opinion for fostering political discontent."

The following is taken from a leading article which appeared in the London *Daily News*:—

"Very little is known in this country concerning the scheme for the partitioning of Bengal as to which our Calcutta correspondent addresses us. Even the India Office is so much in the dark as to the merits and demerits of the proposal that it was unable to provide Mr. Brodrick with an intelligible brief when the question was raised by Mr. Roberts a week ago in the House of Commons. In India the announcement seems to have come as a complete surprise. In 1903 Lord Curzon was compelled to bow to the storm of criticism aroused by a much smaller readjustment of areas, and positive consternation has been created by the present proposal under which twenty-five millions of the people of Bengal are without a word of consultation to be handed over to a new local administration. . . . The inhabitants of Bengal contain a large proportion of educated persons, very many of whom occupy positions of influence and responsibility. What was there to prevent Lord Curzon taking counsel with the leading citizens and ascertaining the views of the localities concerned before enacting this tremendous change? We are afraid the only answer is, that Lord Curzon well knew the views of the people, but declined to argue with them, or to endeavour to persuade them. . . . That re-consideration is desirable, is obvious from every point of view. It cannot be good statesmanship to launch these new provinces in a condition of seething discontent, or to alienate a third of our fellow-subjects in India. There is no suggestion that the matter is a pressing one, and whatever elements of good the scheme may contain are likelier to be appreciated if a truce is called for the present than if Bengal is incontinently hurried up. The cost of the new administration, which is put in some quarters at nearly three millions sterling, calls for special attention at a time when India is suffering from heavy additional charges. We are convinced that Mr. Brodrick would greatly add to the service which he has already done to India if he could call a halt in this matter of the Partition."

Such was the verdict pronounced upon the *efficient* administration of the *brilliant* Viceroy who after seven years of vigorous rule found his unpopularity to be so universal that he advisedly left India as it were by the backdoor without paying even the customary farewell visit to the Metropolis where the historic Viceregal Palace recalled to him, as he himself said the memories of his baronial castle at Keddlestone.

The Congress usually dealt with questions affecting the whole country; but it also occasionally interested itself in matters of special local importance. Although the Partition of Bengal was apparently a provincial grievance, in its wider aspect it was regarded as a national question of the gravest significance, and as such the Congress took it up at its very inception in 1903, and year after year persistently repeated its protest in different centres until the whole country resounded with the voice of that protest. Apart from the special grievances of Bengal the measure involved a question of far-reaching consequences which was in conflict with its propaganda and threatened its ultimate aim of nation-building and national evolution with a collapse. The whole country, therefore, took this flagrant act of high-handedness as a most outrageous flouting of public opinion and a most callous disregard of the feelings and sentiments of the people. Besides it was pointed out that if such could be the fate of Bengal, what guarantee was there that a similar fate might not in future overtake the other provinces also? While, pointed reference was made to Sindh as a probable factor in the not too unlikely contingency that might arise in the case of Bombay. Thus the Parsi, the Maharatta, the Madrasi, the Sindhi and the Punjabi rose as one man with the Bengali to undo the "settled fact." Speaking at the Congress of 1908, the Hon'ble Mr. Krishnan Nair of Madras feelingly observed, "the Partition of Bengal affects the whole country like a deep, bleeding and unhealing wound. So long as such a wound exists in the human body it is difficult, if not impossible, for that body to know peace or enjoy repose." Severe unrest prevailed throughout the country, while a most distressing development of the situation manifested itself both in Bengal as well as in the Deccan. The contemptuous treatment of public opinion by the authorities and their absolute indifference to every proposal of the Nationalists became the theme of public discussion both in the Press as well as on the platforms throughout the country ; while a series of repressive measures inaugurated by the Government of Lord Minto in quick succession to one another instead of providing a remedy for the situation served only to intensify the popular discontent. Advantage was taken of an old obsolete Regulation to deport, without a trial, men whose only fault lay in stubbornly opposing the "settled fact." Sober and dispassionate men like Mr. R. N. Mudholkar from the Berar and Mr. Subba Rao from Madras earnestly appealed to Government for a modification of the ill-starred measure, and none more passionately joined in the appeal than that young lion of the Deccan, Mr. Gopal Krishna Gokhale, who from his place in the Supreme Legislative Council, addressing the Viceroy, said, "My Lord, conciliate Bengal." But in an atmosphere of prejudice and passion, the *fetish* of Prestige was in the ascendant and all the protests and appeals went unheeded. Mr. Gokhale went to England as an accredited representative of the Congress in 1905 and 1906, and on both the occasions he used his great powers of persuasion to impress the authorities as well as the public in England with the extreme inadvisability of persisting in the unpopular measure adopted by the Government of India. Mr. John Morley, who was then the Secretary of State for India, was by no means satisfied with the performance of Lord Curzon. But, although he found that the Partition had gone "wholly and decisively against the wishes of the majority of the people concerned," and openly characterised it as not being a *sacrosanct*, he dismissed the question as being a "settled fact." His predecessor in office Mr. Brodrick (afterwards Lord Middleton) had also in a spirit of half-heartedness, while not fully approving of Lord Curzon's proposals, sanctioned the Partition, and all the voluminous representations submitted to him, including the one containing over 70,000 signatures from Eastern Bengal, went for nothing. It has always been like this in India. She has suffered for things for which she could be hardly held responsible. Mr. St. John Brodrick had to provide an unguent for the wounded pride of a meddlesome Viceroy in the Curzon-Kitchener controversy; while Mr. John Morley, the author of *Compromise*, had to pilot his Reform Scheme through both the Houses of Parliament. There never was perhaps a better case so summarily dismissed in all its stages. People in this country who had all their life worshiped "honest John" with almost idolatrous veneration lost all confidence in him, while men were not wholly wanting who actually went so far as to regard British Liberalism, so far as applicable to India, as a meaningless creed. Men like Sir Henry Cotton, Mr. Hebert Paul and Mr. Keir Hardie, however, kept up a continuous fire over the burning question in the Lower House and it is believed that it was this incessant heckling over Indian questions which was responsible for Mr. Morley's translation to the calmer region of the Upper House and his ultimate resignation of the Indian portfolio. In the Lords also the noble Marquess of Ripon in his old age raised his trembling voice against the infamous measure; while Lord Macdonald openly denounced it as "the hugest blunder committed since the battle of Plassey." And Lord Curzon finding that there was "none so poor as to do him reverence" attempted to throw the responsibility, like a hot potato, on Lord Ampthill and Lord Ampthill on Mr. Brodrick. But although the measure was thus denounced on all hands and there was none so bold as to claim its authorship, it yet seemed to possess a charmed life. At last Lord Morley was succeeded by Lord Crewe and in May, 1911, Mr. Bhupendranath Basu was deputed by the Indian Association, Calcutta, to represent the case of Bengal to the new Secretary of State, as it was felt that the forthcoming Coronation Durbar in India might be a fitting occasion for a satisfactory solution of the situation. No better selection could have been made and the trained lawyer and astute politician performed his mission in an eminently satisfactory manner. With the help of Lord Reay Mr. Basu obtained an interview with Lord Crewe about the end of June and explained to him, with a degree of fulness and clearness hardly possible except in a personal interchange of views, the intolerable situation which had been created by the Partition and the remedy suggested by the people which was calculated not only to mend that situation, but which also afforded the most legitimate solution for the administrative difficulty of the vast Province. Lord Crewe gave him a patient and sympathetic hearing. This was the first practical step taken by the people since the Partition was effected towards the solution of the thorny question which had set the country ablaze and let loose such harrowing miseries and disquietude throughout the country as even the Councial reforms of Lord Morley were unable to remove. At this juncture, happily for India, as well as for England, Lord Hardinge succeeded Lord Minto with the rich legacy of a multitudinous population driven almost mad by a violent disruption of an ancient province and exasperated by a series of repressive and retrograde measures which a bold Indian jurist, enjoying at the time no less confidence and respect of the Government than of the people, openly denounced as "lawless laws." It has been truly said that history repeats itself; and Lord Hardinge like Lord Ripon came at a critical moment holding the olive branch of peace, sympathy and conciliation for the people. Lord Hardinge assumed office in November, 1910, and the leaders of Bengal at once organised a fresh campaign of anti-partition agitation.

Arrangements were made some time in May following for holding a demonstration of United Bengal in the Calcutta Town Hall as a signal for a fresh agitation under a new Secretary of State and a new Viceroy. A police officer was at this time assassinated in the streets of the metropolis evidently by an anarchist; and Lord Hardinge at once sent for Mr. Surendranath Banerjea and asked him not to create further public excitement at such a juncture, adding at the same time that if the object of the proposed demonstration was to draw attention of the Government, then the best course for the people was to submit their case quietly to the Government of India, and he assured Mr. Banerjea that such representation would receive his most careful consideration. The proposed campaign was accordingly dropped and a memorial was drawn up briefly reviewing the history of the disastrous measure and narrating the grievances of the people as well as the disturbances which had flowed from it. The memorial also dealt with the financial aspect of the question which the author of the partition had studiously avoided in the formulation of his scheme and finally, among several alternative suggestions, it earnestly prayed for a re-union of the several provinces of Bengal under a Governor in Council as in Bombay and Madras. The memorial concluded in the following words:—

"In conclusion, we beg to submit that for the first time in the history of British Rule in India His Majesty the King of England will be proclaimed Emperor of India on Indian soil, and His Majesty's loyal subjects in this great dependency look forward to the auspicious occasion with the sanguine hope that it will be marked by some substantial boons to the people. We venture to assure your Excellency, that as far as the bulk of the Bengalees are concerned, no boon will be more warmly appreciated or more gratefully acknowledged than a modification of the Partition of Bengal."

It may be here mentioned that previous to the adoption of this memorial a private conference of some of the leaders of Bengal and of Behar was held at the Indian Association where it was found that Behar could not subscribe to any proposal which did not seek for her divorce from Bengal. The memorial was accordingly drawn up on Bengal's own account, signed only by some of the leading men in the two provinces of Bengal and quietly submitted to the Viceroy on the 12th June, 1911. This was the last representation of the people on the subject. A copy of this memorial was also despatched by one of the members to Sir William Wedderburn as President of the British Committee of the Congress which reached him at a most opportune moment as Sir William had already arranged for an interview with the Secretary of State on the subject. Sir William Wedderburn met Lord Crewe with this memorial and like an honest advocate and a dispassionate mediator laid the whole case before him. It was a most important interview, although Sir William with his characteristic reserve could hardly be persuaded to disclose more than an oracular version of what actually transpired at it. It is to be highly regretted that much of the valuable service actually rendered by him at this juncture must go unrecorded. It was, however, broadly understood in this country that as a result of all the deputations, interviews and the discussions which took place in and out of Parliament.

the authorities in England and the Liberals in particular were fully convinced of the grave injustice which had been done to an innocent and inoffensive people and of the severe unrest for which this ill-advised measure was mainly, if not solely, responsible. It was also believed, that although the question was not free from difficulties, there was no cause for absolute despair and that after all if the people could prevail upon the Government of India to reopen the question and suggest a modification, neither the present Secretary of State, nor the Cabinet would stand in the way of a revision and fresh settlement of the "Settled fact."

It was a strange case of retributive justice both in procedure as well as execution. As in 1905 the partition in its enlarged shape and form was hurled like a bolt from the blue without a warning to the people who ever since their last representation to the Secretary of State were living in a Fool's Paradise fondly clinging to the hope, that nothing so violent could be done by British statesmanship as to go so decisively against the cherished wishes and aspirations of the people concerned; so in 1911 the Indian bureaucracy having a few public buildings hurriedly constructed in the ruined city chosen to be the capital of the new province firmly believed, that the new administration was built upon a rock and that any further struggle on the part of the people was bound to be sheer waste of energies, if not a risky pursuit after a phantom which could afford them no relief, but could only tempt them to greater danger and disaster. In the secrecy of its plan and the abruptness of its execution, the partition met the same fate at its exit as at its entrance and was equally dramatic at its both ends, with this difference that opening with tragic scenes of thrilling interest it ended in a comedy exposing a series of errors productive of the gravest consequences. It would appear that Lord Hardinge had carefully studied the case even before he came out to India and that ever since he received the memorial of the 12th June he was busy working out his scheme for a satisfactory solution of the vexed question and for the restoration of peace and order in the country. This scheme was embodied in a secret despatch, dated the 25th August, 1911, recommending formation of a Presidency Government for re-united Bengal, a separate Lieutenant-Governorship for Behar and Orissa and the transfer of the Imperial Capital from Calcutta to Delhi, with the dominating idea of gradually extending autonomous administration to all the Provinces. All this was, of course, kept a dead secret from August to December. But although nothing definite oozed out, there was persistent rumour throughout the country that a final pronouncement would be made, either one way or the other, on the forthcoming occasion of the Royal visit, the balance of Indian public opinion being of course in favour of a possible modification of the Partition, though the official circle generally scouted such an idea as being a dream and a violent improbability, if not an actual impossibility. The mystery was however soon cleared and it came as a stunning surprise to Anglo-India, both official and unofficial, which firmly believed in its prescriptive right to be in the know in every administrative measure of importance. The pronouncement, however, did not appear in the ordinary garb of a routine work; but was ushered in with quite a dramatic effect. On the memorable 12th December, 1911, at the Coronation Durbar at Delhi, in the midst of an imposing ceremony and in the presence of a gorgeous assembly, His Majesty George V personally and through his Viceroy announced one after another all the boons which were granted on the occasion to the people of India; but there came no response to the wail of Bengal, and the vast crowd of Bengalees, who had gone to Delhi in the earnest expectation of hearing their sore grievance removed, became despondent. At last when the King was about to leave the pavilion upon the close of the ceremony, he stood and said:—

> *" We are pleased to announce to our people that on the advice of our ministers and after consultation with our Governor-General-in-Council, we have decided upon the transfer of the seat of the Government of India from Calcutta to the ancient capital of Delhi and simultaneously, as a consequence of that transfer, the creation at as early a date as possible of a Governorship-in-Council for the Presidency of Bengal, of a new Lieutenant-Governorship-in-Council administering the areas of Behar, Chota Nagpur and Orissa and of a Chief-Commissionership of Assam, with such administrative changes and redistribution of boundaries as our Governor-General-in-Council, with the approval of our Secretary of State for India-in-Council, may in due course determine. It is our earnest desire that these changes may conduce to the better administration of India and the greater prosperity and happiness of our beloved people."*.

The gracious announcement was at once received with tremendous acclamation in which even those who could not be very well pleased with the changes made lustily joined not understanding of course what the announcement really was. One Bengal officer afterwards humourously said, that he did not know that he was cheering his own death-knell. So great was the joy and enthusiasm created by the announcement that after the King left a number of young men, mostly Bengalees, rushed in and kneeling before the throne reverently kissed the footsteps from which the announcement had just been made. The glad tidings were flashed throughout the country and was the signal for an outburst of loyal and enthusiastic demonstration throughout Bengal which was as genuine as it was unprecedented. By a subsequent notification United Bengal was raised to the status of a Presidency Government from the 1st April, 1912, with Lord Carmichael as its first Governor who was specially chosen by the King to take the helm of the new administration.

Thus the single stroke of Lord Hardinge's conciliatory policy, as by a magic wand, at once dispelled the severe unrest which half a dozen repressive measures of his predecessor were unable to cope with. It must here be acknowledged that though Bengal had no doubt fought bravely for six long years under the indomitable leadership of Mr. Surendranath Banerjea, the unstinted moral support which she received from the whole country through the Congress, as well as from its individual members, in the hour of her trials and tribulations, not only largely sustained her in her great struggle, but also added considerable weight and importance to the anti-partition agitation. But for the support which the Congress and the country lent her it seems doubtful if Bengal unaided could have either sustained the agitation, or brought it to a successful termination upsetting a settled arrangement within such a comparatively short period. It should also be gratefully acknowledged, that the support accorded to it by sympathetic Englishmen, in and out of Parliament, was materially helpful in bringing the issue to a successful termination. Nor should it be forgotten that when the matter was discussed in the Cabinet prior to His Majesty's departure for India, Lord Morley did not stand in the way of the proposed unsettlement of his "settled fact."

The anti-partition agitation was not only a successful test of the strength of the cement which the Congress had created for its work of nation-building; but it has also signalised the triumph of public opinion in its trial of strength with a strong bureaucracy. It has resloved India's faith in British justice and her confidence in the ultimate success of constitutional agitation under British rule. It has also inspired the Indian mind with a firm conviction in the strength of public opinion properly organised, wisely directed and zealously carried on within the scope and limits of the British constitution. That constitution yields to no other force but that of moral pressure and answers to no other call than that of public opinion. "Open Wheat" and "Open Barley" would be of no avail. It is the "Open Sesame" of persistent constitutional agitation which alone will throw open the door of its conscience. If the history of the Partition of Bengal has one lesson clearer than another for the Indian Nationalist, it consists in the weight and importance of public opinion which is the irresistible and unresisted master of the British constitution.

HON. PUNDIT MADAN MOHAN MALAVIYA
PRESIDENT, 1909.

SIR HENRY COTTON K.C.S.I.,
PRESIDENT, 1904.

LAL MOHAN GHOSE
PRESIDENT, 1903.

PUNDIT BISHEN NARAIN DHAR
PRESIDENT, 1911.

CHAPTER XVI.

THE INDIAN UNREST AND ITS REMEDY.

The unrest in India has been the theme of earnest and persistent discussions during the past few years both here as well as in England. Whether it be the customary pronouncement of an administrator, or the official report of any branch of the administration; whether it be the criticism of a publicist, or the harrangue of the political agitator on the public platform, and whether it be a debate in Parliament, or the academic discussion in an Indian Legislative Council, nothing passes without, at least, a parting shot at the Indian unrest and without every one in his own way recommending his own specific for its treatment. The unrest is admitted; but while the bureaucracy would fain attribute it to a sudden restlessness among the people owing to an unwholesome development of certain extravagant ideas in their minds, the people with equal emphasis, though not with equal authority, would lay it at the door of that bureaucracy who unable to adapt themselves to the altered state of the country, have lost all sympathy for their legitimate wishes and aspirations and are evidently determined not to guide and control, but simply to curb and crush the rising spirit of a renovated people with old, antiquated methods of reaction and repression. It is, however, a patent circumstance that in a dependency governed like India the people have nothing to gain but everything to lose by unnecessarily irritating the authorities: while an autocratic rule, such as is firmly established in this country, has very little to care about and certainly nothing to fear from any sullen discontent of the people. It is a common saying among the people in this country, which even the meanest among them accepts as a rule of conduct in daily life, that even the lunatic understands his own interest, and agitation which always involves heavy sacrifice of time and energy cannot be a pastime with an Oriental people nurtured upon a philosophy which represents this mundane world as a delusion and guided by religious faiths which preach only eternal peace and repose.

It was Edmund Burke who speaking even of free countries said, that whenever there was a friction between a people and its government it was invariably the case that the former was in the right and the latter in the wrong. It has always been conceded even by their worst critics that the Indians are, by nature, as well as their religious instincts, an extremely docile and a tractable people and that whatever the other defects and blemishes of their character may be it is generally free from the taint of ingratitude. The Indians have always recognised the manifold blessings of the British rule, notably the security of life and property it has secured, the administration of justice it has established and the education it has fostered and extended throughout the country. As regards the development of the internal resources of the country and its economic condition there is no doubt considerable difference of opinion; but there is an absolute consensus of opinion as well as of feeling throughout the country, that but for the British rule it would have been impossible for the various races inhabiting this vast continent to have attained the peaceful progress it has attained in many directions within the last hundred and fifty years. Even the most unrelenting critic is forced to admit, that if India has paid a heavy price for that progress, her gain also has not been inconsiderable, and that *plus* and *minus* the balance of advantage is still on her side. On the other side it is hardly disputed that India was not, correctly speaking, conquered by the sword, but won by the willing allegiance of a people who were unable to govern themselves. If that is so, the question naturally arises, how is it that the Indians have, after a peaceful beneficent rule of more than one and a half century, suddenly developed such a spirit of restlessness and discontent? Can it be Sedition—an earnest desire on the part of the people to overthrow the British Government and establish their absolute independence? If that were so, any attempt on the part of the people to shake off the British yoke would have proved as disastrous a failure as the maintenance of settled Government by Britain herself even for a year despite her naval and military strength. The cry of Sedition was as false as it was senseless and impolitic. There never was in these years a movement anywhere to subvert British rule in India, nor was there a single overt act lending colour to a possible tendency towards such a movement, besides some insane, meaningless, incoherent, inflammatory effusions contained in a few anonymous pamphlets or leaflets which some mischievous urchins might circulate for creating either a fun or a senseless sensation in the country. If a dastardly attempt on the life of Czar Nicholas, or the murder of King Humbert, or the assassination of President Carnot could not be construed into an attempt to overthrow the Russian Empire, or the Italian Monarchy, or the French Republic, it seems difficult to conceive how the secret manufacture of some bombs in a private garden, the assassination of a few police officers, the secret murder of a Magistrate, or even the daring attempt on the life of an innocent Lieutenant-Governor at a public place, however atrocious these acts may be, can be regarded as any evidence of sedition or treason, or how any people outside an asylum could ever dream of driving away the British from India with the help of some bundles of bamboo sticks, a few ounces of picric acid, a few packets of gunpowder, or even of a few dozens of old, rusty smuggled revolvers. The idea is simply quixotic. To whatever lengths human ingenuity may go to strain and stretch the definition of sedition or high treason, common sense must always refuse to believe that a handful of misguided young men, with no other instruments than these in their possession, could really have thought of "waging war against the King." However seriously the situation may have been taken by a bureaucracy placed in a distant foreign land, even the most ardent loyalist in the country regarded the panic as quite mistaken and exaggerated beyond all proportion.

The Indian bureaucracy, particularly the section of it belonging to the Indian Civil Service, may be disposed to regard every member of it as a limb of the Sovereign authority and as such misconstrue every serious offence against any such member to be tantamount to an offence against *lese majeste*, *i.e.*, high-treason. But the Eastern mind draws a sharp distinction between the Crown and its servants, and between an impersonal Government and its personal officers, how highsoever they may be. The expression "Representative of Government" is loosely extended, even sometimes in official documents, to officers whom the people regard as no more than "public servants." A good deal of the misunderstanding seems to be due to an oversight of this distinction on the part of a governing class, every member of which carries in him the natural pride of being a ruler of the country. The late Mr. Kristodas Pal most forcibly and faithfully drew out this distinction prevailing in the Indian mind in his celebrated controversy with the Government of Sir George Campbell who was not inaptly called the Tiberius of the Indian Civil Service. Having been charged, as Editor of the *Hindu Patriot*, with "ill-will towards Government," the great *Tribune* said:—

"The words 'ill-will to Government' are not however explicit. Is the word Government in the phrase intended to mean the Queen's Government or the Local Administration?—the ruling power, or the executive agency?—the Sovereign Mistress of the Empire, or her officers in the country? None is better aware than His Honour that the Supreme Power and the administrative authority are quite distinct; and nowhere is this distinction made so broadly and clearly as in England. When, for instance, Mr. Disraeli denounced the other day the present Government of Her Majesty as "blundering and plundering," it would be a gross perversion of language to interpret this imputation into 'ill-will to Government,' that is, Sovereign authority, the Queen herself. And yet I fear the charge brought against the *Patriot* involves this misuse of words. It would be impertinent in me to remark that if criticisms of public men and measures be construed into 'ill-will to Government,' there is not a single journal in this country, with the slightest pretence to independence, which would not be open to this charge. Constituted as the British Government in India is, in which the governed millions are utterly unrepresented and which is administered by aliens in birth, religion, habits, sentiments and feelings, the Press is the only channel for the communication of the views and wishes of the people,—the safety-valve, so to speak, of the political steam working in the body of the masses. None is better aware than my humble self that the Native Press has many shortcomings; that it has much to learn and unlearn; but nothing, I respectfully submit, could be more unjust than to ascribe to it 'ill-will to Government,' because it considers it its duty to criticise the proceedings of the local administration, or particular officers of Government."

If Krishtodas Pal had been living to-day he would have not only found the charge more lavishly and indiscriminately laid against his countrymen, but also a more forcible illustration for the distinction and the defence; when it has been permissible in our own times for Orangemen, under the organized leadership of a man whom even the King was not precluded from inviting to a conference, to rise in armed rebellion against the established Government of the country without however forfeiting their allegiance to the Sovereign under the constitution. Sedition in the sense of treason really existed nowhere in the country except perhaps in the wild hallucination of a panic-stricken bureaucracy hypnotised by an unscrupulous Jingo Press, and the cry of Sedition was only either a blind man's buff, or a wild goose chase in the country. If an occasion should ever arise to put India's loyalty to a real test it will then be realized how silly and injudicious it was to cry "the wolf" when there was actually no wolf in the field.*

---

* The recent war in Europe has furnished such an occasion and such a test. Whole India has enthusiastically risen in

A question thus arises, what then was this unrest and why was there such constant friction between the people and the Government? And again the dictum of Burke comes to the reply. If it be true as Lord Gladstone has said on a very recent occasion in South Africa that "convulsions could not happen unless there was something gravely wrong," then the cause of the unrest in India was not perhaps too far to seek. As has already been pointed out the stolid indifference and unsympathetic attitude of Government towards popular aims and aspirations, the imperious tone of the bureaucracy and its marked disposition towards opposing even the normal growth and development of the political rights and privileges of the people, the repeated instances of flagrant miscarriage of justice in cases between Indians and Europeans and the recurring famines had long created a deep-seated and widespread feeling of dissatisfaction,—but not *disaffection* unless want of gushing affection is tantamount to it as Justice Strachey would have us believe—throughout the country. The thinking portion of the people laid all these preventible grievances at the door of the Government, while the ignorant mass attributed them to their invisible *Kismat* or inscrutible Providence—the last great argument of the Eastern mind which reconciles it to all worldly sufferings. But the feeling was there every year gaining in its volume as well as in its intensity. Then there came a lull, like the short interlude in a tragi-comic drama, during

---

defence of the Empire and there is now not a man in England who seems to entertain the shadow of a doubt as regards India's devotion to the Imperial connection.

which the people caught fitful glimpse of a struggling ray of hope ; but again the clouds thickened and darkened the atmosphere, when at last a strong, reactionary Viceroy appeared on the scene, who by his rigorous policy put a severe strain upon the patience of an already discontented people, and all discussions of public questions, not only in Bengal but in the other Provinces also, assumed a new tone and complexion. With the Partition in Bengal, the Colonization Bill in the Punjab and the Official Secrets Act, the Press Messages Act and the Universities Act for the whole country, the Indian people were exasperated beyond measure, and a section of the Press also began to give vent to the feeling in the country with a degree of warmth and licence which the authorities construed into Sedition. In the prevailing temper of the bureaucracy repression was prescribed as the proper remedy for the situation, and the Government of Lord Minto went on forging a series of drastic measures, such as the further widening of the Official Secrets Act, the Public Meetings Act, the Press Act, the Sedition Law, the Explosives Act, the Seditious Meetings Act and a number of ordinances and circulars by which the right of free speech and free criticism was practically abrogated ; while quite an army of inefficient and unscrupulous men under the name of C.I.D. officers was let loose upon society, whose impertinent attention did not spare Members of Councils or even of Parliament travelling in the country. Some old, obsolete Regulations, whose existence was nearly forgotten till the Bombay Government discovered it, were brought out of the dusty armoury of Government and several men of note, some of whom were fully believed by the pepole to be quite incapable of any offence, were deported without a trial. In Bombay the Natu Brothers were thus dealt with in 1897; in the Punjab Mr. Lajpat Rai and Sirdar Ajit Singh were deported in 1907; while in the following year, out of a long list of eligible candidates in Bengal, the following nine persons were selected to receive the compliment; *viz.*,—Messrs. Krishna Kumar Mitra, Aswini Kumar Dutt, Shyamsunder Chuckravarty, Subodh Chandra Mullik, Sachindraprasad Bose, Satish Chandra Chatterjee, Pulin Behary Das, Monoranjan Guha and Bhupesh Chandra Nag. All of these men were evidently ready to make whatever sacrifices were demanded of them for the country's cause and a few of them were probably also not a little proud of the advertisement thus given to them. Press prosecutions, proscriptions and confiscations also became very frequent. The *Bande mataram*, the *Jugantar* and the *Sandhya*, a most intemperate and scurrilous paper in Bengal, and several papers in the other provinces were suppressed. Mr. Tilak as Editor of the *Mahratta* was sent to prison; Bromho Bundhab Upadhya, Editor of the *Sandhya*, died in hospital, and Mr. Aurobinda Ghose, the supposed Editor of the *Bande mataram* sought refuge in French territory. Police-raids, house-searches and espionage became the order of the day; while conferences and public meetings were forcibly broken up and suspended in many places, particularly in Eastern Bengal. Even the Education Department so long held almost sacred in the estimation of the public was pressed into a secret service with the "little barbarians" in the schools as political suspects. Like the red rag to the bull, the innocent expression *Bande mataram* became almost intolerable to a certain class of officials. Some interpreted it to mean 'seize and beat the monkey,' others suspected it to be a secret watchword for committing violence; while in point of fact the harmless expression coined by a novelist more than a decade before meant nothing but—'I salute thee, my motherland.' Even the sacred *Geeta* was not spared, and in many a house-search where nothing incriminating could be laid hold on the *Geeta* was eagerly seized and carried away as an important find. The people became incensed and that was but natural. The Swadeshi-Boycott was rightly or wrongly started as the first open protest against this high-handed administration. But to add fuel to the fire the fanatical Mahomedan mass were incited by a class of designing people against the Hindus, and several cases of riot, pillage, desecration, sacrilege and outrage upon women took place in Eastern Bengal and the Punjab. People were not wanting even in official circle who exultantly cited these instances as a foretaste of what might be in store for the Hindus if the strong hand of the Government were either withdrawn or even relaxed; while the bureaucracy generally were not slow complacently to refer all these disturbances to the Swadeshi Boycott movement and the "National Volunteers," as if when that was said all was said against these acts of lawlessness. A suspicion arose in the minds of some people that all these were parts of a settled policy to put down the new spirit and that the Swadeshi movement was made only a scapegoat of that policy. Impartial and independent officers were not, however, altogether wanting to speak out the truth. In Eastern Bengal one European Magistrate, who is now a member of the Bengal Government, openly said that "the Boycott was not the cause of the disturbances," as it could not possibly be since that movement inured more to the direct benefit of the poor low-class Mussalmans who formed the bulk of the weavers and shoemakers in the country; while another Special Magistrate, a Mahomedan gentleman of culture and independence, trying a batch of these Mussalman rioters, remarked in his judgment that "there was not the least provocation for rioting; the common object of the rioters was evidently to molest the Hindus." In another case the same Magistrate observed :—

> "The evidence adduced on the side of the prosecution shows that on the date of the riot the accused (a Mussalman) read over a notice to a crowd of Mussalmans and told them that the Government and the Nawab Bahadur of Dacca have passed orders to the effect that nobody would be punished for plundering and oppressing the Hindus. So, after the Kali's image was broken by the Mussalmans, the shops of the Hindu traders were also plundered."

Again another European Magistrate in his report on another riot case wrote, that "some Mussalmans proclaimed by beat of drum that the Government has permitted them to loot the Hindus;" while in an abduction case the same Magistrate remarked that "the outrages were due to an announcement that the Government had permitted the Mahomedans to marry Hindu widows in *Nika* form." There was, however, yet another and a more disgraceful incident. In 1910 the Metropolis itself was in the hand of a Mussalman mob and for three days and nights the rich Marwari jewellers of the city were plundered with the Lieutenant-Governor himself at Belvedere and an indignant though powerless Viceroy at Government House. And what was still more disgraceful and demoralizing, the Lieutenant-Governor lost no time after the riot was over in coming out with a long winded rigmarole manifesto defending and whitewashing the police. That weak Governor, one of the best in the service, no doubt, soon paid the penalty of his weakness at the hand of a strong Viceroy; but the painful impression produced in the mind of the community by these incidents had its baneful effect. The true explanation, though not the real interpretation, of these harrowing disturbances was, however, to be found in what was called the "Red Pamphlet," which was written by a Mussalman and circulated broadcast among the Mahomedans of East Bengal. This inflammatory leaflet had not the faintest allusion either to the Swadeshi or the Volunteer movement; but it deliberately incited the Mussalmans against the Hindus on racial and religious grounds and upon the supposed bias of Government in favour of Islam; and strange to say, that the man who preached this *Jehad* was tardily brought to trial long after the mischief had been done and only bound down to keep the peace for one year! While instances were not altogether rare where Hindus for writings of less graver description were sentenced to transportation. No sensible Hindu of course believed in the so-called Government Orders, but apparent bias of the local authorities naturally alienated the bulk of the Hindus who were chafing under a sense of unredressed wrongs if not actually "burning with resentment." All this was in Bengal; while in the Punjab, six lawyers of position were placed on their trial at Rawalpindi as political offenders who, according to the alarmist crowd of Sedition-mongers, had by their inflammatory speeches incited violent riots. For six long months these respectable professional men were detained in prison and ultimately they were all honourably acquitted, the special Magistrate trying the case holding that the evidence for the prosecution was "suspicious if not fabricated."

It is a significant fact that these tactics were largely in evidence in the two provinces where the lower elements of the Mussalman population were in the majority. The attempts of the inferior officers of Government to whitewash themselves and make their occupation smooth and easy by referring these disturbances to the leaders of the people, who were nearly all Congressmen, constituted another blunder which went a long way towards alienating the public, and people were not wanting who actually argued that if the popular leaders could be accused of inciting one community to commit disturbances, with equal propriety the local officials could be charged with indirectly fomenting violence among the other community. The natural leaders of the two communities and indeed the upper classes of both throughout maintained their longstanding friendly relation in the least unaffected by these disturbances. If the volumes of confidential reports and cypher messages which came very largely into use at this period could see the light of day, it might be possible to make a fair apportionment of the responsibilities of the situation thus created between the bureaucracy and the people; but to all outward appearances the former made a grievous mistake in making an indiscriminate attack upon all the parties affected—the masses and the classes, the aristocracy and the gentry—and the moderates and the extremists. They were all made the common target of official criticisms and subjected to one sweeping condemnation. In the Swadeshi movement the Mahomedans were actively associated with the Hindus in several places; but they generally received a differential treatment. Anyhow the tension between the Hindus and the bureaucracy became strained almost to the breaking point and even sober, impartial Mahomedans were not wholly wanting who felt that the policy of divide and rule could hardly have been extended more openly or more aggressively in certain direction. A number of thoughtless but impressionable young men were taken of their feet under the influence of some violent speeches and writings of a few enthusiasts and these running amock committed several dastardly outrages which furnished the Government with a legitimate excuse for a series of repressive measures unheard of in this country since the dark days of the Mutiny. The grim spectre of anarchism at last reared its head in a country noted for its piety and overscrupulous tenderness even for the insects and the worms. Secret murders and assassinations took place in towns as well as villages and some secret societies for the commission of crimes were also discovered in the country. In panic the bureaucracy, fanned by a hysterical press, cried out that the country was on the verge of a mutiny. At this critical situation the Indian National Congress and its members rendered a service to the State as well as to the country which, in the heat of passion and prejudice, may not have been properly recognised by either; but which the impartial future historian of this gloomy period will be bound ungrudgingly to record. In a strong adverse current the natural leaders of the people as represented in the Congress stood firm and by their example as well as their influence kept the public under control. Not a few of them on critical occasions flung themselves boldly in the midst of seething disturbances and where the police failed with their regulation *lathies* succeeded in maintaining peace and order by their moving sympathy and persuasive eloquence. But for the firmness and the restraining influence of the Congress and the much-abused Congressmen, the country might have been involved in a much wider and a more serious conflagration. If they were unable to do more, it was more on account of want of confidence in them than any want of earnestness on their part. Unfortunately, however, all the reward that they earned for their services was unmerited calumnies and aspersions on the one hand and wanton insults and opprobrium on the other, and when all was over, the bureaucracy indulged in mutual admiration of the valour, tact and resourcefulness of its members in having successfully averted the repetition of a second chapter of the affairs of 1858.

Unrest had no doubt reached an acute stage and the deadly spirit of anarchism and lawlessness was undoubtedly stalking the streets of cities and towns even in broad daylight; and it was also true that the situation became such as not only to justify but also to make it incumbent upon a civilized Government to take stringent measures for the preservation of peace and order and for the security of life and property. No one could reasonably complain of any legitimate and adequate measure that Government might adopt for the suppression of these heinous crimes. The difference lay only in the means and methods employed. Measures were introduced which made no distinction between the innocent many and the guilty few and in their operation the guity and the innocent were involved in one confusion. In fact, in some cases the rigours of these bad laws were visited mostly upon the peaceful citizens, while the criminals escaped scot-free. For instance, in the case of the Press Laws, the people were perfectly at a loss to understand how the muzzling of a public press could help either in the suppression or in the detection of the dark deeds of the anarchist who moved in secret, hatched his plans in secret and carried them out in secret. In a situation like this the forces of public opinion should have been rallied on the side of the bureaucracy; but they were simply alienated. It was complained, not without some show of reason, that the people withheld their cooperation from the Government; but it was evidently overlooked that Government itself made hearty cooperation practically impossible. Sentiments are often reciprocal, and it is confidence that begets confidence. When the Government evidently distrusted the people and was busy continuously forging fetters for them without distinction it was idle to expect any active co-operation from the people. It is always a bad policy to burn the candle at both ends.

Anarchism was soon followed by another serious crime—Robbery. The truth, however, seemed to be that a section of the bureaucracy were unable to divest themselves of their erroneous impression that both anarchism and robbery were the outward manifestations of an undercurrent of treason. It has been truly observed that when John Bull begins to suspect, he generally begins at the wrong end and that even when the other end forces itself upon his attention he refuses to retrace his step. A little reflection would have shewn that the real objective of the anarchist and the robber in this country has been the police, the approver and the witness, and in one case only it was also the Magistrate in a criminal trial. None but an anarchist need defend anarchism. The anarchist is the common enemy of God and man, and in every age and every climate civilized humanity has refused to recognise the brotherhood of the secret murderer and the dastardly assassin. But anarchism is not one of those tropical diseases which a European need study and investigate in a tropical country at the expense of a tropical people. Its therapeutics ought to be well known to him. Anarchism like plague has undeniably been imported into this country, one from the Far East and the other from the West. They were the unavoidable concomitants of free trade and free communication, and it is the characteristic of both that wherever they find their way they come to stay until the poison has spent itself. A civilized Government is no doubt bound to fight out both ; but in either case the operation should be carefully confined to the rat and not indiscriminately extended to the cat and the kite as well. No sensible man will burn the curtain to get rid of the bug. In this country, however, laws are sometimes made more with a view to make the administration easier than to meet the actual necessities of a situation. The laws of rioting, of accomplices and of conspiracy, all woven with the imaginary thread of a legal fiction, are so many arbitrary inventions for running the administration on convenient lines though at considerable sacrifice of the best interests of justice and fairness, not to speak of the individual rights of free citizenship. One false step imperceptibly leads to another and the law permitting, for the ends of justice in extreme cases, the conversion of an offender to a witness has in recent years been carried too far, particularly in the so-called political trials, at the instance of a police as notorious for its inefficiency as for its corruption. The practice has assumed the proportion of such a scandal as to attract the notice of Parliament and a proposal is actually on foot to amend the law on the subject. The anarchists in this country will generally be found associated with gangs of robbers and secret assassins with no ulterior political object in view. They are a revised edition of the *Thugs* and *Goondals* of a previous generation with this difference that they have ascended a little higher in the scale of society and have taken to more refined weapons of destruction.

Whatever their means and methods may be, their aim generally is the police and the approver—the man who manipulates evidence against them and the man who either betrays their secrets, or securely perjures himself against them. To invest these pests of society with the title of political offenders is to inspire them with an idea of false martyrdom and to indirectly set a premium upon lawlessness.

It has been pointed out that the unrest in India cannot logically be traced to a really seditious or treasonable movement in the country. It is the visible manifestation of a deep-seated and widespread discontent which has gradually accumulated through years of unsympathetic bureaucratic administration and which, in its latest development, is only a rigorous though ill-advised protest against that administration. It may be *disaffection*; but with due deference to the Indian Legislature and the Indian Judges it is neither Sedition nor Treason. The origin and growth of this unrest and the causes underlying it may be summed up as follows:—

The extremely slow and over-cautious movement of the Government and its inability to keep pace with the general advancement of the people to which it at the same time largely contributed may be regarded as the primary cause of the deplorable tension that has arisen between the two parties. The termination of the misrule of the East India Company at the end of a great military rising and with the establishment of a settled Government directly under the Crown marks a turning point in the history of British rule in India. The

Queen's Proclamation of 1858 following a drastic change in Government filled the people's mind with the ardent hope of not only peace and prosperity but also of steady progress and consolidation of their political rights and privileges as British citizens. Peace was restored and justice was firmly established; but the free citizenship was still withheld from them. On the whole, the Government up to 1898 was no doubt a progressive one; but its motion was so slow that for all practical purposes the people regarded it as a fixed body and its immobility became a byword in the country. A complete generation passed away and every reform from time to time proposed or promised proved a source of fresh disappointment; while the occasional shortening of their tether in one direction or another made the people completely distrustful of the administration. This want of confidence led to misunderstanding, and misunderstanding to irritation and discontent.

The next cause which more than any other aggravated the situation, was the racial distinction manifested in the administration of criminal justice. From the trial of Maharajah Nund Coomar down to the latest prosecution of a European upon a charge of murder of a native of the country, the people were never able to divest themselves of the belief that there was invariably a galling failure of justice in cases between Indians and Europeans. Apart from the numerous cases of indigo-planters and tea planters, there was hardly to be found a single instance where a European, whether a soldier or a civilian, voluntarily causing the death of a defenceless Indian did not escape with the payment of a fine not exceeding rupees one hundred only, the usual scale being fifty. A man dragging a live fish or breaking the legs of a crab was sometimes fined Rs. 50 and the spectacle of a European causing the death of a human being and the penalty being the same amount was neither edifying nor conducive to cordial relations between the governing classes and the governed however fragile and enlarged the Indian spleen might be. The Fuller Minute of Lord Lytton, the Resolutions of Lord Curzon in the cases of the Rangoon and Sialkote battalions and the proceedings of the O'Hara case in Bengal may be read to form only an imperfect estimate of the depth of feeling with which the people generally regarded these cases between Indians and Europeans, and, what was still more regrettable, men were not altogether wanting who would quote old *Manu* to justify these proceedings at the present day.

The third and immediate cause of the unrest must be referred to the reactionary policy which asserted itself in the councils of the Empire in recent years. It has been truely remarked by Mr. Henry Nevinson that "although no hard-and-fast line can be drawn in history, the arrival of Lord Curzon as Viceroy on December 30, 1898, marks a fully strong and natural division." During the forty years that elapsed between 1858 and 1898 the Government in its oscillatory motion going backwards and forwards on the whole marked a steady though slow progress. It was Lord Curzon who set back the hand of the clock and reversed the policy into a complete retrograde one. It may be that he was in his own way right in thinking that the policy of 1858 was wrong; but that policy having been accepted and worked upon for nearly half a century with the fullest consciousness of its ultimate results, Lord Curzon was himself in the wrong in trying to change it at this distance of time when the people had outgrown the old system, and as Lord Macaulay had fully anticipated, were with the expansion of their minds, aspiring to institutions, rights and privileges with which that policy had naturally inspired their minds. It was too late. This retrograde policy which sharply manifested itself in almost every branch of the administration and which was received with a chorus of applause by a notoriously Conservative Bureaucracy supported by an equally Conservative Press gave a rude shock to the popular mind and the discontent which had long been brewing in the country burst into a flame. Lord Curzon evidently struck by the magnitude of this discontent attempted to throw the responsibility on his successor saying that there was no disturbance so long as he was in this country; but the popular verdict was unanimous that it was *his* policy which set the house on fire, though he was just lucky enough in successfully making his escape before the smoking fire blazed out.

The repressive policy which Lord Minto adopted to cope with a situation for which he was not himself responsible, was a mistaken remedy and served only to aggravate the situation. The various measures with which he sought to restore peace and order in the country wore the appearance more of a newly conquered territory than of a settled country. The suppression of free speech, the muzzling of the press, espionage, house-searches and police surveillance from which even the most respected in the land were not exempted, became the order of the day; while quite an army of C. I. D. officers mostly recruited from among the refuse of society and who acted more as spies than as detectives made the situation still more intolerable and completely alienated the public. These so-called C. I. D. officers were regarded with distrust both by the people as well as the regular police who, with all their defects, were immensely superior to them both in point of ability as well as efficiency. They in fact served no other useful purpose than that of exasperating the people and in making the situation still more strained which it was the avowed object of the Government to smooth and improve.

A fifth cause underlying the unrest was the supposed policy of stirring up racial jealousy and setting one class against another in the administration of the country. That policy was once tried in favour of the Hindus and against the Mussalmans at an early period of the British rule and was again repeated now only, the order being reversed. Whether in the public services, or in the Municipal and Local Boards, or in the Legislative Councils, the people perceived the working of this racial bias and although the Government was not altogether without some justification in certain cases, the majority of the people were not slow to attribute its actions to the working of a settled policy.

The overbearing and imperious conduct of the bureaucracy was also not a little responsible for the growth of this unrest. Every one cried peace when very few by their act and conduct contributed towards peace. There was more talk than act of living sympathy between the local authorities and the people; while as to mutual trust and confidence both sides were aware that they were simply conspicuous by their absence. In fact to such an extent was official suspicion carried that it sometimes interfered with natural affection and violently disturbed domestic relationship. Cases were neither few nor far between where brothers were forced to break up from brothers and fathers from their sons. While such was the state of things enforced by the condition of the services, the feeling of discontent naturally grew from day-to-day and spread from family to family.

Another cause which has largely contributed to the growth of this unrest was the constant and systematic flouting of public opinion by the authorities in this country. The practice of treating Indian public opinion with perfect indifference and of running counter to such opinion on almost all questions of public importance was often carried to such irritating extent that the average people came to regard it as part of a settled policy. Indeed bitter experience had shown that to anticipate the decision of Government in any important question, one had only to spin out all conceivable arguments against the trend of public opinion and the result of such a process seldom turned out to be incorrect. This not infrequently led cynical publicists sarcastically to suggest that the engine should be reversed and that the very opposite of what the people wanted should be the theme of the public platform and of the public press. Public censure of an officer often acted as a passport to this advancement and, instances were neither few nor far between where the sharp criticism of the acts of an unpopular officer happened to be met by his almost immediate promotion. The popularity of an officer counted only for disqualification. All this was said to be due to the *fetish* of official prestige. The prestige of a Government is no doubt its most valuable asset ; but true prestige does not consist in riding rough-shod over public opinion and in inspiring dread into public mind, but in securing the allegiance and approbation of the popular voice and in enlisting the confidence and co-operation of the people. It is despotism that trusts on its iron will ; but a constitutional government is always founded upon the bed-rock of popular ideas and sentiments.

In the majority of cases where anarchism has developed into robbery and other crimes affecting property, it will be found on careful examination that they are more economic than political in their origin, although the authorities find it more convenient to group them all together with the so-called political offences. The poor but respectable people who generally pass by the name of *bhadralokes* are hit the hardest by the economic condition of the country. They are nobody's care and their position is being gradually more and more straitened. Whether in the Legislature or in the administration their condition receives very little attention ; while driven alike from the soil and the services they have long been a standing menace to society, and it is these people who are now largely in evidence in the *dacoities* that have become rampant throughout the country. They no doubt resort to political cants; but this they do as much to divert official attention from them as to facilitate recruitment of unsuspecting immature youths in their ranks.

The last cause which aggravated the unrest must be traced to the intemperate writings and wild vapourings of a section of the people who found ample opportunities in the unsympathetic attitude of the authorities to foment the irritation which rankled in the minds of the public. These people did not hesitate either to distort facts or to exaggerate situations and create sensation more for self-advertisement than for any real remedy for the actual situation which was bad enough even without them.

Whether this ugly development was due to bureaucratic methods or to a malignant growth in the body politic, or to the economic condition of a certain class of population, its appearance was undoubtedly a grave menace to society and a serious obstacle to orderly progress. Whatever might be the true genesis of these sporadic instances of moral depravity, the question still remained to be considered whether general repression was the proper remedy even in view of a possible outbreak of such a malady. The true remedy for anarchy, says Burke, is conciliation and not coercion; for coercion, however drastic, always leaves room for coercing again. If therefore these disturbances were no more than abnormal developments of crimes the arm of the ordinary law of land was surely long and strong enough to reach and put down these criminals; but if on the other hand they were connected with any political condition in the country, the remedy applied was singularly inappropriate. The first manifestation of this unrest was admittedly political and the present condition of the country amply illustrates the truth of Burke's dictum. It has been admitted even by Sir Valentine Chirol that the Indian political atmosphere has been largely cleared up by the inauguration of a policy of conciliation, which had been so darkly clouded by a policy of repression. If Lord Curzon was primarily responsible for the outbreak, two methods were open to his successors to deal with it, and both the methods were tried one after the other. Lord Minto was advised to resort to repression, and he tried it to the fullest extent, but failed; while Lord Hardinge took to the other method of conciliation and at once succeeded. That is a practical demonstration whose visible result can neither be disputed nor ignored. A question, however, still arises, —has the unrest been completely dissipated and do we now live in perfect sunshine? Are the people and the bureaucracy fully reconciled, and is there no cause for further anxiety? In justice to truth and frankness these unpleasant questions must be answered in the negative. Undoubtedly the situation has vastly improved; but in spite of the prevailing calm and cheering signs of peace all round there is the sore still rankling in the bosom of both the bureaucracy and the people. The loud talk of official sympathy, with which the official documents and utterances resound and which for ought we know, may be perfectly genuine and undefiled at its fountain-source, seems however to touch the heart of the country very lightly. The tension between the executive officers and the educated community is not yet relaxed to an appreciable extent; while in some places the habit of distrust and suspicion and the dogging of the innocents seem to be still in operation. The policy has no doubt changed; but the practice has not fully moved out of its old groove. The repressive measures still stand on the statute book, while occasional reminders are not altogether wanting to apprise the public that there is no intention of even treating them as dead letters. The higher officials have no doubt became in many places more polite and courteous; but it seems extremely doubtful if any real cordiality has been established between the official hierarchy and the leaders of public opinion in the country. Even the serene atmosphere of the legislative assemblies is not sometimes free from the flying dusts of the streets. If the situation is to be radically and permanently improved mere superficial treatment must not be depended on and a more searching enquiry should be made into the real causes of discontent and a genuine effort made to remove them root and branch, though it may involve some sacrifice and a little loss of official prestige.

As regards the remedy it should be borne in mind that although every doctor, and specially the authorized house-surgeon in a hospital, is entitled to his own prescription, the disease really requires but one treatment, and that no surgeon however skilful should resort to Cæsarian operation until all the ordinary rules of midwifery have failed. If the most drastic methods hitherto employed have failed to produce the desired result, there must be other methods which ought at least to have a fair trial. And above all, a correct diagnosis of the situation should be attempted without any bias or prejudice. There are, as has been pointed out by an eminent authority, a number of forces at work in the Indian polity at the present moment which must be so regulated and co-ordinated that their resultant force may make for progress on the line of least resistance or friction. These forces are,—1st, the Parliament, the central body, from which all the other forces radiate and to which all powers, when once created, are supposed to gravitate and which is the ultimate authority controlling the entire system; 2ndly, the Secretary of State or the Minister for India, the seat of Parliamentary power, who holds all the threads of the Indian administration in his hand and directs all its operations from Whitehall, being nominally responsible to Parliament; 3rdly, the Viceroy and the Government of India, the lever which, with the assistance of the local administrations like so many flywheels, works the entire machinery on the spot; 4thly, the Anglo-Indian Bureaucracy, a compact hierarchy dominating the entire administration from top to bottom and mounting guard over every passage and avenue leading to the inner sanctuary of that administration; 5thly, the Indian People as represented by the Indian National Congress, the howling pariah dog that barks out the thief all night to receive in the morning occasional lashes for disturbing the master's sleep with a few crumbs from the refuse of the morning and the evening meals as the reward of his thankless, gratuitous services, and 6thly and lastly, the growing spirit of crimes and lawlessness, the anarchist and the robber, a direct challenge to force No. 4, which being primarily responsible for exercising this evil spirit is now unable to bottle it and in its just endeavour to control it largely tends towards general mischief though in a different direction.

To pursue these points a little further, the first is no doubt the highest and the most important of these forces; but it travels such an immense distance and passes through so many media that its real power is better understood than felt in this country. The parliamentary control over Indian affairs was considerably weakened after the transfer of the sovereignty of the country to the Crown, and it would perhaps be no great exaggeration to say that it has gradually been reduced almost to a vanishing point. "The nearer the Church the farther from faith," is a trite old saying which seems to apply with equal force to the great Mother of Parliaments as any other institution; for as far as India is concerned that august body now sits almost quiescent like the great cosmic force in Hindu philosophy which is supposed to have existence without action and consciousness without volition, a mere silent witness to the wondrous creation around, which however cannot go on without its metaphysical existence. Instances are not wanting where this supreme authority has been not only treated with scant courtesy, but its solemn decision also over-ruled with perfect impunity by authorities admittedly subordinate to it. This has a very unwholesome effect upon Indian minds which regard the British Parliament as a palladium of justice and the final arbiter of the Empire's fate. In the vast and varied organisation of an Empire like that of Great Britain delegation of authority is certainly unavoidable; but delegation is not surrender., any more than that an agent can be an irresponsible substitute for the principal. Abdication of power without the safeguard of necessary control is the surest passport to abuse, and where a helpless subject people at a distance is concerned it is a free license to injustice and corruption. It is doubtless true that the British Parliament has not by any statute divested itself of its supreme authority; but in point of practice its interest in Indian affairs appears to be so feeble and so transitory, that the Indian public are seldom inspired with any great confidence in the justice of its action, or in the earnestness of its intention. At the bar of the House the Indian bureaucracy should be ordinarily considered as put upon its trial; but the position is more often than not reversed, the bureaucracy appearing as the prosecutor and a totally unrepresented people as the accused, and the judgment of the House generally goes *ex parte* against them. The general result of questions and debates in Parliament regarding matters Indian, therefore, produces a very unfavourable impression upon the people, who are thus not unnaturally driven to the conclusion that there is hardly any remedy against the vagaries of the Executive out in this country. The first step towards any improvement of the present situation would, therefore, be for Parliament to assume greater control over the Indian administration and to exercise closer supervision over its management. The theory of the "man on the spot" has been carried to extravagant excess and it is high time that it were thoroughly revised.

The Secretary of State is the real seat of power under the present arrangement. He is assisted by a Council of 9 to 15 retired veterans of the service; but he is, in practice, though not under the statute, a perfect autocrat, although one of the greatest autocrats that India has ever seen since the days of Aurangzeb has at last openly confessed that "anything which has a suspicion of autocracy in a case like that of India" should be carefully avoided and he *humbly submitted* to the House that in India autocracy "would not only be a blunder but almost a crime." That crime, however, has been an outstanding feature of the Indian administration since the battle of Plassey. The India Council is mostly composed of a number of retired Anglo-Indian officials grown grey in Ango-Indian prejudices and strongly saturated with the instincts and traditions of an almost irresponsible Anglo-Indian autocracy. The first Congress in 1885 urged for the abolition of the Council which only worked for mischief by stiffening the Secretary of State against any substantial reform of the Indian administration, and five years after, the sixth Congress also repeated the charge. The only change that has since taken place in the constitution of this Council is the introduction of two Indian members into it by Lord Morley without however any statutory recognition. Lord Crewe attempted to give this improvement the force of a legal provision and make it a permanent feature of the institution; but Lord Crewe's India Council Bill of 1914 has been rejected by the House of Lords. The Bill was not a measure of perfection; but yet it contained some germs of reform which once accepted might have in future years paved the way towards popularizing the Council of the Secretary of State. The proposed nomination of the two Indian members out of a panel of forty elected persons was no doubt a curious invention, although such inventions, like the mock creations of *Viswamitra* of old, were not altogether foreign to the British Indian administration. In the establishment of Trial by Jury Sir James Fitz James Stephen introduced a system of trial with the aid of assessors which was a pure mockery neither sweet nor sour. Then in the reform of the Councils under Lord Cross' Bill of 1892, a system of election was introduced which was subject to the confirmation of Government. Again in the domain of education a novel principle has recently been enunciated by Sir Herbert Risley, which still governs the Educational policy of Government, that "it is not in the interest of the poor (in India) that they should receive high education." India is a proverbial land of surprises, and it has never been her lot to receive a full loaf at a time. It is gravely contended that her soil, her climate and her traditions stand in the way of her normal expansion and development. However that may be, the statutory position of the two Indian members being once secured, it would not have been difficult to remove the panel afterwards. The Conservatives fully grasped the situation, and it is a great pity that they were able to lay their hand on some Indian opinions also in support of their arguments. Thus a great opportunity has been lost for the improvement of the real seat of power in the administration of the country, which may not recur within another decade. Whenever that opportunity comes, it shall be India's case, that although the Viceroy and the Government of India should never be subordinated to any member or department of the India Council, the constitution of that Council should be materially altered, so that not less than one third of its members may be Indians, another third taken from among tried politicians in England totally unconnected with the Indian administration and the rest selected from among a certain class of retired Anglo-Indian officials of experience. Thus there will be one section of the Council faithfully representing the Indian view, another section the view of the bureaucracy, while the third will hold the balance evenly between the two. The present arrangement under which bureaucracy has an overwhelming preponderance in that Council practically sitting in judgment over its own actions may be convenient for the administration, but can never be good for the people. It is not enough that the real seat of power is just; but it is also necessary that its justice should be felt and understood in this country and its people inspired with confidence in the justice of the administration.

Then comes the Viceory, the supreme head of all the local administration and the real representative of the Crown on the spot. He is generally a British statesman of distinction and comes out to India apparently without any bias or prejudice. But once he assumes office he finds himself isolated, or more correctly speaking, hemmed in on all sides by bureaucratic influences which it is his duty to control, but to which he is often bound to succumb. Experience is no doubt a valuable asset in every worldly concern ; but keen insight and sound judgment based upon a dispassionate survey of both sides of a question are of far greater importance towards the success of a great administration. An exaggerated importance seems always to have been attached to local knowledge both in regard to the Council of the Secretary of State as well as the Executive Council of the Governor-General : but in both these cases it is apparently overlooked that local knowledge and experience may often be a bundle of prejudice, begotten of one-sided study of the people and the country, of natural pride of superiority, as well as of the bias of jealousy and selfishnesss. Familiarity often breeds contempt, while class interest sometimes unconsciously magnifies our preconceived notions and ideas. So that "the man on the spot" has his advantages as well as his disadvantages. Nature has its counterpoise in all its arrangements, and so long as the Council of the Governor-General, no less than that of the Secretary of State, is not well proportioned and evenly balanced in its bureaucratic as well as popular influences, the best intentioned and the strongest of Viceroys must fail to give effect to his noblest ideals and projects, and the legitimate aspirations of the people must remain indefinitely postponed resulting inevitably in irritation and discontent. If the administration is to be popularized as a means to secure the real co-operation of the people and thereby shift a portion of the responsibility as well as its unpopularity from the Government to the people, the overwhelming preponderance of the bureaucracy in the Government of India as well as in the Local Governments, must be reduced to a minimum.

The fourth power of the State, the bureaucracy, is the real power felt and understood by the people in every day life in this country. By it the entire weight of the administration is measured and its quality both in tone and character determined. The theory of efficiency has of recent years been carried to extravagant excess, reducing the administration to a lifeless machinery without the initiative of any sentient being. And the working of this machinery is entirely vested in one train of officials all of whom are cast in one mould, trained in one uniform standard and all revolving as it were on a common axis and regulated by a common impulse. Their discipline is exact and praiseworthy and their cohesion almost metallic. It seems impossible to touch this train at any one point without an instantaneous response being transmitted thoughout the entire system. Such a system no doubt secures smoothness of routine work and uniformity in its outturn; but can hardly be progressive. Its power of resistance to innovation is both natural and enormous. Then again, it is not simply the great departments of the State, but also the occasional enquiries into these departments when initiated in this country, are practically vested in the members of the bureaucracy.

If *Canabis Indica* be really a "concentrated food" and as such a remedy for Indian famine, it seems fairly intelligible why a member of the Indian Civil Service should be selected as the President of a *Ganja* Commission; but what special qualification there is for a member of that service to preside over a Sanitary Committee, or an Education Commission or a judicial enquiry, it is rather difficult to appreciate. This centralisation of all authority in one particular service has a distinct tendency towards creating a rigid official caste system, which like all caste systems presents a dead wall against any change and works only for mischief. The result is, that as the bureaucracy generally looks with disfavour upon any proposal of reform advanced by the people, so the people view with distrust any measure inaugurated by the bureaucracy. The first step towards effecting a cordial *rapproachment*, between the two, must therefore be to strike a golden mean where each may meet the other half way, and this can only be done by breaking down the official caste system which is rapidly crystallizing itself and gradually alienating the people from the Government. The subject forms the crucial point of the administration and will be more fully dealt with in a separate chapter.

The next great force is that of public opinion as represented by the Indian National Congress to which the Moslem League is also rapidly coverging. *Vox Populi Vox Dei* may not be fully true of a subject people in a dependency; but no Government however strong or despotic can afford completely to ignore public opinion in the matter of its administration. The voice of the people may not be sometimes wise; but it may often be irresistible; and to keep it within reasonable bounds it becomes necessary to conciliate it by sympathy instead of exasperating it by show of violence or open disregard. Public opinion in this country is not yet sufficiently vigorous to assert itself; but it is gaining strength every day both in volume as well as intensity and is sufficiently pretty strong not to be treated as an altogether negligible quantity. Various grounds may be urged by a stereotyped bureaucracy why every Government cannot be by the people, but even the most cynical bureaucrat has not been bold enough to dispute the proposition that a civilized Government can only be for the people. It therefore follows that in order that a Government may be for the people it must to a large extent conform itself to the views and wishes of that people. A regular tug of war in which the people pull in one way and a close bureaucracy in another, may be an exciting trial of strength; but it always acts as a dead weight to progress and orderly Government; while persistent flouting of public opinion must inevitably let loose forces of disorder in society.

This brings us to a consideration of the sixth and the last force which having recently come into painful operation has been greatly exercising the administration of this country: the force of disorder and lawlessness. Without entering into any discussion as to the orgin of this ugly development and without making any attempt towards an apportionment of the responsibility of the situation between the people and the bureaucracy, it may be pointed out that this new phase is as much a slur upon the administration as it is upon the character of the people themselves. The sinister spirit of heinous crimes seems not to have wholly died out and sporadic cases of assassination and robbery are still reported from different parts of the country. They are mostly actuated either by motives of self-preservation, private grudge, or avarice; but what is most deplorable is, that they are not confined to the habitual criminal population of the country. People who happen to belong to poor but respectable families and who have some pretention to education also, have been drawn into these dark and dismal ways, while even schoolboys in some places appear to have been inveigled to join their ranks under false hopes and absurd misrepresentations. This is a most distressing phase of the situation. Various attempts have been made for the protection of these boys. Education has been officialized, schools have been barricaded and schoolboys segregated and placed under surveillance. Under the ban of political association these boys have been completely dissociated from healthy public influence with the result that they now deem themselves sometimes absolved even from their natural allegiance to their parents. It is the trite old story of "from the frying pan into the fire." To save the youths of the country from the hands of the much abused political agitators these innocents have been driven into the folds of desperate criminals. It is, however, no use crying over spilt milk and abusing one another. Attempts should be made in all earnestness to eradicate the evil, even the latent germs of which unless carefully weeded out, are bound to grow and spread like a catching contagion. Of all the difficulties in practical life the greatest is perhaps that of admitting our own errors and divesting ourselves of our prejudices. The methods hitherto adopted for dealing with this new spirit of crimes have admittedly not succeeded, yet there seems to be no disposition to try other methods. Of the forces mentioned above, the first, second, third and the fifth should be combined and arrayed against the fourth and the sixth, both of which make for mischief though in different lines. The true remedy for the situation does not lie in new inventions, but in proper control and regulation of the forces that are already in existence. It is no doubt the common object of all the other forces to put down the last : but the operation is left entirely to the discretion of one, *i e.*, the fourth, while the other forces stand almost paralysed. Public opinion is wholly discounted except for the purpose of abuse, and the controlling powers are practically led by that one force which dominates the entire administration.

CHAPTER XVII.

THE DEPRESSION.

It is sometimes complained, though not altogether without some show of reason, that the enthusiasm for the Congress is on the wane and that ever since the

Surat imbroglio the response to the call of the national assembly has been growing fainter and fainter every year. This no doubt is painfully true to some extent. But without directly connecting it with the Surat incident it is possible to trace this depression to other causes also. It may be borne in mind that such a state of temporary depression is almost unavoidable in a continued struggle extending over the lifetime of an entire generation. Human nature, says Smiles, cannot perpetually sustain itself on high pressure, or continue to be indefinitely in an elevated plane of existence without occasional breaks in its career. There are ups and downs in national as well as individual life, and an unbroken line of progress is seldom vouchsafed to either. Then it is also clear that upon attainment of some signal success after a protracted struggle human nature seeks some rest for recouping its lost energies. It is apparently with the object of recommending this spirit of relaxation that Sir Valentine Chirol has neively remarked that since the reform of the Legislative Councils has been effected, the Congress has no just ground for its further existence. The Indian public cannot, however, endorse such a view; nor has the success of the Congress probably been such as to justify its members in winding up their business and go into voluntary liquidation. In fact the advantages which they have at last secured ought on the contrary to stimulate them in pursuing those advantages with greater vigour and energy. If they have so far groped their way through the darkness of defeat and despair, they have now to push on with the cheering light of dawning success before them. The promised land is, however, yet far off, and those who have deliberately undertaken to lead a wandering people, through a dreary desert cannot afford to cry out in despair, "How long! Oh, how long is the way to Canan!"

There is another aspect of the depression which, paradoxical as it may seem, may be distinctly traced to the gradual expansion of the movement in different directions. The Congress has in its progress directed the attention of the public to the social, educational, and economic developments of the country which have claimed not a small share of the national energies and thus contributed not a little to divert a considerable volume of the public enthusiasm which originally flowed through the main channel. As in irrigation the rushing current of a mighty river is often reduced both in volume as well as intensity by heavy drains on its resources for the requirements of wet tracts on either side of it, so the superabundance of enthusiasm flowing through the main political bed of the Congress movement has, in its onward course, turned into other channels and found its way into other fields of national activities. This was fully expected and cannot in any way furnish a reasonable ground for regret. In the evolution of a national life all these developments are but hand-maids to one another, and it would be a foolish, if not a futile, attempt on the part of the people to confine their energies exclusively to the political aspect of the situation leaving all other fields of necessary activities as barren, uncultivated wastes. All the phases of a national life are interdependent and no substantial progress can be made in any one of them to the total neglect of the others. They are the different factors of a single problem in the correct solution of which not one of them can be either ignored or eliminated. The relative importance of all these phases may be different and circumstanced as the country is, the political aspect of the situation unquestionably dominates the consideration of all the other issues. It is in fact the main current, if not the fountain-head, through which the other channels of activities receive their supply, force and vitality, and while such a diversion is to certain extent unavoidable, public feelings and sentiments must occasionally be dredged so that the main current may not suffer stagnation leading not only to its own depletion, but also to a serious detriment of the subsidiary channels which it feeds.

Much of the present depression therefore is due to the many-sided activities which the Congress movement itself has created, supplemented by the vexations and disappointments brought about in weaker systems by the extreme slowness of progress and severe moral exhaustion. The situation is not unlike that of a chronic patient who having really lost confidence in himself as well as in his doctors always seeks for new remedies without giving a sufficient trial to any. There is, however, really no lack of enthusiasm in the country. It is more a case of want of self-confidence and of restlessness and impatience. It is a significant fact that public men and measures now receive wider and closer, if also a somewhat more irreverent, attention than they ever did before: Public criticism is undoubtedly on the increase, and it is not only the public associations which are yearly growing in numbers, but even the boarding-houses, restaurants, counting-houses and even railway carriages present the appearance of teeming bee-hives buzzing with discussions of public interest. Conferences and congregations of various denominations are the order of the day, and throughout the country and in every grade of society there is a manifest upheaval of no ordinary magnitude or character. The whole country is in a ferment of agitation undergoing as it were a process of foaming and frothing preliminary to refinement in a boiling cauldron. Unfortunately, however, there is too much of gas and dissipation as are sometimes unavoidable in a period of transition in national evolution. There is more of destructive than of constructive methods in these diverse movements which sometimes counteract one another and not unfrequently tend to hamper and neutralize all of them. There are apparently more men busy each in his own way for discovering the Philosopher's Stone than for patiently and persistently drudging at the ore for the true metal. In this state of things a temporary and partial relaxation in one direction to supplement the supposed requirements of another seems almost inevitable, and it is pretty certain that until the malcontents are made to realize that there is not only no antagonism between these diverse movements, but they are absolutely inter-dependent on one another, the quarrel between the different members of the body politic will not cease and the idle stomach continue to receive its proper nourishments.

Perhaps it may be useful also to bear in mind that the Congress has now worked incessantly for nearly thirty years, and a new generation has sprung up to take the place of those whose rank and file are gradually thinning from death, disease and infirmities of age. The difference in the spirit and temper of the two elements is due largely to the difference of conditions and circumstances in which they are placed. In the estimation of those who have weathered the storm in a dark and dismal night the progress made is sufficiently marked to inspire them with robust optimism and confidence in the future; but a younger generation who have awakened with the dawning light of the grey morning without any experience of the night's adventure and with the vast immensity of heaving expanse still darkly stretching out before them, cannot be expected to be equally impressed with the difficulties that have been overcome, the distance which has been covered and of the ultimate success of the voyage that has been undertaken. This difference in the perspective accounts in no small measure for the scepticism of the younger generations and their want of confidence in the methods which have been so far employed by their more experienced elders. In the race of life foresight is no doubt a great virtue: but the habit of intently looking too much ached regardless of the obstacles that lie immediately in front of one's steps, is the surest way of courting a disastrous fall.

People are not also wanting who unable to bear the strain of the fight as well as of the immense sacrifices it necessarily involves, seek repose in quietly taking a defeat and to cover their own weakness dilate on the utter futility of political agitation in a subject country. These people are generally too precise in their vision to waste their energies in the vain pursuit of unattainable objects and are always ready to dissuade others from doing so. They seem to know more of the future than of either the past or the present and in their innate love for the original, are always busy prescribing their own patents for the treatment of the situation. They apparently forget that an uphill ascent is always a tedious and weary task, and that the higher one ascends the greater becomes the exhaustion and the slower the progress. As there is no royal road to learning, so in practical politics there can be no artificial lift to carry up a people to its destination by a mere switch of the button.

Apart from all natural causes this temporary depression may be referred to some other sources. There are several classes of critics who, in spite of their best intentions, have indirectly contributed not a little to the growth of this depression. Some of them have preferred to attack the Congress from the flank and the rear, the frontal attack delivered by the Anglo-Indian community having been successfully repulsed. They apparently forget that by so doing they are indirectly playing in the hands of their adversaries. It has almost grown into a fashion with some of these critics to indulge in a flow of correspondence through the columns of the press on the eve of every session of the Congress earnestly appealing to the "leaders" to remove all "sources of irritation" and to make it possible, as they say, "for all classes and parties to meet and join hands once again on the Congress platform." What those sources of irritation are, nobody however chooses expressly to state, although a vague reference is invariably made to the Surat incident, as well as to the thrice-told tale of the "Convention Congress." There is, of course, no doubt as to the honesty of purpose and sincerity of intention of these critics; but if half the number of people who seem never tried of indulging in these cants either in public or private life had actually rejoined the Congress, much of the so-called "sources of irritation" would have at once disappeared and the outstanding differences easily solved themselves. But no, the practice has been to keep this real or supposed "irritation" afresh like the proverbial wound of the tiger by constantly licking it. Nobody is able to point out that there is any thing really objectionable either in the creed or in the constitution provided for the Congress in 1908. All that is still urged is, that these were the workings of a Convention which never received the sanction of the Congress. As a matter of fact they were placed before the Congress in 1908 and bodily passed by a whole House in 1911 and again re-affirmed with certain modifications at the Session of 1912. But then the cry is, that they have passed only through a "Convention Congress" and not through a *free* Congress, whatever that may mean. It is only fair to note, that before setting out for the Allahabad Convention the Bengal delegates, at all events, made it perfectly clear that they would solidly vote for whatever constitution the Convention might adopt being formally submitted to the judgment of the whole House at the next Session of the Congress, and they accordingly earnestly requested their colleagues to attend the Convention in sufficient strength to carry the day. It is also well-known that at the meeting of the Convention they lost only by a couple of votes. Now if only three of these critics had, instead of sulkily keeping themselves aloof, taken the trouble to go to Allahabad, they might easily have scored a victory at the outset and much of the powder and shot, which they have since wasted, usefully saved. Then in spite of the initial nervousness of some of the provinces the creed and the constitution provided by the Convention have ultimately passed through the Congress, call it "Convention Congress" or whatever you choose. They could not have been submitted to another bear-garden without running the risk of demolishing the Congress altogether. Besides, what practical difference would it have made in the situation even if such a risky experiment could have been successfully carried out? Do the non-Conventionists mean to suggest that it would have been wiser for their friends, even if they agreed with them in some of the issues raised, to have seceded from the Congress because the majority did not concede to their views and thereby obviously wrecked an organisation which was the result of the labours of a generation and for which such enormous sacrifices had been made? It is presumed that no same man who has the country's cause at heart would have approved of such a course. What then in the name of good sense and patriotism is the objection to join the Congress now on the score of old sores which have practically been healed up, the cicatrices only remaining to remind the combatants of a past conflict of opinions? Such conflicts are sometimes unavoidable even in a well-governed family, and must they eternally rankle in the breast of those who have pledged themselves to fight out a great common cause? If the non-Conventionists are truly inspired by a patriotic impulse, as some of them unquestionably are, there seem to be no insurmountable difficulties in making up their sentimental differences and bodily returning to the common fold for the purposes of strengthening a common cause. If it has been possible for the Ulstermen and the Irish Nationalists to sign a truce to a civil war at their country's call, surely there ought to be no difficulty for the Moderates and Extremists of the Indian Nationalists Party to bury their petty domestic quarrels and re-unite on a common platform. A *rapproachment* may easily be made by mutual surrender of some fanciful positions on either side, unless these positions are sought to be maintained as a mere pretext for carrying on a suicidal controversy. In practical politics in every country and under every popular constitution it must always be a question of majority as well as of expediency, and where differences arise the policy must be one of *give-and-take*. Where there is a practical agreement in aim and object, a mere difference in procedure ought not to divide those whose unity is their only strength. A man's principles are no doubt his religion ; but it were well to remember that principles, like religion, carried to excess are sometimes apt to degenerate into bigotry and fanaticism. It is all very well to talk of fighting for principles ; but it seems allowable even without going the actual length of saying with the shrewd French philosopher, that *prejudices* and *principles* are sometimes merely interchangeable terms in controversies between parties of opposite views, to point out that even in the case of people more favourably circumstanced than ourselves accepted principles have not unoften to conform themselves to practice and expediency according to the exigencies of a situation.

Then as regards the contemptuous expression "Convention Congress," any one acquainted with the history of the Congress must know that it had its being in a Convention and that the Constitution of 1908 was not an innovation, but only a repetition and amplification of the original Constitution with which it was started in 1885. As has already been pointed out, early in 1885 a Union was established by a dozen leading people under the name and style of the National Union, and it was this National Union which called the Indian National Congress into existence with the following express declaration of its object and its method, *viz* :—(1) That "unswerving loyalty to the British Crown shall be the keynote of the institution," and (2) that "the Union shall be prepared, when necessary, to oppose by all *constitutional methods* all authorities high or low, here or in England, whose acts and omissions are opposed to those principles of the Government of India as laid down from time to time by the British Parliament and endorsed by the British Sovereign." Now let any honest critic say if the Constitution framed by the Convention of 1908, after a most regrettable incident, was anything new or retrograde in its character or whether those who had been thoroughly loyal to the Congress down to 1906 had any just cause to secede from it since 1908? The declaration and subscription to the creed was a mere matter of form necessitated by the exigencies of a painful situation and adopted with a view to ensure the due observance of the Constitution. If that Constitution be accepted in principle, it is difficult to conceive where the shoe pinches, or what reasonable objection there may be to signify that acceptance in writing. The misfortune is, that there is too much logic in this country and particularly in Bengal. No practical people, much less a subject race, can afford to live in the dreamland of Utopia, or indulge in fighting upon bare theories wholly divorced from practice. The country has admittedly reached a stage of its evolution, where all its strength and available resources should be concentrated and brought to bear upon decisions of issues which are as momentous in their character as are the contending forces with which they are confronted stubborn and irresistible. At such a grave situation for a weak and helpless people to flitter away their energies in fruitless controversies and academic discussions over mere theories and procedure seems to be little short of reckless dissipation altogether unworthy of men who have put their hands into serious business and are responsible for the future of the country. It is high time that these unseemly squabbles were ended and as practical men all parties in the country presented a solid, united front sinking all their differences in the name of the Motherland.

There is another class of critics who with equal vagueness urge the Congress to be directed on "practical lines." They maintain with perfect sincerity that the Congress should now devote its energies to the practical development of education, sanitation and various kinds of industries. This no doubt in the abstract is a "counsel of perfection"; but is it also practical within the scope and capacity of the Congress? These critics apparently forget that the Congress is essentially a huge deliberative body of a vast continent which can and does formulate ideas, generate impulses and also indicate the lines on which the energies and activities of the people may be directed for the amelioration of their condition. It can and does also urge upon the country as well as the Government to adopt measures which in its opinion are calculated to foster education, improve sanitaion and develop indigenous industries. But it has neither the means, nor the organisation, to establish schools, open drains, provide watter-supply or build industries, and cannot possibly be asked to undertake any of these operations, throughout the country. It can, as it always does, enunciate principles and lay down lines upon which the national energies are to be directed and the methods by which they are to be guided.

and controlled. It also allows petitions and representations to Government; but it is a gross mistake to characterize its policy as mendicant. Its prayers are all demands based upon rights and its appeals to the people are exhortations to them to stand on their own legs in defence of such rights. The Petition of Rights is the strongest bulwark of the liberties of the British people, and the highest function of the Congress is to initiate the people into the secrets of those means and methods by which that people has acquired its valued rights of free citizenship. The Congress is a great school for the national education of the people and its practicability can no more be questioned than those of the other educational institutions in the country. But beyond these, what practical measures are actually open to the Congress it is difficult to conceive. Even in politics the Congress can only formulate the legitimate rights and privileges of the people and press for the removal of their grievances and disabilities. The Congress is a great force-centre where the united intellect and moral strength of the country generate steam and give the impetus necessary to move the body politic; but there must be other machineries and appliances to utilise these forces and turn them into proper account. The Congress seeks to represent the entire country with its diverse races and communities, and beyond indulging in vague generalities and vaguer platitudes no one has yet suggested how it may be possible for such an organisation to go into practical details for working out sanitary, educational or industrial reforms applicable to each particular community or province. Perhaps an attempt in that direction, even if it were possible, would only lead to a disintegration of the units which the Congress has so far laboured to combine. After all, if those who find fault with the Congress as not being *practical* were to cease firing at a long range and come to close quarters with a view to associate themselves with it and submit any practical scheme of work suited to its constitution, there is no reason why they should not receive a patient hearing and respectul consideration.

There is yet another class of critics of the Congress who would kick the ladder behind them. They seem to fancy that if the Congress had any use, it was for their individual or class advancement and when that is satisfied it has no more claim to its earthly existence. Most of these arm-chair critics come from the official rank who owe no allegiance to the Congress, but seem to have the largest claim to its services. Outside the official circle these critics are mostly like the cynic Diogenes walking in broad daylight with the lamp of their own unerring intellect in the vain quest of a single capable man in the country. They have neither the sincerity nor the earnestness of the other two classes of critics and are ready at all times to indulge in tirades and raphsodies which are as inflated as they are violent and sweeping in their denunciations. They represent the destructive and not the constructive element of society; and not having taken any part in building it up, they are for the most part for demolishing the Congress altogether. In their impotent vanity and conceit these cynics regard the Congress as perfectly "useless" and "almost unnoticeable" and denounce the Indian leaders as "no politicians," but as mere "mimic actors on the political stage." They would take exception even to Mr. Montagu or Mr. Asquith denominating them as "bad politicians," for to be a "bad politician" one must first of all be "a politician." Erostratus acquired a lasting notoriety by burning the temple of Ephesus on the birthday of Alexander the Great and all incendiaries may well imitate the example of their prototype to leave their names in history. Sharp criticism of notable men and measures is no doubt one of the cheapest methods for mediocre intelligence getting into prominent notice; but such wild effusions as those above noticed can serve no other useful purpose than that of a hawker's advertisement. It seems high time that these flambuoyant critics were disabused of the impression, which was at one time rather too common in this country, that such advertisements also pay. Sir Chareles Dilke has neatly disposed of these traducers of the Congress in his own trenchant style. In his "Problems of Great Britain" that shrewd statesman observes :—

"Argument upon the matter is to be desired and not invective, and there is so much reason to think that the Congress movement really represents the cultivated intelligence of the country that those who ridicule it do harm to the imperial interest of Great Britain, bitterly wounding and alienating men who are justified in what they do, who do it in reasonable and cautious form and who ought to be conciliated by being met half-way. The official class themselves admit, that *many of the natives who attack the Congress do so to ingratiate themselves with their British rulers and to push their claims for decorations.*"

Now, whatever these various classes of critics may or may not say, it seems as useless, as it is harmful, to disguise the fact, that there has come some sort of depression in the country which is necessarily reflected in its national assembly. The fault is not in the shadow, but in the substance behind it. Whether it be due to the despicable tyranny exercised by the dastardly proceedings of a few gangs of unhinged fanatics, or the result of unremitted hammerings of a series of repressive measures unknown in this country even in the dark days of the Mutiny, the popular mind has visibly received a rude shock from which it is bound to take some time to recover. The bureaucracy may rejoice over this set-back; but it cannot fail to create some anxiety in the minds of responsible statesmen. For, the normal growth of a people cannot be stunted with impunity by any violent artificial process, and when under any abnormal pressure national life begins to stagnate, the forces of disorder must gain strength and become rampant in society. It is a dangerous experiment which has had its fair trial in almost all despotic governments, whether in ancient or modern times, and invariably ended in disastrous results. It is not the Congress alone that is likely to suffer by this inanition, but the general state also stands the imminent risk of falling into a deadly relapse. As for the Congress itself, it has to be borne in mind that the rank of its veterans must be thinning away every year from death, illness and infirmities of age; while some of its best members are occasionally taken away to the services; but fresh recruits are neither so adequate, nor sufficiently strong to supply their deficiency. It is almost the same old familiar faces that are seen on the

Congress platform every year. Politics is a science which requires careful study, deep thought and strong practical common sense. It embraces a much larger area than any other practical science and commands a keener insight and broader vision of the social as well as economic condition of a people. It fact, as the Lord Mayor of London once felicitously observed, there is scarcely a phase of life where politics does not in one shape or another play an important part. Then with a people circumstanced like ourselves progress must necessarily be slow and inadequate, and consequently there must be sufficient asset of patriotic impulse and spirit of self-sacrifice to counterbalance all our losses, defeats and disappointments. It is for our young men to study soberly the political as well as the economic condition of the country, to indulge less in platitudes and to have greater faith and confidence in their leaders. A spirit of honest enquiry is good, but a tendency towards hair-splitting arguments is a positive evil. Original ideas in this world are not so plentiful as blackberries, so that any one who passes by may pick them up. No one deprecates fair criticism, but captious criticism is a kind of dissipation which weakens the intellect and inebriates the mind. Besides, it cannot be too carefully borne in mind that in depreciating great men and measures we may sometimes unconsciously indulge in arguments simply to cover our own incapacity to follow them, or as a pretext for our inability to make necessary sacrifices. Every generation has its common succession of rights and responsibilities, and no generation can therefore safely indulge in intellectual profligacy without serious prejudice to the general estate and ultimate ruin and bankruptcy to its posterity. There are no doubt almost irresistible moments of depression in the life of a nation as of an individual; but it is also as true of the individual as of the nation, that the correct test of its strength does not consist in never falling, but in rising every time it falls. As this depression often proceeds from physical as well as mental and moral exhaustion, a rising people should be the quickest in shaking it off lest it should supervene in a collapse. The means by which the national life may be cured of its present depression and galvanized into fresh activities may be considered separately.

CHAPTTR XVIII.

REORGANIZATION OF THE CONGRESS.

A little reflection on the narrative as given in the foregoing chapters will probably shew that the history of the Congress so far roughly divides itself into four periods. The first three sessions held in Bombay, Calcutta, and Madras may be taken as the period of its inception during which the Congress propaganda was formulated and submitted, to the judgment of the country. From 1888 to 1896 was the period of its development during which that propaganda was, with the sanction and approval of the country, actively preached both in India as well as in England, the British Committee was established, an Indian Parliamentary Party organised and its organ '*India* started. In India the movement was properly organised by the establishment of provincial committees and a network of district organisations all working under the control and guidance of a central body known as the All-India Congress Committee. It was a period of vigorous adolescence marked by the zeal and earnestness of a rising spirit during which all the national forces and energies, were unfolded and brought to bear upon the realization of the ideal which had dawned upon the minds of the people. Roused to a full consciousness of the situation and with a comprehensive view of the endless restrictions and entanglements by which their normal growth and expansion as a nation were found closely barred, the people rapidly sunk all their differences and eagerly rallied under a common standard. In fact, many of the older institutions and associations were readily merged and absorbed in the swelling current of the new movement. It was a period of incessant activities in course of which the movement extended and received fresh reinforcements from every direction both here as well as in England. It was a sacred task for which no labour was deemed too exacting and no sacrifices either too onerous or too burdensome. This period was certainly not marked by any appreciable success, but the people were still borne up by unbounded hope and confidence.

The next decade from 1897 to 1908 was a prolonged period of a deadly struggle marked by the stubborn resistance of a reactionary government and the growing discontent of a people almost driven to despair by a series of violent, retrograde measures designed to curb the new spirit. Lord Curzon came to rule the country with an iron hand and set back the hand of progress in every direction. Beginning with the enactment of a fresh law of Sedition and a curtailment of Local Self-Government by the emasculation of the premier Municipal Corporation in the Metropolis and ending with the officialization of the Universities and the dismemberment of the foremost province of the Empire, the Earl of Keddlestone gave clear notice to the people that he was not going to tolerate the new spirit, and then as the situation became more and more acute with the inauguration of still more drastic repressive measures under the government of Lord Minto and the appearance of anarchy and lawlessness in the country, the people and the Government were almost at the parting of their ways and the Congress found itself placed between the devil and the deep sea. It, however, sat tight at the helm steering clear of all shoals and sands until superior British statesmanship was roused to a sense of the impending danger when at last there appeared like a silver lining in the threatening cloud the reform scheme of Lord Morley, which marked the first milepost in the fourth stage of the progress of the national movement. From 1908 starts a new chapter in the history of the Congress. The reform of the Councils was not however altogether a voluntary concession, and as it was practically wrung from Government it naturally lacked that generous and ungrudging support from the local authorities which alone could have ensured its full measure of success and secured an adequate appreciation of its benefits from the people. It has been truly said that even "rich gifts wax poor when givers prove unkind." Ever since then the policy of Government has been one of oscillation swinging forward and backward and attempting to treat the situation as it were with alternate dozes of concession and repression—a curious application of heat and cold as in a Turkish bath. That is the stage at which the movement has arrived after thirty years of patient labour. The duty of the Congress at this juncture is neither to fall back, nor to relax its energies; but to push forward with renewed zeal and earnestness to arrest this vacillation of Government which once removed it is bound to maintain a steady course of uniform progress.

Whether the success so far attained by the Congress be regarded as either gratifying or disappointing, it must be fairly conceded that the great task of nation-building in which it is engaged has been fairly started. It cannot be gainsaid, that if its progress has been slow and tedious, it has so far fairly succeeded in collecting men and materials, laying out a proper plan and in digging out a concreate foundation for the superstructure. It would be as grievous a mistake to regard its past labours as a wholesale failure, as to count the few outpost skirmishes it has won as complete victories. With the reform of the councils it may be said to have only driven the thin end of the wedge, and it is the duty of its members, however exhausted they may feel themselves, to screw up all their strength and strike ever more vigorously than before if all their past labours are not to be thrown away. With the changed situation its plan of action must however be somewhat modified to meet its altered condition. The old desultory method of the Congress was not without its use; but it has done its work for the preliminary stage of its operation by rallying the people under a common standard and mobilizing them for a regular campaign. It is now time for the movement to organize and direct the forces it has created to a regular and systematic course of action continuous in its nature, persistent in its character, and vigorous in its policy. It has now got to create fresh enthusiasm for its new operations and to galvanize itself for its future activities. The Congress must, therefore, be now re-organized on a permanent and substantial working basis. Its annual session must no doubt be maintained: but it should only be in the nature of an anniversary where it will review its year's work, take measure of the distance it has covered and then provide for the next stage of its advance. As at present carried on the annual session practically constitutes its sole existence. The All-India Congress Committee is no doubt a very useful organization; but from the very nature of its constitution it is adapted only to the requirements of a purely deliberative assembly without however an efficient executive agency behind it. That Committee can take no initiative, carry out no programme of action and discharge no function besides that of doing the work of a post office throughout the year and, if required ultimately, selecting a president for the Congress. But such a constitution is no longer permissible at the present stage of the national movement.

If the Congress is to make further progress and fulfil its mission, it must now be provided with a strong Executive Council with a fixed headquarter and an efficient staff regularly and systematically working out its programme all the year round. From an annual effervescent display the Congress should now be converted into a permanent living organization constantly at work and perpetually in session. The Congress has already got a complete network of territorial organizations in the Provincial Committees and the District and Taluka Associations established in all the provinces and throughout the country. Most of these have relapsed into a moribund condition, and it is high time that they were again galvanized and once more put into active operation to further the work of the Congress. The annual session of the Congress having formulated its programme of action, it should be the duty of the proposed Council or Committee, by whatever name it may be designated, to give effect to this programme by moving from time to time both the Government as well as Parliament, by organizing agitations whenever necessary, both here as well as in England with the help of its established agencies, by publishing tracts and leaflets circulated broadcast among the masses not only on matters political, but also bearing on social, educational, economic as well as sanitary improvements for the country, by establishing a regular mission for the spread of the Congress propaganda and by adopting such other means as may from time to time be found best calculated to further the cause of national development in all directions. Having the foregoing observations in view, the following practical suggestions may be made for a fresh revision of the Congress organization. There is no claim to any originality for any of these suggestions; nor is perhaps much of originality needed for an organization which has stood the test of nearly thirty years' experience.

It has already been pointed out in an earlier chapter that much of the lost enthusiasm for the movement is attributed by a section of the people to the hard-and-fast constitution provided for it by the Convention of 1908. Whether such an assumption is correct, or how far a relaxation of this constitution is likely to conduce to a substantial improvement of the situation, is a point on which there is ample divergence of opinion. For, while the non-Conventionists still maintain that their secession from the cause is due to that constitution, the bulk of the nationalist party hold that the constitution was necessitated by a wave of reaction which had already set in to wreck the movement and which has not as yet fully spent itself. Whether the Convention was really the cause or the effect of the waning of genuine enthusiasm in the cause is a perfectly unprofitable discussion in which no one need now indulge. Those who lightly indulge in threats that unless the rules and regulations of the Congress are modified the movement is "destined to die a natural death," ought to remember that there are those who are not so much afraid of a *natural* death as of a *violent* death for the movement. However there seems to have arisen during the last few years a genuine desire for a *rapproachment* between the two parties. There seems to be no longer any difference of opinion

RAO BAHADUR R. N. MUDHOLKAR
PRESIDENT, 1912

HON. NAWAB SYED MAHOMED
PRESIDENT, 1913

GOPAL KRISHNA GOKHALE, C I.E.,
PRESIDENT, 1905.

ANANDA MOHAN BOSE
PRESIDENT, 1898.

as to the main article of the constitution commonly called the creed of the Congress. The point of difference now seems to lie only in certain rules which though somewhat relaxed by subsequent Congresses are pressed for a further modification to meet the scruples of the Separatists. The first of these objection refers to the subscription to the creed and the second to the electorates of the Congress. The first is no doubt a purely sentimental objection, since the creed is admitted on all hands to be perfectly legitimate and unquestionable. But here the wishes of the non-Conventionists can easily be met by a provision to the effect that any one accepting a delegation to the Congress *shall be deemed to have subscribed to the constitution in all its details.* There seems to be no charm in a pen and ink signature unless there is sufficient guarantee in the personal honesty and character of a delegate; for there is nothing else to prevent a delegate from signing a declaration on the back of a six-inch piece of printed form and then after securing his admission into the *pandal* treat it as a scrap of paper used only as a passport. The real check, however, seems to lie in the electorates, and it is sufficiently safeguarded by the rules which limit the franchise to recognized associations and public meetings organized at the instance of such associations. This is sufficiently wide to admit of the election of everybody who is anybody in the country honestly to associate himself with the deliberations of the Congress. To ensure a proper observance of the last clause of this rule it may be necessarv to make the convening of such public meetings compulsory on the requisition of certain number of residents within a certain area, provided that not more than one such meeting shall be held for any such area and not more than a fixed number of delegates shall be elected at such a meeting. To throw open the election of delegates to every association or any kind of public meeting might not only expose the organization to further dismemberment, but would evidently take away much from the weight of its representative character. Anyhow if there is a reasonable spirit of mutual concession on both sides, a re-union does not appear to be at all difficult at the present stage, and it is a consummation which is devoutly to be wished for at an early date. The material gain of such a step may not ultimately prove to be very marked, but the moral gain will undoubtedly be quite considerable.

Another point which deserves earnest attention of the Congress is the development of its strength in another direction. It must have occurred to every thoughtful observer of the situation that the bulk of the landed aristocracy in the country have largely suffered a most deplorable relapse in their enthusiasm for the national movement. In the early stages of the movement they were inspired as any other community with a remarkable zeal for the advancement of the common cause. Maharajah Sir Luchmeswar Singh Bahadur of Durbhanga, the princely houses of Paikparah, Bhukaliash, Sova-Bazar and Utterparah, the Maharajah of Natore, the lineal representative of the historic Rani Bhavani, Maharajah Suryakanth Acharyee

Bahadur of Mymensingh and Maharajah Manindra Chandra Nandi of Cossimbazar and many other magnates in Bengal; Rajah Rampal Singh and the scions of not a few of the other historic Taluqdars of Oudh; Sirdar Dayal Singh of the Punjab ; the Rajah of Ramnad, the Zamorin of Calicut in whose territories the Parsis first found a hospitable refuge, Rajah Sir T. Madhava Rao and many others in the Southern Presidency, and last not the least, the merchant princes of Bombay, were all bodily with the national movement during the first period of its existence. It was since the Allahabad Congress of 1888 that like the Mahomedans they began gradually to secede from the movement, and the causes which led to their defection were very much similiar to those in the case of the Mussalmans. They were taught to think that their interests did not lie in the popular movement, although they were dubbed with the title of the "natural leaders" of the people. The more astute among them no doubt clearly saw through the game ; but there were other sinister influences at work which in their peculiar circumstances they were unable to resist though they heartily resented them. If the stories of some of these cases could be unearthed and brought to light there might be such a revelation as would probably scandalize a civilized administration and compromise not a few among the responsible authorities in the country. If the people were openly repressed, the landed aristocracy felt not a little the pressure of secret and subtle coercion. The case of the "conduit pipe" which is so well-known was only a typical illustration of many such cases which have gone unrecorded. Any how the bulk of this important community have fallen back, and it should be the earnest endeavour of Congressmen to strengthen their position by recovering their powerful help and co-operation. These fortunate possessors of wealth and influence ought also to remember that in a country where happily there neither is nor can be a permanent hereditary aristocracy any attempt on their part to establish after the Western model and artificial class by themselves is a delusion and a snare. Their legitimate position is at the head of the people from whose rank they rise and into whose rank they fall, and with whom they are indissolubly linked in blood and society. With all its defects there is in the mechanism of Indian social organization a democratic force which it is not possible even for the strongest to overcome. Besides, these wealthy men ought gratefully to acknowledge that the position of real power and authority, to which they have been recently admitted in the higher administration of the country, they owe primarily to the exertions of the people, and it may be no disparagement to them to say that these privileges, like the rich heritage which they enjoy, are practically unearned acquisitions for which injustice to themselves and to the country they ought to make a fair contribution to the common stock. The material help rendered by them as a class towards the beginning of the movement, is well-known and fully recognized; and if their stake in the country is much greater than those of others they cannot fairly refuse to make at least proportionate sacrifices for the common cause. They must have had sufficient experience of the insecurity of their isolated position and if they want really to safeguard their own interests they must cast in their lot with the people and abandon their ostrich-like policy. Many of them are men of culture and education, and they must know the difference that exists between marching in manly dignity at the head of one's own people and being dragged at the tail of guilded equipages for the glorification of other and stronger men with however no other recognition than that of a side glance with a smile or an empty title for all the indignities to which they are sometimes subjected. The British people with all their defects are a manly race and nothing is really more repugnant to their ideas and instincts than cringing servility and fawning hypocrisy.

It has already been observed that the movement stands in need of a readjustment and revision of its method of working. It is no doubt a deliberative body and it cannot be altogether divested of its deliberative character. But it has also a practical side in which it has to preach its propaganda, educate the mass, generate fresh enthusiasm and take definite steps towards the attainment of its objects. For doing all this in an efficient manner it must be provided with a permanent active organization working all the year round and throughout the country. If it is to have an active propaganda, it must have a permanent mission to carry it on. It ought to be provided with a permanent office at a fixed centre and a sufficient establishment regularly to carry on its work. The establishment must be paid. Honorary duties lack in vigour and persistency and carry no sense of responsibility with them. It may be found useful to attach this office to the All-India Congress Committee, which should have a responsible paid executive secretary working under the guidance and control of the Joint General Secretaries assisted by the General Committee. The Joint General Secretaries may be elected every year from the province in which the Congress is to hold its next session; but the Executive Secretary must be a whole-time permanent officer. From this office and under the sanction and authority of the All-India Congress Committee, approved tracts and leaflets translated into the vernacular languages of the country should be issued and circulated broadcast among the masses bearing on political, social, economic, sanitary and educational problems engaging the attention of the Congress and thereby a strong healthy public opinion should be created in the country on all the phases of the national life. Much may be done through these publications to direct a campaign against anarchism and other acts of lawlessness which are not only a stigma on the national character, but have also proved serious impediments to many a reform of the administration. Above all, there ought to be a systematic missionary work carried on in all the provinces explaining and impressing upon the public the real nature of the work upon which the Congress is engaged and upon a proper solution of which the future destiny of the country so largely depends. It has almost grown into a fashion among a certain class of people to decry the art of speaking. The cry is a meaningless, mischievous cant. Word without action may no doubt be useless like powder without shot; but the shot is equally ineffective without the use of the powder. Practical politics cannot be taught in Deaf and Dumb Schools by mere signs and symbols.

This missionary work cannot, however, safely be entrusted to immature and irresponsible agencies. It should be undertaken, at all events, at the outset by the leaders themselves. Each Provincial Committee may be left to choose or elect its own missionaries with their jurisdictions or circles defined and allotetd to them through which they must make occasional tours holding meetings and conferences for the dissemination of the Congress propaganda. If properly arranged, this need not very much interfere with the ordinary avocation of the missionaries themselves, while it is sure to bring them into closer touch with the people and secure for them a stronger hold upon the popular mind. While our public men are ever so justly persistent in their complaints against the aloofness and the unsympathetic attitude of the executive officers of Government, they cannot themselves consistently with their protestations live in a state of splendid isolation from their own countrymen. None of the leaders, not even the tallest among them, should consider himself above this work and grudge whatever little sacrifice it may involve, if the flame which they themselves have lighted is to be kept burning. The annual session of the Congress should thus become an anniversary of the movement at which the works done during the year by the entire organization should come under review and the operations of the next year carefully planned and laid before the country. Without being guilty of pessimism it seems permissible to draw the attention of the leaders of the movement even more pointedly to the future than to the present. The assets of a national life cannot be the subject of a free gift or a testamentary bequest: They must be the heritage of natural succession. Every generation of a nation succeeds to the acquisition of its past and, whether augmenting it with its own acquisitions or depreciating it by its own extravagance, is bound to transmit it to the next. The training of a succeeding generation is also an imperative task in the work of nation-building which cannot be accomplished in a single generation. If Rome was not built in a day, the Roman nation was not built even in a century. Those who have laid the foundation of a new structure in this country upon the shapeless ruins of its departed glories and upon whom the shadows of the evening are deepening may well pause for a moment and seriously consider whether they have sufficiently trained those upon whom their mantle will shortly fall. Of course "there may be as good fishes in the sea as ever came out of it"; but those who have spent their life-blood in the undertaking cannot better close their career than with a clear knowledge and confidence that they are leaving the work to successors who will carry on the work, raise it higher and if they cannot themselves complete it will at all events leave it far advanced for those who will come after them.

The next step in the reorganization of the movement must be directed to its work in England. The British Parliamentary Committee which after a brilliant career has ceased to exist should be restored. The euphimistic platitude that every one of the Six Hundred and odd members of the House, including of course Sir J. D. Rees, was a member for India, was only a paraphrase of a sounder and truer dictum that very man's business is no man's business, and Congressmen cannot forget that India received the largest amount of attention in England when the Parliamentary Committee was at its highest strength. In a Liberal House of Commons there are no doubt apparent difficulties for the maintenance of such a special body; but where both sides of the House can conveniently agree to treat India as being outside the scope of party politics, the existence of such a body, to watch the special interests of India, cannot be deemed either superfluous or anomalous. On the contrary, its absence is sorely felt in this country when the Liberals are apparently disposed to take long holidays under the spell of a nominal improvement of the situation which needs not only consolidation, but is also threatened with a reverse from underground sapping and mining operations in this country. In this as in every other operation at the main theatre of the struggle in which the Congress is engaged, its British Committee is its principal ally and no sacrifice can be deemed too heavy to maintain it in an efficient condition. That Committee ought also to be strengthened from time to time by the addition to its roll of prominent

Englishmen who evince a genuine interest in Indian problems. Sir William Wedderburn who has so long been the moving spirit of the Committee as well as of the Parliamentary Party and who has ever so freely and ungrudgingly sacrificed his time, energies and resources for the cause of India would probably be only too glad to undertake both these reforms if only the Indians themselves could make up their minds to supply him with the sinews of the operations. Mr. Dadabhai Naoroji, Mr. W. C. Bonnerjee and Mr. R. C. Dutt, practically settled in England, proved a tower of strength to the British Committee, and an earnest attempt should again be made to instal a couple of well-posted Indians at the seat of power to pilot the course of that important body. And lastly the paper *India* which is the sole organ of the Congress in England ought to be considerably improved and popularized in both countries. It must of course be conducted in England and by an Englishman thoroughly conversant with British politics and in full touch with the trend of British public opinion; but to make it more interesting and serviceable a few Indian publicists either as sub-editors or contributors ought regularly to co-operate with the editor in purveying Indian views on all important questions and making its columns more weighty and attractive to the British public.

Another remedy, though of an adventitious character, which suggests itself from some of the foregoing observations, refers to the concentration and co-ordination of all the public movements among which all the national forces are now distributed. The social and the industrial conferences are already closely associated with the Congress movement. But there are many other organizations which have sprung up in the country which are all crowded within the Christmas week at different places in absence of more convenient occasions. If it is not possible to deal with all of them, the Moslem League at all events should be held every year at the same centre and if possible in the same pavilion where the Congress is held either on successive or on alternate days. By this means not only all the communities may be brought into closer touch with one another but a greater enthusiasm may be secured for all of them. Since the League has already come into a line with the Congress, such an arrangement may not be at all difficult if the leaders of both the organizations will put their heads together and work out the details of the scheme.

It may be said that the above suggestions form a very large order; but large or small, some such order must be substantially complied with if the struggle is to be continued and further success achieved. To carry out a scheme of action which has for its object the regeneration of a nation through a process of evolution in which all the moral and intellectual forces on a subject people have not only to be called out and harmonized, but also arrayed against the colliding interests of a powerful dominant race, is no light work and cannot be approached with a light heart. The first and foremost condition of such a scheme is that of ways and means. A national organization must have at its back a national fund. As no sustained movement is possible without a well-defined organization, so no organization can subsist for any length of time without the sinews of war. If there is any depression in the movement it is largely due to the stagnation with which it is threatened in the absence of such an effective organization. It is no small surprise to many, that the movement has not collapsed within this sufficiently long period without a solid financial foundation for its basis. For thirty years it has fought out its way on a precarious dole annually voted to it and its agencies, the tardy realization of which has not a little hampered its progress. Its vitality is no doubt due to the intense patriotic sentiment that has been its underlying motive power ever since the movement was started; but even patriotism requires a healthy nourishment unless it is to degenerate into a spasm of fitful excitement and then die out like a flame fed only on straw. So early as 1889 it was proposed to establish a Permanent Congress Fund and a sum of Rs. 59,000 was voted to form the nucleus of such a fund. Out of this a small sum of Rs. 5,000 only was realized and deposited with the Oriental Bank which was then considered as the strongest Exchange Bank in India. In the Bombay crisis of 1890 the bank however went into liquidation and the small sum thus credited to the fund was lost. Ever since then no serious attempt has been made to re-establish this fund, and the undignified spectacle of one of the leaders at every session stretching out his beggarly "Brahminical hand" and the Congress going out hat in hand for a precarious subsistance allowance towards the maintenance of its British agency and its office establishment has contributed not a little to the bitter sarcasm of its critics, as much as to the mortification and discouragement of its supporters. The messages of Sir William Wedderburn alternately coaxing and threatening for financial help every year for the work of the British Committee seem to have lost their sting, and the whole business is carried on perfunctorily in an atmosphere of uncertainty and despondency. Complaints are often heard that the British Committee is no longer as efficient as it used to be. But whose fault is it if it has really fallen off from its pristine vigour and energy? It has certainly not deteriorated either in form or substance. Its weakness lies in its financial embarrassment created by our own inability to regularly meet its requirements for useful action. It is a bad policy to try to cover one's own failings by throwing dirt upon others. It cannot be denied that although the Congress has many critics, it is at present maintained only by the devotion and self-sacrifice of a small band of its supporters, who have always borne the brunt of the action, and strange as it may seem, its loudest detractors are to be found generally among those who have been least disposed to make any sacrifice in its cause and at the same time most exacting in their demands for its account. If the members of the Congress seriously mean, as they no doubt mean, to carry on its work and not throw away the immense labour and sacrifice of an entire generation, they should lose no more time in providing it with a permanent working organisation and investing it with a solid permanent fund sufficient to carry on the work before it efficiently and in a thoroughly methodical and business-like manner. The work before the Congress is much stiffer than its work in the past, and its present equipment must necessarily be of a more efficient and substantial character. If the Congress has so far successfully carried on a guerilla campaign it has now arrived at a stage where it must be prepared to fight the real issue involved in the struggle at close quarters, and for this no sacrifice in money or energy can be too great. In a country where fabulous sums are still available for a memorial hall, or a ceremonial demonstration, surely a decent contribution for the emancipation of a nation ought to be so difficult a task as to be beyond the capacity of genuine patriotic self-sacrifice. It would be a stigma and a reproach on our national character and a sad commentary on our patriotic fervour if after having advanced so far the national energy were to break down at this supreme moment with all tne sacrifices made, grounds gained and the prospects opened lost for ever.

CHAPTER XIX.

THE RECONSTRUCTION OF THE INDIAN CIVIL SERVICE.

Having so far cursorily dealt with the past career of the national movement and glanced over its present condition, a brief survey of the difficult task which awaits its future labours may not be deemed altogether out of place. Following the question of the reorganisation of the Congress, there is another very serious question which must sooner or later press itself upon the closest attention of its members: It is the question of the Indian Civil Service in which is vested the actual internal administration of the country. The Congress has so long discussed the questions of simultaneous examinations for the recruitment of that service, its age-limit, and the comparative importance of the various subjeccs of that examination from the Indian point of view. But these are all side issues forming, as it were, the mere fringes of the real crux of the case, which, divested of all shuffling and circumlocution, resolves into the plain question,—Is the Indian Civil Service, as at present constituted, to be the permanent basis of the Indian administration, or whether the time has not long arrived when that service should be thoroughly overhauled and reconstructed not only with reference to its own defects, but also in the light of the vast changes which the country has undergone and the enormous difficulties which have grown round the Indian administration? A little consideration of only three of the most vital points upon which the Congress has so far directed its main operations may afford a sufficient clue to the right investigation of this important question.

At the outset, the leaders of Indian public opinion appear to have strongly believed that the real remedy for nearly all the grievances of the people lay in the reform of the Legislative Councils and in that view their energies were largely directed towards the expansion of these Councils on a representative basis. Lord Cross' reforms of 1892, though it would be quite unfair to characterize them as mere lollypops, practically turned out to be very unsubstantial; while, eighteen years after, the very substantial reforms initiated by Lord Morley, also met with a similar fate. Although Lord Morley most gratuitously taunted the Indian public at the time with asking for "the moon," a prayer which they in their senses could never venture to make even to any one who may be supposed to be nearer that orb, yet people are not altogether wanting in this country who only after five years' experiment have come to regard his great reforms of 1910 as no more than mere moon-shine. The failure of these reforms, manacled and maimed in their operations by a set of Regulations framed in this country, has revealed the fact that there is one powerful factor which has to be seriously reckoned with in dealing with any real reform of the Indian administration. That factor is the strong, stereotyped Indian bureaucracy which stands between the Government and the people and can always make or mar the prospect of peaceful development of the country. The object of the best-intentioned legislative enactment may easily be defeated by those who must be ultimately entrusted with its practical application, and so the most generous measure of the British Parliament granted after full half a century of cool and collected deliberation has been allowed to be practically stranded on the bed-rock of bureaucratic opposition in India. The Councils, upon which the people built their hopes and pinned their faith, have been reformed and the popular representatives in much larger numbers armed with powers of interpellation, as well as of moving resolutions and dividing the Councils upon them; but the cry still is that these privileges have proved quite disappointing if not altogether illusory. The debates in these councils still retain their academic character, the results being generally a foregone conclusion. The most modest prayers of the representatives are sometimes summarily rejected and their most reasonable resolutions treated with scant courtesy or consideration; while, with a highly inadequate representation of the interests of the educated community on the one hand and a mischievous communal representation on the other, the real strength of the non-official members of these Councils has been reduced almost to an irreducible minimum.

Again, on the vexed question of the separation of judicial from executive functions, although there was apparently none to oppose the much desired reform, while every one seemed to be unreservedly in favour of it, a mysterious force has in spite of all the authoritative promises and pronouncements succeeded in shelving the proposal with the flimsiest of excuses and evasions which cannot deceive even the most credulous of schoolboys.

Then there is yet another question of vital importance upon which the Congress has directed its energies ever since its beginning: The admission of the children of the soil into the higher offices of the State having regard to their fitness and capacity for such appointments. It would be uncharitable not to recognise the fact that Government has in recent years shown a laudable disposition to admit, though very sparingly, the just and natural claims of the Indians to participate in the administration of their own country. But here again the galling injustice manifest in almost every department and which is the root cause of the popular dissatisfaction may easily be traced to a common source from which mainly flow all the other grievances of the people and the unpopularity of the administration. What is that source of mischief and where lies the remedy? Upon a closer examination of the situation, it will be found that the real obstacle to all substantial reforms in this country is the bureaucracy. It is the same narrow, short sighted and close-fisted official hierarchy which crippled Lord Ripon's early measure of Local Self-Government by a set of model Rules, practically over-riding the spirit if not the letter of the law, that has again successfully defeated Lord Morley's great scheme of national Self-Government by a set of Regulations circumscribing and barricading the measure in such a way as to render it almost important in substance though not in form. And it is this bureaucracy which in its nervousness, no less than in its blind selfishness, has stood bodily in opposition to the judicial reform and the admission of the children of the soil into its close preserves to which it believes to have acquired an exclusive and indefeasible right by virtue of its prescriptive enjoyment. The Indian Civil Service forms the citadel and the stronghold of this bureaucracy, and that service is so deeply saturated with selfish prejudices and so highly inflated with the legend of its natural superiority that it cannot heartily entertain any proposal of reform which necessarily militates against its vested interests and which if forced upon it by higher statesmanship naturally excites its secret opposition. The entire administration from the Government of India down to the smallest district charge, is practically vested in one train of officials who belong to this Service and who as such form a compact fraternity. They are, with honourable exceptions, traditionally conservative in their ideas and exclusive in their habits and manners, while their systematic training in the arts of autocratic government leaves little or no room for the development of those instincts which might go to curb their insular pride and inspire confidence and respect for those whom they are called upon to govern. In vain would one try to find a single instance in which, with very rare exceptions, the members of this Service have supported any great measure of reform of the administration which they as a body naturally regard either as an infraction of their status or as a reflection upon their capacity for good government. They apparently do not believe in the dictum of their own statesmen who have repeatedly held that no good government can be a substitute for a government by the people themselves. Very well-intentioned British statesmen coming out as Viceroys or Governors find themselves in the hands of the veterans of this Service and however strong they may be, they can hardly be sufficiently strong to overcome the deep-rooted prejudices and the all-pervading and overpowering influence of the bureaucratic atmosphere into which they are placed. Unless and until that atmosphere is cleared, it would be useless to expect any great results either from any parliamentary measure or from the ablest of Viceroys and Governors whom England may send out for the administration of her greatest dependency.

Nobody denies that the Indian Civil Service has a brilliant record in the past. It was eminently adapted to a period of consolidation when by its firmness and devotion to duty it not only established peace and order, but also inspired confidence in its justice and moral strength. But an archaic institution is ill-suited to a period of development in an organised administration and is an anomaly in an advanced stage of national evolution. The Indian Civil service has long outlived its career of usefulness, and however benevolent may have been the patronising methods of its administation in the past, those methods are neither suited to the present condition of the country nor are they appreciated by the people. Besides, people are not wanting who honestly believe that the halcyon day of the Indian Civil Service has long passed away, that it no longer commands the characteristic virtues of the sturdy Anglo-Saxon race and has largely degenerated into a mutual-admiration-society, demoralized to no small extent by the unrestrained exercise of its extensive powers and the extravagant adulations lavished upon it in season and out of season and sometimes beyond all proportion. It is no wonder that in the circumstances under which they are trained from youth to age in bureaucratic methods, the members of the Service should become obstinate, conceited and impatient of criticism. It is the system, more than any individual, that seems to be responsible for the decadence of this once magnificent Service. In point of compactness, the Service has been organised into a rigid caste system where it is impossible to touch it even in its remotest extremities without exciting the susceptibilities of the entire system. From the Lieutenant-Governor to the rawest assistant magistrate there seems to be established a magnetic current which is responsive to the mildest touch on the hereditary prerogatives of the service, and the highest demands of justice and fairness are sometimes cruelly sacrificed on the altar of a blind prestige, the maintenance of which appears to be the paramount consideration of the administration. Instances are not wanting where a young civilian insulting an Indian gentleman of position for no other offence than that of intruding upon his august presence without taking off his shoes, or walking before him with an open umbrella in his hand, is broadly justified by the head of a provincial administration; while the forcible ejection of an Indian member of a Legislative Council from a first class compartment in a railway carriage is hardly considered sufficient to call even for a mild rebuke. On the contrary, such is the idolatrous veneration for the *fetish* of prestige and so undisguised is the contempt displayed towards public opinion, that a stronger public censure passed upon the vagaries of an erring member of the Service has come to be regarded almost as a passport for his advancement rather than as a drawback in his official career. Young men just above their *teens*, who are probably bad enough for the Home Service and not good enough for the Colonial, are generally supposed to be drafted for the Indian Civil Service and, placed in important positions of trust and responsibility, they learn more to depend upon the extensive powers, privileges and immunities attaching to that Service than upon the art of governing well. Whip in hand, they learn only to sit tight without acquiring the easy grace of an accomplished rider. They are often placed when only a few months in the country in charge of sub-districts, some of which are larger than an English county and as they rise with the official tide, they carry with them the accumulations of their earlier training. They generally seem to have a peculiar ethics of their own in which conciliation is tabooed as a sign of weekness and popularity as a disqualification. They love more to be dreaded than to be respected. Such is the obstinacy of their infallibility that once a suspect always a suspect. A man may be honourably acquitted by the highest tribunal in the land; but if he is fortunate enough not to be rearrested upon some other charge as soon as he leaves the dock, he is sure to be dogged all the rest of his life until that life becomes a burden to him and he is goaded to desperation. The success and delight of the administration seem to consist more in chasing the criminal than in reforming the society. In every civilised country, the courts of justice have the last word on every difference between an administration and the people; but here in India the bureaucracy seems to have very little scruple to sit at times in judgment over His Majesty's judges, and committees and commissions of the members of the Service who are ordinarily subordinate to them are sometimes appointed to review the decision of even the highest tribunals in the land. The spectacle is neither decent nor dignified which slowly undermines all respect for the administration of justice in the country. All this constitutes what is termed the efficiency of the administration. These may be called little accidents; but they mark the trend of a decaying Service and point to the source of the unpopularity it has so largely earned. The greatest loss which England has suffered in her connection with India is perhaps the moral deterioration she is silently undergoing in the manly dignity of her national character in exchange for her material gains. It is neither army nor commerce, but it is moral greatness, that constitutes the most valuable and enduring asset of a nation, and if England has to fear from any quarter it is mostly from the "voluntary exiles" who having passed the best portions of their lives in the enervating climate of India and getting themselves practically divorced from lofty British principles, every year go to swell the colonies at Chelmsford and Bayswater.

It is persistently claimed for the Indian Civil Service that it is the best Service which human ingenuity has ever devised for the administration of any country in this world. The Indians have, however, no experience of any other system, and as such they are equally precluded from either implicitly accepting or summarily rejecting such a strong verdict. It seems, however, incomprehensible to the average Indian intellect what peculiar charm there may be in any particular stiff examination in certain subjects, which are taught all over the civilised world, so as to make every one successfully passing that examination proof against all lapses and failures in practical life. It cannot be argued that there is anything mysterious in the method or manner of that examination which necessarily sifts the grain from the chaff in British society and turns out what is best or noblest in British life. And where is the evidence that any other system of recruitment for the Indian Civil Service would not have served the purpose equally well if not better? Is the Civil Service in Great Britain less efficient because it is not trained in the methods of a close bureaucracy? Then what becomes of the hollow fallacy underlying this boasted claim for the Indian Civil Service when the open competitive examination for the Subordinate Civil Service was found after a brief experiment not to be congenial to the Indian administration? Probably it will be urged that what is sauce for the goose is not sauce for the gander.

The real crux of the case, however, appears to be this: The Indian Civil Service, however glorious its past record may be, is, after all, one of the *services* of the State and it ought never to have been allowed to usurp the function of the State itself. The duties of a service are to carry out the policy of a government and to discharge with efficiency and devotion the functions entrusted to it in the general distribution of work of the State. In the Indian administration the covenanted Civil Service not only administers the work, but also dictates the policy, distributes the work and supervises it. In short, the State is merged in the Service and all distinction between the Service and the State has practically disappeared. The best candidates who successfully pass the Civil Service Examination every year are generally retained for the Home Service and yet they are nowhere in the Government and have no hand in determining the policy of the State. In India, however, the term *Service* is a misnomer: for the Service and the State are interchangeable, or, more correctly speaking, the one is entirely lost in the other. Wherever such a condition prevails, principles of constitutional government fly through the windows and the establishment of bureaucratic rule becomes an imperative necessity.

The most orthodox argument invariably advanced in support of the Indian Civil Service is that experience has shown that it is best suited to the condition of the country and that its past achievements are a guarantee to its future success. But in this it is apparently ignored that the country itself has undergone stupendous changes in point of education, political training and economic development. An entirely new generation has come into existence inspired by a lofty sense of duties and responsibilities, as well as of the rights and privileges, of true citizenship; while there is no dearth of men who, by their education, training and character, are quite capable of holding their own against the best men in the Service. The ideas of rights and liberties, as well as of self-respect, of this new generation of men is quite different from those of their predecessors who were content to eke out their existence purely under official patronage. The overdrawn picture of Lord Macaulay has not the slightest resemblance to the present condition of the country and its people, who have undergone a complete transformation within the last half a century of which the British nation ought to be justly proud instead of being either jealous or nervous. And is it to be supposed that, amidst all these changes and evolutions of time, the one Service in which the Government of the country has been vested since the days of Tippoo Sultan and Lord Cornwallis is to remain immutable and unchangeable? Granting that the Indian Civil Service has a splendid record behind it and admitting that it has produced in the past excellent public servants whose "devotion to duty is unparalleled in the history of the world," do not the marked changes which both the people and the Government have undergone during the life-time of two generations call for even a revision of that Service? The Indian Civil Service was organised in 1858, and can it be decently contended that any human institution, particularly an administrative machinery, can be so perfect as not to admit of some modification in more than fifty years at least to adapt itself to its shifting environments? It would evidently be a most extravagant claim even for a scientific invention or discovery.

The indictments thus preferred against the proud Service, which forms the pivot of the Indian administrative machinery and which a recent Royal Commission has been asked to recognise as the accepted basis of its investigation, may be regarded in some quarter as rather too strong. But whether strong or mild, the indictments are not perhaps an unfaithful reflex of the Indian view of the situation ;- and if Government is really anxious to ascertain public opinion on the merits of its administration, they may not be regarded as either offensive or altogether gratuitous. Then, these charges do not appear to be altogether unsupported by facts and arguments to which competent opinions, other than Indian, have also from time to time subscribed in no uncertain language. Mr. D. S. White, the late president of the Eurasian and Anglo-Indian Association, who but for his premature death would have certainly adorned, like Mr. George Yule, the distinguished roll of the Congress presidents, was present among the distinguished visitors at the first Congress held in 1885. Speaking, however, on the question of the Indian Civil Service which was being hotly discussed by the delegates, Mr. White said :—

"The proposition contains an application for raising the competitive age in England of candidates for the Civil Service, and for holding examinations simultaneous in India. On both the points I differ. I do not think the remedy is in raising age, but in procuring the gradual abolition of the Civil Service. What we need, I think, is that the future importation of boys should be put a stop to. The real education of these boys takes place in India and the State is put to enormous expense in connection therewith, while there is no need for the expenditure. The State now has at hand indigenous talent, educated at its own expense, either locally or in England and should take advantage of it, and if it requires special talent from England it may import it just as men ready-made are imported for the Educational Department. For the Judicial Service, the Bar in India offers itself, and why boy-civilians should be paid for years to learn to become judges is a matter not easily understood."

Mr. White was clearly of opinion that the competitive system should be abolished and that "men of eminence and skill alone, in any profession, should be brought out on limited covenants." This was said thirty years ago by a man who was universally respected for his sobriety of views and dispassionate judgment. It cannot be disputed that both India and the Government of India to-day are as different from what they were in 1885 as the butterfly is from the catterpillar, and yet how strange that methods, arrangements and conditions which were considered ill-adapted even to the rearing of the larva are sought to be applied without any amendment for its nourishment in its full-grown form. Sir Henry Cotton, who with just pride recalls that for a hundred years his family have been members of the Indian Civil Service and himself a most distinguished member of that service, who by sheer force of his character and abilities rose to the position of the head of a provincial administration, has quite recently again brought the question prominently to the notice of the public. It is now nearly thirty years that Sir Henry with his characteristic frankness and intimate knowledge of the Indian administration raised his warning voice that "the Indian Civil Service as at present constituted is doomed." Then in 1888, while giving evidence before the Indian Public Service Commission, he formulated a reconstructive policy;

but he was brushed aside as a "visionary." Now that another Royal Commission has been appointed to enquire into the Indian Public Services, Sir Henry Cotton has again returned to his charge. Writing in the *Contemporary Review* and commenting on the terms of reference to the Commission, which apparently assume the existing constitution as the permanent basis of Indian administration, Sir Henry Cotton says:

> "But what is wanted now is no scheme for bolstering up the decaying fabric of a Service adapted only to obsolete conditions which have passed away and never can return."

Calmly considered, without passion or prejudice, the question would appear to be, no longer one of repair, but of reconstruction. A sudden drastic change may, however, be found as impracticable as it may be inexpedient. At the same time it should be recognised that any attempt to revitalize a system which has long run its normal course by means of a variety of make-shifts, proposed by those who are naturally interested in anyhow preserving the ancient monument to which they are deeply attached by tradition and sentiment as well as by the supreme instinct of self-love, is bound to be a costly failure. The inadaptability of that system to the present condition of the country is writ large in almost every page of the records of an administration extending over the lifetime of a generation, and instances are neither few nor far between where a truly benevolent Government has often incurred unnecessary odium owing chiefly to its lingering affection for a spoilt service. That affection has now practically grown into a blind superstition under the spell of which none dare take any serious step towards its correction. Speaking of the *morale* of the administration, Sir Henry Cotton frankly observes:

> "When once the sacred name of *prestige* has been sounded as a civilian war-cry by such a bureaucracy as we have in India, with vested interests clamouring for protection, it is no simple matter to solve any problem of reconstruction. No Viceroy has hitherto been strong enough to deal with the question."

For thirty years the people have cried hoarse for the separation of judicial from executive functions. Successive Viceroys and Secretaries of State have repeatedly declared themselves in favour of this "counsel of perfection." But successfully has the Indian bureaucracy resisted the proposal upon the sole ground that it would impair its prestige, the only other plea of double expense having been neatly disposed of by the various practical schemes formulated by the different provinces for an effective separation of the two functions. This prestige, however, the Indian public understand as meaning nothing more than the immunity which the bureaucracy enjoys in the exercise of its arbitrary powers and the protection which the unholy combination affords against its incompetency to carry on the administration in the ordinary way. Nowhere is this incompetency more glaringly disclosed than in the judicial administration of the country. If the queer experiences of practising lawyers in the country could be collected and published it would form a very amusing, though somewhat grotesque and humiliating, catalogue of the strange vagaries and colossal ignorance of the young civilian judges as regards the law and procedure of the country; and these young civilians are as a rule called upon not only to control the subordinate judiciary, but also to sit in judgment over the decisions of veteran Indian officers of established reputation and long experience. The disastrous result of such a system may easily be imagined.

"The Bar in India," says the high authority just quoted, "is daily becoming stronger than the bench, and the ignorance of law and practise exhibited by junior civilians who are called on to preside over the judicial administration of a district—not to speak of the executive tendencies which are the inevitable accompaniment of their earlier training—has become a source of danger which will not be remedied by a year's study in a London barrister's chamber, or by passing the final examination at an inn of court."

Like all old orthodox institutions, the Indian Civil Service has become saturated with strong prejudices against all popular aspirations and even the rawest recruits for that Service are not often free from conceited notions of their superiority and importance much above their desert. It may be no exaggeration to say that like Narcissus of old that Service is so enchanted with the loveliness of its own shadow that it has neither the leisure nor the inclination to contemplate beauty in others. Its devotion to duty may be unquestioned; but its superstitious veneration for its own prestige is much stronger. It is generally opposed to change and is always afraid of being regarded as weak. It has acquired all the characteristics of an antiquated institution which, unable to adapt itself to its modern environments, is always great in the worship of its great past. "The Indian Civil Service," says Sir Henry Cotton, "is moribund and must pass away after a prolonged period of magnificent work to be replaced by a more popular sytem which will perpetuate its efficiency while avoiding its defects." Rightly understood, there is no censure or disparagement in this ; for every human institution has its rise, its progress and its decay and the world is ever marching onwards through a process of changes and evolutions.

It is admitted on all hands that the Indian administration is the most costly and elaborate in the world and unless means are devised for an early revision of this huge and expensive machinery it stands the risk of being threatened with a collapse. The most obvious remedy lies in the reconstruction of the entire Civil Service, by gradually replacing the Covenanted Service by uncovenanted indigenous materials which may be found cheaper and not less efficient. There is no longer any dearth of such materials in the country although the bureaucracy is naturally ever so loud in their disparagement and in the advertisement of its own superior stuff. There is scarcely a department of the civil administration where, given the opportunity, the Indians have not proved their fitness and capacity to hold their own against foreign competition. Of course where any special qualification or expert knowledge may be needed it may be imported on a limited covenant ; but surely no country can be in such an awful plight as to be unable to do for a century without an army of covenanted officers on extravagant salaries with Exchange Compensation Allowances for the administration of its domestic concerns.

It is suggested that as a first step towards the reconstruction of the Indian Civil Service, the Judicial branch should be completely and effectively separated from the Executive branch of the service and the former recruited from the Bar as in England, though other sources must also be availed of at the experimental stage to avoid violent disruption as well as possible injustice to existing vested interests. The subordinate civil Judiciary is no doubt at present primarily recruited from the Bar, though it is afterwards crystallized into a rigid orthodox body beyond the charmed circle of which its members cannot move. But the original recruitment being mostly from among the inferior and inexperienced elements of the Bar, the subsequent outturn of the present system necessarily fails, with of course honourable exceptions, either to command the respect and confidence of the public, or adequately to satisfy the demands of the public service. The subordinate criminal judiciary, as at present constituted, is still more unsatisfactory. The competitive examination which annually used to introduce into the service a fair leaven of distinguished graduates of the Universities having been abolished, for reasons widely known throughout the country, that service is now entirely founded on the patronage of the bureaucracy naturally leading to a state of demoralization which has practically reduced the rank and file into three-quarters executive and only one-quarter judicial officers of the State. As a preliminary, therefore, to the reorganisation of the Indian Civil Service the judicial service being completely separated and reconstructed on the lines indicated above, the entire Judicial administration should be vested in the High Courts, which to be worthy of the British constitution should be at once freed from the trammels of bureaucratic provincial administrations. The administration of British justice, more than the British arms, has been the bulwark of the British Empire in the East, and they are the greatest enemies of that Empire who either directly or indirectly work towards undermining that basal strength of its greatness. If the Indian Nationalist wants to make definite progress and to secure himself against disappointment even after a victory, he must go to the roots of the question and boldly face the situation however stiff the fight may be. The Indian National Congress has at last arrived at a stage when it can no longer burke the question of the reorganisation of the Indian Civil Service, and if it has necessarily to proceed step by step, it cannot afford to loose sight of its real objective and avoid the great struggle as well as the great secrifices to which it has committed itself and the nation.

CHAPTER XX.

INDIAN REPRESENTATION IN BRITISH PARLIAMENT.

The reform of the Legislative Councils is no doubt justly regarded as a great triumph of the Indian National Congress. It has for the first time recognised the elective principle in the government of this country and invested these councils with the form, though not the substance, of representative institutions. But although it may be somewhat premature to hazard an opinion as to the probable outcome of this scheme, the comparative ease and freedom with which it has been allowed to be circumscribed, mutilated and crippled in its operation at the hands of a nervous bureaucracy, have furnished no small excuse for the disappointment and scepticism evinced by a section of the people as regards the ultimate result of such an experiment. Apart from its immediate results, the value of which need not be either under-rated or over-estimated, it seems fairly permissible to these critics to ask, whether any further expansion of these councils, on the only lines upon which such expansion appears to be possible in the existing temper of the bureaucracy, can be very much counted upon to lead to a substantial reform of the administration, or to any appreciable development of the political status of the people? That the reform scheme pointed to such an aim there can be no mistake, and that it was fully intended to operate towards that end there need be no doubt. But the point is, does the reform scheme, as actually carried out, really provide a constitution which in its normal development is likely to bring about the desired improvement either in the one or the other? Lord Morley quite superfluously observed, that he could not give us the moon; for no one in this country ever asked for the moon. But has his Lordship ever enquired, whether the great scheme of reform which he took so much pains to carry through both the Houses of Parliament has or has not been practically converted into stone when the people cried for bread? Supposing, for instance every district in a province were allowed, in course of a gradual expansion of this reform, to return a member to the local council and the number of members for the Supreme Council were raised from 75 to 750, would the people gain or the bureaucracy lose an inch of ground under such an expansion if the official element were always to maintain its corresponding level proportionate to this increase? Then again the right of interpellation and the right of moving resolutions are no doubt valued rights; but even if the representatives of the people were to be armed with the right of moving a vote of want of confidence in the Government, would these rights mean much unless they were capable of influencing the policy of the administration? A resolution *carried* is as good as a resolution *lost* when it carries no binding force with it and all the animated discussion in a council serves only the purpose of letting out a quantity of extra steam or of gratifying a Governor's admiration for eloquence. If the power of the purse is ever to remain a forbidden fruit to the people, of what earthly good is it for their representatives to annually enter into a mock-fight over the budget? The whole atmosphere of the reformed councils as they stand is one of unreality and largely of dramatic interest. The normal expansion and development of such rights and privileges for any length of time cannot, therefore, be calculated very much either to advance the status of the people, or to popularize the administration. A proper exercise of such rights may no doubt occasionally produce a certain amount of moral pressure; but moral pressure by itself is of very little consequence in practical politics, particularly such politics as are commonly practised by a bureaucratic administration in a subject country. Lastly, the incalculable mischief which the Regulations have done, by providing water-tight compartments in representation and creating vested interests, is a serious blow to the national development from which the country is not likely to recover either very soon, or without the united efforts of the people.

The wholesome changes initiated by Lord Morley's Act of 1909 and the impetus it has generated in the body politic in this country must, therefore, be supplemented by other forces not only to counteract the retrograde policy of the Regulations, but also to prevent the reforms granted, like so many other reforms neutralised almost in their inception, from relapsing into a lifeless, rigid official formula to be mechanically repeated for another generation without any variation and in compliance with the letter without the spirit of these reforms. The most effective of these forces must no doubt come from within and not without. The people must train themselves in the art of evolving constructive policies and not merely indulge themselves in destructive criticisms. They must learn calmly to weigh the two sides of a question and take the most practical and not the most dramatic view of a situation. And, above all, they must be thoroughly characterised by honesty of purpose and firmness of determination and inspired by a spirit of lofty, patriotic self-sacrifice which is calculated to sink all differences and merge all personal considerations into the common well-being of the nation. Proper discipline is as much needed in national development as in military organisation, and the Indian bureaucracy furnishes the most striking object-lesson of the value of such discipline. The evolution wrought by the national movement during the last thirty years is no doubt very remarkable; but it would be a grievous error not to recognise the serious defects which still underlie our national character and constitute its weakness. A robust, healthy public opinion, divested of prejudice and passion and founded upon impartial observation and careful study, carries with it not only a highly educative effect; but is the most potent safeguard against national demoralization. It is the only censor of all lapses and aberrations in public life. It is as useless, as it is harmful, to disguise the fact, that the public in this country are still much given to carping criticism and abuse. Self-confidence is indeed a virtue, but self-conceit is a vice which, like a slow deleterious poison imperceptibly undermines the intellectual and moral constitution of an individual as well as of a nation. The habit of thinking the oneself is indeed to be diligently cultivated; but the practice of immature young men sitting in judgment over the decisions of veteran public men and lightly formulating chimerical ideas of which they can have no clear conception is very much to be deprecated in their own interest as well as in the interest of the public of whom they are the future asset. Honest emulation is indeed to be desired, but not arrogance. True patriotism is not a mere passive sentiment, but an active energy which in its proper exercise strengthens the nerves, stimulates the will, broadens the vision and purges nature of all its dross. It is the most valuable asset of national existence. With the loss of this one supreme virtue, India had once lost nearly all the glories of her past and with its revival dawns her present regeneration. At this renaissance there is indeed no lack of bright examples of patriotic devotion to duty; but it cannot be denied, that there is also no want of cracked coins still in circulation in this country. These false currencies are not only a deception but also a sure token of the moral trupitude of a nation. In an enlightened community thoroughly imbued with a stern sense of public responsibility, it should be practically impossible for all milksops and blotting papers to secure public trust as a means to their personal advancement at the sacrifice of public interest. For all these, the people themselves must be held responsible, and the pace of their progress must be graduated by the scale of their development of these national virtues.

But while it is perfectly true that most nations get as good a government as they deserve, it cannot be disputed that the conditions of a subject people are materially different from those of a free country, and that as such the development of both cannot be governed precisely by the same rules. In a free country the government itself is based upon public opinion and cannot but be guided by that opinion in its adaptation to the demands of public interest which is the very essence of its existence. In a subject country, particularly where the overning class and the governed are perfect aliens to each other, there is always some amount of colliding interest which naturally precludes a fusion of the two elements and thus deters the progress of the people which accordingly becomes more largely dependent on the support of the Government. Where the State is perfectly independent of the people, the political advancement of the latter becomes almost an impossibility without proper facilities and opportunities afforded by the former. The people must, therefore, look to the supreme authority from which has emanated the present reforms for their future growth and expansion. It is the British Parliament which must apply the necessary force to correct the defects of the present system and remove the various impediments which have been thrown to arrest the progress of its future development. The British public are mostly ignorant of the actual state of affairs in this country, while the British Parliament is naturally disposed to content itself with the thought that when a reform has once been granted, it is bound to take its usual course and that the administrations in India may be fully depended upon loyally to carry out its policy. Unfortunately, however, such is not the case, and the Indian public are driven to the necessity of constantly knocking at the gate of the House which is always so carefully guarded by some well-trained Cerberuses, not a few of whom have fattened themselves upon the salt of India, but owe no allegiance to her, that their most reasonable complaints are easily drowned in the howling raised by these watch-dogs. But the people must knock and knock, until the gate is opened to them.

If India is to be redeemed through British connection, the battle of India must be fought on British and not Indian soil. It is to the British public and the British Parliament that India must look for her ultimate redemption.

The best means therefore of having Indian's voice heard in England is to have some persons directly to represent her in Parliament. As has already been pointed out, Henry Fawcett was the first to assume the title of "Member for India," although he too had to apologise to his constituency for devoting some portion of his time and attention to the affairs of India. Next came Charles Bradlaugh, to whom the title was conceded by his colleagues more as a nickname than as a genuine compliment. But perhaps the highest representation which India ever obtained in the House of Commons was through the Parliamentary Committee which was so successfully organised mainly through the efforts of the much-abused British Committee of the Congress. This Committee at one time counted upon its roll no less than 200 members of Parliament, and a careful student of Indian politics will have no difficulty in finding that they were a tower of strength to India and that the persistent agitations which they kept up in the House were at the root of most of the reforms which have recently been inaugurated in the administration of this country. Those were the halcyondays of the Congress. But that Committee has been dissolved and it has naturally ceased to exist under a Liberal Parliament and is not likely to be fully revived even under the next Conservative Government.

The question of direct representation for India in the British House of Commons therefore comes to the forefront of the future programme of the Congress. The question is not altogether a new one. It was first noticed by Mr. Dadabhai Naoroji in his presidential address at the Lahore Congress of 1893. But for ten years the Congress apparently took no notice of it until 1904 when it unanimously adopted the following Resolution :—

"That in the opinion of the Congress the time has arrived when the people of this country should be allowed a larger voice in the administration and control of the affairs of their country by (*a*) the bestowal on each Province or Presidency of India of the franchise of returning at least two members to the British House of Commons."

The Resolution was tacked on to the more immediate questions of the expansion of the Legislative Councils and the appointment of Indian members to the India Council as well as to the Executive Councils of the Government of India and the Presidency Governments of Bombay and Madras. It was again repeated in 1905 ; but owing partly to the immediate pressure of reforms nearer at home and partly because of the serious troubles into which the country was plunged since 1905 this important question was allowed to be dropped from the programme of all subsequent Congresses. But the spirit in which the expansion of the councils has been carried out and the manner in which effect has been given to the reform of the Executive Councils, from which popular leaders of exceptional abilities appear to have been carefully excluded for reasons which are not perhaps too far to seek and which the bureaucracy apparently does not care much to conceal, would seem to call for the revival of the question with all the the vigour and earnestness which it obviously demands. It is the high pressure of Parliament which is absolutely needed to keep an obstructive bureaucracy abreast of the times and to enforce ungrudging compliance with its supreme mandates. And it goes without saying, that such a pressure can be generated only by India's own representatives in the House. If it be true, that "it is not England's heart that is steeled against India, but it is her ear that is deaf to her cries," then it follows that the highest endeavour of the Indian nationalist should not be confined to the loudest cries raised in India, but directed towards their gaining access to the ear of England.

The tremendous influence of Parliamentary representation may be judged from two sources. The labours of Sir Henry Cotton, Sir William Wedderburn and the other members of the unofficial Indian Parliamentary Committee are well known to the public and it must be remembered that they were all Britishers and constitutionally represented certain British constituencies only. Mr. Dadabdai Naoroji was the first Indian who ever sat in a British Parliament. He too sat not for Bombay, but for Central Finsbury. But such was the moral influence of the presence of this "black man" in the House that it at once excited the jealousy and nervousness of a conservative premier and led to the hasty return of another black man who was none the whiter because he was set up in the conservative interest.

The other and the more potent example is furnished by Ireland. Ireland like India has been fighting for her national emancipation for a much longer time and with much greater determination and unquestionably with incomparably superior advantages on her side. Yet Ireland, with Parnell on one side of the Irish Channel and Gladstone on the other, was unable to make one-tenth of the impression which she has now made upon Great Britain with Redmond in Ireland and Asquith in England. Nobody would ever venture to suggest that the present great leader of the Irish Party and the present distinguished premier of England are stronger personalities than the "uncrowned king of Ireland" and the "Great Commoner" of England; but nevertheless the success of the former is more decided and remarkable than the failure of the latter. It is the seventy odd Nationalist members in the House who holding the balance of power in their hands have turned the scale and decided the question of Irish Home Rule. It is practically the same question with which the Indian Nationalist is concerned :—It is National Self-Government within the Empire, or Home Rule for India. And the Indian people must be armed with similar weapons to carry the struggle to a successful conclusion. If two dozens of Indian representatives were to be admitted into the British House of Commons, they would not only by themselves form an important factor in the House; but a party would naturally grow round them which would undoubtedly exercise considerable influence in shaping the policy of Government and doing adequate justice to India. It would then be impracticable for the Indian bureaucracy to tamper or tinker with the wholesome provisions of any Parliamentary statute or to impede the normal growth of Indian nationalism. Bureaucracy may shudder at the prospect of such an innovation, but true statesmanship can hardly fail to realise that it would form a permanent cement and a bond of indissoluble union between England and India, the value of which, as the most precious assets of Great Britain, even the most blatant jingo would be bound to admit. It must be a process of gradual fusion and not of increasing dominance that will permanently secure British rule in India.

India certainly desires British connection; but it is a connection of co-partnership based upon mutual trust and confidence and comradeship in rights and responsibilities but not of permanent subjection which she aims at. The kind of connection commonly known as liege-lordism was sought to be enforced by Western civilisation in America, Africa and in other dark corners of the world, and it led to the extirpation of the weaker races. But India possesses a civilisation and literature older than that of Greece and Rome and even older than that of Egypt and Phœnicia which are still the admiration of the modern world. She still boasts of cities and towns which flourished before Babylon and Nineveh came into existence. She has withstood the revages of time and revolutions of ages which have swept over her often leaving their deep scars upon her; but neither the one nor the other have succeeded in wiping her out of existence, or even in disfiguring her beyond identification. She possesses a wonderful vitality which has, on the contrary, assimilated and absorbed most of the civilisations which came in contact with her and which she was unable either to resist or counteract. And to-day she is the common home of the Hindu, the Mussalman, the Parsi, the Jain, the Buddhist and the Christian. Such a country may be conquered, but not held in prepetual bondage. None of her many conquerors succeeded in doing so, and it would be a grievous mistake if Great Britain should either intend or attempt to make such an experiment. Militarism can subjugate countries, but cannot enslave a civilised people. India, emancipated and consolidated into a federal unit, will constitute the strongest cement of the British Empire; whereas emasculated, impoverished, distrusted and discontented, she is bound to be a standing menace to her true greatness and is likely to prove her greatest weakness in an hour of danger. England must be prepared to admit India into the Councils of the Empire if she is to be honestly treated as an integral part of that Empire. She must cease to be her greatest Dependency and rise to the dignity of her foremost Dominion, and her people should be treated not as paying subjects but as privileged citizens of that Empire. The misfortune is that so few Englishmen know much of ancient Indian History and fewer still command an insight into ancient Indian civilisation and have, therefore, so little sympathy and respect for Indian aspirations.

Reverting to the immediate question of Parliamentary representation, it may be pointed out that from the Queen's Proclamation down to the latest Royal declaration of George V, there was not a single authoritative pronouncement made which did not hold out the hope that the Indian people would be treated in all respects as "equal subjects" of Great Britain and entrusted with rights and privileges of British citizenship to which they by their position and education may be found entitled: and the people would naturally resent it as an evasion of these solemn pledges if, after they have been tried and found not unworthy of representative institutions, they should be still debarred from their legitimate position of representing their country's interest in the supreme Legislative assembly of the Empire of which they form such an important factor. Besides, if France has found no difficulty in extending such an important franchise to her handful of Indian subjects and thereby recognising them as free citizens and co-partners of the great Republic, it is no small or fancied grievance of the three hundred and odd millions of British Indian subjects, that they should stand carefully excluded from a fair participation in the rights of the British Empire although they have to bear more than a fair share of its responsibilities. It cannot be, and will perhaps never be, contended that Chandernagore is more advanced than Calcutta, Pondicherry than Madras, or Mahe than Bombay; or, that French Government have lost either in strength or prestige or efficiency by reason of the admission of their Indian and African subjects, either in the army or in the

Chamber of Deputies. Vigorous efforts should, therefore, be made to secure proper and adequate repesentation for India directly in the British House of Commons.

CHAPTER XXI.

INDIA IN PARTY POLITICS.

There is another question of difficulty which must shortly engage the attention of the Congress and its members. As often as an important question of Indian reform is raised for discussion, a studied, stereotyped cry is invariably raised both in the British Parliament as well as in the British Press, that India must be kept outside the pale of party politics in England. This earnest solicitude can evidently mean one of two things: It may either mean that India is regarded as too "great and solemn a trust of Providence" to be entrusted to the wrangling and rancorous spirit of the two hostile political parties which decide the fate of the rest of the British Empire; or it may mean, that India is a rich preserve in common held under a common agreement and for the benefit of both the parties which cannot, therefore, be allowed to be an apple of discord between them. Whatever may be the correct interpretation of the pléa thus advanced, its one effect has always been to perpetuate India's wrongs and to defer Indian reforms by either party in England. The grim humour of the situation, however, lies in the fact that India must alternately come under a Liberal or Conservative Government and be ruled by a Liberal or Conservative Secretary of State, while the anomaly is sometimes allowed to assume a most awkward position when a conservative Viceroy is permitted to govern India under a Liberal Government in England. The result of such an arrangement has invariably been found to involve a partial surrender of Liberal principles and a consequent sacrifice of India's best interests. Individual members may have occasionally nobly fought for justice to India; but seldom has Parliament risen to the height of such occasions for an adequate redress of her wrongs. The best of fights for India on the floor of the House has in recent years ended in a compromise where neither party has suffered any defeat and both parties have come out triumphant, as in a mock military tournament, at the sound of the warning note of 'party politics.' The story, however, is as old as the sovereignty of the British Crown in India. In 1858, when Lord Palmerston introduced his first India Bill for the reform of the Indian administration, Mr. Disraeli, who was then the leader of the Opposition in the House of Commons, elaborately dwelt on the desirability of having "the representative principle applied to the Government of India," and objected to the Bill on the ground that it did not provide sufficient check for the protection of India's interest and for "that redress of the grievances under which she suffered which British protection ought to ensure." But soon after when upon the sudden defeat of Lord Palmerston, Lord Derby came into power, the same Benjamin Disraeli in introducing *his* India Bill "regretted that the unsettled state of the country did not admit of a representation of the people in India," and both sides of the House complacently agreed to his dictum. The same process of "promising to the ear and breaking to the hope" has long been repeated with unfailing precision and uniformity by both parties in Parliament in dealing with India and the Indian people: and it was this painful display of a tragi-comic farce that led Mr. George Yule candidly to observe that "the 650 odd members who were to be the palladium of India's rights and liberties have thrown 'the great and solemn trust of an inscrutible Providence' back upon the hands of Providence to be looked after as Providence itself thinks best." It was the same sophistry to which in more recent years Sir Henry Fowler gave utterance, when as the Minister for India he said that every one of the said 650 odd members in the House, whether liberal or conservative, was a Member for India," which (according to the trite old saying that everybody's business is nobody's business) in simple unsophisticated Indian phraseology, was as much as to say that as in a letter so in spirit there was absolutely no member for India in the British Parliament. These platitudes have led not a few Indians, however erroneous they may be, honestly to believe, that the British people are entirely liberal as far as Great Britain is concerned; they are divided into liberals and conservatives when Ireland comes into question, and with few honourable exceptions, they close their ranks and stand solid as conservatives when the fate of India has to be decided.

The question, therefore, whether India should be drawn into English party politics does not appear to be free from difficulties. Mr. Dadabhai Naoroji speaking so early as 1885 said, that "the Conservatives are not so bad as that they will never do a good thing, nor are the Liberals so good that they never did a bad thing. In fact, we owe good to both and we have nothing to do with them yet as parties." This may be perfectly correct; but it seems equally clear that whenever the Conservatives have done a good thing by India, they have mostly done so under pressure from the other side. It is also commonly pointed out that the great Proclamation was the gift of a Conservative Government, though subsequent acts and declarations of responsible ministers of the Conservative rank have shown, that it is hardly accepted by them as the gift of any Government, but that of a female Sovereign addressing her distant alien subjects upon her assumption of power after a great revolution, and it did not probably cost a Conservative minister much to draw up a liberal manifesto in his "inimitable style" under the express dictation of that Sovereign. If that Proclamation has ever been respected as a sacred document, it has been so done only by liberal ministers and administrators. Current of events in recent times has, however, brought home to the Indian mind, that although it may not matter much to India which of the two parties is in actual authority in England, it matters a good deal whether the members who form the Government for either party are or are not individually men of more generous instincts, wider sympathies and broader statesmanship in dealing with the affairs of an Empire which covers nearly one-sixth of this habitable globe. It is the saying of one of the greatest political philosophers the world has produced that "a great Empire and a little mind go ill together." Then India being a subject country without any voice in her own affairs, it is only natural that those that are imbued with liberal principles and democratic ideas, "Little Englanders" as they are called, who are more likely to be in sympathy with her than the lordly Impearialist who unreservedly talks of India having been conquered by the sword and who openly preaches that it must be retained by the sword.

Lord Cromer, who was perhaps the first open advocate of this doctrine of Indian neutrality, had no doubt his reasons for the occasion when he asked the House not to drag India into a party question; but is India really kept outside party politics? Is it not a fact, that although Great Britain is alternately governed on Liberal or Conservative principles, India is permanently ruled on Conservative lines? Parties rise and fall, ministers change and Viceroys come and go; but the bureaucracy in which the Indian adminisitration is permanently vested, is an essentially conservative institution as unchangeable in its methods as it is unimpregnable in its policy. A time must, therefore, come when the Congress will have to face the situation and decide the question whether it should not openly cast in her lot with one of the political parties in England.

CHAPTER XXII.

THE EDUCATIONAL PROBLEM.

The highest problem for solution in the evolution of a nation is perhaps Education. As it is the essence of civilization, so it is the very backbone of progressive humanity; while the force and stamina of a national life, as much as its longevity and capacity for action, are largely determined by the nature and extent of the development and expansion of its educational system. Education is the main stock-in-trade of a civilized people and the working capital ofits administration. In every well-regulated country, therefore, the State assumes the charge and control of public education as its paramount duty towards its subjects. Administration of justice and protection of life and property are no doubt among the primary functions of a Government; but these are discharged in one shape or another by every form of government that cares for its own existence. Even in early stages of society these elementary duties were fully recognised in all communal or feudal systems of administration where the educated few held the ignorant many in bondage in return for the peace and security guaranteed to them. It is, however, the highest aim of civilization to emancipate humanity from this forced subjection and restore to it the rights and liberties which are the common heritage of mankind. And education is the only means towards that end: It, is the only weapon with which to fight out the intellectual slavery and the moral turpitude of a people. As it is the sole test of a people's fitness to participate in the management of its own concerns, so it is the only standard by which a civilized government is to be judged and justified in its assumption of authority to rule over its destinies. The highest claim of Britain to the gratitude of the people of this country is, therefore, not founded either upon its elaborate system of efficient administration, or upon its extensive railways or other means of communication. Nor is that claim based upon the development of the country's resources and the expansion of its trade. All these are no doubt fully appreciated as the blessings of a civilized and enlightened rule; but the people know and feel that these blessings are purchased not without the payment of a price for each and all of them. The real source from which that gratitude flows lies deeper and is to be traced to the Educational policy which the British Government solemnly undertook to carry out, and which it has to no small extent carried out in the administration of this country ever since the assumption of its sovereignty. In recent years the educational policy of the Government has admittedly undergone remarkable changes leading to a considerable divergence of opinion, as regards not only the aim, but also the effect of that policy upon the general education of the country. While the Government maintains that these changes are intended to improve education, the people are unable to divest themselves of the belief that they are all retrograde measures calculated seriously to restrict and hamper educational progress. A brief survey of the history of that policy, therefore, appears to be necessary for a clear understanding of the issues involved in the discussion, as also of the merits of the contention on both sides.

It is a grievous mistake to assume, as not a few among the Englishmen have rather too hastily assumed, that when India passed into the hands of England she was found sunk deep in one unbroken darkness of ignorance and superstition ; that public education was foreign to the instinct and tradition of the people, and that educational institutions were imported from the West with the advent of the British, India was neither South Africa, nor the West Indies. Older than Rome and Greece and even older than Egypt and Phœnecia, India was in the dim and distant past the only one bright spot when the rest of the world was enveloped in darkness. She was the cynosure of all eyes and in spite of all the fanciful attempts of modern researches to prove the contrary, she still stands out in bold relief as the centre of all the earliest culture and enlightenment of the world. Even in later periods Chinese travellers from the East, and Grecian and Roman travellers from the West bore eloquent testimony to the unrivalled advancement and civilization of the Indian people. Coming down to modern times the Mahomedan historians have also ungrudgingly testified to their superior knowledge and culture. Since the Mahomedan conquest, India made further acquisition of Arabic and Persian enlightenment, and it seems absurd to suppose that towards the middle of the eighteenth century all this civilization and culture of ages were suddenly swept away by some mysterious agency, leaving the country involved in one impenetrable darkness. India with her vanished glories still retained the hall-mark of her proud and peculiar civilisation when she came in contact with the modern civilization of the West. She was even then rich in her Sanskrit and Persian literature, not to speak of the various Vernacular dialects of these classical languages, and though very much deficient in the knowledge of applied sciences, she possessed an indigenous system of education, both primary as well as secondary, spread throughout the country as the decaying fabric of the past—the crumbling relic of the vanished glories of her Nalanda and other Universities. We have it on the authority of the Education Commission of 1882, that prior to 1854, when the first Educational Despatch of Sir Charles Wood was issued, there were more than 900,000 or nearly a million of boys in British India, receiving elementary education in reading, writing and arithmetic including surveying, mensuration, square and cubic measures as well as equation. These primary instructions were systematically imparted in *Patshalas* and *Muktabs*; while higher education in literature, philosophy, logic, theology, medicine and astronomy was amply provided for in *Tols* and *Madrassas* established throughout the country, unsupported by any State-grant and uncontrolled by any State-agency, The customary recitation of the historical epics on festive and other occasions was another means of popular education. Medical science, including anatomy; surgery and chemistry, which is one of the highest products of civilization, had reached such a degree of efficiency, that in recent years with increased knowledge of ancient Indian civilization it has extorted the wonder and admiration of European scientists; while, in the domain of astronomy, although the latter-day Indians had ceased to make any fresh discoveries, the precision and accuracy with which they were still able to utilise their old stock of knowledge for the purpose of calculations and the many observatories which were in existence at Benares and other places down to the eighteenth century bore no mean evidence of the people's acquaintance with the wonders of the stellar world. Indian music still holds its place among the fine arts of the civilized world; while India's architecture and sculpture, of which eloquent testimony is still borne by the Taj at Agra, so well described as a "dream in marble, designed by Titans and finished by jewellers," and the grand mausoleum at Chunar which Bishop Heber characterised as "embroidery in stone," and by the numerous caves and temples still extant in Orissa as well as in Central and Southern India, gave unquestionable evidence of her technical knowledge of no mean order. The futile attempts of Western pride to attribute these wonderful works of art to either European or Byzantine civilization only add to their matchless glory and unrivalled superiority. India's maritime trade even in the sixteenth century was not inconsiderable; while her far-famed textile fabrics, particularly of cotton and silk, were largely in demand in the courts of Europe even in the eighteenth century. Scientific appliances she had none; but it was want of patronage, more than the competition of superior scientific machineries of

Europe, which crushed her finer industries and overpowered her in the end. Such was the country that was practically ceded to Great Britain towards the middle of the eighteenth century by a people torn by internal dissensions, distracted by mutual jealousy and spite, and tired of the misgovernment of a hundred inefficient principalities and administrations which had become accustomed to look more to their own pomp and grandeur than to the comforts and well-being of their subjects, and which had, as such, systematically neglected public instruction as a State duty. Of course the system of education at the time was very defective as there was hardly any method in the system; while the higher studies were generally of an unprofitable character. All this was due to the fact that there was no authority to guide or control education, and the people were left entirely to their own initiative and resource to educate their children as best as they could and as the circumstances of the country either permitted or required. The genius and aptitude of the people for education was, however, never extinct.

The government of the East India Company, which was mainly directed by purely mercantile considerations and from the highest to the lowest animated by a spirit of exploitation, naturally marked a very slow and slight advance in the direction of Education. The Board of Control from time to time no doubt urged for larger provisions being made for the education of the people, yet the largest grant ever made in any one year for education was not more than *one lakh* of rupees, which the Board strongly insisted on being put down in one of the Budgets of the Company towards the close of its administration. Full twelve years were taken in deciding the controversy which raged between those who were called the 'Orientalists' aud the 'Anglicists,' that is, persons who were opposed to the introduction of English education and urged for the encouragement of the study of the Oriental languages, and those on the other side, who advocated Western education and as such insisted on the English language being accepted as the medium of education in India. In this vital controversy, Rajah Rammohun Roy, strongly supported by David Hare, took a leading part and threw himself heart and soul at the forefront of the Anglicist party. We may not at this distance of time fully agree with the great Indian reformer in all that he said against the study of Sanskrit and Arabic languages which he strongly denounced as being barren and unprofitable studies, and we may even doubt if he actually anticipated the remarkable changes which his mother-country would undergo in the next hundred years ; but that his prophetic vision clearly foresaw that India's future destiny lay in the acquisition of modern knowledge and that such knowledge could be adequately and efficiently purveyed only through the medium of a living Western language cannot certainly be disputed. The question was finally decided during the government of Lord William Bentinck, when by a Resolution dated the 7th May, 1835, it was declared that although elementary education was to be confined to the Vernacular languages, higher education in India must be imparted in the English language. It was a most decisive point gained which paved the way for the future evolution of Indian Nationalism by providing a common language for the whole country. The Company, however, still moved at a very slow pace towards the educational development of the country when, worried and wearied by the systematic evasion of its mandates, the Board at the instance of Parliament at last laid down a definite policy of education to be pursued in India. The famous Despatch of the 19th July of 1854, commonly known as the despatch of Sir Charles Wood, afterwards Lord Halifax,—then President of the Board of Control—was the first declaration of that Policy and it is justly regarded as the great charter of education in India. The Despatch opened with an unreserved declaration of the Government accepting the responsibility of education of the people as a State duty. The declaration runs as follows :—

> "It is one of our most sacred *duties* to be the means, as far as in us lies, of conferring upon the natives of India those vast moral and material blessings which flow from the general diffusion of knowledge and which India may under Providence derive from her connection with England."

"The Despatch, after formulating its general scheme, went on to prescribe the following means for the attainment of its objects :—(i) The establishment of Universities at the Presidency cities ; (ii) the constitution of a Department of Education for each Presidency; (iii) the maintenance of the existing Colleges and High Schools whose number was very small and the increase of their number; (iv) the establishment of middle schools and of training institutions for teachers; (v) provisions for increased facilities towards the expansion of elementary education among the masses; and (vi) the introduction of a grant-in-aid system for the development of education. Provision was also recommended for a system of State scholarships to connect the lower schools with the higher, and the higher schools with the colleges.

It was a grand and comprehensive scheme, and one now naturally feels inclined to inquire as to how far it has been carried out. Three years after this programme was taken in hand and immediately as the first university was established in Calcutta, the Mutiny broke out which again set in motion a retrograde policy and caused a set-back in education. A party of Anglo-Indians, who were never so zealous in the cause of education, if they were not actually opposed to it from the very beginning, came forward to denounce education as being mainly responsible for the attempted revolution. The question was neatly disposed of by Sir Frederick Halliday, the first Lieutenant-Governor of Bengal, in a minute of 1858 on a letter of Lord Ellenborough, as President of the Board of Control, to the Court of Directors, who had found in the disturbance ample excuse for reverting to their old policy of inaction and issuing a peremptory order upon the Government in India not to "sanction any increase of expenditure in any part of India in connection with Education" without their authority previously obtained. Sir Frederick Halliday wrote:

"On the question of the connection between education and the rebellion, our wisdom, no less than our duty, is to persevere in what we have begun and not to turn our backs upon Bihar or any other parts of our territory, because there is difficulty or danger in the path of improvement. It is certain, however, that both the difficulty and the danger are exaggerated and look imposing only to those who keep at a distance from them and view them through the delusive mist of prejudice and mis-information. As to difficulty, the progress of Bengal, even within the memory of living witnesses, is a proof of the aptitude of the people and of their plastic docility. And though it is not uncommon in these days to attribute the recent mutinies to our educational operations, and even to propose to draw back from them for fear of similar consequences in future, the error of this opinion is like that of a man who after unwisely and incautiously exposing a barrel of gunpowder to all kinds of dangerous influences and having by good luck, and in spite of bad management, long escaped without an accident, should, at last, when the fatal and inevitable explosion takes place, blame neither the gunpowder nor his own rashness and indiscretion, but rather lay the whole mischief to account of some one of many little sparks flying about, and talk of limiting the use of fire and candle in future to prevent similar occurrences."

No more statesmanlike view of the situation or crushing reply could have been advanced, and the Government of Lord Canning made a firm stand against the insensate, hysteric cry of an alarmist crowd. It will be seen a little later on, that the same cry has again been raised in recent years and has contributed not a little to the shaping of the present educational policy of the Government, with this difference that there is neither a Halliday nor a Canning to take a dispassionate perspective of the situation and boldly adhere to the noble policy of 1854. By Statute 21 and 22 Victoria, passed on the 2nd August, 1858, the weak and vacillating misgovernment of the East India Company was brought to an end and on the 1st November of the same year, the great Proclamation was issued from Allahabad notifying the assumption of the Government of India directly by the Crown. That Proclamation is universally regarded as the *Magna Charta* of British India.

The second great Despatch on Education was issued on the 7th April, 1859, shortly after the transfer of the Government from the Company to the Crown. After reviewing the working of the earlier Despatch, the policy of which it whole-heartedly re-affirmed and accepted as the policy of the Crown, it went on to point out that although much had been done to stimulate a desire for education and the people had evinced a great aptitude for Western knowledge, the progress made was indeed very slow and inadequate; and while fully endorsing the policy of encouraging all indigenous efforts towards the expansion of education, the practice of educational officers demanding contributions from the people, which had largely come to a vogue as a condition precedent to the establishment of Vernacular schools, was declared both undignified and ine pedient. Doubts were also expressed as to the suitability of the grant-in-aid system for the supply of Vernacular education to the masses of the population, which, it was suggested, should be provided by the direct efforts of the State. The question of levying an educational rate for the provision of elementary education was also recommended by this Despatch of the careful consideration of the Government.

At this period, the Christian Missionaries acted as strong auxiliaries towards the spread of education, and though their primary object was to facilitate the propagation of the Christian Gospel, the schools and colleges which they founded in connection with the

Universities became powerful adjuncts to the cause of secular education also. But by far the greatest efforts were perhaps made by the people themselves, particularly as regards secondary and high education, though they failed largely to co-operate with the Government in promoting elementary education .among the masses. A number of enlightened Indian gentlemen, mostly inspired by the lofty teachings of Rajah Rammohun Roy, one after another took the field in different parts of the country which became soon studded with schools and colleges, some of which to this day stand as the proudest monuments of their patriotic labours and self-sacrifice. The names of Pandit Iswar Chandra Vidyasagar, Prisonno Coomar Tagore, Gow Mohan Addy, Bhudev Mukherjee, Peary Churn Sircar, Mahomed Moshin, Maharanee Swarnamoye and many others in Bengal, of Dababhai Naoroji, Bal Gangadhar Shastri, Roychand Premchand and Mahadev Govinda Ranade in Bombay, of Sir Syed Ahmed in the United Provinces of Pachyappa Mudaliar and Gopal Row in Madras and of the saintly educationist Dayananda Swaraswati in Benares are embalmed in the grateful memories of their countrymen.

The next landmark in our educational histhory was the Education Commission of 1882, appointed by the Government of Lord Ripon under the presidency of Sir William Hunter, which reviewed the progress the country had made during a period of thirty years since the first Education Despatch of 1854. Although the province of Bengal was found to be much ahead of the other provinces, defects were noticed in the entire system which loudly called for the earnest attention of the Government. The number of schools and colleges was still found to be inadequate and the provision for education insufficient. It was recommended by the Commission that the support and countenance afforded by the Government to indigenous schools, whether of elementary or of higher instruction, and the encouragement given to private enterprise by grant-in-aid rules should be further extended; that the Government should be reluctant to open Government institutions whenever private institutions could be expected or encouraged to do the work; that more liberal rates of aid should be granted to private colleges; and that primary education having been still very much neglected closer supervision and larger grants were needed for the education of the mass of the population. The Commission proposed an increased expenditure of 10 *lakhs* of rupees a year for the promotion of primary education. All these recommendations were of course generously accepted on principle; but only such effect could be given to them in practice as was possible under the eternal cry of financial difficulties, though of course neither the increase of the administrative machinery, universally admitted to be the costliest in the world, nor of the army, nor of the Home charges could afford to wait for their periodical expansion in an unfailing progressive ratio. And the official reports almost invariably winded up with the euphemistic platitude that "the recommendations of the Commission received the *fullest* attention *compatible with the necessity of avoiding any considerable increase of expenditure.*" Comment upon the rhyme and reason of language like this is perfectly superfluous.

Then came the Local Self-Government scheme of Lord Ripon, and the Government found an opportunity of relieving itself of the charge of primary education which, with certain petty and fluctuating receipts, was transferred to the Municipalities, the District, and the Taluqa Boards. This was no doubt a wise measure taken towards the development of elementary education; but its efficiency was largely impaired by the crippled resources of the local bodies overburdened by an army of inspecting establishment which in some places swallowed up nearly 45 per cent. of the grants for education.

Having thus largely relieved itself of the charge of Primary Education, the Government set to deal with higher education. A tendency had become manifest for some time past to view high education with a degree of suspicion and distrust and in certain quarters even with positive disfavour. It was the educated community which clamoured for increased rights and privileges and it was their agitation which was supposed to be responsible for the increased difficulties of the administration. The smoothness with which that administration was carried on from the middle of the eighteenth to nearly three-quarters of the nineteenth century was very much disturbed by the growing consciousness of a people who, in the prophetic words of Lord Macaulay, having their minds and ideas expanded by Western education, were aspiring to Western institutions and methods of administration. It was indeed the dawning of the "proudest day" of England though unfortunately, however, the just pride of British rule in India was at this stage slowly, though perceptibly, deteriorating into unworthy jealousy and spite, and the lessons of broad statesmanship gradually yielding to the dictates of a narrow, short-sighted policy. In 1902 Lord Curzon appointed a Universities Commission, and the Universities Act of 1904 was the outcome of the recent retrograde policy of education in India. With the ostensible view of securing *efficiency*, for which the government of Lord Curzon stood in every department of the administration, the Universities were officialized and their growth and expansion at once curbed to suit the purposes of the general administration. While it was apparently intended to secure a serene atmosphere of pure study, free from all political influences, it was entirely a political move to checkmate the Nationalist party who were the bugbear of the Indian bureaucracy. The whole programme of education was recast and the existing institutions were forced to conform themselves to a set of Regulations which placed them, as it were, upon the bed of Procrastes if they meant to exist. Some of the institutions died out on account of the stringent operation of these Regulations; while the growth of new ones was tightly fettered by their expensive requirements in a country notorious for its extreme poverty. To justify the new policy, the aim of which was unmistakably to restrict high education, it was pointed out that education was expanding in area at the sacrifice of depth and that in not a few cases it was conducted by private enterprise more as commercial business than as philanthrophic undertakings. It was further urged that in the case of both the colleges as well as the high schools, the majority of the students lived in a suspicious atmosphere of uncontrolled and unrestricted independence incompatible with the healthy growth of their moral and intellectual development. Above all, it was contended that the Universities stood in urgent need of thorough overhauling both as regards the subjects of studies as well as the conditions of affiliation of colleges and recognition of high schools; while it was fairly proposed that if it was actually impossible to convert the existing Universities into teaching institutions like those of Europe, it should be the aim of a sound policy gradually to impart such a character to them by opening out fresh avenues for researches and post-graduate studies and establishing new chairs and professorships directly under these Universities. Most of these arguments were perfectly plausible, while some of them were simply unasssailable; and the sudden change in the educational policy of the Government would not have been unwelcome to the people and become subject to much adverse public criticism if it had not been evidently dictated by a political object to divest the Universities of their popular character and place them entirely under bureaucratic control, and to restrict high education and sap the growth of indigenous enterprise which had largely contributed towards the expansion of education in the country. The new policy was, to all intents and purposes, a retrograde movement, and behind its charming frontispiece there was the same lurking suspicion and distrust of education and of the educated community which manifested themselves after the Mutiny of 1857, with this difference that while the old servants of the Company, who were largely responsible for the outbreak, were then kept well in hand by superior British statesmanship, the servants of the Crown forming an invincible bureaucracy now got the upper hand of that statesmanship, and under more favourable auspices succeeded in completely reversing the policy of Government. It is not denied that in certain directions the policy of 1904 has achieved remarkable progress, while at least one of the Universities has, under the guidance of a very capable and energetic Vice-Chancellor, aided by the philanthropy and patriotism of some of its noblest products, well-nigh risen to the rank of a teaching University of high order; but in the estimation of the public, these solitary advantages are completely overshadowed by the sinister spirit of that policy which seeks to improve by reduction and foster by curtailment of education in a country whose educational requirements are admittedly so vast and yet whose educational status is still indisputably so weak and miserable, compared with the rest of the civilized world. Under the policy of 1854 the Government, fully conscious of its own weakness, was most anxious to supplement its efforts by offering all possible encouragements to private enterprise; but under the new policy of 1904 it assumed the full control of education not only without making any adequate provision for its progress, but by actually forging serious restrictions to its normal expansion and development. If the earlier policy was purely educational in its character, the later policy has been politico-educational in its essence as well as substance. Even the large subsides which it has in some cases forced upon private bodies and individuals have been influenced rather by political than educational considerations. If the redeeming features of such a policy have failed to commend themselves to the appreciation of the people, it is more their misfortune than their fault. The improvements effected in certain directions are naturally regarded in the light of the improvised Chinese shoes for the improvement of Chinese beauty however maimed and crippled the subjects may be under its painful operations.

The next important step, in the history of education in the country, was the creation of a separate portfolio of Education in 1910 with an independent minister in charge of it. Although the Despatch of 1854 had established a separate Education Department for each of the provinces, it occupied a subordinate position where, in the words of Mr. Gokhale, "educational interests rubbed shoulders with jails and the police in the all-comprehensive change of the Home Department." For the first time in 1910, Education received its due recognition as an important and independent department of the State. But the fullest results of the working of this department can hardly be expected until it is released from the fetters of the policy of 1904. Sir Harcourt Butler's Educational Resolution of 1913 clearly emphasises the necessity at least of a partial revision and relaxation of that policy, and it is perfectly clear that if the creation of a new ministry for education is to have any meaning, the minister in charge must have a wider scope and greater freedom of action than the policy of 1904 apparently allows.

Lord Hardinge's scheme for the establishment of a residential and teaching University at Dacca is no doubt a movement in the right direction if the proposed University is to be conducted on the lines of the Universities of Great Britain. But if it is to have any territorial jurisdiction, however small, its usefulness will be considerably reduced; while if its standard in any way becomes lowered, it is bound to act as a setback rather than as an impetus to the advancement of high education in the country. The demand for high education is so great in the country that both the Hindus and the Mussalmans have come forward to found two independent Universities of their own. Their aim and scope have become the subject of considerable speculation among the people; but these attempts are a proof positive of the fact that the number of Universities in the country is too small to satisfy the demand of the people and that there is large room for additional adjuncts for the advancement of high education in the country.

The above is a short summary of the history of the educational policy of British rule in India, the net results of which up-to-date may now be briefly discussed. These results may broadly be considered under three heads: (1) High Education, (2) Secondary Education, and (3) Primary or Elementary Education. The first and second may be taken together as the one is complimentary to the other. High education is imparted under the control of five examining Universities of which the first was established in Calcutta in 1857, the second and third in Madras and Bombay in 1858, the fourth at Lahore in 1882 and the fifth at Allahabad in 1887. The five Universities between them command 128 Arts Colleges for males and 10 Arts Colleges for females. These Colleges are fed by 1,278 High Schools for boys and 144 High Schools for girls. According to the statements furnished by the Hon'ble Member for Education in March, 1914, the number of scholars in the 138 Arts Colleges (both for males and females) amounted in 1912-13 to 33,249, and the 1,422 High Schools counted on their rolls a population of 446,697 pupils and students. As regards the products of the five Universities it will be found, counting only once graduates holding more than one degree, that the Calcutta University has so far turned out about 21,000, Bombay 12,000, Madras another 12,000 and the two youngest Universities of Lahore and Allahabad, about three to four thousand graduates in Art, Science, Law, Medicine and Engineering. The total number of graduates turned out by the five Universities during the last 57 years does not, therefore, come up even to 50,000. These figures standing by themselves may not appear to be altogether inappreciable; but taken with the vast extent and population of a country which, compared with the countries of Europe, with the exception of Russia, looms as large as a continent, they become practically lost to the view. Taking the total population of the country under the last census at 255 millions, the percentage of scholars in Colleges, eliminating the odd figures on both sides, would be about '012, and that of the students in the High Schools 174 per cent. of the population; while the percentage of graduates of more than half a century hardly works upto '018 only. This is the result of nearly 60 years' labours, and it has to be noticed that the highest increase in high education has been attained only in recent years. Now, in the face of this stunted growth and slow progress of the country in high education, can it be reasonably argued that the time has arrived for the application of the pruning knife? Pruning is good; but pruning before a plant has struck deep its roots and sufficiently put forth superfluous offshoots and branches can only help in hastening its destruction. So it has been with high education in India. With a total number of graduates which yields no percentage to the population until it is pursued down to two places of decimal fraction, an alarm has been sounded that the country is swamped by an army of "discontented graduates" and that a remedy must be provided against the yearly influx of these "disappointed place-seekers." To justify these retrograde movements, a responsible minister of the Government has openly enunciated a principle, which, in its originality no less than in its boldness, bids fair to mark a new departure in the history of the civilized world. It is confidently stated that "it is not in the interest of a poor people to receive high education." It is generally recognised in all civilised societies that poverty is no crime for which a special penalty need be provided by any Government; while it can hardly be disputed, that not many centuries ago, most of the advanceed countries in the West were as poor as, if not much poorer than, India and that it is only through the falling off of education in the one case and advancement in the other that their economic conditions have become reversed. Germany since her prostration at Jena and France after her crushing defeat at Sedan would not have been the Germany and France of to-day but for the expansion and development of high education, which made such rapid strides in these countries since the disasters which overtook them alternately; while the continued prosperity and strength of Great Britain are to be traced primarily to her Oxford and Cambridge, Leeds and Bermingham, Edinburgh and Glasgow, and Sandhurst and Woolwich. Poverty and ignorance may be hand-maids to each other, but they are neither inherent in nor inseparable accidents of the climatic condition of a people: these are conditions imposed upon a nation by the invasion of ignorance or of superior knowledge and culture. Besides, it would be the barest pretension on the part of any Government to evince such overwhelming anxiety for its poor subjects as not to further impoverish them by allowing them to have higher education without making adequate provision for their employment. Nobody expects the Government to make such a provision for a multitudinous population even on temporary occasions of drought, famine or flood, and far less is it reasonable to hope that Government should be able to absorb more than a very small percentage of the educated community into its limited services. Education has a value of its own, and even where it is not sought for its own sake, it somehow solves the economic problem of its possessor. It may be useful to remember that more than two-thirds of the colleges and nearly four-fifths of the high schools are private institutions, and where the people are so eager for education it is not for the State indirectly to impede its progress even if it cannot directly contribute towards its advancement.

The School Final Examination, which has already been introduced in some of the provinces and is sought to be introduced in others, is another standing menace to high education. It is already diverting a considerable number of boys from the Universities under the inducement of petty employments at small expense and is working a double mischief. As it is on the one hand weakening the colleges, so it is on the other hand impairing the efficiency of the minor services. The improvement of these services, which were at one time notoriously corrupt and inefficient, has been the work of generations during which the Government has systematically raised the standard of educational qualification and increased the value of the services, so that it is now the pride of not a few of them to count among their ranks graduates and under-graduates of the Universities. To discount the value of education and reverse the forward movement would be to undo a noble work done and demoralize the services as well as the people to no small extent. The people are afraid that, with the restrictions already imposed on the expansion of high education and the school final thrown in as a sop to a poor people, accompanied with a transfer of the power of recognition of the high schools from the Universities to the Education Departments of Government, the prospect of high education may be regarded as sealed. Government has at no time like Japan or China either very materially helped or encouraged the people in receiving higher education in foreign countries, while signs are not wanting that even in the British Universities, the Indian students are often regarded with racial jealousy and spite. How intensely the serene atmosphere of Education has become saturated with racial and political considerations may be judged from the fact that the colour bar still sharply divides even the educational Service into what are called Imperial and Provincial branches, and distinguished Indians whose fame for original researches and discoveries in the domain of science has travelled to Europe and America are made to wear the badge of this invidious distinction apparently for no other offence than the colour of their skin. Owing to a most regrettable manifestation of lawlessness among a certain class of misguided young men in the country, into which immature school-boys were treacherously decoyed in some places, the high schools have been placed under a state of surveillance, the effect of which is equally demoralising to the teachers as well as to the taught. On the whole, the serenity of the educational atmosphere has been disturbed, the growth and expansion of colleges and high schools impeded, and the entire system of education has been largely subordinated to the political exigencies of the State.

As regards Primary or Elementary Education, the subject was completely threshed out with remarkable ability by Mr. G. K. Gokhale in connection with the famous Resolution which he moved in the Supreme Legislative Council in 1910 and the Elementary Education Bill which, in the following year, he introduced in the same Council. Himself a devoted educationist, who voluntarily sacrificed his high material prospects to his ardent love for education and a saintly politician who to serve his country declined an unsolicited honour for which many may be secret candidates and not a few would gladly sacrifice all that they possess if they could only attain it, Mr. Gokhale dealt with the subject so luminously and with such characteristic force that his remarkable exposition drew the unstinted admiration of the whole Council, while Sir Guy Fleetwood Wilson, then Finance Minister, went so far as to compare him with Mr. Gladstone in his mastery of facts and marshalling of figures. Mr. Gokhale pointed out that in 1882 (the year of Lord Ripon's Education Commission) there were 85,000 Primary Schools recognised by the Department with about 2,150,000 pupils attending these schools, which, with another 350,000 attending the unrecognised indigenous schools, gave a total of 2,500,000 of boys and girls receiving elementary education in the whole country at the time. That means that only 1·2 per cent. of the entire population were at school in 1882. In 1910 the number of Primary Schools rose to 113,000 and the number of pupils in recognised schools to 3,900,000 which, with another 1,600,000 attending unrecognised schools, made the figure stand at

4,500,000 or only 1·9 per cent. of the total population. Speaking in 1910, Mr. Gokhale had necessarily to take the census return of 1901 for the basis of his calculation; but if the population of 1910 had been available to him, he could have shewn that this percentage was still less. However that may be, we are now in a position to consider the state of elementary education in the further light of the census of 1911 and the Educational Statements of 1912-13 as furnished by the Member for Education in March, 1914. According to these statements, there are at present 113,955 primary schools for boys and 13,694 schools for girls giving a total of 127,649 schools with a total strength of 5,261,493 boys and girls receiving instruction in these schools. This works out to little over 2 per cent. of the entire population. There has been some slight improvement in the other provinces; but in Bengal, the most forward province in point of education, there has been a steady falling off in mass education. Mr. Hornell's Report for 1912-13 shows a loss of 513 schools with a decrease of 17,292 boys and 2,974 girls among Hindus and 5,421 boys and 1,588 girls among Mahomedans. The proportion of pupils to children of school-going age (reckoned at 15 per cent. of the population) is little over 18 per cent.; that is nearly five out of every six children are allowed to grow up in ignorance. That is how elementary education stands in the country after 150 years of British rule in India, and yet Mr. Gokhale's modest Bill was thrown out with a few complimentary platitudes.

Now, taking the total number of scholars in public institutions of all grades (both for males and females), the figures stand at 6,488,824, and the grand total including unrecognised institutions amounts to 7,149,669. This gives a percentage of 2·8 to the whole population of the country. This then is the net result of more than half a century during which the Crown has assumed the supreme control of education and systematically tried to foster it. It took nearly thirty years to raise the percentage to 1·2 in 1882 and it has taken another thirty years to increase it by 1·6 per cent. in 1913. Thus even with a normal increase in population, this rate of educational progress in the country must prove a veritable race between the hare and the tortoise to enable the one to overtake the other; and how many generations must pass before even half the population can be rescued from absolute darkness! Mr. Gokhale conclusively pointed out that whether it be the extent of literacy among the pupulation, or the proportion of those actually under instruction, or the system of education adopted, India lags far behind any other civilised country in the world. She occupies a worse position than even the Philippine Islands, which came under American rule only fifteen years ago, and Ceylon and the principality of Baroda, while the small State of Mysore may alse be shortly expected to beat her in the race. According to the last census, barley 7 per cent. of the population of India are literate, while in Russia, the most backward of European countries, the proportion of literates is more than 25 per cent. In the Philippines the proportion of children at school is 6 per cent. and in Ceylon it is 6·6 per cent. of the entire population: while in India it is little over 2 per cent. only. In the State of Baroda in the year 1912-13 about 80 per cent. of the boys and 48 per cent. of the girls of school-going age were at school, as against 28 per cent. of boys and 5 per cent. of girls in British India as shown in the statement of March 1914 referred to above. The Report of Mr. Masani, Director of Public Instruction, Baroda, on the educational progress of the State in 1913-14, reveals a still more remarkable advance made in all branches of education. During the year, as reported by the *Bombay Chronicle*, the educational institutions of all descriptions in the State rose from 3,045 to 3,088, the total number of pupils attending them rose from 207,913 to 229,903 or an acquisition of 22,000 new pupils, which is a remarkable record indeed for a single year for such a small State as Baroda. Out of this total, 550 were in the Arts Colleges, 8,079 in the secondary schools, and the remaining 221,274 attending Primary Schools. Of the total number of children, 147,413 were boys and 82,490 were girls. The number of Primary Schools increased by 39 and the number of pupils attending primary institutions by 21,680. The remarkable increase in a single year was mainly due to the raising during the year of the statutory age limit for boys to 14 and that for the girls to 12 and the statutory standard limit from the Fourth to the Fifth Standard. The result of this reform has been that "fully 93·2 per cent of the boys of the school-going age are attending school to-day in Baroda,"—a state of things which is far, far in advance of the conditions in British India or any of even the most progressive States. The State spent on education about 1·9 per cent. of the total revenues, which must be pronounced to be a fair, or even more than fair, proportion for spending on education. What a sad commentary this to the state of things in British India !

As regards the State expenditure on education, Mr. Gokhale's statement showed that while Russia spent 7½*d* per head of population, the Indian expenditure was barely one penny. It must be admitted that in recent years educational grants have been largely augmented by the Government of India and the Education Member's statement quoted above, gives the total expenditure on Education from all sources in 1912-13 at Rs. 9,02,09,000, which would out work at about 4*d* per head of the population. But with reference to this large increase it has to be borne in mind, that it has gone more towards the increase of inspecting establishments, improvements of school buildings and subsidies to existing institutions than to the increase of schools and colleges or to other extension of existing facilities for further development of education. The objects to which the bulk of these increased grants have been devoted may be perfectly legitimate ; but in a country where education is at such low level, every available income should be utilised more towards extension and expansion of education than towards the supervision of the inspecting staff and the improvement of buildings. Indians are accustomed to receive instructions even under the open sky, sitting in the cool shade of a village tree or temple; and although a decent and well-ventilated school house is always preferable, India is in more urgent need of extended facilities than of improved but limited accommodation for education. Supervision is no doubt wanted; but an army of inspecting officers, out of all proportion to the number of institutions and of the pupils, constantly in motion recording statistics and indulging in criticisms, each in support of his own fad, is a serious obstacle to real progress if not a positive nuisance. The whole system is working like a machinery without any life or spirit to inspire it to a higher ideal or nobler aim; while underlying that system there seems to be a secret dread of higher as well as universal education for the people. Repeatedly has the Crown solemnly declared its policy of trust and confidence in the people and its earnest desire to sweeten their homes with the blessings of education, and at no time perhaps was such declaration marked by greater solemnity or inspired by more profound solicitude for the true well-being of the teeming millions of this vast country than when in December 1911, His Gracious Majesty George V announced from the Durbar Throne at Delhi, the choicest of his boons—the grant of 50 *lakhs* of rupees for the education of his Indian subjects. Unfortunately, however, whether it be the fault or misfortune of India, the veil of suspicion and distrust has never been wholly removed from her administration. Even conceding for argument's sake that there are dark corners here and there requiring to be carefully watched, it is clearly the duty of a wise Government to clear them up by throwing in more light than to deepen the gloom by withdrawing all light from them. Education is certainly to the body-politic what light and air are to living organism. With the increase of education the Indians will no doubt clamour for greater rights and privileges; but with the growth of education they are also bound to grow in their intelligent attachment to the British connection. It is the educated community which has a correct appreciation of British rule, which is in a position to form a comparative estimate of the relative strength, status and genius of other civilized Governments, and however unsparing or disagreeable its comments and criticisms at times may be, it is this community alone which can and does weigh the serious consequences of a change of hands in the Government of the country. It is the dictates of self-interest—the highest of impulses in human nature—which draw the educated Indians towards the British connection. Theirs may not be love and loyalty in the sense in which an English man loves England and is loyal to her: but it is through the British connection that educated India aspires to rise in the scale of civilized nations and rank herself as a component part of the Empire, united by common ties of partnership and consolidated into a federation with the other units of that Empire on terms of equal rights and responsibilities of British citizenship. She aims not at separation but union, not at independence but amalgamation. She indeed wants to throw off the badge of a

Dependency but only to be ranked as a Dominion of the British Crown. Education is the only cement of that union, and if ever a crisis comes it will then be recognised how valuable an asset education is to British rule in India.

Nor can the Indian National Congress have a nobler aim or a higher destiny than the educational regeneration of the multitudinous population, whose interest and well-being it seeks to represent. Education is the problem of problems before it, and if the Congress can satisfactorily solve this one problem, the other problems will solve out themselves in no time. It is the main engine which gives motion to all the other wheels, and according as it moves backward or forward, the entire machinery is bound to have either a retrograde or progressive motion. With the engine reversed, neither wind nor tide, however favourable, will enable the nation to reach its destination. It is neither a dream nor a phantom that is alluring Educated and New India ; it is the glorious vision of a reality that inspires her in the evolution which has already set in and is silently shaping her destiny in the noiseless march of Time.

CHAPTER XXIII.

INDIAN RENAISSANCE.

Although it has been found somewhat difficult to give a precise definition of Renaissance, it has been aptly and significantly described as the spring-time of a nation's life. However different may be their durations, as well as their intensities, in differect latitudes and longitudes, every civilized nation has its budding spring, its bright summer, its leafless autumn and its frosty winter. Again the description is also quite apposite in as much as the evolution of the world has not followed from the dawn of creation in one uninterrupted line of progress; but it has spun out itself in cycles of revolutions which have come and gone like waves of seasonal changes. The absurd hypothesis of Christian speculation which assigned to creation a brief age of only four thousand years has long been exploded even by Western scientific investigations, and it is now almost universally admitted that there were ancient civilizations which, having repeatedly attained a much higher elevation than many of the modern European States, had as often to pass through their autumn and winter, leaving their treasures burried under the debris of a ruined past unknown to later ages, or ruthlessly destroyed by the rushing tides of ignorance and barbarism which have again and again flooded the world and enveloped her in the abyss of darkness. Egypt, Carthage, Assyria, Phenœcia and Persia—all had their palmy days; while the Celestial Empire, possessing the greatest longevity among the living nations of the earth, has undergone a succession of revolutions during a period within which the world has witnessed the meteoric rise and fall of hundreds of smaller nations on her surface. In Europe, Platonism was succeeded by the barren subtleties of the schoolmen, which were in their turn overthrown by Roman civilization, which shed its lustre over the entire old world for centuries until the great Empire itself was over-run by Teutonic and Celtic barbarism. Then there followed a dark and dismal period gradually developing into what is now known as the Middle Ages with its feudalism, its knight-errantry, its papacy and its monasteries, until the Reformation came before whose dawning light the 'misty twilight of the Middle Ages slowly faded away. It was the commencement of modern European Renaissance, and since then Europe has step by step risen to the pinnacle of her material greatness and established her supremacy over the four continents of the habitable globe. She has no doubt long passed her vernal equinox; but whether the shadows of autumn have begun to fall upon her, or she has yet to pursue a longer summer course to attain the solstitial altitude of her greatness, time and events alone can prove. She has, however, evolved through Science a system of materialism, the resources of which seem to be almost inexhaustible, and as spiritualism appears to play such an insignificant part in this evolution, it seems extremely problematical if her attention will be readily directed to a higher evolution of her destiny until she is overtaken in her mad but majestic career by some catastrophe which will open her eyes to the yawning gulf which lies immediately below the lofty precipice upon which she has taken her stand.

India of all ancient countries has passed through vicissitudes of changes perhaps unparalleled in the history of mankind. She has, in her evolution, undergone strange transformations through cycles of ages of which there is hardly any authentic or chronological record besides such as may be gleaned through the pages of her vast and ancient literature and the silent testimony of her widely-scattered stone monuments. Beginning with the sublime revelations of the *Upanishads* and ending with the profound philosophy of the *Geeta*, it covered a glorious period of Aryan civilisation. After the great War of Kurukshetra, India was over-run by barbarism and her high civilization was almost wiped out by successive waves of vandalism such as in later years dismembered the Roman Empire. She again reared her head and attained the highest summit of her material grandeur during the Buddhistic period, when her imperial sway not only influenced the Asiatic continent, but also extended beyond the seas. It was the Augustan period of Indo-Aryan civilization. Her arts and commerce travelled far and wide, while her culture and civilization attracted to her courts Greek historians from the West and the Chinese travellers from the East. She was at this period the Queen of the habitable globe. But after nearly four centuries of her undiminished splendour, she had to suffer another relapse during which she gradually again sunk into the depths of a terrible degeneration, losing all her arts and sciences, her culture and civilization. It was at this period that a decadent people, unable to maintain its pristine greatness, began, like the schoolmen in Europe, to revel in dogmas, absurd theories, crudities and subtleties, which, in absence of any chronological accuracy, were in latter years jumbled up with the higher civilization of an earlier age. All this furnished easy and ostensible grounds for the ill-informed, hasty and egotistic antiquarians of the West summarily to dispose of one of the highest civilizations the world has ever attained as being only a confused conglomeration of dreamy ideas, phantasies, visions, inconsistencies, absurdities and monstrosities and to characterize the profoundest philosophy that human mind has yet evolved as "the babblings of child humanity." The object of these remarks, however, is not either to establish the superiority of ancient Indian civilization or to encourage vanity in a useless retrospect of its vanished glories. They are intended only to draw attention to the fact that the evolution of the world is not marked by one continuous line of progress in which each successive step has been an advance over the past; but that it has been the result of a succession of alternate changes not unlike its diurnal course passing through darkness to light and light to darkness. India has not been an exception to this universal law of nature: She too had gone through several such revolutions before she came in contact with Western civilization for her third or fourth re-birth in the evolution of her national life.

Modern Indian Renaissance may be said to have commenced from the time of Rammohun Roy. As in the morning of the world light travelled from the East to the West, so towards the beginning of the last century the returning light began to proceed from the West to the East. The present Renaissance of India is essentially a product of Western civilization. Every Renaissance has several aspects,—religious, social, literary, economic and political. Rammohun Roy primarily took up the first three for his programme. The first he attempted to build upon the sacred scriptures of the ancient Hindus, while the second and the third he would construct upon the model of modern Europe. But his one great idea was to ingraft and not to supplant. In the task of religious reformation he was closely followed by the saintly Maharshi Devendranath Tagore, Keshab Chandra Sen and Dayanand Saraswati, the founder of the Arya Samaj; while on the social and the educational sides his mantle fell upon the renowned Pundit Iswar Chandra Vidyasagar, Prosonno Coomar Tagore, Mahomed Moshin, Sir Syed Ahmed, Roychand Premchand, Bal Gangadhar Sastri, Gopal Row and many other distinguished men who, in quick succession, took up and advanced the great master's work. But the Educational Renaissance was firmly established in the country with the creation of the Universities in 1857-58, which, besides imparting Western knowledge, were largely instrumental in reviving the Vernacular languages and stimulating literary activities of remarkable vitality and fecundity. The economic or industrial Renaissance may be said to date from the time of the American Civil War when, as has already been stated, Bombay made a dashing attempt to turn the cotton crisis of the world to her advantage. She at first no doubt paid the penalty of her wreckless misadventure; but the energies of a renovated people succeeded in shortly rehabilitating their equilibrium and inaugurating an epoch of industrial enterprise which has seized the popular mind throughout the country. Madras, Bengal and the Punjab have all awakened to a full consciousness of the economic prostration of the country and each in her own way is struggling to revive her trade and industry into fresh life and activity. The progress so far achieved may not be much but the spirit evoked and the energies roused without the legitimate support of the State are sufficiently encouraging for a period of healthy and vigorous Renaissance.

The political Renaissance of modern India is of later growth. Although clearly foreshadowed by the unerring vision of the great reformer of Modern India, and heralded by a number of political evangelists among whom may be mentioned men like Ramgopal Ghose, Hurrish Chandra Mukherjee, Kristodas Pal, Digumbar Mitter, Juggonauth Sunkersett and Naoroji Furdoonji, that Renaissance did not clearly dawn until the birth of the Indian National Congress. The Congress has, as has already been pointed out, awakened a new consciousness in the country, united its scattered units, infused into them a new life and spirit, generated new forces and evolved a nationality out of a chaos. The Gospel it has preached has become the accepted creed of a country ten times the size of France and containing five times the population of Great Britain and Ireland. Whatever the future destiny of the country may be, there can be no denying of the fact that it has roused a slumbering people from the torpor of ages, opened out to their astonished gaze the world's panoramic progress towards Liberty, Equality and Fraternity, and sounded the trumpet-call to them to join in the march for a fair share in the common heritage of mankind.

At this momentous period of transition, there are not a few dangers and difficulties which cannot be too carefully watched, nor too zealously guarded against. At a time of regeneration the fresh energies and the new impulses of a renovated people have in the exuberance of a new consciousness a tendency to run to excesses. Impatient idealism sharpens the imagination and soaring ambition warps the judgment of youthful minds. There are no more hidden rocks or drifting icebergs in the ocean than in the wide expanse of the political field. The slightest deviation from the charted line may gradually lead to the widest divergence in its course and ultimately end in disasters to even the stoutest national life. Unfortunately, however, at this early period of her Renaissance, India was not able completely to avoid the shock of this impatient idealism. From whatever causes it may be, an ugly development manifested itself in the country when a few bands of misguided young fanatics got out of hand, ran amock and gave way to violence and dastardly outrages. It was the spirit of anarchism imported along with many other commodities from the West. Like the mythical Empedocles, these political fanatics rashly attempted to leap into the flame in the false delusion of being returned to the gods, little reckoning that the gods in their wrath were capable of drawing the entire people to the crater and throwing them into the consuming fire. If they really had any political object in view they apparently overlooked the fact, that history does not present a single instance where a righteous cause has ever been advanced by unrighteous methods, and that, either anarchism, or nihilism has anywhere succeeded in achieving its desired end. These pests of society and avowed enemies of order and progress in the country were, however, promptly dug out like rats from their dens and their gangs broken up though not without considerable damage done to the country and the people who innocently suffered in the operation. There are now only the scattered remnants of these secret organisations which still haunt the people like plague and pestilence which die hard wherever they once find their way.

Without entering into any unprofitable discussion about the genesis of this pestilential development, or indulging in any apportionment of the responsibility between the Government and the people, it may be permissible to express some regret for the attitude which the bureaucracy still maintains towards the perfectly legitimate political movement in the country and the eagerness with which it seizes every opportunity to cry it down by ingenuously associating it with this ugly development. An official communique, a gubernatorial speech and a general administration report—all find in it a target for criticism and a wide mark for its indiscriminate fling. Recently a committee of civilians was appointed to advice Government upon its pre-arranged plan of partitioning some of the bigger districts in the re-united province of Bengal. The Committee's report does not contain a single suggestion which was not a foregone conclusion, or which throws any new light on the administrative problems of the country; but this District Administration Committee, as it was styled, has made quite an original discovery that anarchism was confined to the Hindus. What secret satisfaction they derived from this ethnological analysis, or what connection it had with the geographical boundaries of a few districts, it is not possible for the outside public to discover; but the propriety of raking up the dying embers of a controversy which was supposed to have been long buried may be seriously questioned. True statesmanship nobody expects from an old and effete bureaucracy of the kind and quality as is established in India; but an exercise of bare common sense and discretion would have disclosed not only the absurdity, but also the mischievous character, of such a generalization. Because a handful of fanatics at one time and under a peculiar circumstance belonged to a particular community, therefore that kind of fanaticism is the characteristic of that community, is a piece of logic which will probably be difficult for any other people outside the Indian Civil Service easily to swallow. Then was it historically true that anarchism in India was confined to the Hindus who had unfortunately fallen on evil times and upon evil tongues? Without intending in the least to cast the slighest reflection on any community, it may be pointed out that the first assassin who drew his dagger against a popular Chief Justice in the country was not a Hindu, nor the yet more desperate miscreant who assassinated a noble Viceroy. The Rye House Plot and the story of Guy Fawkes are matters of history, and were not three abortive attempts made within living memory even on the sacred life of the most virtuous Queen that ever adorned the British Throne? It is apparently overlooked that these anarchists in fact belong to no country, nationality or community. They are a race which stands by itself and is the common enemy of humanity throughout the world. They are monster-births and, whether owing to any abnormal condition in their phrenological structure, or any convolutions of their brains, they belong to the destructive elements of nature. The deadly spirit may have travelled from the West to the East; but these scourges of society are neither Europeans or Asiatics, nor Bengalees or Mahrattas. They are neither American, nor Italian, nor Indian in their origin. The Indian anarchist belongs to the same stock to which the murderers of Garfield, Lincoln and Sadi Carnot belonged, and it would be positively as unfair to brand the Hindus, or the Bengalees and the Mahrattas, with anarchism as to charge the Christians, or the Americans and the

Italians, with it. Civilized humanity in all ages and in all countries has positively refused to recognise the kinship and brotherhood of secret murderers and dastardly assassins, and no men probably have greater reasons than the Indian public to deplore the present situation which has not only cast a deep stain on their national character, but has also considerably reduced the security of their lives and properties and, above all, cruelly blasted the splendid opportunities which they had created with patient labours and sacrifices of a complete generation for the orderly progress and development of their national life; and those who lavishly indulge in indiscreet and light-hearted criticisms of that situation, wounding the feelings and alienating the people, simply add insult to injury without serving any useful purpose either to the administration or towards the proper solution of that situation.

But if the people have their grievances they cannot divest themselves of the responsibility which belongs to them in helping the administration for effectively eradicating the evil which has secured such a pestilential foothold in the country. There have been enough of complaints and protestations on both sides. The authorities have not been tired of accusing the public of apathy, indifference and want of co-operation, while the public have not been either slow or remiss in charging the authorities with want of sympathy, trust and confidence. Wherever the true line of demarcation may lie, it ought not to be at all difficult in laying down a *via media* where both sides may meet half way. The Government has certainly a right to expect co-operation from the people; but the people have also a just claim to the ways and means which Government alone can supply towards successful co-operation. The people must be treated as useful adjuncts of the administration before they can be expected to co-operate for its success. Take the case of lawlessness which has become the ground of universal complaint. It is as ridiculous on the part of the authorities to urge the public to face armed gangs of desperate assassins and robbers with bows, arrows, brickbats and other primitive weapons of defence, as it would be extravagant on the part of the public to ask Government to divest itself of all legitimate control over the administration. A reasonable relaxtion and not the abrogation of the very stringent provisions of the Indian Arms Act seems to be urgently demanded by the exigencies of the situation. There are obvious objections to the granting of free and unrestricted licences to all people, and no reasonable man could ask for such a free hand in the matter. What, however, seems to be necessary is a reasonable modification and relaxation of the very strict rules under which licences are so very sparingly granted only to an extremely limited number of the people and that under conditions which practically operate as a wholesale disarmament of the public. But there seems to be no disposition either on the part of Government or of the authorities to treat the question with any degree of consideration. Real co-operation is begotten of mutual trust and confidence. It can never be the product of one-sided activity, nor can it be manufactured to order. It seems as absurd to try to extort hearty co-operation where there is no conciliation, as an attempt to extract honey out of a hornet's nest. Probably what the Government really wants is not co-operation, but passive submission. All the same, the people are bound to reckon with the existing condition of things and try to make the best of the slender opportunities presented to them to help the administration. In all their trials and tribulations, vexations and disappointments, let them beware of desperate thoughts and let New India at this renaissance always remember that with all the progress they have made they have yet to travel very long distances through dreary moors and arid deserts before the promised land can be in their sight and that the path is not free from the treacherous *ignis fatuus* or the delusive *mirage* which can neither guide them to their proper destination, nor afford them any shelter or relief, but can only tempt them to danger and disaster.

There is another danger which requires careful circumspection at this period of Renaissance. The current of a rising national life, like that of a river, generally seeks its old bed. Every revivalism has a tendency to revert to old institutions and every nation that has a past tries to rebuild its future on the ruins of its departed greatness. This tendency has generally the effect of introducing the good with the bad, the pure with the baser metal, into the composition of a revived national life. The temptation is too great and the tendency too strong, and a conservative reaction has burst upon this country with all the force and impetuosity of youthful imagination. It would be absurd to claim perfection for any system of civilization.

Besides, in India, successive revolutions have at different times introduced different forms of thought, observances, and practices, and all that should not be allowed to go down as the expression of the highest Indian culture and enlightenment. No attempt to revive all these dirts and filths of a dark and dismal period under ingenuous explanations and interpretations can by any means further the cause of progress or be credited to true patriotism. These attempts may feed vanity and pander to the boast of ancestry; but can never conduce to legitimate pride or true national advancement. On the contrary, such a frame of mind may run riot and serve to create a distaste for fresh investigation and a contempt for superior intelligence. At the present momentous period of transition, this tendency to reproduce the past without any amendment appears to have been very excessive, and people are not wanting who would fain revive many of the objectionable practices which have grown like parasites round the civilization of the ancients and give currency to many a counterfeit in the great demand that has arisen for old coins in the country. Nothing should honestly be done to counteract the influence of the new spirit which has not only opened out the political vision of a long disenfranchised people and inaugurated industrial enterprise in an exhausted and impoverished agricultural country, but also silently worked out a revolution in their social organisation under the spell of which even the old hide-bound caste system has become considerably relaxed and the orthodox prejudices of a conservative people are rapidly crumbling to pieces. Where the dead body of a *Tili* youth could be carried for cremation on the shoulders of Brahmins, Vaidyas and Kayasthas in a procession of thousands of people eager to do honour to real or supposed martyrdom and to defeat the last indignity of the law, the depth and intensity of the force of the new spirit may be easily conceived, and it would be neither wise nor patriotic to suppress or divert this rising spirit. Prejudices are said to die hard; but they often die violent death in the hands of those who have long harboured them.

There is another class of people who in their imperfect knowledge of the world seem to believe that all the discoveries of modern sciences and arts were anticipated by the ancients. They are ready to prove that electricity, magnetism, steam-engine and even wireless telegraphy and aerial navigation were not quite unknown to the ancient Hindus. In fact, in their fertile imagination they are able to trace every invention, as it is advertised, to the genius of their mythical ancestors. But what avail these academic disquisitions when we have to learn these mysteries of nature either from the past or the present, unless their aim and object, as well as their tendency, be to stimulate our energies to a fresh acquisition of their knowledge and use? There are irrefragable evidences that in certain branches of knowledge both the Hindu and Islamic culture had at one time attained a high level of perfection. If, in some branches of useful knowledge, they had few their equals and none their superiors in the ancient world, it can by no means be a reflection on their genius that thousands of years after them, other people have added to the stock of human knowledge and made fresh acquisitions in the domain of applied sciences. The higher philosophy of life evolved by the ancients still remains unexplored by modern culture, while many of their arts are admitted to have been lost. It is the world's evolution in course of which yet higher culture and nobler civilization must be the heritage of unborn ages. If we are really anxious to elevate ourselves and participate in the world's progress, we must think more of the present and the future than of the past. A legitimate pride of ancestry is no doubt a noble source of inspiration: but no nation can be truly great only in the blind worship of a great past.

On the other hand, any attempt to Europeanize India would be a great disaster and a failure. Herbert Spencer's advice to the Japanese applies with equal, if not greater, force to the Indians. Every great nation has a genius of its own, and its renovation to be permanent and effective must be based upon that genius. Materials may be imported from other sources and knowledge gathered from other people; but no nation can be recast in an altogether new mould. Man is no doubt an imitative creature; but imitation without assimilation produces a kind of mental and moral indigestion which gradually impairs and ultimately breaks down the national constitution. It is physically impossible for one people to divest itself of its essential characteristics and completely assimilate those of another—born, bred and brought up under different climatic conditions, nurtured for centuries on different modes of thoughts, ideas and sentiments and acclimatized for ages to a different moral, intellectual and social atmosphere. Nature itself would be opposed to such a transformation. Foreign dress and style may be adopted, certain habits and manners may be changed, and even some outlandish forms and fashions may be cultivated; but it is no more possible to change the character of a people completely than to evolve quite a new species of animal out of a different one by any process of culture. Besides, even European testimony is not wanting, that Western civilization, with all its recommendations, has failed in many respects particularly on the social and moral sides, and India cannot wholly profit by a radical transformation even if it were possible. No doubt that which is really good in European civilization and particularly those virtues which have made Europe what it is at the present day ought to be cultivated by our people; but they must be ingrafted on our national genius and made to grow on our ancient civilization. It is only those characteristics of Western culture which are of universal application and those traits of Western civilization which can be properly assimilated into our national system that are deserving of our closest attention, and we cannot be too careful in sifting the grain from the chaff and the metal from the dross in all our importations from the West. Above all, in our craze for the cheap chemical manufactures of European civilization, let us not throw away the real gold that is in our own system because it does not possess the lustre of a finished article.

The present is no doubt the age of European supremacy, and in the wheel of fortune that has been incessantly turning round since the dawn of the world's civilization, Europe has admittedly come to occupy the uppermost position to-day and everything bearing the hall-mark of European civilization has therefore a charm and attraction for the rest of the world. But where European civilization has admittedly failed to satisfy the highest claims of human nature and in cases where even Europeans themselves, in the midst of their superior culture and enlightenment, have come to realise and proclaim the failure of their institutions as a means to human progress and happiness, it would be a grievous mistake for the Indians to discard even that which is good in their own system and blindly adopt a garb which the Europeans themselves after a fair trial would fain throw away. The true European is neither in the dress nor in the colour of the skin; nor yet in his manners and customs; but in those qualities of the head and heart which have made him what he is. These virtues are no monopolies of any climate, or new acquisition to humanity, but the common natural heritage of mankind which, in the usual vicissitudes of time, have passed away from the East to the West. It is these virtues which should be cultivated, fostered and assimilated in our own system where, ingrafted on the spirituality of that system, they are bound to evolve a higher and nobler civilization not only for the regeneration of a fallen race, but also as a further step in advance towards that co-ordination of the Mind, Matter and Spirit which is so essential for the establishment of true Liberty, Equality and Fraternity throughout the civilized world.

CHAPTER XXIV.

THE AIM AND GOAL OF THE CONGRESS.

Again and again it has been asked both by friends as well as critics,—what is the ultimate goal of the Indian National Congress and what is the final destiny of India which it seeks to attain? Does the Congress aim at sovereign independence for India, or does it seek to secure only adequate peace, security, justice and prosperity for the people as a permanent subject race? What there may be in the womb of invisible time and in the dispensation of an inscrutable providence no one can foretell: but again and again has the Congress declared in no uncertain voice, that neither the one nor the other is its final object in view. The real aim of the Congress is to attain Self-Government within the Empire and the destiny of India which it professes to secure is a great Federal Union under the ægis of the British Crown,—the establishment of a United States of India as an independent unit and an equal partner of the British Empire. With a truly representative legislative assembly for each province, from which the lion's share by *nomination* shall be wholly excluded, and with a popular Executive Council, not an autocratic official hierarchy which once created at once becomes the unaccountable and irresistible master of the situation, but a representative Council strictly responsible to and controlled by the legislative assembly, dealing freely and independently with their respective provincial concerns, the establishment of a federal Parliament holding the reins of the supreme Government by and for the people under the suzerainty of Great Britain is the ideal which the Indian nationalist cherishes with pious hope and confidence. It is in this hope and confidence that he lives, works and suffers, and it is this hope and confidence which bear him up in the great struggle into which he has deliberately plunged himself and solemnly committed his posterity.

There have been "birds of evil presage" who have often shaken their heads and gravely observed that the idea is a dream and an impossibility. But they apparently forget that there can be no dream without a substratum of reality behind it and that the history of the world bears repeated testimony to the fact that the dream of one age has been the reality of another. The Roman Empire must have been a dream when Romulus built his mud walls on the Palatine Hill, and was not the British Empire also a dream when the Anglo-Saxon Barons wrested the *Magna Charta* from an unwilling English sovereign on the field of Runneymede ? If more than a dozen principalities of Germany, with all their differences of laws, customs, constitutions and even of dialects, could, after centuries of internecine strife and struggle coalesce and form into one of the strongest powers in modern times ; if Canada inhabited by a people of French, Dutch and British descent could constitute a self-governing dominion in the new world ; if the Boer and the

Briton could, even after a sanguinary conflict, establish a Union Government in the dark continent; and, why go further, if England, Scotland, Wales and Ireland, with their distinct and different nationalities, could after centuries of mutual jealousies and conflicts be blended into one Kingdom, perhaps the mightiest in the world, then is there any insurmountable difficulty why India —India of the Hindus, Mussalmans and Parsis— cannot be brought into a federation under a common rule? The Indian people have a common interest and are guided by common aspirations. In each province they already form an autonomous entity and there is no reason why, with further spread of education, development of national ideas, growth of patriotic sentiments and the cultivation of mutual trust and confidence, they cannot form into a harmonious, if not a homogeneous, whole. If the question of Ulster can be solved, as it will be solved, by a grant of Home Rule within Home Rule, the solution of the Indian problem cannot be regarded as beyond the region of practical politics.

The British Empire itself is a mighty federation of diverse peoples, and a strong tide has already set in for the autonomous and independent development of its component parts. It is in this far-sighted, vigorous policy that the British constitution proposes to differentiate itself from the Roman Empire and build itself upon a firmer basis. Once the Irish Home Rule is effected, the grant of Home Rule for Scotland, Wales and even England cannot be long deferred. If the whole of the Empire be thus spilt up into its separate autonomous units, can it be reasonably contended that India alone will remain to a distant day a common pasture for the rest of Empire? And then to which of the three parent states, supposing Home Rule is granted also to England, Scotland and Wales, will India form an appendage? It must cease to be a *khas mehal* of all if it is to cease to be such to any one of them. If the immobility of the present stiff bureaucracy once breaks down and the short-sighted policy of *divide-et-impera* fails, as it is bound to fail at no distant date, the blind superstition about the so-called eternal difference between the East and the West will be dissipated and the federation of British India under one union parliament will no longer appear as a nightmare in a dream. And what a glorious federation it would be, more glorious than South Africa and Australia and even more glorious than the Dominion of Canada, when with the vast and almost illimitable resources which she has at her command and with the inspiriting tradition which is behind her teeming millions to guide and stimulate their renovated energies, India would march towards the consummation of her destined goal to the eternal triumph of Justice and Truth, as well as to the glory of England.

Bombay, the cradle of modern Indian industries and enterprise and the gate to the world's commerce with the East; the obscure island city, the gift of a marriage dower of a foreign princess, which within two hundred years has, from the collection of a few fishing hamlets, risen to the proud position of the "Star of the East," and which, with its magnificent harbour and its splendid lagoons and causeways, is stronger than Boston and more beautiful than Venice; the presidency which is the home of the wealthy Bhatia and the enterprising Guzerati, of the adventurous Parsi and the intellectual Mahratta and is justly proud of Poona, the centre of Mahratta activity and the capital of the Peshwas, of Surat, "the treasury" of the immortal Shivaji, of Ahmedabad, the industrial centre of the "garden of Western India" and of Karachi, the glory of Sindh and the future emporium of India, as also the probable terminus of the Trans-Persian Railway connecting the East with the West; Bombay of Jamsetji Nusservanj Tata, Jamestjee Jeejeebhoy, Naorojee Furdoonji, Mangaldas Nathubhoy and Juggonath Sunkarsett; Bombay of Dadabhai Naoroji, Kashinath Trimbak Telang, Budruddin Tyabji, Pherozeshah Mencharjee Mehta and Dinshaw Edulji Wacha; of Mahadev Govinda Ranade, Gopal Krishna Gokhale, Bal Gangadhar Tilak, Ibrahim Rahimtullah, Behramji Malabari, Ramakrishna Bhandarkar, Narayan Ganesh Chandavarkar, Balchandra Krishna, R. P. Paranjpye and last not least Bombay of Mohandas Karamchand Gandhi, the liberator of Indian Settlers in South Africa,—where can you find a province and a people so rich, so industrious, so practical, so patriotic and so philanthropic?

If the Congress was born in Bombay and met its grave at Surat, it attained its resurrection in Madras—Madras where the first light came from the West; where in modern times the Dutch, the French and the English contested for supremacy in India and where the first

British flag was planted within an enclosed factory built upon the first territorial possession of England in India and christened as Fort St. George; sober and steady Madras,—Madras, the home of Ramanuja and Sankara and the land of temples and sanctuaries; Madras of Sir Salar Jung and Sir T. Madhava Rao, of Pachyappa Mudaliar and Gopal Rao, of Bhashyam Iyengar, Subramania Iyer, Ananda Charlu, Subba Rao, Krishnaswami Iyer, Sankaran Nair, Syed Mahomed, Sabapathi Mudaliar, Veeraraghava and Vijayaraghava Achariar, of Sivalai Ramaswami Mudaliar and of G. Subramania Iyer who turned the first sod on the Congress soil by moving the first Resolution of the first Congress;—where can you find a people at once so devoted and unostentatious, so firm and resolute, so cautious, yet so steadfast and untiring in its onward step?

The Punjab, the sacred land of the five rivers, the ancient home of the Aryan settlers where the pilgrim fathers came chanting the *Vedas* and carrying the first implements of civilization in the early morning of this world; Punjab of Guru Nanak and Guru Govind Singh who first preached the gospel of unity and fraternity in modern India, and organised a wonderful brotherhood, combining religion with politics; the Punjab of the brave *Pathans* and the valiant *Sikhs*; Punjab of Prithwi Raj and the lion-hearted Runjeet Singh, of Sirdar Dayal Singh Mejhatia, Lala Lajput Rai, Lala Murlidhar and Mahomed Ali; Punjab of Kurukshettra and Panipat, of Indraprastha and Delhi, of Amritsar and Taxila; Punjab of the Gurukul and the Arya Samaj which have created a revolution in modern

Hindu society and for the first time broken the charmed circle of an ancient exclusive religious organisation and evolved out of it a wide and comprehensive proselytising movement, reviving, as it were, the inspiration of the long lost treasures of the Vedic times; Punjab hoary with her ancient glories and bearing testimony to the rise and fall of countless dynasties;—where is to be found such a cradle of the brave and the true?

The United Provinces of Oudh and Agra containing the holy city of Benares, older than Babylon and Nineveh, the seat of a bygone University which Phœnix-like is about to rise out of its ashes; Benares, the centre of Hindu civilization and culture for untold centuries, and which sanctified with the memories of the learned and of the saints, that carry back human imagination to the dim and distant past when the rest of the habitable globe was involved in darkness, still holds its undiminished sway upon the life and teachings of one of the oldest, if not the oldest, branch of the Aryan family; Benares, the heart of Hinduism, the nursery of ancient philosophy, of the *Vedas* and the *Vedantas*; the province which is proud of one of the Seven Wonders of the World and other relics of Hindu and Moghul greatness; a province which is justly proud of men like Dayanand Saraswati, Pundit Ajudhya Nath, Gangaprasad Varma, Sundarlal, Madan Mohan Malaviya and Wazir Hossein;—where can you find a place and a people in whom loyal conservatism is so happily blended with robust liberalism in such strange harmony and co-ordination?

Behar the youngest of the self-contained provinces and yet one of the oldest in its traditionary greatness; Behar the *Maghad* and *Videha* of the ancients, the birthplace of Buddha Goutam, the greatest and mightiest of inspired reformers the world has ever produced, whose lofty teachings govern the lives of more than one-fifth of the entire population of this planet of ours; Behar of Chandra Gupta and Asoka of the Mauryan dynasty, whose dominions extended beyond the seas and in whose court Megasthenes sat and Pliny wrote; Behar of Pataliputra and Nalanda; Behar which has in recent times produced men like Luchmeswar Singh, Mazr-ul-Haque, Tejnarain Singh, Ali Imam and Hassan Imam; —where can you find a province where Hindus and Mussalmans live in such amity and concord, working hand in hand for the common motherland?

As Europe is unthinkable without France, so India would be unthinkable without Bengal. If the people of the Western and Southern presidencies are more like the level-headed Britons, the people of the Gangetic delta are more like the dashing French. In their passionate love and pride for their country, in their fiery impetuosity, in their originality of ideas and quickness of perception, in their fervid eloquence and glowing imagination and in their sensitiveness as well as fickleness, the Bengalees present a much nearer approach to the great Latin race than any other people of India. Alert, keen-sighted, enthusiastic, acute, fiery, go-ahead Bengal is the fountainhead of ideas and the centre of patriotic inspiration, Bengal where six centuries before *Jimutvahana*, the eminent Judge under the Sen kings of

Bengal, rebelling against the orthodox Mitakshara, the *Code de Napoleon* of India, laid down advanced legislation; where five hundred years ago Sri Chaitanya proclaimed the message of love, fratenity and equality from the Ganges to the Narbadda; Bengal where the famous twelve chieftains made the last brave stand for independence against the great Moghul in the seventeenth century; Bengal where the ruins of Gour bear testimony to her departed glories and where the "City of Palaces," homaged by the splendid shippings of all nations and guarded by the grim fortress of Fort William, rears her proud head as the Queen of the East; Bengal where Gadadhar established the subtle *Naya* philosophy and Gangadhar resuscitated the rusted medical science of the ancient Hindus; Bengal the granary of India where Nature has poured her bounties from the highest mountains in the world and artistically laid a magnificent network of highways for trade and commerce; Bengal of Ram Mohan Roy, of Iswar Chandra Vidyasagar and Mahomed Moshin, of Krishna Mohan Banerjee and Rajendralal Mitra, of Dwarkanath and Romesh Chunder Mitter, of Woomesh Chunder Bonnerjee and Romesh Chunder Dutt, of Devendra Nath Tagore and Keshab Chandra Sen, of Ramgopal Ghose, and Surendra Nath Banerjee, of Harish Chandra Mukerjee, Kristodas Pal and Shishir Kumar Ghose; of Monomohan Ghose and Anand Mohon Bose, of Taraknath Palit and Rashbehary Ghose, of Gurudas Banerjea and Ashutosh Mukerjee, of Michael Madhusudan Dutt and Hem Chandra Banerjea, of Jagodish Chandra Bose and Praphulla

Chandra Roy, of Ramkrishna and Vivekananda;—where can you find a land so fertile and a people so sharp in intellect, so subtle in perception, so persuasive in eloquence, so cosmopolitan in ideas and so sanguine in patriotic fervour? With all her faults and frailties Bengal has always held the beacon-light to the rest of modern India and marched at the van of all movements—religious, social and political.

For a country possessed of such potential units and such vast and varied resources, both economic as well as moral and intellectual, a country which on account of its diverse physical features and climatic conditions, varying from the torrid to the frigid region, with its magnificent rivers and sublime mountains, before which the highest peaks in other continents appear like ant-hills, with all its products comprising the varieties of different countries and climates, has justly been described by competent authorities as an "Epitome of the World," the attainment of a political federation cannot be a dream or a phantom of hope. Whatever fanciful theories may be invented by interested politicians for the justification of unjustifiable wrongs, and however much obdurate pessimism may indulge in the convenient belief that the East is by nature an uncongenial soil for the growth of democratic institutions, it cannot be denied that it is from the East that light travelled to the West and that it is from Asia that civilization marched to Europe and thence to the rest of the world. If religion is the supreme test of a nation's moral and intellectual capacity, it cannot be honestly denied that both Islamism and Hinduism

THE HON. BABU BUPENDRANATH BASU
PRESIDENT, 1914.

DR. SIR RASH BEHARI GHOSE
PRESIDENT, 1907 & 1908.

HON. SIR S.P. SINHA
PRESIDENT, 1915,

HON. BABU AMVICA CHARAN MAZUMDAR
PRESIDENT, 1916,

in their essential conceptions are the most democratic religions the civilised world has yet evolved. The two religions which have successfully moulded the life, thought and conduct of its followers to a wonderful disregard of material prosperity, levelling princes and peasants to a uniform standard of judgment and inculcating passive submission to temporal powers only as a means to secure peace and order and not for conquest of territories or for extinction of other people but for the attainment of spiritual welfare and for the expansion of God's Kingdom on earth, ought not to be lightly condemned as being incompatible with democratic ideas and institutions. If the followers of these two religions have through centuries yielded ungrudging submission to the will of their despotic sovereigns, they have always offered greater allegiance to their saints who, in their humble cottages, have not unoften defied crowned heads in their fortified palaces. A merely superficial knowledge of the inner life and civilization of the Hindus and the Mussalmans, coupled with the too hasty generalisations of a spirit of arrogance which marks the undisputed and indisputable superiority of modern Europe in the physical world, is largely responsible for the accentuation of a number of fallacies and sophistries which have grown up round a superstition about a supposed or assumed inherent difference between the East and the West. There can be no rational charm in the point of a circular compass where the East in one way is the West in another. Besides, where is the charter of Providence by which a monopoly of civic rights and institutions is reserved within certain geographical limits and circumscribed by either climatic or racial considerations, or, for the matter of that, defined by the colour of the skin? What was Europe before the fifteenth century when the whole Christendom prostrated before the Pope and even the crowned heads trembled on their thrones for fear of an autocratic Pontificate? Where was democracy in the land of the Saxons or the Franks, of the Teutons or the Slavs, when the people stood absolved from their allegiance to their sovereign as the mandate of the Bull or Dispensation? Brahminical hierarchy, however galling it may appear to-day, was never half so tyrannical in the exercise of its arbitrary powers as the papacy of Europe up to the thirteenth century of the Christian era. Then, besides Great Britain and France, is there any country even now in Europe where democratic instincts are better developed than in India? What was Italy up to the middle of the eighteenth century? The Germans who are supposed to be the most intellectual and progressive people in Europe are still a congeries of nations living under the domination of a military despotism which does not admit of a civilian citizen, no, not even of a civil judge or a magistrate, smiling at a subaltern in his uniform. In spite of her universities, her sciences and her arts, there seems to be very little of true democracy in the constitution of Germany as has been amply demonstrated by the recent Zabern incident. That constitution still "turns helmets into crowns and sabres into sceptres." In point of fact, the supremacy of Russia, Germany and Austria consists not in any great democratic development of those countries, but upon their material resources and military strength. The defeat of the strongest power among them has raised the "little Jap" in the estimation of the world and no achievement is now deemed too high for his brains or arms. If China can successfully stand on her legs, the "heathen Chinee" will also be recognised as fit for the highest form of democratic institutions.

Then, where stands the false generalisation about the East and the West and the differentiation between the coloured races and the white as regards democratic institutions? Difference there is at the present moment between the Orient and the Occident, but such difference is due to difference in condition, training and opportunities, and not to any organic peculiarity. It may be the just pride of England that she has been training India in the art of self-government and that she has sown the seeds of democratic institutions on an Eastern soil; but it seems a mistake to suppose that she is making a desperate experiment of cultivating them altogether in a hot-house. India is by no means a more uncongenial soil for the growth of free institutions than any other part of His Majesty's Dominions beyond the seas. There is the latest testimony of no less an authority than Lord Glastone who, from his high place as the Governor-General of South Africa, recently oserved, that

"He had made special study of Indian history and had later visited India. He wished more South Africans could go there, and by so doing rise to the highest appreciation of what the Indians were. They would then think less of India as a country which sends its coolies to the South African coast, In fact, India had developed perhaps far above the line attained by some parts of the British Empire in its civilization and efforts to rise to a higher life."

Nor is it reasonable to attribute the aspirations of the Indian people to a want of proper appreciation of the manifold blessings which the British rule has already conferred upon them. Those aspirations, on the contrary, are an open acknowledgment of the benevolent spirit of that rule and a declaration of the confidence reposed in its justice and generosity. It is England which has deliberately created those aspirations in the minds of a people whose destiny a mysterious Providence is said to have committed to her care, and, however much she may tug and twist, she cannot wriggle out of a position into which she has thrust herself either voluntarily or in her absent-mindedness. Now the fate of India and of England is indissolubly linked together, and it would be a futile attempt to maintain the existence of the one at the expense of the other. Let England cheerfully rise to the height of her greatness which she owes in no small measure to her connection with India, and the horrid spectre which at times seems to haunt her imagination will at once vanish. King George, who appears to be a greater statesman than his party ministers, truly observed on a historic occasion that there is no people easier to govern than the Indians. Love, affection and gratitude play a more important part in the life and conduct of a people who are mystic in their ideas, romantic in their conceptions, and intensely spiritual in their aims and aspirations. Those who lightly talk of "driving discontent underground" seem not to realise that it is England's moral greatness more than her military strength that laid the foundation of her Indian Empire, and it is that greatness alone which can ensure its existence broad-based upon the love and affection of a contented and grateful people.

To even a superficial observer it will appear that a world-wide current has set in throughout the four quarters of the habitable globe. From armed and aggressive Europe to the peaceful Philippines in the Pacific Ocean, everywhere there is a ceaseless struggle going on for existence, and every people is seized with a burning desire to assert itself in a world which is rapidly changing every day. The most despotic governments which have withstood the ravages of immemorial ages are crumbling to pieces, and empires and monarchies which have stood the test of revolutions of centuries are in the course of a single revolution of the earth in its diurnal motion quietly surrendering to *vox populi*, the hereditary occupants of the thrones taking their exits as in a dramatic stage without a struggle and without shedding either a tear or a drop of blood. The bloodless revolutions which have in recent years taken place in Spain and Portugal, in Norway and Sweden and above all, in Turkey, Persia and China, would have been unthinkable only a hundred years ago, and it would be simply unreasonable to expect that India alone could have escaped being caught in the current of this universal tide. Fortunately for India it is neither a bore, nor a sweeping rush of the sea; but a slow rising tide quite normal in its condition and unalarming in its volume or intensity.

That tide has, however, entered every creek and estuary of Indian life, leading to answering movements in almost every direction. It is the duty of a wise government to place itself at the head of these movements and judiciously and sympathetically guide them into proper and useful channels rather than imperiously command, "thus far and no farther."

CONCLUSION.

It was probably the late Lord Salisbury who observed that the success of a people who know how to wait was always assured. Patience is truly the secret of success, while impatience is another name for weakness. The Congress is well conceived and is being guided on right and sound lines. It is the duty of those on whom its mantle now rests as well as of those who form its rank and file to work harmoniously and vigorously to push on its work and extend its healthy influence to the masses with the gradual spread of education among them. The Mahomedans have been galvanized into life and they have awakened themselves to a sense of self-consciousness. They are visibly coming on in a line with the Congress movement, and if the two great communities of the Indian people can unite, as they will and must unite at no distant date, "there is no force on the surface of the earth," as Sir Ibrahim Rahimtullah observes, "which can resist its just and legitimate demands." It may be necessary for the Moslem League to work independently for some time for the consideration of the special requirements of its own community; but in the meantime a *rapprochement* between the Congress and the League should be sedulously fostered by the members of both the organisations on the basis of mutual goodwill and co-operation. It may be found useful to constitute a joint Board to settle all differences between the two communities which unfortunately still lead to occasional friction and misunderstanding. It is, however, a most humiliating spectacle for either of the communities to have always recourse to the authorities for the settlement of their social and religious differences and even to go so far as to apply for a legislative measure for their control. If a "Conciliation Board" is necessary, why not establish it among ourselves? While it is difficult to gain an inch of ground in the political world, it is certainly not expedient or politic to voluntarily abdicate our birthrights even in matters of our social and religious observances and ceremonies and call for official interference. What a commentary this on our claim for self-government and what a sharp weapon in the hands of our adversaries! "United we stand and divided we all" is a trite old maxim which is never so strikingly illustrated as in the case of national evolution.

It is through reverses that success is often achieved in this world and a people that has made up its mind to rise must be prepared, to take many a defeat before it can make any tangible advance. It has been justly observed, that true greatness does not consist in never falling, but in rising every time we fall. It is only in the nature of weak people to be always highly calculating and where courage fails, to take shelter either under philosophic indifference or absolute hopelessness. Many people would fain pass for wise men and even as prophets when in reality they are unable manfully to grapple with difficulties of a situation. If optimism sometimes errs in raising extravagant hopes and ideas, pessimism is largely responsible for creating depression and fostering scepticism by magnifying dangers and difficulties beyond their real proportions. With a virile people a defect only serves to stiffen their backs. It should be remembered that in nature the struggle for existence is only a war of exhaustion and those that can endure the longest are bound to triumph in the end. The Indian nationalists ought to know that the journey they have undertaken through a wilderness under a divine call is steep and long, and that the promised land must continue to be completely out of their sight, though they may be all the same advancing by degrees, until they are within a measurable distance from it, and it would be a grievous mistake to abandon the march because at every step some faint outlines of its magnificent columns and spires are not visible to the naked eye to encourage them. Their sacred scripture says—Thou only canst *work* and shalt live by *work*; and the Indian nationalists must be prepared devotedly to work in the spirit of that scripture if the ultimate *result* is to come to those who are coming after them as a reward for their labours.

It was truly observed by the great "Father of the Congress" that "every nation gets almost as good a government as it deserves." A civilised government can and often does educate the people and stimulate their energies towards a healthy development of their national existence; but the civic rights and liberties of a people have always to be acquired and can never be the subject of free gift from a Government. Under a despotic rule they are often attained through *revolution*, while under a constitutional Government they are acquired through a process of *evolution*. But in both cases it is the people who must work out their own destiny. Self-help is the key to success in individual as well as national life, and whether the weapon employed be active pressure or passive resistance, a people that wants to rise in the scale of nations must learn to stand on its own legs. Above all, we must be true to ourselves. Those who are false to themselves can never expect others to be true to them. Confidence in one's own self and trust in righteousness constitute nearly half the success of a cause. However difficult the voyage may be, those who have launched out in the name of god and the Motherland cannot afford to turn back. Rolling and pitching, tempest-tossed and even with masts broken and riggings gone, they are bound to proceed onwards. Resolute in their purpose, firm and unswerving in their devotion and invincible in their faith, they must be pledged to sacrifice themselves in the cause of the country, looking for no other reward for their labours than the blessing of God and the approbation of their own conscience. Mutual jealousy and spite, suspicion and distrust, and envy and malice are the cankers of national life, and these secret pests have to be carefully guarded against, particularly in the early stage of its growth. To the Indian Nationalists, the country must be their religion "taught by no priests, but by the beating hearts," and *her* welfare their common faith "which makes the many one." And the one prayer in which they should ever join in a spirit of sincere humility is contained in the touching words of that pious divine who cheerfully sacrificed himself in the cause of suffering humanity :—

"Lead kindly light amid the encircling gloom.
Lead thou me on!
The night is dark and I am far from home,
Lead thou me on!
Keep thou my feet, I do not ask to see
The distant path, one step's enough for me."

CHAPTER XXV.

POSTSCRIPT.

INDIA AND THE WAR.

Since the foregoing chapters were mainly written and partly placed in the hands of the publishers, a terrible war has broken out in Europe which in its developments has drawn all the five continents of the globe into the vortex of a titanic struggle unparalleled in the history of the world. As in the middle ages the Goths and Vandals overran the Roman Empire and towards the middle of the fifteenth century the Tartar hordes of Czenghis Khan carried fire and desolation through Central and Southern Asia, so has German militarism, backed by a Teutonic confederacy, raised a world-wide conflagration in its insatiable thirst for a world-wide Empire. Solemn treaties have been openly flouted as mere "scraps of paper," sacred rights of inoffensive neutrality wantonly violated under the infernal maxim that "necessity knows no law" and a "chosen people," the boasted "salt of the earth," hurled into the fray, like herds of dumb driven cattle, to sweep away centuries of civilization by the sheer dint of the "mailed-fist" and the "shining armour." The shrieks of agonizing humanity and of outraged civilization all over the world have risen above the thunder of roaring guns and the clashing of steels, while land, sea and air are all filled with infernal engines of destruction, the proudest products of Western culture. European civilization which has ruled the world for centuries has at last stood unmasked in its grim nakedness. The outstanding figures of this terrible game up to the present form a rule of three K's—Kaiser, Krupp and Kultur—the unknown value of the fourth quantity of which has yet to be solved. England and France, while sharing in no small degree the gluttonous appetite of Europe for territorial aggrandisement and glory, are the only two countries which have ever stood in defence of Freedom's cause and the just rights of other nations, and both of them have flung themselves at the brunt of this conflict as much in their own vital interest as in justice to universal humanity and for the peace of the world. India, true to her genuine devotion to the British connection, has, forgetting all her domestic differences, risen as one man in defence of the Empire. From the princes to the peoples all are animated by a spirit of chivalry, self-sacrifice and patriotism, and as a result there has been such an outburst of loyal enthusiasm, throughout the country as has almost staggered the British public. That public had long been treated to highly coloured rigmaroles about lurking treason in India as a plausible justification of the repressive methods of its administration. The absurdities of these stories were largely exposed during the King's visit to this country in 1911, and what remained of the figments of these gross lies and libels have been completely swept away by the wave of enthusiasm which is now surging from one end of the country to the other. This spontaneous outburst of loyalty has not only for the time being silenced the Indian bureaucracy, but has come as a complete surprise upon the deluded British public. The grim humour of the situation is not, however, without its lessons. The reactionaries who had so long cried sedition to justify a repressive policy have now come forward singing hallelujahs over the efficiency and popularity of the Indian administration which it is now claimed to have evoked such gushing loyalty to the British Throne. When the cry of sedition could no longer be sustained, these resourceful critics cleverly turned round to say, lo and behold! how much the bureaucratic rule in India has done to evoke such a sentiment throughout the country! They seem to be perfect adepts in the art of burning the candle at both ends and in playing the well-known game of "head I win, tail you lose." But with the better minds of England the surprise must be not a little due to a living consciousness, if not a sincere conviction, that how little that administration has actually done to produce such a thrilling vibration throughout the country. Even the *Times*, the leading organ of conservative opinion in England, has been struck at this unexpected demonstration and frankly admitted that the Indian problem must be henceforth looked at from a different point of view. "On our part," says the great journal, "when we have settled account with the enemy, India must be allowed a more ample place in the councils of the Empire." Men like Sir Valentine Chirol and Lord Curzon, who are so well-known exponents of conservative policy and such staunch advocates of bureaucratic interests, have naturally become alarmed at the note sounded from such an unexpected quarter and have promptly entered their caveat, lest judgment should hereafter go against them either by default or non-traverse. Evidently conscious of the weakness of their hollow claim for the success of the bureaucratic rule they have also returned to their old, favourite charge against the educated community as a second string to their bow, and have taken upon themselves to inform the British public that that community have no influence with the masses (they should have spoken with some reservation to conveniently meet some other contingency) and are altogether unaffected by the wave of the popular enthusiasm evoked by the war. These pronounced exponents of uncompromising imperialism are of course not insidious German spies ; but their reckless utterances require to be as strictly censored as those of the correspondents at the front. At a critical time like the present, every other consideration, whether present or prospective, should be subordinated to the supreme needs of the Empire, and any one indulging in foolish diatribes calculated to wound the feelings and alienate the sympathies of any section or community within that Empire must be guilty of a most unpatriotic conduct. Any honest man who has the slightest claim to Indian experience would readily admit that the distinction between the masses and the classes in India in matters political is not as sharply drawn as in Western countries and that the loyalty of the Indian masses who are densely ignorant is a passive sentiment, the active expression of which is furnished by the intelligent and educated section of the population. The masses know as much of the Germans as of the man in the moon, and if German militarism were to win, they would settle down as quietly under the "mailed fist" as they are securely ensconced behind the British Lion. It is the educated community that know and understand the difference between the two and it is this section of the people alone who feel that the future destiny of India can only be attained under a democratic constitution and not under an inflated junker rule. If it is the educated men of India who adversely criticise the Government, it is because they alone are capable of appreciating the spirit of the British constitution and are desirous of improving the Indian administration by bringing it into line with that constitution and thereby securing a permanency for it. And at this time of imperial calamity it is these responsible people who are keeping the masses straight, disabusing them of disquieting rumours, and inspiring them with confidence in the strength as well as the justice of the British cause. The educated community in India is mainly composed of the middle classes, and it is these classes whom the war has hit the hardest. Yet these are the very people who have been most forward in not only offering their services to the Crown, but also in raising throughout the country as much war relief as was possible within the scope of their limited resources. The Hospital Ships fitted up by Madras and Bombay and the Ambulance Corps raised in Bengal for service in Mesopotamia are mainly the works of the educated community and of the middle classes. It is deeply to be regretted that men pretending to having a wide Indian experience and who ought to have known better should only to serve an ulterior object, come forward at this juncture to feed fat their ancient grudge against educated India.

It is all very well for blind imperialists to flatter themselves upon their shortsighted and retrograde policy based upon old-world ideas of Government; but it is a matter of no small gratification to learn that responsible British statesmanship is fully alive and equal to the situation. Both Mr. Montagu and Mr. Roberts, as Under-Secretary for India, have from time to time expressed themselves in no uncertain voice as to the correct lines upon which the Indian administration requires to be revised and modified. Mr. Montagu's honest interpretation of Lord Hardinge's despatch of August 1911 is well-known; while Mr. Roberts, speaking from his place in the House of Commons, has frankly acknowledged that with the intellectual classes in India this outburst of loyalty is "a reasoned sentiment based upon considerations of enlightened self-interest," and has at the same time asked the British public to alter "the angle of vision" in their perspective of the Indian problem. Following the *Times*, the *Review of Reviews*, has in one of its latest numbers, fairly admitted that :

"India to-day occupies a higher place in the Empire than ever before, and has materially advanced her claims towards self-government, and it is inevitable that, after the war her outstanding demands should receive the most sympathetic consideration." "We have", the *Review* adds, "made promises of self-government to Egypt, and it is inconceivable that we should deny the same privileges to India. At present India is not pressing her claim, but patiently awaits her just due, not as a reward, but as a right which her conduct has shown her worthy of possessing."

Lord Haldane, a prominent member of the last Liberal Cabinet, at a reception by the Indian students in England, said :—

"The Indian soldiers were fighting for the liberties of humanity, as much as we ourselves. India had freely given her lives and treasure in humanity's great cause, hence things could not be left as they were. We had been thrown together in the mighty struggle and had been made to realise our oneness, so producing relations between India and England which did not exist before. Our victory would be victory for the Empire as a whole and could not fail to raise it to a higher level."

These pronouncements represent a correct appreciation of the Indian situation, and in arriving at a real and correct solution of the phenomenal demonstration of Indian loyalty. England must first thoroughly disabuse herself of her pre-conceived prejudices, abandon an ostrich-like policy and direct her vision more to the future than to the past.

The demonstration proceeds from two causes both potential in their nature, though one is positive while the other is negative in its character. India's aims and aspirations are indissolubly bound up with democratic ideas and institutions, and the people are thoroughly convinced that it is the gradual development of these ideas and institutions which alone can enable her to realise her destiny in the evolution of her national life. Starting from this hypothesis, one of these causes is not far to seek. Before the outbreak of the war the world was full of admiration for German culture, German enterprise and German erudition; but educated India was not very much impressed with German democracy. The inability of Germany to conciliate and Germanize two of her conquered provinces equally civilized within a period of nearly half a century, and the disgraceful incident which recently took place at Zabern incontestably proved that amidst all her grandeur and greatness acquired since the war of 1870, Germany possessed little or nothing of popular liberty. Her Reichstag is only a mock imitation of the British Parliament or the French Chamber and a little better than an enlarged edition of the Indian Legislative Councils which can freely indulge in academic discussions, ask questions and move resolutions, but for practical purposes can no more shape the policy of a despotic government than it can control the action of a still more despotic sovereign. The moral strength as well as the political status of a people must be extremely doubtful whom it is possible to dupe in this age of reason and common sense by one man, how high his position and however strong his hold upon their imagination may be, by openly announcing that "the spirit of the Lord has descended upon him" to lead his "chosen people" to victory like the wandering Israilities of old and whose blasphemous tongue is not afraid of declaring, as it is reported to have declared on the memorable 3rd of August, that:

> "It is my imperial and royal intention to give consideration to the wishes of God with regard to Belgium when I shall have executed my imperial and royal will with regard to France and the pestilent and contemptible English."

Vanity of vanities before High Heavens! His imperial and royal Majesty may be perfectly free to execute, if he can, his imperial and royal will as regards the future of France and "contemptible England"; but to have the hardihood to say that it is his imperial and royal intention so to condescend as to vouchsafe his kind "consideration to the wishes of God" must be regarded, if the report be true, as the height of a mental derangement bordering on dangerous lunacy. It has been truly said that pride goeth before fall and vanity before destruction. Even the great Napoleon, whose equal in military genius the world has not yet produced, was never guilty of such arrogance not to speak of such profanation, although kingdom after kingdom, including Germany, fell prostrate before him and his invincible legions with such astounding rapidity as the world has never witnessed whether in ancient or modern times. But after all what must be the *morale* and the status of a people who can believe in the *superman*, merge their existence into the State surrendering all their personal rights and liberties and ungrudgingly acquiesce in the methods of military despotism? Question of barbarism apart, which seems to be no insignificant feature of German militarism, these facts constitute a severe indictment of German culture and enlightenment. Indian loyalty may not proceed from an affection for British rule, but it certainly proceeds from a dread of something very much worse under German militarism. Here lies the negative origin of the phenomenal demonstration which has taken place in this country irrespective of colour, caste and creed.

On the positive side, there is much to be said in favour of the British constitution though not in favour of the Anglo-Indian administration. It is of course not to be supposed even for a moment that a people who have for the life-time of a generation bitterly complained against the methods of a bureaucratic rule have been suddenly transformed into an admiring crowd by the magic wand of a repressive policy. On the contrary, their opposition to the bureaucracy is only a milder reflex of their stronger hatred for German despotism. But the people are thoroughly impressed with the superiority of the British constitution and the morality of the British nation. That constitution, being essentially democratic, naturally appeals to the sentiment and imagination of a people whose national evolution is so largely dependent upon the growth and development of democratic ideas and institutions, and which can only be fostered by a people who have themselves fought for personal rights and liberties and tasted the sweets of free citizenship. Educated India knows and understands that with all its faults the British nation as a whole is inspired with a sense of justice and regard for truth. If in times past there ever was ruthless spoliation in India, it had also been occasionally followed by relentless impeachment in England. If in the roll of Indian Viceroys there have been reactionaries like Lord Dalhousie and Lord Curzon, there have been also brilliant names like those of Canning, Bentinck, Ripon and Hardinge. It is a nation for whom Milton wrote and Sidney died not in vain, and in whom the spirit of Howard and Wilberforce still works with undiminished sway. That nation cannot be fairly judged by the spirit of the Indian bureaucracy or the Anglo-Indian press. If the repeated vexations and disappointments of India have been very great, her hope and confidence in England are still greater. The task of ameliorating her condition is not an easy one. What a mass of prejudices have grown round the policy of the administration of the country, what an accumulation of superstitions have found place in the tradition of the government, how many vested interests, not unoften incompatible with the true well-being of the people, have asserted themselves in places of power and authority, what an invincible entanglement of barbed wire-fencings have been drawn for the protection of those interests at every assailable point, what an atmosphere of suspicion and distrust has been created, how deep and wide trenches have been dug out to keep the people outside the pale of an official hierarchy, and above all, what a solid bureaucracy governing the body-politic from top to bottom has been firmly established. These enormous difficulties have to be overcome for a satisfactory solution of the Indian problem. The war has opened unforeseen conditions and a splendid opportunity for the solution of that problem. It has at once dissipated the dark and threatening clouds of suspicion and distrust and cleared the vision of the British public. It has inspired the Indian mind with hope and confidence in the fruition of her long-deferred destiny within the Empire, and it is in this hope and confidence that a correct explanation has to be sought for the positive side of the Indian demonstration and not in the achievements of an effete and unpopular bureaucracy which has so far rather hindered than helped the growth of Indian attachment to the British connection. Correctly understood, the present attitude of India is a strong and successful protest against the theories and principles of that bureaucracy, Lord Crewe apparently made a great mistake in addressing a number of young recruits for the Indian Civil Service in the old orthodox style that he did on a recent occasion. The extravagant tribute he paid to that service was altogether wide of the mark and has given great offence to the people of this country. If he really believes that the unique outburst of loyalty which the great war has called forth in India is due to the bureaucratic administration, then his Lordship must have completely misread the history of the Indian administration during the last thirty years or more. The Indian princes are beyond the pale of the Indian Civil Service; while during the whole of that period there has been a continuous stand-up fight between the people and the bureaucracy. Whatever merits that bureaucracy may claim as regards their efficiency in other directions, conciliation is certainly not one of them. Indeed they have never cared to conciliate the people and have always spoken contemptuously of driving discontent underground.

They have throughout cried sedition and sought to repress. Repression may coerce, but cannot manufacture loyalty and particularly such an outburst of that sentiment as is swaying the Indian mind at the present moment. For a responsible minister of the Crown, who holds in his hand the reins of the Indian Government, to get up an unnecessary ceremony to compliment the bureaucracy in such a style and at such a time was, to say the least of it, highly impolitic, and people are not wanting who have received it as a great disappointment, if not as rude shock, to their sentiments. Taking the various pronouncements recently made in England both for and against their cherished hopes and aspirations and reading between them in the light of the fate of Lord Crewe's Bill for the reform of the India Council and of the Royal Proclamation for the establishment of an Executive Council for the United Provinces, the people are apt to take a somewhat gloomy and despondent view of the situation, and not unnaturally apprehend that it may all end in another repetition of what is known as breaking to the hope while promising to the ear. But after all the pronouncement of the Secretary of State may be nothing more than a conventional compliment intended more to encourage a batch of young men in the honest discharge of their duty than to operate as a judgment on the pending issues between the people and the bureaucracy. People of the Chirol-Curzon School may no doubt enter their protests in anticipation; but the educated community in India who have studied the British constitution and closely followed the trend of the British democracy may yet possess their souls in patience and confidently await a fair and impartial decision in their case when it is ripe for judgment.

Good often cometh out of evil and calamitous as the war is, it is not without its lessons for the future of the world. It has dissipated the wildest dreams of the materialist for the establishment of universal peace upon the basis of international commerce and the fondest hopes of the socialist to establish universal brotherhood by preaching against increase of armaments of war. Both these prescriptions have served only to aggravate the war-fever and intensify international jealousy and spite. A system of armed neutrality was devised under the cloak of which all the powers in Europe were running a constant race for political supremacy in the name of progress and enlightenment. Civilization, culture and even religion were made to contribute to that one end, and while every one cried peace, all were intent on disturbing the peace of the world. A fierce collision under such circumstance was inevitable and the armed powers of Europe have at last met to play the last scene of the tragic drama which they had so long laboured to put on the stage. The war has revealed in a ghastly light the overwhelming preponderance of barbarism which the world still retains, amidst all her progress and advancement, and has clearly demonstrated that both the conception as well as the ideal of modern civilization must be thoroughly revised by those who profess to hold the future of the world in their hands if they really aim at peace, prosperity and happiness of God's creation. They must, to begin with, curb their consuming ambition and gluttonous appetite which have so far served to civilise the world largely by a process of exploitation and extinction and by substituting specimens of refined savagery for inoffensive barbarism of weaker people. Pillage, plunder, incendiarism, massacre and other unutterable and shocking offences on women and children are as rampant in modern warfare as they were in the days of Alexander, and if the Thracian robber had been living to-day he might well have hesitated to choose between the ancient Macedonian and the modern Teuton. Looking from the standpoint of universal humanity and a higher ideal of human evolution it must be painfully admitted that modern science and civilisation have contributed more to the material than to the moral progress of the world; and if the present war succeeds in revealing to the West some of the higher aspects of the philosophy of the East, its appalling sacrifices in men, money and treasures of art will not have been incurred wholly in vain.

The first outstanding feature of the war is the co-operation and fellowship of the different units of a consolidated Empire. It has dissipated the longstanding colour prejudices under which Europe claimed an inherent and permanent superiority over the inhabitants of Asia and Africa and refused comradeship with them even in the grave. France, which seems to have developed the highest power of assimilation, has derived no small advantages from her solid possessions in Africa, as Great Britain has done from her vast territories in India. Turcos, Zuaves, Moors and the Senegalese have added as much weight to the French army as the Sikhs, the Gurkhas, the Jats and the Pathans have strengthened the British Expeditionary Force to the Continent. Fighting side by side with and against white races, these brave soldiers of Africa and India have incontestably proved that the colour of the skin is entirely due to climatic conditions and does not at all connote any essential distinction in the physical, intellectual and moral fabrics of any race whether residing in the torrid or the tropical zone. Differences no doubt exist; but they are mostly the result of forced conditions and artificial barriers irrespective of all considerations of latitudes and longitudes. For the first time in the history of Europe the martial races of India have been admitted into comradeship with the British and the colonial forces of the Empire and the entire population of India made to take a noble pride in the defence of that Empire. The war has made the Indian people recognise their position as well as their responsibility as a distinct unit—not merely a dependency, but a component part—of the huge fabric which goes by the name of the British Empire. In fact, the imperial conception of that fabric is based upon the possession of India, and India naturally expects to be recognised as an equal partner both in the rights and liabilities of the Imperial Federation which the war is likely to bring about as the psychological development and the highest strength of the British Empire. Without the cement of fellowship and equality no union can be either solid or lasting; and weak in one point, whether at the base or in the superstructure, the hugest fabric devised by human skill is liable to collapse either in course of natural decay or whenever subjected to a test of its strength.

In the next place it has to be considered that it is neither possible nor desirable for India to aim at sovereign independence at the present stage of her evolution, and whether such a state is or is not attainable at some remote future period need not very much concern us at present; while it seems extremely doubtful if consistently with her higher aspiration for the establishment of an All-Indian Nationalism, India can ever attempt at such a consummation without the disruption and disintegration of those forces with which she has set to work in building an Indian nation. It is no doubt a long and laborious task requiring patience and perseverance. In the work of nation-building every generation has its appropriate task and if every generation were only to contemplate the carvings and mouldings for the finishing touch of the edifice, where would be the less attractive foundation underground and the barren superstructure upon it? The work must be built up from the base to the top and no rational people can think of reversing the process. There may be revolutionaries who, in their inability to grasp this higher conception of an All-India Confederacy, dream of perfect independence as the goal of their nationalism; while people are not wanting who seem to indulge in the belief that in the fullness of time England herself will out of her free will retire from the field leaving the people to govern the country as a free and independent nation. The idea is perfectly Utopian and if those who entertain it are at all sincere in their expression, they must be quite mistaken in their views.. No nation in this world, whether in ancient or modern times, has ever shown such an example of philanthropy, and the British people cannot be expected to do that which is not in human nature. Besides, nations are not born, but by themselves are made. If the people of India do not by degrees learn to govern themselves, it is inconceivable that a time should ever come when the people of Great Britain will find an opportunity of relieving themselves of the "white man's burden," or of fulfilling "the sacred trust of Providence" of which so much has been said and written. Freedom and independence cannot be the gift of one people to another. They have to be acquired and sometimes, also extorted; but they can never form the subject of a voluntary conveyance. Given the opportuuities presented by the situation created by the European War, it should be the highest endeavour of the Indian nationalists calmly and vigorously to press forward for an adjustment of their outstanding claims as well as for a fair apportionment of their liabilities and responsibilities arising out of that situation. The highest statesmanship in England should also frankly, recognise the necessities of that situation and be ready to consolidate the Empire on firmer basis. The Government is certainly bound to proceed with caution and circumspection; but it is also expected to proceed with genuine trust and confidence in the people. It is not enough that justice should be done to them, but the people should be made to feel that they do not live under a foreign domination. One Indian administrator has told us that it would be inconsistent with Eastern character and tradition to expect a reward for humble and loyal services rendered at the present juncture. He has of course not gone the length of reminding us of the story of the Lion and the Crane; but the appeal is quite characteristic of the bureaucratic sympathies for the hopes and aspirations of the Indian people. But what people are there in this world who do not naturally expects a reward for their services? Besides, the claim of the Indians for self-government is not in the nature of a reward for their participation in the present war, but as of right which they had advanced long before this war broke out. There may be people who are eager to seize every opportunity to work upon the spiritualism of the Indian character to turn its attention from the material aspect of a situation; but they must be very much mistaken to think that the Indians of to-day can be made to reconcile themselves to their lot with the mere bribe of eternity. England must be prepared in her own interest to admit India into an equal partnership of the Empire.

As words without thoughts never go to heaven, so promises without performance can never touch the heart of a people. In fact, in practical politics, promise unredeemed is much worse than no promise at all. England has plunged herself into a desperate struggle for the honour and sanctity of a "scrap of paper." The Charter Act of 1833, the Queen's Proclamation of 1858 and the two gracious messages of Edward VII. and George V. all demand that they should not be allowed to be considered in any quarter as mere "scraps of paper." Now an opportunity has arrived for the redemption of the solemn pledges which have been so often repeated but never fulfilled. A great nation's word is its bond and England cannot consistently with her honour and greatness resile from the position to which she has voluntarily committed herself. Judging however by the fate of Lord Crewe's India Council Bill and of Lord Hardinge's Proclamation for the establishment of a Council Government for the United Provinces, not an inconsiderable section of the Indian people are getting nervous as to the ultimate result of the many promises held out to them recently in England. The "angle of vision" may be changed after the war; but whether it is the angle of vision of the Indians or of the British people that may have to be altered, events alone can prove. If the former be the case, it may not require too much of the gift of prophecy to say that the result will be simply disastrous. Of course there are those who sincerely indulge in the belief that as India has been won by the sword so it must be maintained by the sword, and that the grant of autonomy to India would be the first notice to quit given, to England. On the other hand, there are those who with equal emphasis, though not with equal authority, maintain that a permanent occupation of India by England is only possible upon grounds of perfect reciprocity as in the case of the colonies. History does not present a single instance where one nation however powerful has succeeded in permanently holding another nation under subjection except through a process of assimilation and amalgamation. The Dominion of Canada, the Commonwealth of Australia and the

Union of South Africa, which have now materially contributed to the strength of Great Britain, all furnish a striking contrast to the results of a policy of coercion which Edmund Burke in his prophetic vision so clearly foresaw and to avert which he vainly pleaded for conciliation of America.

THE NEW SPIRIT AND SELF-GOVERNMENT FOR INDIA.

It has already been shewn that with the inauguration of the reactionary policy of Lord Curzon, a New Spirit arose in the country. It is a serious mistake to confuse this new spirit with the ugly developments which took place about this time as a result of that policy. For a long time the people had lost confidence in the progressive character of the administration and a feeling was steadily gaining ground in certain quarters that the passive method of the Congress had exhausted all its resources. And no further result could be expected to flow from it. The futility of petitions and prayers was advanced as a strong argument to undermine the constitution of the Congress and weaken its hold upon the public mind. The position of the leaders at this period was one of extreme difficulty and embarrassment. On the one hand they had to contend against opposing forces working from within and on the other to repel incessant bureaucratic assaults delivered from without. The firmness and fortitude with which they however held their position at this critical stage bear remarkable evidence of their judgment, political insight and capacity of no mean order. Although the Congress from its very inception had started with the basel idea of representative institutions for India, it began with the internal reforms of the administration hoping to build up from the bottom to the top. For twenty years it was mainly engaged in spade work, clearing the ground and removing the roots and branches of all the thorny questions that beset the situation. The very indifferent and inadequate success which attended this labour coupled with an unsympathetic and reactionary policy naturally led to a state of unrest and largely contributed to the growth of the new spirit, which has now manifested itself in a clear and open demand for self-government. Those who complacently advise the people still to work at the base apparently forget that they want them to retrace their step and proceed upon a line which has long been tried and found infractuous. Congressmen have found to their bitter experience that all attempts at irrigating and fructifying the plain without securing the supply of the fountain-head and removing the impediments and obstructions to an uninterrupted flow of the stream are vain and delusive; for strike as hard as you can and dig as long as you may choose, if the source spring will refuse its supply all your efforts are bound to end in disappointment. The constitution of a government is the only key to unfold its internal administration. It is the "open sesame" to a bureaucratic rule whose iron portals will yield neither to "open wheat" nor "open Barley" however patiently and persistently u may cry it.

The Congress which had so long urged for an expansion of the Legislative Councils now acquired a deeper insight and grasped a more definite idea for the realization of its aims. In 1904 it formulated a resolution for an effective Representation of the people in the higher administration of the country and this resolution was re-affirmed in the Congress of 1905. But it was not until the memorable session of 1906 that a formal demand for Self-Government within the Empire was plainly and definitely put forward. The Partition of Bengal proved to be the last straw on the camel's back and the New Spirit burst forth throughout the country. Small section of fiery youngmen seized with the ideas of the Irish *Sein Fein* got out of hand and a series of repressive measures followed in quick succession. The Congress, however, held on firm and unassailable. The split at Surat no doubt weakened its rank ; but the New spirit which was perfectly legitimate and quite as wide of any revolutionary ideas as the poles as under continued to gather strength both in and outside the Congress in spite of the many adverse circumstances which beset it. It inspired both the moderates and extremists and recognised self-government as the only remedy for the evils from which the country suffered. The waning enthusiasm for the Congress was however not due to the operation of the repressive measures but to two other causes both internal in their character. In the first place, it was the suicidal defection of one entire wing of the Nationalist party, and in the second place the serious aloofness which still possessed the important Mahomedand community. Attempts were however made from time to time both through the press as well as the platforms to remove these causes until the Allahabad Congress of 1910 when Sir William Wedderburn made a vigorous effort not only to reunite both the wings of the Nationalists, but also to remove the wedge which had been driven deep to split up the Hindu and the Mussalman communities *en bloc.* The communal representation in the one case and the convention creed in the other were the two main stumbling blocks in the way of the settlement of these vexed questions. The labours of some of the advanced and patriotic Mahomedan leaders towards the solution of the Hindu-Mahomedan question were most helpful to the common cause. The first step towards an effective *rapproachment* was however not taken until 1915 when the Congress under the presidency of Sir S. P. Sinha and the Moslem League under the presidency of Mr. Mazar-ul-Haque simultaneously held their session in Bombay. But though this was a decisive step in advance, an unforeseen incident for which neither the Hindus nor the Moslems were responsible advanced the cause of union still further. The local authorities, as is often the case with a short-sighted and nervous bureaucracy, most imprudently interfered with the proceedings of the League and this at once dispelled what remained of the fantastic delusion of the Moslem community for a separate and independent realization of their destiny. Both the League and the Congress now formed Committees to formulate a common scheme for the attainment of their common destiny within the Empire.

At this stage a masterful personality appeared on the scene. Mrs. Annie Besant who had long consecrated her life to the services of her adoptive motherland now came out with her proposal for starting a Home Rule League for India. In 1915 she consulted a number of Congress leaders, many of whom approved of the idea and advised her not to launch it as a distinctly independent organization but only as supplementary to and working in harmony with the Congress movement. To this she readily agreed and a number of Congressmen, including the Grand Old Man, expressed their adherence to this plan of her campaign. There were of course some among the old Congressmen who regarded her as being extremely impulsive and viewed her method with distrust, although none questioned the honesty, integrity and sincerity of her purpose.

The new spirit thus gained considerable strength from different sources and directions ; while a devastating war broadened its vision as regards the immediate future destiny of the country as a component unit of the Empire. Self-Government had long been the aim of the Congress as being the true remedy for the grave situation in this country. It now became its watchword and battle-cry in the bloodless evolution which was silently marking its progress upon the dial of its destiny,

During the following year both the All-India Congress Committee, in consultation with its various Provincial Committees, and the representatives of the All-India Moslem League worked strenuously and after many a stormy debate arrived at a solution of the vexed question of communal representation which was raised in some of the Provinces and nowhere was this thorny question more hotly contested or keenly debated than in the United Provinces. The whole scheme was finally submitted to the decision of a joint Conference of the leaders of all the communities, which met at Lucknow on the eve of the thirty-first session of the Congress and the ninth session of the All-India Moslem League.

In the meantime the Government of Lord Chelmsford was understood to have arranged for a despatch to the Secretary of State for India touching some of the post-war reforms for this country and the non-official members of the Imperial Legislative Council who were then at Delhi at once hastened to submit to the Government a memorandum based on the lines formulated by the various Committees of the Congress and the League. The finishing touch to this new movement inaugurated by a new spirit was however reserved for the next session of the Indian National Congress which was the most brilliant session ever held since its birth. The 31st Indian National Congress held at Lucknow on the 28th, 29th, 30th and 31st December 1916 was not only an epoch-making session, but it fully indicated its title as a truly *national* assembly. The Hindus and Mussalmans for the first time openly joined hands and the moderates and extremists who had parted company since the Surat split again closed their ranks to make a united demand for self-government under the ægis of the British Crown. Men like Sir Rashbehary Ghose, Surendra Nath Banerjee, Madan Mohan Malaviya, Bhupendra Nath Basu and N. M. Samarth sat side by side with Messrs. Tilak, Khaparde, Govinda Raghava Iyer and others; while the indomitable Mrs. Annie Besant who had grown grey in the service of her adoptive Motherland, came there accompanied by her trusted disciples Messrs. Arundale and Wadia and true to her Celtic blood raised the cry of "Home Rule for India". Mahomedan leaders like the patriotic Rajah of Mahmudabad, Mr. Mazar-ul-Haque, Mr. A. Rusaul and Mr. Mahomed Ali Jinnah worthily represented their community. The two South African heroes, Messrs. Gandhi and Polak, were also there and then took an active part in its deliberations. Thus it was a unique session of the Congress in which all classes and communities, as well as every political school in the country, were fully represented. An entire day was given for the discussions of the Subjects Committee which finally settled the scheme of self-government formulated by the committees of the Congress and the League and very nearly the whole of a day was taken in the Congress by a full-dressed debate upon this vital question. The scheme was read clause by clause and almost all the leading men in the various provinces took active part in the discussion. At the close of the prolonged and interesting debate a resolution embodying the scheme which laid down the demands of the people to be given effect to in the readjustment of the Empire after the close of the war was unanimously adopted, the whole of the vast assembly of delegates and visitors standing in response to a call from the chair and cheering with repeated and deafening shouts of *Bande Mataram.* On the following day this scheme was also adopted by the All-India Moslem League without a division. The Congress adopted a further resolution calling upon the various Congress Committees and other organised bodies and associations to start propagandist work throughout the country to give effect to the scheme. The whole country at once caught the fire and rang with the cry of self-government and no province took up the question earlier or with greater earnestness than Madras under the auspices of the Home Rule League of which Mrs. Besant was the central figure and the guiding spirit.

As in Bombay so at Lucknow an unpleasant incident took place which was quite illustrative of the nervous meddlesomeness of the Indian bureaucracy which like the proverbial tiger, has the habit of aggravating its own sore by constantly licking it. Shortly before the Congress week a most gratuitous and offensive letter was issued from the U. P. Government Secretariat warning the Chairman of the Reception Committee and its General Secretary against the use of any seditious speeches at the Congress and apparently so great was the anxiety of the authorities that a copy of this letter was served also on the President-Elect through the Government of Bengal. The Chairman and the Secretary gave a firm and pertinent reply to this uncalled for communication, while the President took no notice of it. Judging from the recent strange proceedings of the Bombay and the Berar Governments prohibiting Mrs. Annie Besant from entering their territories many were the people who apprehended that this letter of the U. P. Government was only a prelude to a still more untoward development at Lucknow. The good sense of the Lieutenant-Governor, however, prevailed and averted any further unpleasantness. On the second day Sir

James Meston accompanied by Lady Meston and attended by his staff came to the Congress. The President gave him a fitting welcome on behalf of the Congress and Sir James gave a most sympathetic reply. Thus the last lingering mist of suspicion and irritation which still hung over the delegates was at once removed, and the work of the Congress, as well as the League, to which also Sir James Meston paid a similar visit, went off smoothly and without a hitch.

The remarkable success of the historic session of the Congress was as far as its local interest was concerned largely due to the untiring zeal and patriotic devotion of two men—the Rajah of Mahmudabad, one of the premier Taluqdars of Oudh, and Mr. Gokaran Nath Misra, the energetic General Secretary of the Reception Committee, who stumped the whole province and roused the people to a pitch of enthusiasm unsurpassed in the history of the Congress. Mr. Bishen Narain Dhar who had been fitly selected as the Chairman of the Reception Committee suddenly died and Mr. Jagat Narain, another sound and silent worker in the cause of the Congress, at once stepped to fill the vacant chair and worthily did he fill it. But above all it was the visible manifestation of the new spirit, which had taken a full decade slowly but steadily to develop itself amidst repeated defeats and disappointments that at last burst upon the country with a world-wide struggle between Imperialism and Democracy and raised the cry of constitutional freedom for India within the charmed circle of the great British Empire, as being the only rational solution of the Indian problem and the concrete basis of a permanent settlement of the indissoluble link between Great Britain and India.

It ought to be fairly recognised that India disenfranchised, emasculated and discontented is a source of weakness to Great Britain. India is no doubt the most valuable asset of her imperial greatness; but all her immense internal resources both in men as well as materials stand at present practically as a dead stock in her balance-sheet. A vast country like India with her teeming millions numbering five times the population of Germany should alone have furnished at the present juncture an effective reply to German militarism and closed all discussion about compulsory military service in Great Britain. These facts never received any serious consideration until the present crisis forced them upon the attention of responsible men in England. At a meeting of the Royal Colonial Institute presided over by the Right Hon'ble Mr. Hobhouse, who was the President of the Royal Commission on Decentralization and not long ago a member of the Cabinet, Colonel Sir Francis Younghusband with his intimate knowledge of India and the characteristic frankness of a soldier said, that "as regards the future of India it could safely be predicted that new conditions would arise, the old demand of Indians for commissions in the army would be pressed; there would be demands for a more definite share in the Councils of the Empire, a larger part in the management of their own affairs, right to bear arms and to volunteer and a more equal social position." Then at a recent meeting held at Guildhall at the instance of the Lord Mayor, Mr. Asquith, the premier, and Mr.

Bonar Law, the rest while leader of the Opposition and both now united in a coalition ministry, have given a joint pledge for the readjustment of India's position in the Councils of the Empire after the war is over. But, to quote the words of Mr. Bonar Law, why the thing should not be done "while the metal was still glowing red-hot from the furnace of the war," and the promised rewards of India's comradeship and co-operation should be all relegated to the indefinite future and not one of them even shadowed forth in the present programme of the Imperial Government, seems to be inexplicable; while here in India there seems to be not the slightest indication of a disposition to treat the situation otherwise than as quite normal in its conditions and requirements. Sceptics are not, therefore, altogether wanting in this country who gravely shake their heads at the future prospects supposed to have been at last opened out by this terrible revolutionary war and warn the bulk of the people not to be over-sanguine in their expectations to avoid the rude shock of a bitter disappointment.

The military career which after 30 years of vain but persistent efforts has recently been opened to the Indians is a great step in advance towards the formation of a national militia and it would be a fatal blunder if the people notwithstanding all the defects, disabilities and discouragements of the system do not ungrudgingly seize this opportunity to establish their first claim to a legitimate and adequate share in a responsible government for the country.

Everything turns on the question of mutual trust and confidence. If England really believes in the fidelity of India and is more deeply inspired by a higher policy of prospective greatness than by any short-sighted consideration of immediate loss and gain, the dictates of self-interest alone will induce her carefully to tend and nourish the goose that lays the golden egg. But if, on the other hand, her feeling towards India be such as to dispose her to hand her over even to her worst enemies rather than to the Indians themselves, no amount of argument will satisfy her that she has not muddied the water and need not, therefore, be condemned to the last penalty for her action. It is, however, only fair to presume that a nation that sacrificed millions upon millions for the liberation of enslaved humanity and which has always stood forth to defend freedom's cause wherever threatened by the vaulting ambition of military despotism, is not likely easily to go back upon its solemn pledges, falsify its best traditions and stultify itself before the eyes of the world. Great Britain does not appear to have passed the meridian of her greatness and a nation in its ascending node with all its lapses has always a motion upwards. Besides, if the longivity of a nation, like that of an individual, is to be judged by its achievements and not simply by its earthly duration, the question easily yields to but one solution. Then if at some remote period in the fullness of time and in the dispensation of Providence the inevitable hour should come when Great Britain must fall, may she so fall fulfilling her "divine mission" and covered with imperishable glory blazing forth through distant ages in the annals of an emancipated people. *Bande Mataram.*

APPENDIX A.

CONSTITUTION

OF THE

INDIAN NATIONAL CONGRESS ORGANISATION.

(As adopted by the Congress of 1908, amended by the Congress of 1911, and further amended by the Congress of 1912.)

ARTICLE I.

OBJECTS.

The objects of the Indian National Congress are the attainment by the people of India of a system of government similar to that enjoyed by the self-governing members of the British Empire and a participation by them in the rights and responsibilities of the Empire on equal terms with those members. These objects are to be achieved by constitutional means by bringing about a steady reform of the existing system of administration and by promoting national unity, fostering public spirit and developing and organising the intellectual, moral, economic and industrial resources of the country.

ARTICLE II.

Every delegate to the Indian National Congress shall express in writing his acceptance of the objects of the Congress as laid down in Article I. of this Constitution and his willingness to abide by this constitution and by the rules of the Congress hereto appended.

SESSIONS OF THE CONGRESS.

ARTICLE III.

(*a*) The Indian National Congress shall ordinarily meet once every year during Christmas holidays at such town as may have been decided upon at the previous session of the Congress.

(*b*) If no such decision has been arrived at, the All-India Congress Committee shall decide the matter.

(c) An extraordinary session of the Congress may be summoned by the All-India Congress Committee, either of its own motion or on the requisition of a majority of the Provincial Congress Committees, wherever and whenever it may deem it advisable to hold such session.

(d) It shall be open to the All-India Congress Committee to change the venue of the Congress to some other town when such change is deemed by it to be necessary or desirable owing to serious or unforeseen difficulties or other contingencies of a like nature.

COMPONENT PARTS OF THE ORGANISATION.

ARTICLE IV.

The Indian National Congress Organisation will consist of:—

(a) The Indian National Congress.

(b) Provincial Congress Committees.

(c) District Congress Committees.

(d) Sub-divisional or Taluka Congress Committees affiliated to the District Congress Committees.

(e) Political Associations or Public Bodies recognised by the Provincial Congress Committees.

(f) The All-India Congress Committee.

(g) The British Committee of the Congress; and

(h) Bodies formed or organised periodically by a Provincial Congress Committee, such as the Provincial or District Conference or the Reception Committee of the Congress or Conference for the year.

ARTICLE V.

No person shall be eligible to be a member of any of the Provincial or District or other Congress Committees unless he has attained the age of 21 and expresses in writing his acceptance of the objects of the Congress as laid down in Article I. of this Constitution and his willingness to abide by this constitution and by the rules of the Congress hereto appended.

PROVINCIAL CONGRESS COMMITTEES.

ARTICLE VI.

(a) To act for the Province in Congress matters and for organising Provincial or District Conferences in such manner as it may deem proper, there shall be a Provincial Congress Committee with its headquarters at the chief town of the Province in each of the following nine Provinces:—

1. Madras. II. Bombay. III. United Bengal. IV. United Provinces. V. Punjab (including N. W. Frontier Provinces). VI. Central Provinces. VII. Behar and Orissa. VIII. Berar; and IX. Burma.

ARTICLE VII.

Every Provincial Congress Committee will consist of :—

(*a*) Such persons in the Province as may have attended as many sessions of the Congress as delegates as may be determined by each Provincial Congress Committee for its own Province.

(*b*) Representatives elected in accordance with its terms of affiliation by every affiliated District Congress Committee.

(*c*) As many representatives of recognised Political Associations or Public Bodies referred to in Clause (*e*) of Article IV. as each Provincial Congress Committee may think fit to determine.

(*d*) All such ex-Presidents of the Congress or ex-Chairmen of Reception Committees of the Congress as ordinarily reside within the jurisdiction of the Provincial Congress Committee and may not have been enrolled as members of the said Committee in accordance with Clause (*b*) of Article VI. or by virtue of the provisions contained in any of the foregoing Clauses of this Article.

(*e*) The General Secretary or Secretaries of the Congress ordinarily residing within the jurisdiction of the Provincial Congress Committee, such General Secretary of Secretaries being added as *ex officio* member or members of the said Committee.

ARTICLE VIII.

Every member of the Provincial Congress Committee shall pay an annual subscription of not less than Rs. 5.

DISTRICT OR OTHER CONGRESS COMMITTEES OR ASSOCIATIONS.

ARTICLE IX.

The Provincial Congress Committee shall have affiliated to itself a District Congress Committee or Association for each District, wherever possible, or for such other areas in the Province as it deems proper, subject to such conditions or terms of affiliation as it may deem expedient or necessary. It will be the duty of the District Congress Committee or Association to act for the District in Congress matters with the co-operation of any Sub-divisional or Taluka Congress Committees which may be organised and affiliated to it, subject in all cases to the general control and approval of the Provincial Congress Committee.

ARTICLE X.

Every member of the District Congress Committee or Association shall either be a resident of the District or shall have a substantial interest in the District and shall pay an annual subscription of not less than one Rupee.

ARTICLE XI.

No District Congress Committee or Association or Public Body referred to in Clauses (c) & (e) of Article IV. shall be entitled to return representatives to the Provincial Congress Committee or Delegates to the Congress or to the Provincial Conference unless it contributes to the Provincial Congress Committee such annual subscription as may be determined by the latter.

ARTICLE XII.

Each Provincial Congress Committee shall frame its own rules not inconsistent with the constitution and the rules of the Congress. No District or other Congress Committee or Association mentioned in Article IX shall frame any rules inconsistent with those framed by the Provincial Congress Committee to which it is affiliated.

THE ALL-INDIA CONGRESS COMMITTEE.

ARTICLE XIII.

The All-India Congress Committee shall, as far as possible, be constituted as hereinbelow laid down:—

15	Representatives of	Madras.
15	" "	Bombay.
20	" "	United Bengal (including Assam).
15	" "	United Provinces.
13	" "	Punjab (including N. W. Frontier Provinces).
7	" "	Central Provinces.
15	" "	Behar and Orissa.
5	" "	Berar; and
2	" "	Burma

provided, as far as possible, that 1/5th of the total number of representatives shall be Mahomedans.

All ex-Presidents of the Congress residing or present in India, and the General Secretaries of the Congress, who shall also be *ex-officio* General Secretaries of the All-India Congress Committee, shall be *ex-officio* members in addition.

ARTICLE XIV.

The representatives of each Province shall be elected by its Provincial Congress Committee at a meeting held, as far as possible, before the 30th of November for each year. If any

Provincial Congress Committee fail to elect its representatives, the said representatives shall be elected by the delegates for that Province present at the ensuing Congress. In either case, the representatives of each Province shall be elected from among the members of its Provincial Congress Committee, and the election shall be made, as far as possible, with due regard to the proviso in Article XIII.

ARTICLE XV.

The names of the representatives so elected by the different Provinces shall be communicated to the General Secretaries. These together with the names of the *ex officio* members shall be announced at the Congress.

ARTICLE XVI.

The President of the Congress at which the All-India Congress Committee comes into existence shall, if he ordinarily resides in India, be *ex officio* President of the All-India Congress Committee. In his absence the members of the All-India Congress Committee may elect their own President.

ARTICLE XVII.

(*a*) The All-India Congress Committee so constituted shall hold office from the date of its appointment at the Congress till the appointment of the new Committee.

(*b*) If any vacancy arises by death, resignation or otherwise the remaining members of the Province, in respect of which the vacancy has arisen, shall be competent to fill it up for the remaining period.

ARTICLE XVIII.

(*a*) It will be the duty of the All-India Congress Committee to take such steps as it may deem expedient and practicable to carry on the work and propaganda of the Congress and it shall have the power to deal with all such matters of great importance or urgency as may require to be disposed of in the name of and for the purposes of the Congress, in addition to matters specified in this constitution as falling within its powers or functions.

(*b*) The decision of the All-India Congress Committee shall, in every case above referred to, be final and binding on the Congress and on the Reception Committee or the Provincial Congress Committee, as the case may be, that may be affected by it.

ARTICLE XIX.

On the requisition in writing of not less than 20 of its members, the General Secretaries shall convene a meeting of the All-India Congress Committee at the earliest possible time.

ELECTORATES AND DELEGATES.

ARTICLE XX.

The right of electing delegates to the Indian National Congress shall vest in (1) the British Committee of the Congress; (2) Provincial or District or other Congress Committees or Associations formed or affiliated as hereinabove laid down; (3) such Political Associations or Public Bodies of more than two years' standing as may be recognised in that behalf by the Provincial Congress Committee of the Province to which the Political Association or Public Body belongs; (4) Political Associations of British Indians resident outside British India of more than two years' standing recognised by the All-India Congress Committee, and (5) Public Meetings convened by Provincial or District Congress Committees or other recognised bodies.

ARTICLE XXI.

All delegates to the Indian National Congress shall pay a fee of Rs. 10 each and shall be not less than 21 years of age at the date of election.

RECEPTION COMMITTEE OF THE CONGRESS.

ARTICLE XXII.

(*a*) The Provincial Congress Committee of the Province in which the Congress is to be held shall take steps to form a Reception Committee for the Congress. Everyone, who ordinarily resides in the Province, fulfils the conditions laid down in Article V. of this Constitution and pays such contribution as may be determined by the Provincial Congress Committee, shall be eligible to be a member of the Reception Committee.

(*b*) No one who is only a member of the Reception Committee but not a delegate, shall be allowed to vote or take part in the debate at the Congress.

(*c*) The Reception Committee shall be bound to provide the necessary funds for meeting all the expenses of the Congress as also the cost of preparing, printing, publishing, and distributing the Report of the Congress.

ELECTION OF THE PRESIDENT.

ARTICLE XXIII.

(*a*) The several Provincial Congress Committees shall by the end of June suggest to the Reception Committee the names of persons who are in their opinion eligible for the Presidentship of the Congress, and the Reception Committee shall in the first week of July submit to all the Provincial Congress Committees the names as suggested for their final recommendations, provided that such final recommendation will be of any one but not more of such names, and the Reception Committee shall meet in the month of August to consider such recommendations. If the person recommended by a majority of the Provincial Congress Committees is accepted by a majority of the members of the Reception Committee present at a special meeting called for the purpose, that person shall be the President of the next Congress. If, however, the Reception Committee is unable to accept the President recommended by the Provincial Congress Committees or in the case of emergency by resignation, death or otherwise of the President elected in manner the matter aforesaid shall forthwith be referred by it to the All-India Congress Committee, whose decision shall be arrived at, as far as possible, before the end of September. In either case, the election shall be final:

Provided that in no case shall be person so elected President belong to the Province in which the Congress is to be held.

(*b*) There shall be no formal *election* of the President by or in the Congress, but merely the adoption (in accordance with the provisions in that behalf laid down in Rule 3, Clause (*b*) of the "Rules" hereto appended) of a formal resolution requesting the President, already elected in the manner hereinabove laid down, to take the chair.

SUBJECTS COMMITTEE.

ARTICLE XXIV.

The Subjects Committee to be appointed at each session of the Congress to settle its programme of business to be transacted shall, as far as possible, consist of:—

Not more than	15	Representatives	of	Madras.
"	15	"	"	Bombay.
"	20	"	"	United Bengal.
"	15	"	"	United Provinces.
"	13	"	"	Punjab (including N. W. F. Province).
"	7	"	"	Central Provinces.
"	15	"	"	Behar and Orissa.
"	5	"	"	Berar.
"	2	"	"	Burma.
"	5	"	"	British Committee of the Congress.
And additional	10	"	"	the Province in which the Congress is held.

All the above-mentioned representatives being elected, in accordance with Rule 9 of the "Rules" hereto appended, by the delegates attending the Congress from the respective Provinces.

The President of the Congress for the year, the Chairman of the Reception Committee of the year, all ex-Presidents of the

Congress and ex-Chairmen of Reception Committees, the General Secretaries of the Congress, the local Secretaries of the Congress for the year, not exceeding six in number, and all the members of the All-India Congress Committee for the year, shall in addition be *ex officio* members of the Subjects Committee.

ARTICLE XXV.

The President of the Congress for the year shall be *ex officio* Chairman of the Subjects Committee, and he may nominate 5 delegates to the Subjects Committee to represent minorities or to make up such deficiencies as he may think necessary.

CONTENTIOUS SUBJECTS AND INTERESTS OF MINORITIES.

ARTICLE XXVI.

(*a*) No subject shall be passed for discussion by the Subjects Committee or allowed to be discussed at any Congress by the President thereof, to the introduction of which the Hindu or Mahomedan delegates, as a body, object by a majority of ¾ths of their number; and if, after the discussion of any subject, which has been admitted for discussion, it shall appear that the Hindu or Mahomedan delegates as a body, are by a majority of ¾ths of their number opposed to the resolution which it is proposed to pass thereon, such resolution shall be dropped; provided that in both these cases the ¾ths mentioned above shall not be less than a 4th of the total number of delegates assembled at the Congress.

(*b*) In any representations which the Congress may make or in any demands which it may put forward for the larger association of the people of India with the administration of the country, the interests of minorities shall be duly safeguarded.

VOTING AT THE CONGRESS.

ARTICLE XXVII.

Ordinarily, all questions shall be decided by a majority of votes as laid down in Rule 21 of the "Rules" hereto appended, but in cases falling under Article XXX. of this Constitution or whenever a division is duly asked for in accordance with Rule 22 of the "Rules" hereto appended, the voting at the Congress shall be by Provinces only. In cases falling under Clause (1) of Article XXX, each Province shall have one vote to be given as determined by a majority of its delegates present at the Congress. In all other cases of voting by Provinces, the vote of each Province, determined as aforesaid, shall be equivalent to the number of representatives assigned to the Province in constituting the All-India Congress Committee.

THE BRITISH COMMITTEE OF THE CONGRESS.

ARTICLE XXVIII.

The Reception Committee of the Province, in which the Congress is held, shall remit to the British Committee of the Congress through the General Secretaries of the Congress half the amount of the fees received by it from delegates, subject to a minimum of Rs. (3,000) three thousand.

GENERAL SECRETARIES.

ARTICLE XXIX.

(*a*) The Indian National Congress shall have two General Secretaries who shall be annually elected by the Congress. They shall be responsible for the preparation, publication and distribution of the Report of the Congress, and they shall submit a full account of the funds which may come into their hands and a report of the work of the year to the All-India Congress Committee at a meeting to be held at the place and about the time of the session of the Congress for the year; and copies of such account and report shall be previously sent to all the Provincial Congress Committees.

(*b*) The All-India Congress Committee shall make adequate provision for the expenses of the work devolving on the General Secretaries, either out of the surplus at the disposal of the Reception Committee or by calling upon the Provincial Congress Committees to make such contribution as it may deem fit to apportion among them.

CHANGES IN THE CONSTITUTION OF RULES.

ARTICLE XXX.

No addition, alteration or amendment shall be made (1) in Article I. of this Constitution except by a unanimous vote of all the Provinces, and (2) in the rest of this Constitution or in the "Rules" hereto appended except by a majority of not less than two-thirds of the votes of the Provinces, provided, in either case, that no motion for any such addition, alteration or amendment shall be brought before the Congress unless it has been previously accepted by the Subjects Committee of the Congress for the year.

RULES

FOR THE CONDUCT AND REGULATION OF THE

INDIAN NATIONAL CONGRESS MEETING

(*As adopted by the Congress of 1908, 1911 and 1912.*)

---

1. The Indian National Congress shall ordinarily hold an annual session at such place as may have been decided upon in accordance with Article III. of the "Constitution" and on such days during Christmas week as may be fixed by the Reception Committee. An Extraordinary Session of the Congress shall be held at such town and on such days as the All-India Congress Committee may determine.

2. Each Congress Session shall open with a meeting of the delegates at such time and place as may be notified by the Reception Committee. The time and place of subsequent sittings of the Session shall be fixed and announced by the President of the Congress.

3. The proceedings on the opening day and at the first sitting of each Congress Session shall, as far as possible, consist of :—

   (*a*) The Chairman of the Reception Committee's inaugural address of welcome to the delegates.

   (*b*) The adoption of a formal resolution, to be moved seconded and supported by such delegates as the Chairman of the Reception Committee invites or permits, requesting the President elected by the Reception Committee or the All-India Congress Committee, as the case may be, to take the chair, no opposition by way of a motion for amendment, adjournment or otherwise being allowed to postpone or prevent the carrying out of the said resolution.

   (*c*) The President's taking the chair and his inaugural address.

   (*d*) Reading or distribution of the Report, if any, of the All-India Congress Committee and any statement that the General Secretaries may have to make.

(e) Any formal motions of thanks, congratulations, condolence, etc., as the President of the Congress may choose to move from the chair.

(f) The adjournment of the Congress for the appointment of the Subjects Committee and the announcement by the President of the time and place of the meetings of the delegates of the different Provinces for the election of the members of the Subjects Committee and also of the first meeting of the Subjects Committee.

4. No other business or motions in any form shall be allowed at the opening sitting of the Congress Session.

5. The Chairman of the Reception Committee shall preside over the assembly at the first sitting until the President takes the chair. The President of the Congress shall preside at all sittings of the Congress Session as well as at all meetings of the Subjects Committee. In case of his absence and during such absence, any ex-President of the Congress present, who may be nominated by the President, and in case no ex-President is available, the Chairman of the Reception Committee shall preside at the Congress sitting; provided that the Subjects Committee may in such cases choose its own Chairman.

6. The President or the Chairman shall have, at all votings, one vote in his individual capacity and also a casting vote in case of equality of votes.

7. The President or Chairman shall decide all points of order and procedure summarily and his decision shall be final and binding.

8. The President or Chairman shall have the power, in cases of grave disorder or for any other legitimate reason, to adjourn the Congress either to a definite time or *sine die*.

9. The election of the members of the Subjects Committee shall take place at meetings of the delegates of the different provinces held at such place and time as may be announced by the President. Each such meeting, in case of contest shall have a Chairman who will first receive nominations, each nomination being made by at least two delegates, and then after announcing all the nominations he may ask each delegate to give in a list of the members he votes for, or he may put the nominated names to the vote in such order as he pleases, or if there are only two rival lists, he shall take votes on these lists and announce the result of the election and forthwith communicate the same to the General Secretaries of the Congress.

10. The Subjects Committee shall deliberate upon and prepare the agenda paper for the business to be transacted at the next

Congress sitting. The General Secretaries shall, as far as practicable, distribute among the delegates a printed copy of the agenda paper for each sitting before the sitting commences.

11. At each sitting of the Congress, the order in which business shall be transacted shall be as follows :—

(a) The resolutions recommended for adoption by the Subjects Committee.

(b) Any substantive motion not included in (a) but which does not fall under Article XXX, of the "Constitution" and which 25 delegates request the President in writing before the commencement of the day's sitting to be allowed to place before the Congress, provided, however, that no such motion shall be allowed unless it has been previously discussed at a meeting of the Subjects Committee and has received the support of at least a third of the members then present.

12. Nothing in the foregoing rule shall prevent the President from changing the order of the resolutions mentioned in Rule 11 (a) or from himself moving from the chair formal motions of thanks, congratulations, condolences or the like.

13. The proposers, seconders and supporters of the Resolutions recommended for adoption by the Subjects Committee shall be delegates and shall be selected by the said Committee. The President may allow other delegates to speak on the resolutions at his discretion and may allow any distinguished visitor to address the Congress. Nothing in the foregoing, however, shall prevent the President from moving from the chair such resolutions as he may be authorised to do by the Subjects Committee.

14. An amendment may be moved to any motion provided that the same is relevant to the question at issue, that it does not raise a question already decided or anticipate any question embraced in a resolution on the agenda paper for the day and that it is couched in proper language and is not antagonistic to the fundamental principles of the Congress. Every amendment must be in the form of a proposition complete in itself.

15. When amendments are moved to a motion, they shall be put to the vote in the reverse order in which they have been moved.

16. A motion for an adjournment of the debate on a proposition may be made at any time and so also, with the consent of the President or Chairman, a motion for an adjournment of the House. The President or Chairman shall have the power to decline to put to vote any motion for adjournment if he considers it to be vexatious or obstructive or an abuse of the rules and regulations.

17. All motions, substantive or by way of amendment, adjournment, etc., shall have to be seconded, failing which they shall fall. No motions, whether those coming under Rule 11 (*b*) or for amendment, adjournment, closure, etc., shall be allowed to be moved unless timely intimation thereof is sent to the President with the motion clearly stated in writing over the signatures of the proposer and seconder with the name of the Province from which they have been elected as delegates.

18. No one who has taken part in the debate in Congress on a resolution shall be allowed to move or second a motion for adjournment or amendment in the course of the debate on that resolution. If a motion for adjournment of the debate on any proposition is carried, the debate on the said proposition shall then cease and may be resumed only after the business on the agenda paper for the day is finished. A motion for adjournment of the House shall state definitely the time when the House is to resume business.

19. A motion for a closure of the debate on a proposition may be moved at any time after the lapse of half an hour from the time the proposition was moved. And if such motion for closure is carried, all discussion upon the original proposition or amendments proposed to it shall at once stop and the President shall proceed to take votes.

20. No motion for a closure of the debate shall be moved whilst a speaker is duly in possession of the House.

21. All questions shall be decided by a majority of votes, subject, however, to the provisions of Articles XXVII. and XXX. of the "Constitution." Votes shall ordinarily be taken by a show of hands or by the delegates for or against standing up in their place in turn to have the numbers counted.

22. In cases not falling under Article XXX. of the "Constitution" any twenty members of a Congress sitting may demand a division within 5 minutes of the declaration of the result of the voting by the President and such division shall be granted. Thereupon the delegates of each province shall meet at such time and place as the President may direct and the Chairman of each such meeting shall notify to the President the vote of the Province within the time specified by the President.

23. Every member of a sitting of the Congress or of the Subjects Committee shall be bound (*a*) to occupy a seat in the block allotted to his Provinces, save as provided for in Rule 30; (*b*) to maintain silence when the President rises to speak or when another member is in possession of the House; (*c*) to refrain from hisses or interruptions of any kind or indulgence in improper and and un-Parliamentary language; (*d*) to obey the chair; (*e*) to with-

draw when his own conduct is under debate after he has heard the charge and been heard thereon, and (*f*) generally to conduct himself with propriety and decorum.

24. No member shall have the right at a Congress sitting to speak more than once on any motion except for a personal explanation or for raising a point of order. But the mover of a substantive motion (not one for amendment or adjournment) shall have the right of reply. A person who has taken part in a debate may speak upon an amendment or motion for adjournment moved after he had spoken. The President or Chairman shall have the right to fix a time-limit upon all speakers, as also to call to order or stop *any speaker* from further continuing his speech even before the time-limit expires, if he is guilty of tedious repetitions, improper expressions, irrelevant remarks, etc., and persists in them in spite of the warning from the President.

25. If a person does not obey the President's or the Chairman's orders or if he is guilty of disorderly conduct the President shall have the right, with a warning in the first instance, and without a warning in case of contumacious disregard of his authority, to ask such member to leave the precincts of the House and on such requisition the member so ordered shall be bound to withdraw and shall be suspended from his functions as a member during the day's sitting.

26. If the President considers that the punishment he can inflict according to the foregoing section is not sufficient, he may, in addition to it, ask the House to award such punishment as the House deems proper. The Congress shall have the power in such cases of expelling the member from the entire Congress Session.

27. The Reception Committee shall organise a body of such persons as it may deem fit for the purpose of keeping order during the meeting of the Congress or of its Subjects Committee or at divisions. There shall be a captain at the head of this body and he shall carry out the orders of the President or the Chairman.

28. Visitors may be allowed at the sitting of the Congress on such terms and conditions as the Reception Committee determines. They may at any time be asked to withdraw by the President. They shall be liable to be summarily ejected from the House if they enter the area marked out for the delegates, or if they disobey the Chair, or if they are guilty of disturbance or obstruction, or if they are in anywise disorderly in their behaviour.

29. The meetings of the Subjects Committee shall be open only to the members of that Committee and the meetings of the delegates of each Province at divisions shall be open to the delegates of that Province only, subject in either case to the provisions of Rule 27.

30. The Chairman of the Reception Committee and the President as well as the Secretaries may, at their discretion, accommodate on the Presidential platform: (1) Leading members of the Congress. (2) Distinguished visitors. (3) Members of the Reception Committee. (4) Ladies, whether delegates or visitors, and (5) Members of the All-India Congress Committee.

31. The foregoing rules shall apply, *mutatis mutandis*, to the Provincial or District Conferences organised by the Provincial Congress Committees as provided for in Article VI. of the "Constitution."

CONSTITUTION

OF THE

INDIAN NATIONAL CONGRESS

(Adopted at the Meeting of the Convention Committee held at Allahabad on the 18th and 19th April, 1908.)

ARTICLES I-XXX. Same as in the Constitution subsequently adopted by the Congress and as set forth above.

TRANSITORY PROVISIONS.

ARTICLE XXXI.

(*a*) The Committee appointed by the Convention at Surat on 28th December 1907 for drawing up a constitution for the Congress should exercise all the powers of the All India Congress Committee till the formation of the latter at the next session of the Congress.

(*b*) The Secretaries of the said Convention Committee shall discharge the duties of the General Secretaries of the Congress till the dissolution of the next session of the Congress.

(*c*) The President and Secretaries of the Convention Committee should, in consultation with the Secretaries of the several Provincial Sub-Committees, arrange for the holding of a meeting of the Congress during Christmas next in accordance with this Constitution.

(*d*) For the year 1908, the Reception Committee, may in electing the President, consult the Provincial Congress Committees in the beginning of October, before the end of which month, the Provincial Congress Committees, on being so consulted, shall make their recommendations and the rest of the procedure prescribed in Article XXIII, should be followed and completed, as far as possible, before the end of November.

RASHBEHARY GHOSE,
President, Convention Committee.

DINSHAW EDULJI WACHA,
DAJI ABAJI KHARE,
Hony. Secretaries, Convention Committee.

The rules for the conduct and regulations of the Congress as framed by the Convention Committee were substantially the same as those subsequently adopted by the Congress and as set forth above.

TENTATIVE RULES

IN REGARD TO CERTAIN MATTERS CONNECTED WITH THE

INDIAN NATIONAL CONGRESS

(Framed by the Committee appointed by Resolution I. of 1887.)

I.

There shall be yearly, during the last fortnight of each Calendar year, a meeting of the delegates of the people of India which shall bear the name of *The Indian National Congress.*

II.

It shall from year to year assemble at such places and on such dates as shall have been resolved on by the last preceding Congress ; it being, however, left open to the Reception Committee (Rule XII.) (should any real necessity for this arise) to change, in consultation with the several Standing Congress Committees (Rule III.), the place fixed by the Congress for some other locality.

III.

There shall be, as resolved at the 2nd National Congress (XIII. of 1886), Standing Congress Committees at all important centres. These Committees are at present as in Appendix I., but the Congress may at any sitting add to or diminish the number of these Committees, or alter their jurisdiction. The delegates from any jurisdiction attending a Congress shall form the Standing Congress Committee for that jurisdiction for the ensuing year and they shall have power to add to their number and appoint their own executive. There is at present a General Secretary holding office at the pleasure of the several Congress Committees but henceforth a General Secretary shall be elected at each Congress for the ensuing year.

IV.

It shall be the primary duty of all Standing Congress Committees to promote the political education of the people of their several jurisdictions *throughout the year*, and to endeavour, by the circulation of brief and simple tracts and catechisms written in the vernacular of that people, by the holding of public meetings at important centres and by sending competent men round to lecture and explain these subjects, and by all other open and laudable means, to imbue the intelligent and respectable classes everywhere with a healthy sense of their duties and rights as good citizens. Care has to be especially taken to impress the people with a conviction, 1st, of the immense benefits that the country has derived from British rule, and of the sincere desire that pervades the British nation to do the very best they can for the people of India; 2ndly, with the same idea of the more important shortcomings of that rule, due partly to the unavoidable ignorance of the rulers of the real condition of the ruled, and partly to the failure of these latter to make known in a definite and intelligible form their wants and wishes, and 3rdly, with the knowledge that all defects in the existing form of the administration may surely, though perhaps slowly, be amended, if the people will only unite in loyal, temperate and persistent demands for the redress of grievances through such persons as they may choose as exponents of their views.

V

To enable the several Committees to carry out his great work successively, they are empowered to create as many sub-committees, (to each of whom a definite sphere of action be assigned), within their jurisdictions, as may be necessary and possible, and they are further empowered to associate themselves with any existing Associations and work with them and through their various branches and sub-committees.

VI

Each year, each Standing Congress Committee shall report fully the work that it has done during the year, accompanying the same, as far as may be practicable, by English translations of all the tracts, leaflets and the like that it may have issued during the year; such reports shall be in English, and shall be so despatched as to reach the Secretary of the Reception Committee (Rule XII.) on or before the 15th of December, and shall be laid before the Congress and duly considered thereat.

VII

It shall be the duty of all Standing Congress Committees, in consultation with their Sub-Committees, and as many of the leading men resident therein as may be possible, to divide their several jurisdictions into such electoral circles as may to them seem to be most likely in the existing state of the country to secure a fair representation of the intelligent portion of the community, without distinction of creed, caste, race or colour. Such circles may be territorial, or where local circumstances require this, may each include one or more castes, or professions, or Associations of any kind. Except in the cases of Associations, all delegates shall be elected at Public Meetings held for the purpose. In the case of Associations, delegates shall be elected at General Meetings specially convened on that behalf.

VIII

Delegates may be of any creed, caste or nationality, but must be residents in India and not less than 25 years of age.

IX

It shall be the duty of all Standing Congress Committees to send out, three months before the date fixed for the Congress, special notices to each of their electoral divisions calling upon each to elect the number of delegates assigned under their scheme to such division, as also one or more provisional delegates who will, in case of the death or inability to attend to any of the elected delegates, take the places of these without further election, and to forward to them—the Congress Committee—a full list of such delegates with all particulars in the form given in Appendix II. It will be the duty of the Standing Congress Committees not only to issue such notices, but see that they are acted upon, deputations from their number proceeding, where necessary, to the centres of the divisions. Provided that in case any electoral division fails to elect the required delegates, the Committee is empowered to cancel such division and create in its place another division more ready to do its duty. Each Standing Congress Committee shall forward a complete list (in the form given in Appendix III.) of all delegates and provisional delegates elected for their entire jurisdiction to the Reception Committee, so that the same may reach the latter on or before the 15th of December, and it shall be the duty of the Reception Committee to remind the Standing Committee that they are due, and failing to receive these lists to telegraph for them persistently and to bring to the notice of the Congress any serious neglect of this rule.

X

It shall be the duty of each Standing Congress Committee, at least one month before the date fixed for the Congress, to ascertain the cheapest and best routes and modes of conveyance by which the several delegates of their jurisdictions can reach the Congress, the time that will be occupied in transit, and the cost of the journey by both 1st and 2nd class, single and return, and to notify the same to each of the delegates and provisional delegates elected within their jurisdiction.

XI

It shall be the duty of each Standing Congress Committee to notify, so that such notification shall reach the Reception Committee on or before the 1st of November, the subjects that the people of their several jurisdictions desire to see discussed. Provided that such subjects shall be of a national character, that is to say, of a nature affecting the whole country, and not provincial, and that in regard to each subject the exact resolution which it is desired to pass be also transmitted, along with, whenever the latter is practicable, the names of the gentlemen who are prepared to propose or support such resolutions.

XII

The Standing Congress Committee of the jurisdiction in which the Congress is to be held shall, not less than six months before the date fixed for the Congress, associate with itself all the leading inhabitants of the place where the Congress is to be held, who may be willing to take part in the proceedings, and with them constitute itself a Reception Committee.

XIII

It shall be the duty of the Reception Committee (*a*) to notify to all the Standing Committees their appointment, and to invite them to proceed to call for delegates and to send in before the appointed date the list of the subjects which the people of their jurisdiction desire should be discussed as required by Rule XI; (*b*) to collect and provide the funds necessary for the entertainment of the delegates and other purposes essential to the holding of the Congress; to arrange for a suitable Meeting Hall; for the suitable lodgment of the delegates of other jurisdictions; for the food of the delegates during their stay, due regard being had to the customs, local or religious, of each, and generally to arrange for everything necessary for their convenience and comfort, and (*c*) to maintain a constant correspondence with all the Standing Congress Committees, and generally, so far as may be, assure themselves that the necessary work is duly proceeding in all jurisdictions.

XIV

It shall be the duty of the Reception Committee to *obtain*, from the several Standing Committees the list of subjects referred to in Statute XI, reminding them and giving them ample warning that lists not received by the 1st of November cannot be attended to, and on the 1st of November to proceed to consider such lists and after eliminating all subjects (if there be any such) of a clearly provincial character, or unsupported by definite resolutions intended to be proposed in regard to them, to compile the rest into one list in the form given in Appendix IV, and print and despatch the same by the 15th of November in sufficient numbers to the several Standing Committees to enable these to distribute copies to each delegate and provincial delegate, and the several Standing Committees shall be responsible for their immediate distribution accordingly.

XV

It shall be the duty of the Reception Committee, as soon as possible after its constitution, to select and communicate to the several Standing Congress Committees the names of those gentlemen whom it considers eligible for the office of President, and in correspondence with them to settle who shall be invited to fill that office, and thereafter when, and agreement thereon has been come to, to communicate with the gentlemen finally approved by all, or a considerable majority of the Standing Committees, and generally to do all that may be necessary to settle the question of the Presidentship at least one month before the Congress meets.

XVI.

Of the subjects circulated under Rule XIV, for information, only those shall be brought forward and discussed at the Congress which shall be finally approved by a committee (to be called the Subjects Committee) consisting of the President-Elect and one or more representatives of each jurisdiction (selected by all delegates who may be then present at the Congress station) which shall meet on the day previous to the inaugural sitting of the Congress. Provided also that this Committee shall be empowered to add any subjects to those included in this list that may for any reasons appear to them specially deserving of discussion, framing at the same time the resolutions that they desire to see proposed in regard to them, and further, to modify as may appear to them necessary, any of the resolutions propounded in regard to the subjects included in the list which they have accepted for discussion. Provided further, that the Committee shall at the same time settle, so far as may be possible, those gentlemen who are to be invited to propose, second and support the Resolutions, and shall put themselves into communication with them, and that they shall at once frame a list of the approved subjects and resolutions in the form given in Appendix V. and shall print the same so that a copy may, if possible, be placed in the hands of each delegate at the inaugural sitting of the Congress.

XVII.

It shall be the duty of the Chairman of the Reception Committee to preside at the commencement of the inaugural sitting of the Congress, and after delivering such address as he and the Reception Committee may consider necessary to call upon the assembled delegates to elect a President and after such election to instal the said President in the chair of office.

From and after the installation of the President, he shall direct and guide the entire proceedings of the assembly, he being empowered in all cases, except as hereinafter provided, in which differences of opinion arise or doubts occur, either himself, to rule what course should be taken when his ruling shall be final, or to take a vote from the assembly, when the decision of the majority shall be final.

Until the subjects and resolutions approved by the Subjects Committee have been discussed (and this in such order as the President may direct) and disposed of by the adoption, rejection or modification of such resolutions, no other business shall be brought before the Congress. But after this, if there be time for this, any delegate who shall have given notice in writing at the commencement of the sitting to the President, of his desire to have a particular subject discussed, and definite resolution, which he sets forth, proposed shall have *a right* and a delegate who at *any* time previous to rising shall have given such notice *may*, with the permission of the President rise and ask the President to take the sense of the assembly as to whether such subject shall be discussed. No speaking at this stage shall be allowed. The President shall simply read out the subject and the proposed resolution and make any such remarks as he considers essential and take a vote of the assembly as to whether the subject shall or shall not be discussed. If the vote is in the affirmative the proposer shall then set forth the subject and the resolution he therein proposes with such explanations as he considers necessary. and then, after due discussion, the question shall be disposed of in the usual way. If the vote is in the negative, the subject shall be at once dropped.

ADDENDA.

ADDENDUM TO RULE XII.

It is to be distinctly understood that the Reception Committee cannot provide accommodation or food for any one but delegates and at most for one servant each for any delegates who absolutely require such attendance. All delegates who *can* do without a special servant of their own should do so, the Reception Committee will provide attendance for their guests. If any delegate desires to bring with him friends or family or more than one servant he must notify the same at least 20 days before the Congress meets to the Reception Committee, stating the number of persons he intends to bring, the number of rooms or the kind of house he requires and the amount he is willing to pay for the same, and the Committee will endeavour to have the required accommodation ready. Unless such timely notice be given, the Committee, though they will still try to assist their guest's friends, can take no responsibility in regard to them. Under no circumstances can any one not a delegate, or the one servant of a delegate, be accommodated in any of the quarters provided by the Reception Committee for the delegates.

RULE XVI.—(*Revised*).

Of the subjects circulated under Rule XIV. for information, only those shall be brought forward and discussed at the Congress which shall be finally approved by a Committee (hereinafter designated the Subject Committee) consisting of the President-Elect, the General Secretary and one or more of the representatives of each jurisdiction which shall meet as early as possible on the day previous to the inaugural sitting of the Congress and with necessary intervals for food and rest continue sitting until the work is completed. It shall be the duty of each Standing Congress Committee to select specially and arrange for the despatch of one or more of its delegates, so that he or they may arrive in good time for and represent their views at the Subject Committee which besides these specially selected delegates may include a limited number of gentlemen selected by the other delegates present at the time, should the President-Elect consider this necessary to ensure an adequate representation of all sections of the community. It shall not be open to any delegate or body of delegates or any Standing Congress Committee, not present or represented at the opening of the Subject Committee to question later on, its proceedings or demand that the work of selecting subjects be done over again, but it will be open to any and all who may be dissatisfied with the programme of the Committee to propose amendments to any or all the resolutions they have approved, or when all the subjects approved by them have been disposed of, to move for the discussion for other subjects, as provided in other rules. The Subject Committee is empowered to add any subjects to those included in the last circulated under Rule XIV. that may for any reasons appear to them specially deserving of discussion, framing at the same time the resolutions that they desire to see proposed in regard to them, and further, to modify as may appear to them necessary, any of the resolutions propounded in regard to the subjects included in the list, which they have accepted for discussion. The Committee shall at the same time settle, so far as may be possible, those gentlemen who are to be invited to propose, second and support the resolutions, and shall put themselves into communication with them, and they shall, before separating, frame a list of the approved subjects and resolutions in form given in Appendix V. and shall print the same so that a copy may, if possible, be placed in the hands of each delegate at the inaugural sitting of the Congress.

RULE XVIII.—A

It is desirable that the President should have, sitting with him on the platform, and constituting a sort of Council, that he can consult in case of necessity, one or more of the leading delegates from each jurisdiction. There are places on the platform according to the standard plan, for 22 such Councillors, and these shall be apportioned as follows to the jurisdictions of the several Standing Congress Committees, *viz*, to that of Calcutta 4 of Bankipore 1, of Benares and Allahabad taken together 2, of Lucknow 2, of Lahore 2, of Karachi 1, of Surat 1, of Bombay 3, of Poona 1, of Nagpore 1, of Madras 4. The delegates of each jurisdiction present on the morning of the inaugural sitting, must elect these their representatives and notify their names before noon on the day of such sitting to the Secretary of the Reception Committee. The Chairman of the Reception Committee and a special Secretary, to be selected by the President, will also occupy the platform on the immediate right and left of the President.

RULE XVIII.—B

On or before noon of the day of the inaugural sitting, the President-Elect, in consultation with the Chairman of the Reception Committee, shall nominate 8 or more gentlemen not themselves delegates, as wardens of the assembly and shall invest them with a conspicuous badge and a wand of office. It shall be the duty of these wardens throughout the Congress to see that the delegates take the places assigned to them; that the pathways are kept clear, the arrangements of the Reception Committee rigidly respected and generally order maintained in all particulars. It shall be the duty of all delegates to comply at once and unhesitatingly with any requests made to them by the wardens.

RULE XVIII—C

No one, not a delegate, shall be allowed to address the Congress or vote on any matter before it. No delegate shall be allowed to address the assembly except from the platform. The Subject Committee will usually have arranged for proposers, seconders, and supporters, and at times for other speakers on each resolution, and these will, when no amendment is proposed, have precedence of other persons who desire to speak, but after these have spoken, these others shall be called on to speak in the order in which they may have submitted their names (very clearly written in full, in ink) to the President. Provided that when it seems clear that the Congress is of one mind on any subject and does not desire further speaking, the President may, at the close of any speaker's address take the sense of the assembly as to whether further discussion is necessary and proceed accordingly. When one or more amendments have been duly notified, then after the proposer and seconder of the original resolutions have spoken, the proposers and seconders of the amendments shall be called on in the order in which the amendments were filed, and after this the supporters of the original resolution and the amendments shall speak in turn, and after these, again, all other speakers in the order in which their names have been registered.

No original proposer of a resolution shall, without the express permission of the President previously obtained, speak for more than 15 minutes. No other speaker shall, without the express permission of the same officer previously obtained, speak for more than 10 minutes and, as a rule, speakers are expected to confine themselves to five minutes. The President will touch a gong once to warn each speaker when the time allotted to him is drawing to a close, and he will touch it a second time when that period has elapsed and he considers that the speaker should cease speaking, and when the President does thus a second time touch his gong, the speaker shall thereupon, then and there close his address and leave the platform unless called upon by the assembly generally to proceed. Each speaker on ascending the platform for the purpose of speaking shall give one card on which his name is very clearly written in full in English, as also the name of the jurisdiction to which he belongs, to the Short-hand Reporter employed by the Congress and similar card to the President's Secretary, and the latter shall read it out distinctly to the assembly before the speech commences.

RULE XVIII.—D

When considerable difference of opinion is proved, by the course of the discussion, to exist in the assembly in regard to any question before it, the President may, at any time, temporarily suspend business and inviting to the platform such other delegates as he considers necessary, with these and his Concillors, as a Special Committee, proceed to endeavour to work out a solution of the difficulty which will commend itself to all parties, or to the great majority of these. Should this prove impracticable he will resume business and take the sense of the assembly as to whether further discussion shall be allowed or the several amendments (the last, first, and so on) put in the usual way. But should, as will generally be the case, a compromise be arrived at by the Special Committee, unanimously or by majority of at least two-thirds he shall, on resuming the chair, first read out the resolution thus arrived at and then either himself explain its bearings on the matters in dispute, or call upon some one else to do so, and after such explanation put this at once to the assembly. If it be not carried, he will proceed as above directed, but if carried, the discussion will be considered closed and assembly will proceed to the next subject and resolution on the programme. Such resolutions will appear in the summary, as "Proposed by a Special Committee and carried by a majority unanimously, or, by acclamation"—as the case may be.

RULE XIX.—A

Without the special permission of the President, which shall only be granted, when this appears to him essentially necessary, no amendment shall be proposed, of which due notice in writing signed by at least five delegates shall not have been given to the President at the time of his taking the chair or before business commences, on the day on which the resolution which it is proposed to amend is discussed. The notice shall set forth the resolution, to which it is proposed to move an amendment, the exact words of the amendment, and the whole resolution as it would stand were the amendment carried. In introducing each resolution for discussion the President shall mention fully each amendment thereon of which he has received notice, so that all delegates may clearly realise the points which are to be in debate, and all including the proposers, etc., of the original resolution frame their speeches accordingly,

RULE XIX.—B

To allow for the presentation of notices of amendment and the like, including general protests by all the Hindu, or Mahomedan delegates as a body against the proposing of any particular resolution, the President shall always take his seat one half hour before business commences.

RULE XIX.—C

The President may at any time during a debate himself explain or call upon the proposer, or any other delegate, to explain more fully the whole or any portion of an original resolution, which appears to him to be being misunderstood by the speakers or the assembly.

RULE XIX—D.

It may sometimes occur that in the hurry and heat of debates where but little time can be conceded to each subject, (especially where amendments on amendments are admitted by the President), that the resolution actually passed by Congress, though perfectly clear and intelligible, are yet needlessly involved, tautological, or otherwise verbally defective. It shall, therefore, be the duty of the President, in consultation with the General Secretary, if possible, day by day, otherwise at any rate immediately at the close of the session, to review most carefully each of the resolution and while preserving intact their meaning, to correct so far as may appear to him really necessary, all literary and verbal oversights, retaining in all cases so much of the exact original wording as may be possible, consistent with the proper discharge of the duty above imposed upon him.

SUGGESTIONS *
FOR THE
STANDING CONGRESS COMMITTEE

(1) The Standing Congress Committee must, under the Tentative Rules, consist in the first instance of all those delegates who attended the last Congress, and these should associate with themselves all those gentlemen who attended as delegates at any previous Congress and all other leading members of the circle who sympathize in the movement. Of course the large body thus formed cannot be expected to work at details. The majority of the members have not the time to attend to a huge series of these. If any matter of great importance arises, they must of course assist with advice, and if required money also, but the regular routine

---

* These suggestions are the result of the practical experience gained in working out the electoral system in Madras and must of course be only taken *quantum valeant* and open to such modifications as each Standing Committee finds necessary or expedient.

work, of which there will necessarily be a good deal, must be done by a small number of real workers whom the committee must appoint: men whose circumstances permit to give a fair share of time and attention to the work, and who are so really and earnestly interested in this that they will not grudge either.

(2) The first point, then for every Standing Congress Committee, as soon as it is constituted, is to appoint a secretary or secretaries and a *small*, strong, Executive Committee—all of them men of the class just referred to—with instructions to hold a meeting *without fail*, one *every* week, on a fixed *day*, at a fixed *hour*, at a fixed *place*, two to form a quorum. All work pertaining to the Standing Congress Committee to be disposed of by these weekly meetings, by such members of the Executive Committee as are at present. No one should afterwards be competent to question such decisions on the score, that only 2 or 3 were present; if more were not present, that is their own fault, and all must cheerfully accept, and be bound by the decision of those who did take trouble to be present.

(3) The most important work of the Executive Committees is to create (if this has not already been done) and consolidate the electoral division. The electoral divisions must be so arranged as to cover every portion of the circle * and include every section of the community. One main object in elaborating them is to insure that delegates shall fairly represent every creed, class, race, and section of the community inhabiting the circle. This can only be achieved in most circles by constituting electoral divisions of two classes, *viz.*, first, territorial, each to include, (*a*) a portion of a city, or (*b*) a whole city or town (*c*) with a portion of district adjacent to it, or (*d*) a town with the entire district to which it pertains, or (*e*) in very backward portions of the country, a town together with 2 or more neighbouring districts, and, second, sectional, each to include a special community or an association, or groups of either of these. A glance at the Appendix will show how this has been managed at Madras, it being noted that the divisions printed in Italics, though duly constituted, have not yet agreed to act, but letters have been addressed to them which with such replies as they may elicit, will later be published.

Of course the divisions must, as a rule, be worked out in consultation with leaders in each, and these must be constituted Sub-Committees. The very essence of the scheme is that there should be a *working* local Sub-Committee in and directly responsible for each division, whether Territorial or Sectional, and as the divisions are created so must there Sub-Committees be created.

---

* The circle is that tract of country over which the standing Congress Committee has jurisdiction.

In constituting divisions, regard must be had to the men available for Sub-Committees. The smaller and more manageable the divisions, the better no doubt—but then it is no use constituting a division unless you have in it men who will form a Sub-Committee and *work* the division. Very often, therefore, divisions will have to consist of entire districts at the headquarters of which alone can men of the requisite education and public spirit be found.

The divisions settled, the numbers of delegates that each should return as a minimum (which each is absolutely pledged to send, no matter how far off the Congress be held), should be fixed by dividing the total number for the circle (at 3 per million for the total population thereof) over the several divisions with due advertence to their relative importance and the advance that they have made in political and general education and then adding thereto as will be necessary in all metropolitan circles at any rate, such additional delegates as may be essential to secure a really comprehensive representation of all the interests embraced in the circle.

It may be that some of the divisions such, for instance, as the European Chambers of Commerce, the Jewish Community in Bombay, the Armenian Community in Calcutta, the European Planters in Assam, Sylhet and Cachar—the Universities (which are to a great extent official, the fellows being nominated by Government, and not elected by the graduates as they should be), etc., may decline to co-operate and act, but they must be none the less invited and pressed to do this and constitute divisions. Only, in the schedule, those declining to act must be printed in Italics.

The schedule thus prepared should have the formal assent of the entire Standing Congress Committee, or if every member cannot, as often happens, be got hold of, of a large majority thereof—a copy of it should then be sent to the General Secretary. This schedule will represent what the circle is pledged to; it will be open to the circle, until at any rate the entire Congress rule otherwise hereafter, to send as many *more* delegates on any occasion it finds necessary or desirable.

The schedule thus worked out, the Executive Committee next have to bring home to each Sub-Committee* its responsibility for

---

* Each Sub-Committee can add to its numbers such leading residents of its division as are willing to co-operate heartily in the work, and each must appoint a Secretary for correspondence with the Executive Committee.

its division making it clear to them that there are two main branches of their responsibility—(*a*) in regard to delegates, (*b*) in regard to the education of the people.

As to (*a*), they are answerable for causing the selection, not in a hurry at the last moment, but, during the year, after the consultation with all the most influential and intelligent of the inhabitants of their division of really suitable delegates to attend the Congress. They must in this selection weigh all matters; they must look to position, influence, intelligence, education and unblemished character. They must try and have all combined; but if this be not possible, they must remember that the last is the most important, the last but one the next most important, and so on. They must, of course, arrange either that the delegates selected are well able to bear the expense of the journey, etc., or that the necessary funds for the purpose are duly collected in the division.

So far as may be possible all persons selected as delegates should understand English sufficiently well to be able to take an intelligent part in the proceedings of the Congress, without the need of any one to explain or interpret to them.

Beside the 1, 2, or 3 delegates that they are required to send up from their division by the electoral scheme, the Sub-Committees should also always select one or more extra or provisional delegates, who, in case of death, sickness, or other restraining cause, preventing the attendance of any delegate, may be prepared at once, without further action, to take the defaulter's place.

Of course, in all places where there are a good number of Mahomedans, they should endeavour to have at least one delegate a Mahomedan.

As to (*b*) they should charge themselves with the political education of all the respectable inhabitants of their division. They need not, at present, trouble themselves with the quite ignorant low caste people, labourers, and the like, who have virtually no stake in the country, and no sufficiently developed intelligence to be as yet associated in the work; but all respectable ryots, petty shopkeepers, artizans, as well as the higher classes, should be made to understand something of their rights and duties as good citizens—something of the leading political question of the day—something of the support that in their own interest they are bound to accord to those who are endeavouring to secure for their fellow-countrymen and themselves, rights, privileges and power, that will enable them to do away with many of the chief grievances of which the country now justly complains.

Now they can do this partly by the wide circulation of elementary tracts, and partly by going round their divisions and lecturing from place to place on these matters.

As to tracts, the Congress Catechism, in simple language, in all the vernaculars of the circle, will be provided for them by the Executive Committee, but they will have to realise and pay to this Committee the 10 or 20 Rs. that the 1,000 to 2,000 copies that they will need for their divisions will cost. As to lecturing they must enlist in the work every competent man within their divisions, and arrange amongst themselves, so that at least every town and village that contains 500 inhabitants and upwards, is visited and lectured in by *some one* not less than once a year.

These are the principal duties of the Sub-Committees but besides this they must keep themselves in communication with the Executive Committee, and carefully carry out all subsidiary instructions that they receive from them.

(4) The Executive Committee should arrange for holding a Conference at some suitable central locality of all the Sub-Committees and take care that these are all made to understand and realise thoroughly their duties and their responsibility to their country and countrymen for the due performance of these.

(5) The Executive Committee must *at once* arrange for the translation of the catechism into all the vernaculars of its circle, taking care that the language is simple, and adapted to the comprehension of the ordinary ryot, and adding in the last two replies, all such local matter as they consider necessary for the guidance of their people. They must get these clearly printed, and as cheaply as possible (the cost ought not to exceed Rs. 10 per 1,000. and they must then insist on the Sub-Committees speedily providing the funds for the number of copies requisite for their several divisions, which will range from one to two thousands, probably according to number and degree of advancement of their people.

(6) Each member of each Standing Committee must contribute a small sum of Rs. 5 or 10 each. as may be settled locally, to the Executive Committee to put them in funds for printing these catechism and other papers, and where copies are obtained from other Executive Committees, paying for these. But as explained, the major portion of this will be recovered from the Sub-Committees, so that it will not often be necessary to apply to the Standing Congress and it is believed that no member of this will grudge this small donation once in a way.

(7) The Executive Committee should draw up a regular scheme so as to ensure every single electoral division being visited,

at least once in every twelve months, by a competent member of its own body or of the General Standing Committee, who should deliver one or more lectures at its headquarters, and satisfy himself that the Sub-Committees are really doing their duty or if not, put them in the right way. If there be any difficulty in getting members, each to attend to, say one division once in the year, it will be a matter for deep regret. Every true-born son of India *ought* to be proud of the opportunity of thus promoting the enlightenment of his fellow-countrymen, and strengthening his country's cause, even at some minute sacrifice of time, comfort and convenience, such as the required work entails.

(8) Further the Executive Committee, in consultation from time to time with the members of the Standing Committee, must thoroughly mature a scheme for raising, when the time comes to make a call for this, a Permanent Congress Fund, at a rate of not less than Rs. 3,000 or more than Rs. 5,000 per million of population.

(9) It will be observed, that, realising the fact that the Standing Congress Committees will, in many places, mainly consist of leading public men already fully occupied, these suggestions contemplate relieving them of all detail work, and of all compulsory attendance (though each and all *when able to do so*, can attend and take part in the regular fixed weekly meetings of the Executive Committee) at ordinary meetings. But it is expected of them that they shall, once in a way, when they can afford the leisure, satisfy themselves that the Executive Committee are really carrying out the work efficiently that—they shall individually be at all times ready to afford to the Secretary, or the member of the Executive Committee, advice on any special point, or the support of their influence in any special matter—and that they shall at the outset make a small donation to place the Executive Committee in funds for their printing works.

In the case of any really important matters having to be decided, a general meeting of the Standing Congress Committee will be called by the Executive Committee after personal enquiries from as many of the members as possible, so as to ensure the fixing of the most generally convenient date and hour. One such meeting will certainly be required some time before the next Congress takes place and possibly, one or two others, but the Standing Committee will be troubled as little as possible, only in fact when it is really necessary and when consequently none of them will grudge either the time or the trouble.

If at any time any 3 of the members of the Standing Committee consider, for any reason, that a general meeting should be called, they will notify the same to the Executive Committee, explaining their reason for the same in writing and the Committee will arrange accordingly.

On the 1st of May, and each succeeding month, the Executive Committee will report progress, succinctly circulating the report, which should be informal, confidential and as brief as possible, to each member of the Standing Congress Committee, who shall be answerable for reading and *promptly* sending it on.

It is very desirable that a copy of this Report should be simultaneously sent to the General Secretary for record and for the information, where necessary, of other circles.

APPENDIX B—SURAT PAPERS.

I. THE CONVENTION.

After the adjournment of the 23rd Indian National Congress *sine die* under the most painful circumstances on the afternoon of the 27th December, a large number of the leading delegates met the same evening at about 4 p.m. in Sir P. M, Mehta's quarters to consider what steps should be taken to continue the work of the Congress.

At this meeting it was unanimously resolved that a National Convention be held at Surat on the next day (28th Dec.,) and the following notice calling the Convention was issued :

The 23rd Indian National Congress having been suspended *sine die* under painful circumstances the undersigned have resolved with a view to the orderly conduct of future political work in the country to call a Convention of those delegates to the Congress who are agreed :—

(1) That the attainment by India of Self-Government similar to that enjoyed by the self-governing members of the British Empire and participation by her in the rights and responsibilities of the Empire on equal terms with those Members is the goal of our political aspirations.

(2) That the advance towards this goal is to be by strictly constitutional means by bringing about a steady reform of existing system of administration and by promoting *National Unity*, fostering public spirit, and improving the condition of the mass of the people.

(3) And that all meetings held for the promotion of the aims and objects above indicated have to be conducted in an orderly manner with due submission to the authority of those that are entrusted with the power to control their procedure, and they are requested to attend at I P.M. on Saturday the 28th December 1907 in the Pandal lent for the purpose by the Working Committee of the Reception Committee of the 23rd Indian National Congress.

(Signed) Rashbehari Ghose. Pherozeshah M. Mehta. Surendranath Banerjee. G. K. Gokhale. D. E. Wacha. Narendranath Sen. Ambalal Sakerlal Desai. V. Krishnaswami Iyer. Tribhovandas N. Malvi. Madan Mohan Malaviya. Daji

Abaji Khare. N. M. Samarth. Gokuldas K. Parakh. Chimanlal H. Setalwad. Hari Sitaram Dikshit. Ambica Charan Muzumdar. A. Chowdhury. Ganga Persad Varma. Mulchand Fessumul, Abbas Tayabji. Tulsidas Shewandas. A. Nundy. S. Sinha. Bhalchandra Krishna. Gokaran Nath Misra. Sangamlal. Govind Sahay Sharma. Teji Bahadur Sapru. V. Ryru Nambiar. Deora Vinayak. Hussain Tyabji. M. V. Joshi. R. N. Mudholkar. J. F. D'Mello. J. B. Petit. Ishwar Sha Ran. Parmeshvar Lall. N. Subba Rau. Krishna Kumar Mitra. J. Chowdhry. A. H. Ghazanavi. L. R. Gokhale. C. V. Vaidya. Ram Garudh. R. P. Karandikar and others.

II. THE EXTREMISTS' VERSION.

A Press Note containing an official narrative of the proceedings of the 23rd Indian National Congress at Surat has been published* over the signatures of some of the Congress officials. As this Note contains a number of one sided and misleading statements, it is thought desirable to publish the following account of the proceedings :—

PRELIMINARY.

Last year when the Congress was held at Calcutta under the presidency of Mr. Dadabhai Naoroji, the Congress, consisting of Moderates and Nationalists, *unanimously* resolved to have for its goal Swaraj or Self-Government on the lines of the Self-Governing Colonies, and passed certain resolutions on Swadeshi, Boycott and National Education. The Bombay Moderates, headed by Sir P. M. Mehta, did not at the time raise any dissentient voice, but they seem to have felt that their position was somewhat compromised by these resolutions, and they had since then been looking forward to an opportunity when they might return to their old position regarding ideals and methods of political progress in India. In the Bombay Provincial Conference held at Surat in April last, Sir P. M. Mehta succeeded by his personal influence in exlcuding the propositions of Boycott and National Education from the programme of the Conference. And when it was decided to change the venue of the Congress from Nagpur to Surat, it afforded the Bombay Moderate leaders the desired-for opportunity to carry out their intentions in this respect. The Reception Committee at Surat was presumably composed largely of Sir Pherozshah's followers, and it was cleverly arranged by the Hon. Mr. Gokhale to get the Committee nominate Dr. R. B. Ghosh to the office of the President, brushing aside the proposal

---

* For this Official Note, see page 109.

for the nomination of Lala Lajpat Rai, then happily released, on the ground that "we cannot afford to flout Government at this stage, the authorities would throttle our movement in no time." This was naturally regarded as an insult to the public feeling in the country, and Dr. Ghosh must have received at least a hundred telegrams from different parts of India requesting him to generously retire in Lala Lajpat Rai's favour. But Dr. Ghosh unfortunately decided to ignore this strong expression of public opinion. Lala Lajpat Rai, on the other land, publicly declined the honour. But this did not satisfy the people who wished to disown the principle of selecting a Congress President on the above ground, believing as they did that the most effective protest against the repressive policy of Government would be to elect Lala Lajpat Rai to the chair.

The Hon. Mr. Gokhale was entrusted by the Reception Committee, at its meeting held on 24th November 1907 for nominating the President, with the work of drafting the resolutions to be placed before the Congress. But neither Mr. Gokhale nor the Reception Committee supplied a copy of draft resolutions to any delegate till 2-30 P.M., on Thursday the 26th December, that is to say, till the actual commencement of the Congress Session. The public was taken into confidence only thus far that a list of the headings of the subjects likely to be taken up for discussion by the Surat Congress was officially published a week or ten days before the date of the Congress Session. This list did not include the subject of Self-Government, Boycott and National Education, on all of which *distinct* and *separate* resolutions were passed at Calcutta last year. This omission naturally strengthened the suspicion that the Bombay Moderates really intended to go back from the position taken up by the Calcutta Congress in these matters. The press strongly commented upon this omission, and Mr. Tilak, who reached Surat on the morning of the 23rd December, denounced such retrogression as suicidal in the interests of the country, more especially at the present juncture, at a large mass meeting held that evening, and appealed to the Surat public to help the Nationalists in their endeavours to maintain at least the *status quo* in these matters. The next day a Conference of about five hundred Natianalist Delegates was held at Surat under the chairmanship of Srijut Arabindo Ghose where it was decided that the Nationalist should prevent the attempted retrogression of the Congress by all constitutional means, even by opposing the election of the president if necessary; and a letter was written to the Congress Secretaries requesting them to make arrangements for dividing the house, if need be, on every contested proposition including that of the election of the President.

In the meanwhile a press note signed by Mr. Gandhi, as Hon. Secretary, was issued to the effect that the statement, that certain resolutions adopted last yeat at Calcutta were omitted from the Congress programme prepared by the Surat Reception Committee, was wholly unfounded; but the draft resolutions themselves were still withheld from the public, though some of the members of the Reception Committee had already asked for them some days before. On the morning of 25th December, Mr. Tilak happened to get a copy of the draft of the proposed constitution of the Congress prepared by the Hon. Mr. Gokhale. In this draft the object of the Congress was thus stated; "The Indian National Congress has for its ultimate goal the attainment by India of Self-Government similar to that enjoyed by the other members of the British Empire" and etc. Mr. Tilak addressed a meeting of the delegates the same morning at the Congress Camp at about 9 A.M. explaining the grounds on which he believed that the Bombay Moderate leaders were bent upon receding from the position taken up by the Calcutta Congress on Swaraj, Boycott and National Education. The proposed constitution, Mr. Tilak pointed out, was a direct attempt to tamper with the ideal of Self-Government on the lines of the *Self-Governing* Colonies, as settled at Calcutta and to exclude the Nationalists from the Congress by making the acceptance of this new creed an indispensable condition of Congress membership. Mr. Tilak further stated in plain terms that if they were assured that no sliding back of the Congress would be attempted the opposition to the election of the President would be withdrawn. The delegates at the meeting were also asked to sign a letter of request to Dr. Ghosh, the President-Elect requesting him to have the old propositions on Swaraj, Swadeshi, Boycott and National Education taken up for reaffirmation this year; and some of the delegates signed it on the spot. Mr. G. Subramania Iyer of Madras, Mr. Kharandikar of Satara and several others were present at this meeting and excepting a few all the rest admitted the reasonableness of Mr. Tilak's proposal.

Lala Lajpat Rai, who arrived at Surat on the morning of that day, saw Messrs. Tilak and Khaparde in the afternoon and intimated to them his intention to arrange for a Committee of a few leading delegates from each side to settle the question in dispute. Messrs. Tilak and Khaparde having agreed, he went to Mr. Gokhale to arrange for the Committee if possible; and Messrs. Tilak and Khaparde returned to the Nationalist Conference which was held that evening (25th December). At this Conference a Nationalist Committee consisting of one Nationalist delegate from each Province was appointed to carry on the negotiations with the leaders on the other side; and it was decided that if the Nationalist Committee failed to obtain any assurance from responsible Congress officials about the *status quo* being maintained, the Nationalists should begin their opposition from the election of the President. For the retrogression of the Congress was a serious step, not to be decided upon only by a bare accidental majority of any party, either in the Subjects Committee or in the whole Congress (as at present constituted), simply because its session happens to be held in a particular place or province in a particular year; and the usual unanimous acceptance of the President would have, under such exceptional circumstances, greatly weakened the point and force of the opposition. No kind of intimation was received from Lala Lajpat Rai this night or even the next morning regarding the proposal of a Joint Committee of reconciliation proposed by him, nor was a copy of the draft resolutions supplied to Mr. Tilak, Mr. Khaparde, or any other delegates to judge if no sliding back from the old position was really intended.

On the morning of the 26th December, Messrs. Tilak, Khaparde, Arabindo Ghose and others went to Babu Surendranath Banerjee at his residence. They were accompanied by Babu Motilal Ghosh of the *Amrita Bazar Patrika* who had arrived the previous night. Mr. Tilak then informed Babu Surendranath that the Nationalist opposition to the election of the President would be withdrawn, if (1) the Nationalist party were assured that the *status quo* would not be disturbed; and (2) if some graceful allusion was made by any one of the speakers on the resolution about the election of the President to the desire of the public to have Lala Lajpat Rai in the chair. Mr. Banerjee agreed to the latter proposal as he said he was himself to second the resolution; while as regards the first, though he gave an assurance for himself and Bengal, he asked Mr. Tilak to see Mr. Gokhale or Mr. Malvi. A volunteer was accordingly sent in a carriage to invite Mr. Malvi, the Chairman of the Reception Committee, to Mr. Bannerji's residence, but the volunteer brought a reply that Mr. Malvi had no time to come as he was engaged in religious practices. Mr. Tilak then returned to his camp to take his meals as it was already about 11 A.M.; but on returning to the Congress pandal an hour later, he made persistent attempts to get access to Mr. Malvi but could not find him anywhere. A little before 2-30 P.M., a word was brought to Mr. Tilak that Mr. Malvi was in the President's camp, and Mr. Tilak sent a message to him from an adjoining tent asking for a short interview to which Mr. Malvi replied that he could not see Mr. Tilak as the presidential procession was being formed. The Nationalist Delegates were waiting in the pandal to hear the result of the endeavours of their Committee to obtain an assurance about the maintenance of the *status quo* from some responsible Congress official, and Mr. V. S. Khare of Nasik now informed them of the failure of Mr. Tilak's attempt in the matter.

FIRST DAY.

It has become necessary to state these facts in order that the position of the two parties, when the Congress commenced its proceedings on Thursday the 26th December at 2-30 P.M., may be clearly understood. The President-Elect and other persons had now taken their seats on the plateform; and as no assurance from any responsible official of the Congress about the maintenance of the *status quo* was till then obtained, Mr. Tilak sent a slip to Babu Surendranath intimating that he should not make the proposed allusion to the controversy about the presidential election in his speech. He also wrote to Mr. Malvi to supply him with a copy of the draft resolutions if ready, and at abut 3 P.M. while Mr. Malvi was reading his speech, Mr. Tilak got a copy of the draft resolutions which he subsequently found were published the very evening in the *Advocate of India* in Bombay clearly showing that the reporter of the paper must have been supplied with a copy at least a day earlier. The withholding of a copy from Mr. Tilak till 3 P. M. that day cannot, therefore, be regarded as accidental.

There were about thirteen hundred and odd delegates at this time in the pandal of whom over 600 were nationalists, and the Moderate majority was thus a bare majority. After the Chairman's address was over, Dewan Bahadur Ambalal Sakarlal proposed Dr. R. B. Ghosh to the chair in a speech which though evoking occasional cries of dissent, was heard to the end. The declaration by the Dewan Bahadur as well as by Mr. Malvi that the proposition and seconding of the resolution to elect the President was only a *formal* business, led many delegates to believe that it was not improbable that the usual procedure of taking votes on the proposition might be dispensed with; and when Babu Surendranath Banerji, whose rising on the platform seems to have reminded some of the delegates of the Midnapur incident, commenced his speech, there was persistent shouting and he was asked to sit down. He made another attempt to speak but was not heard, and the session had, therefore, to be suspended for the day. The official press-note suggests that this hostile demonstration was pre-arranged. But the suggestion is unfounded. For though the nationalists did intend to oppose the election, they had at their Conference held the previous day expressly decided to do so only by solidly and silently voting against it in a constitutional manner.

In the evening the Nationalists again held their Conference and authorised their Committee, appointed on the previous day, to further carry on the negotiations for having the *status quo* maintained if possible, failing which it was decided to oppose the election of Dr. Ghose by moving such amendment as the Committee might decide or by simply voting against his election. The Nationalists were further requested, and unanimously agreed, not only to abstain from joining in any such demonstration as led to the suspension of that day's proceedings, but to scrupulously avoid any, even the least, interruption of the speakers on the opposite side, so that both parties might get a patient hearing. At night (about 8 P.M.) Mr. Chuni Lal Saraya, Manager of the Indian Specie Bank and Vice-Chairman of the Surat Reception Committee, accompanied by two other gentlemen, went in his un-official capacity and on his own account to Mr. Tilak and proposed that he intended to arrange for a meeting that night between Mr. Tilak and Mr. Gokhale at the residence of a leading Congressman to settle the differences between the two parties. Mr. Tilak agreed and requested Mr. Chuni Lal if an interview could be arranged to fix the time in consultation with Mr. Gokhale, adding that he, Mr. Tilak, would be glad to be present at the place of the interview at *any* hour of the night. Thereon Mr. Chuni Lal left Mr. Tilak, but unhappily no word was received by the latter that night.

SECOND DAY.

On the morning of Friday 27th (11 A.M.) Mr. Chuni Lal Saraya again saw Mr. Tilak and requested him to go in company with Mr. Khaparde to Prof. Gajjar's bungalow near the Congress Pandal, where by appointment they were to meet Dr. Rutherford who was trying for a reconciliation. Messrs. Tilak and Khaparde went to Prof. Gajjar's, but Dr. Rutherford could not come then owing to his other engagements. Prof. Gajjar then asked Mr. Tilak what the latter intended to do; and Mr. Tilak stated that if no settlement was arrived at privately owing to every leading Congressman being unwilling to take any responsibility in the matter upon himself, he (Mr. Tilak) would be obliged to bring an amendment to the proposition of electing the President after it had been seconded. The amendment would be to the effect that the business of election should be adjourned, and a Committee, consisting of one leading Moderate and one leading Nationalist from each Congress Province, with Dr. Rutherford's name added, be appointed to consider and settle the differences between the two parties, both of which should accept the Committee's decision as final and then proceed to the *unanimous* election of the President. Mr. Tilak even supplied to Prof. Gajjar the names of the delegates, who in his opinion should form the Committee, but left a free hand to the Moderates to change the names of their representatives if they liked to do so.* Prof. Gajjar and Mr. Chunni Lal undertook to convey the proposal to Sir P. M. Mehta or Dr. Rutherford in the Congress Camp and asked Messrs. Tilak and Khaparde to go to the pandal and await their reply. After half an hour Prof. Gajjar and Mr. Saraya returned and told Messrs. Tilak and Khaparde that nothing could be done in the matter, Mr. Saraya adding that if both the parties proceeded constitutionally there would be no hitch.

It was about 12-30 at this time, and on the receipt of the above reply Mr. Tilak wrote in pencil the following note to Mr. Malvi, Chairman of the Reception Committee :—

"Sir,—I wish to address the delegates on the proposal of the election of the President after it is seconded. I wish to move an adjournment with a constructive proposal. Please announce me.

Yours Sincerely,
B. G. TILAK,
Deccan Delegate (Poona)."

This note, it is admitted, was put by a volunteer into the hands of Mr. Malvi, the Chairman, as he was entering the pandal with the President-Elect in procession.

The proceedings of the day commenced at 1 P.M., when Babu Surendranath Banerji was called upon to resume his speech, seconding the election of the President. Mr. Tilak was expecting a reply to his note but not having received one up to this time asked Mr. N. C. Kelkar to send a reminder. Mr. Kelkar thereupon sent a chit to the Chairman to the effect that "Mr. Tilak requests a reply to his note," But no reply was received even after this reminder, and Mr. Tilak who thought he was allotted a seat on the platform was sitting in the front row of the delegates' seats near the platform-steps, rose to go up the platform *immediately* after Babu Surendranath, who was calmly heard by all, had finished his speech. But he was held back by a

---

* The names given to Pro. Gajjar were as follows :—United Bengal—Babu Surendranath Bannerjee, A. Chaudhari, Ambikacharan Mazumdar, Arabindo Ghose, Ashwinikumar Dutt. United Provinces—Pandit Madan Mohan, Jatindranath Sen. Punjab—Lala Harkisenlal, Dr. H. Mukerji. Central Provinces—Roaji Govind, Dr. Munje. Berars—R. N. Mudholkar, Khaparde. Bombay—Hon'ble Mr. Gokhale, B. G. Tilak. Madras—V. Krishnaswami Iyer, Chidambaram Pillai ; Dr. Rutherford. This Committee was to meet immediately and decide on the question at issue. The names of the Nationalist representatives in the above list, except Mr. A. K. Dutt, were those of the members of the Committee appointed at the Nationalist Conference on the previous day.

volunteer in the way. Mr. Tilak, however, asserted his right to go up and pushing aside the volunteer succeeded in getting to the platform just when Dr. Ghosh was moving to take the President's chair. The Official Note says that by the time Mr. Tilak came upon the platform and stood in front of the President, the motion of the election of Ghose had been passed by an overwhelming majority; and Dr. Ghose being installed in the Presidential chair by loud and *prolonged* applause, had risen to begin his address. All this, if it did take place as alleged, could only have been done in a deliberately hurried manner with a set purpose to trick Mr. Tilak out of his right to address the delegates and move an amendment as previously notified. According to the usual procedure Mr. Malvi was bound to announce Mr. Tilak, or if he considered the amendment out of order, declare it so publicly, and to ask for a show of hands in favour of or against the motion. But nothing of the kind was done; nor was the interval of a few seconds sufficient for a prolonged applause as alleged. As Mr. Tilak stood up on the platform he was greeted with shouts of disapproval from the Members of the Reception Committee on the platform, and the cry was taken up by other Moderates. Mr. Tilak repeatedly insisted up on his right of addressing the delegates, and told Dr. Ghose, when he attempted to interfere, that he was not properly elected. Mr. Malvi said that he had ruled Mr. Tilak's amendment out of order to which Mr. Tilak replied that the ruling, if any, was wrong and Mr. Tilak had a right to appeal to the delegates on the same. By this time there was a general uproar in the pandal, the Moderates shouting at Mr. Tilak and asking him to sit down and the Nationalists demanding that he should be heard. At this stage Dr. Ghose and Mr. Malvi said that Mr. Tilak should be removed from the platform; and a young gentleman, holding the important office of a Secretary to the Reception Committee, touched Mr. Tilak's person with a view to carry out the Chairman's order. Mr. Tilak pushed the gentleman aside and again asserted his right of being heard, declaring that he would not leave the platform unless bodily removed. Mr. Gokhale seems to have here asked the above mentioned gentleman not to touch Mr. Tilak's person. But there were others who were seen threatening an assault on his person though he was calmly standing on the platform facing the delegates with his arms folded over his chest.

It was during this confusion that a shoe hurled on to the platform hit Sir P. M. Mehta on the side of the face after touching Babu Surendranath Bannerji, both of whom were sitting within a yard of Mr. Tilak on the other side of the table. Chairs were now seen being lifted to be thrown at Mr. Tilak by persons on and below the platform, and some of the Nationalists, therefore, rushed on to the platform to his rescue. Dr. Ghose in the meanwhile twice attempted to read his address, but was stopped by cries of "no, no" from all sides in the pandal, and the confusion became still worse. It must be stated that the Surat Reception Committee, composed of Moderates, had made arrangements the previous night to dismiss the Nationalist Volunteers and to hire *Bohrah* or Mahomedan goondas for the day. These with lathis were stationed at various places in the pandal and their presence was detected and protested against by the Nationalist Delegates before the commencement of the Congress proceedings of the day. But though one or two were removed from the pandal, the rest who remained therein now took part in the scuffle on behalf of their masters. It was found impossible to arrest the progress of disorder and proceedings were then suspended *sine die;* and the Congress officials retired in confusion to a tent behind the pandal. The police, who seem to have been long ready under a requisition, now entered into and eventually cleared the pandal; while the Nationalist Delegates who had gone to the platform safely escorted Mr. Tilak to an adjoining tent. It remains to be mentioned that copies of an inflammatory leaflet in Gujrathi asking the Gujrathi people to rise against Mr. Tilak were largely distributed in the pandal before the commencement of the day's proceedings.

It would be seen from the above account that the statement in the official note to the effect that Dr. Ghose was elected President amid loud and prolonged applause before Mr. Tilak appeared on the platform, and that Mr. Tilak wanted to move an adjournment of the whole Congress are entirely misleading and unfounded. What he demanded, by way of amendment, was an adjournment of the business of the election of the President in order to have the differences settled by a joint Conciliatory Committee of leading delegates from both sides. Whether this was in order or otherwise, Mr. Tilak had certainly a right to appeal to the delegates and it was this consciousness that led Mr. Malvi and his advisers to hastily wind up the election business without sending a reply to Mr. Tilak or calling upon him to address the delegates. It was a trick by which they intended to deprive Mr. Tilak of the right of moving an amendment and addressing the delegates thereon. As for the beginning of the actual rowdyism on the day some of the members of the Reception Committee itself were responsible. The silent hearing given by the Nationalists to Mr. Surendranath on the one hand, and the circulation of the inflammatory leaflet and the hiring of the goondas on the other, further prove that if there was any pre-arrangement anywhere for the purpose of creating a row in the pandal, it was on the part of the Moderates themselves. But for their rowdyism there was every likelihood of Mr. Tilak's amendments being carried by a large majority and the election of President afterwards taking place smoothly and unanimously. But neither Dr. Ghose nor any other Congress officials seemed willing to tactfully manage the business as Mr. Dadabhai Naoroji did last year.

Dr. Ghose's speech though undelivered in the Congress pandal had been by this time published in the Calcutta papers, and telegrams from Calcutta received in the evening showed that he had made an inoffensive attack on the Nationalist party thereon. This added to the sensation in the Nationalist camp that evening, but the situation was not such as to preclude all hope of reconciliation. Srijut Motilal Ghose of the *Patrika*, Mr. A. C. Moitra of Rajshahi, Mr. B. C. Chatterji of Calcutta and Lala Harkisen Lal from Lahore accordingly tried their best to bring about a compromise, and, if possible, to have the Congress session revived the next day. They went to Mr. Tilak on the night of 27th and the morning of 28th to ascertain the views of his party, and to each of them Mr. Tilak gave the following assurance in writing :—

"Surat, 28th December, 1907.

"Dear Sir,—With reference to our conversation and principally in the best interests of the Congress, I and my party are prepared to waive our opposition to the election of Dr. Rash Behari Ghose as President of 23rd Indian National Congress, and are prepared to act in the spirit of forget and forgive, provided, *firstly* the last year's resolutions on Swaraj, Swadeshi, Boycott and National Education are adhered to and each expressly reaffirmed; *Secondly*, such passages, if any, in Dr. Ghose's speech as may be offensive to the Nationalists Party are omitted,

Yours &c., B. G. TILAK."

This letter was taken by the gentlemen to whom it was addressed to the Moderate leaders but no compromise was arrived at as the Moderates were all along bent upon the retrogression of the Congress at any cost. A Convention of the Moderates was, therefore, held in the pandal the next day where Nationalists were not allowed to go even when some of them were ready and offered to sign the declaration required. On the other hand, those who did not wish to go back from the position taken up at the Calcutta Congress and honestly desired to work further on the same lines met in a separate place the some evening to consider what steps might be taken to continue the work of the Congress in future. Thus ended the proceedings of the 23rd Indian National Congress;

and we leave it to the public to judge of the conduct of the two parties in this affair from the statement of facts hereinbefore given.

B. G. TILAK.
G. S. KHAPARDE.
ARABINDO GHOSE.

SURAT.
31st December, 1917.

H. MUKERJEE.
B. C. CHATTERJEE.

Appendix to the Extremists Version.

HOW THEY WANTED TO GO BACK.

THE CONGRESS IDEAL.

At the Calcutta Congress, under the presidentship of Mr. Dadabhai Naoroji, it was resolved that the goal of the Congress should be Swaraj on the lines of the Self-governing British Colonies, and this goal was accepted by all Moderates and Nationalists without a single dissentient voice. The resolution on Self-Government passed there is as follows :—

" *Self-Government* :—This Congress is of opinion that the system of Government obtaining in the Self-Governing British Colonies should be extended to India and that as steps leading to it, urges that the following reforms should be immediately carried out." (Here followed certain administrative reforms such as simultaneous examinations in England and India, reform of Executive and Legislative Councils, and of Local and Municipal Boards.)

The Congress Reception Committee at Surat did not publish the draft Resolution till the commencement of the Congress Sessions ; but a Draft Constitution of the Congress, prepared by the Hon'ble Mr. Gokhale, was published a day or two earlier. In this draft the goal of the Congress was defined as follows :—

" The Indian National Congress has for its ultimate goal the attainment by India of Self-Government similar to that enjoyed by other members of the British Empire and a participation by her in the privileges and responsibilities of the Empire on equal terms with the other members ; and it seeks to advance towards this goal by strictly constitutional means, by bringing about a steady reform of the existing system of administration, and by promoting national unity, fostering public spirit and improving the condition of the mass of the people."

"Those who accept the foregoing creed of the Congress, shall be members of the Provincial Committee."

"All who accept the foregoing creed of the Congress . . . shall be entitled to become members of a District Congress Committee."

"From the year 1908, delegates to the Congress shall be elected by Provincial and District Congress Committees only."

Remarks:—It will at once be seen that the new Constitution intended to convert the Congress from a national into a sectional movement. The goal of Swaraj on the lines of the Self-governing colonies as settled last year, was to be given up: and in its stead Self-Government similar to that enjoyed by other members (not necessarily self-governing) of the British Empire was to be set up as the *ultimate* goal evidently meaning that it was to be considered as out of the pale of practical politics. The same view is expressed by Sir Pherozeshah Mehta in his interview with the correspondent of the *Times of India* published in the issue of the *Times* dated 30th December, 1907. The Hon'ble Mr. Gokhale must have taken his cue from the same source. The *reform* of the existing system of administration, and not its gradual replacement by a popular system, was to be the immediate object of the Congress according to this constitution; and further no one, who did not accept this new creed, was to be a member of provincial or district committees or possibly even a delegate to the Congress after 1908. This was the chief feature of retrogression, which Sir P. M. Mehta and his party wanted to carry out this year at a safe place like Surat. It is true that the old resolution on Self-Government was subsequently included in the Draft Resolutions published only after the commencement of the Congress Session. But the Draft Constitution was never withdrawn.

SWADESHI MOVEMENT.

The Calcutta Resolution on the Swadesi Movement was as follows:—

"The Congress accords its most cordial support to the *Swadeshi* Movement and calls upon the

At Surat, the Draft Resolution on the subject was worded as follows:—

"This Congress accords its most cordial support to the Swadeshi Movement, and calls people of the country to labour for its success by making earnest and sustained efforts to promote the growth of indigenous industries, and to stimulate the production of indigenous articles by giving them preference over imported commodities even at some sacrifice."

upon the people of the country to labour for its success by earnest and sustained efforts to promote the growth of indigenous industries and stimulate the consumption of indigenous articles by giving them preference, where possible, over imported commodities."

Remarks :—Last year the words "even at some sacrifice" were introduced at the end after the great discussion and as a compromise between the two parties, The Hon. Mr. Gokhale or Sir P.M. Mehta now wanted to have these words expunged, converting the old resolution into a mere appeal for preference for the indigenous over imported goods.

BOYCOTT MOVEMENT.

The Calcutta Resolution was as follows :—

"Having regard to the fact that the people of this country have little or no voice in its administration and that their representations to Government do not receive due consideration, this Congress is of opinion that the Boycott Movement inaugurated in Bengal by way of protest against partition of that province was and is legitimate."

The proposed Resolution at Surat was :—

"Having regard to the fact that the people of the country have little or no voice in its administration and that their representatives to the Government do not receive due consideration, this Congress is of opinion that the boycott of foreign goods resorted to in Bengal by way of protest against the partition of that Province was, and is legitimate."

Remarks :—This subject was not included in the list of subjects published at first but seems to have been subsequently inserted in the Draft Resolutions, when the first omission in the list was severely noticed in the press. The words *Boycott Movement* in the old Resolution have, however, been changed into *Boycott of foreign goods.*

NATIONAL EDUCATION.

The Calcutta Resolution was as follows :—

"In the opinion of this Congress the time has arrived for the people all over the country earnestly to take up the question of National Education for both

The proposed resolution at Surat runs thus :—

"In the opinion of this Congress the time has arrived for the people all over the country earnestly to take up the question of National Education for both

boys and girls and organise a system of education—Literary, Scientific, Technical—suited to the requirements of the country on National lines and under National control."	boys and girls and organise an independent system of education, Literary. Scientific, Technical—suited to the requirements of the country."

Remarks :—The change is significant inasmuch as the word " on National lines and under National control" are omitted in the Surat draft, for " control " is the most important factor in this matter. The phrase " an independent system " does not convey all that is desired.

K.P,P.

III. MR. GOKHALE AND THE EXTREMISTS' VERSION.

The Extremist version of what occurred at Surat, which was under preparation has at last been published. It is full of gross mis-statements, some of which concern me personally, and these, with your permission, I would like to set right in your columns.

1. The version says :—"It was clearly arranged by the Hon. Mr. Gokhale to get the (Reception) Committee to nominate Dr. R. B. Ghose to the office of President, brushing aside the proposal for the nomination of Lala Lajpat Rai." Dr. Ghose had been nominated for the office of President by all the Provinces consulted except Berar. The overwhelming preponderance of opinion in the Reception Committee at Surat was also in his favor. The reason why I attended the meeting of the Reception Committee at which the nomination took place was that rowdyism had been threatened to make its proceedings impossible as at Nagpur unless the proposal of the Extremists to elect Lala Lajpat Rai was accepted. The Reception Committee had barely a month at its disposal for making the required preparations, and any hostility to it on the part of a section however small would have meant abandoning the Congress Session at Surat. I went there as Joint General Secretary of the Congress in the interests of harmony, and for the time may appeal to those who wanted to bring forward Lala Lajpat Rai's name proved effective. The harmony brought about lasted till Mr. Tilak's emissaries from Nagpur repaired to Surat and stirred up trouble about a week after the meeting of the Reception Committee.

2. I am charged with "brushing aside the proposal for the nomination of Lala Lajpat Rai" on the ground that "we cannot afford to flout the Government at this stage. The authorities would throttle our movement in no time." This unscrupulous distortion of stray sentences from a private conversation, taken apart from their context, has now been pushed to such lengths that it is necessary to put aside the feeling of delicacy that has hitherto restrained me in the matter. The conversation was with two Extremist gentlemen of Surat with whom I discussed the situation at some length prior to the meeting of the Reception Committee on the 24th November. I pointed out to these gentlemen the unwisdom of bringing forward Lala Lajpat Rai's name for the Presidentship of the Congress, and this I did on three grounds :—

First, that with only a month at disposal of the Reception Committee for making arrangements which, in other places, had taken at least three to four months, any division among the workers at Surat was most undesirable as it was sure to hamper the progress of their work.

Secondly, that there was absolutely no chance of their carrying their proposal about Lala Lajpat Rai, their strength being only five or six out of about two hundred, who were expected to attend that afternoon's meeting and that the rejection of Mr. Lala Lajpat Rai's name would only be a painful and wanton humiliation for him and thirdly and lastly, that though Lala Lajpat Rai had been personally restored to freedom, the larger question of principle involved in his deportation had yet to be fought out, and it would best be fought out by keeping up the feeling of the country united and intact behind him, and that this feeling was sure to be divided if one section of the Congress tried to run him as a party candidate. I next pointed out that there were other ways in which we could all honour Mr. Lajpat Rai, and then I added, "if your object is simply to flout the Government, I can understand your proposal." To this one of the two gentlemen said, "Yes, even if we do nothing else, we want to show that we are prepared to flout the Government." I thereupon said, "I don't believe in such flouting. The Congress must, of course, express its condemnation of Government measures when necessary, but it has other important work to do. We cannot do without the help and co-operation of Government in many matters at our present stage." The conversation then turned to what our goal should be, and what the Congress should try to do. And the gentleman in question—a young man who had only recently returned from England.—urged on me his view that the Congress should work for absolute independence, and that it should try to teach the people of the country to hate the present foreign Government as much as possible. It was in reply to this that I said, "you do not realise the enormous reserve of power behind the Government. If the Congress were to do anything such as you suggest, the Government will have no difficulty in throttling it in five minutes." It is out of this conversation that the story which has been kept going for some time past with a hundred variations has been concocted. There were about twenty people present when the above conversation took place.

3. "The Hon. Mr. Gokhale was entrusted by the Reception Committee at its meeting held on the 24th November 1907, for nominating the President with the work of drafting the Resolutions before the Congress."

This is not correct. No resolution whatever was passed on the matter at the meeting of the Reception Committee. About the beginning of December, when I went to Bombay from Poona, I was informed by one of the Secretaries of the Reception Committee, Mr. Manubhai Nanabhai, that the Working Committee had decided to ask me to undertake the drafting of the Resolutions to be laid before the Subjects Committee. I was at that time pressed with other work, and so I suggested that the draft should, in the first instance, be prepared by either Mr. Manubhai himself or by his colleague Mr. Gandhi, and that I would then touch them up if required. Mr. Gandhi wrote back at once to say that that he could not undertake the work as he had no time. Mr. Manubhai began to collect the material necessary for drafting the resolutions, but he was so terribly overworked that he too could not give any time to the actual work of preparing the drafts, and at last about the 15th December, he told me that I should have to do the whole work in that respect myself.

4. "Neither Mr. Gokhale nor the Reception Committee supplied a copy of the Draft Resolutions to any delegates till 2-30 P.M. on Thursday, the 26th December." This was due to the fact that printed copies were not till then available. On the 15th December, I settled the headings of the Resolutions in Bombay, but I could get no quiet there for the work of drafting, and so I went to Poona on the 19th December to prepare the drafts. It was by no means easy work. The Resolution that gave the greatest trouble was about the proposed reforms. I wrestled with it as well as I could in Poona, but I could not produce a satisfactory draft. When I arrived in Surat on the morning of the 24th, the Draft Resolution on the proposed Reforms was still not ready. I then gave the other drafts to Mr. Gandhi, Secretary of the Reception Committee, in charge of this work, who immediately sent them to the press.

For the draft on the Reform proposals I asked for a day more. There were, however, a thousand things to distract one's attention and though I gave to the draft all the time I could spare on the 24th and the morning of the 25th I was not able to finish it. So, with much regret, I asked Mr. Gandhi to get the other drafts printed leaving a blank in the place of the Resolution on Reform proposals. Now Surat is a small place and its printing resources are not equal to those of Calcutta, Bombay or Madras, and the press took a day to give printed copies of the drafts to Mr. Gandhi. It was only when I went to the pandal at 2-30 P.M. on the 26th that I learnt from Mr. Gandhi that copies had arrived from the press, and the first printed copy which I myself saw was the one which I procured from Mr. Gandhi to pass on to Mr. Tilak who had just then asked Mr. Malvi for a copy. The copies were available in good time for the deliberations of the Subjects Committee which, in the usual course, was expected to sit that afternoon and for whose use alone the drafts have always been prepared.

Three things must here be noted. First, though the Draft Resolutions have in previous years been published beforehand, whenever there has been time to do so, it is not true that they have *always* been so published. Last year, for instance, at Calcutta, some of the Draft Resolutions were not ready till the last minute, and this, in spite of the fact that our Calcutta friends had much more time at their disposal than the one month in which Surat had to make its preparations.

Secondly, never before in the history of the Congress was an attempt made as at Surat to attach an absurdly exaggerated importance to the Draft Resolutions. Everyone knows that these drafts bind nobody, and that they are merely material laid before the Subjects Committee for it to work upon. I don't remember a single Congress at which the Subjects Committee did not make important and sometimes even wholesale alterations in the drafts placed before it by the Reception Committee. The final form in which Resolutions have been submitted to the Congress has always been determined by the Subjects Committee and the Subjects Committee alone.

Thirdly, no Reception Committee has ever in the past merely reproduced the Resolutions of the previous Congress on its agenda paper for the Subjects Committee. The Calcutta Reception Committee of last year did not merely reproduce the Benares Resolutions, neither did the Benares Committee reproduce the Bombay Resolution. Every Reception Committee has exercised its own judgment as to the wording of the Draft Resolutions, and the Surat Committee or those who were working for it were merely following the established practice when they prepared their own drafts.

5. "While Mr. Malvi was reading his speech, Mr. Tilak got a copy of the Draft Resolutions, which he subsequently found were published the very evening in the *Advocate of India* in Bombay, clearly showing that the reporter of the paper must have been supplied with a copy at least a day earlier." The reporter must have procured a copy from Mr. Gandhi as soon as copies arrived from the press and must have wired the Resolutions to his paper, or it is possible that he may have obtained a proof from the press before copies were printed. Certainly no printed copies were available to me till I went to the pandal on the 26th. I wanted to give a copy to Lala Lajpat Rai that morning, but could not do so as no copies had arrived from the press till then.

I now come to the wording of the Draft Resolutions.

Coming to the wording of the Draft Resolutions, I would like to point out at the outset that the cry set up by Mr. Tilak in connection with these drafts was his third attempt to discredit the Surat Congress since the middle of November.

He began by denouncing the change of venue from Nagpur to Surat and by misrepresenting, beyond all recognition, the proceedings of the All-India Congress Committee which decided upon the change—and this, without even the excuse of ignorance, since he was personally present at the meeting of the Committee and knew exactly what had taken place.§

When he found that he could not make much impression on the country by these attacks, he played his second card. He started his agitation to have the election of Dr. Ghosh set aside in favour of Lala Lajpat Rai. In this, however, he was foiled by Lala Lajpat Rai's own letter which put an effective extinguisher on the agitation.

Then the cry was raised that it was the intention of the Reception Committee to drop certain resolutions altogether this year. The ball was set rolling by a telegram from Poona to certain Madras and Calcutta Papers about a week before the meeting of the Congress that the Reception Committee had made up its mind to omit certain resolutions from its agenda paper and that there was intense indignation in the "Nationalist circles" in consequence. This manufacture of "Nationalist indignation" was pushed forward so energetically that, when I went to Bombay on the 22nd December, I found a considerable amount of feeling stirred up in certain quarters against the Reception Committee on this account. On that day I met Lala Lajpat Rai and he asked me what the truth was about the resolutions in question. I told him that the resolutions were all there with slight verbal alterations made in one or two of them to remove ambiguity and that the Subjects Committee would decide in what form they should finally be submitted to the Congress. I understand that Lala Lajpat Rai communicated the substance of this conversation that same evening to Mr. Tilak. In spite of this communication, Mr. Tilak definitely and deliberately stated at the Extremists' Conference at Surat on the 24th December that the Reception Committee had decided to omit the resolutions and this naturally caused great excitement among the delegates assembled! Mr. Gandhi, the local secretary in charge of the resolutions, came to know of this in the evening and he immediately issued a Press Note contradicting Mr. Tilak's statements as wholly unfounded.

But the cry was kept up the whole of the next day, *i.e.*, the 25th. On that day, in the afternoon, Lala Lajpat Rai, who was going to visit the Extremist Camp, asked me if he might personally assure the leaders on that side that they were under a misapprehension about the resolutions and that they would find them all on the agenda paper when it arrived from the press. I readily agreed and Lala Lajpat Rai went and gave the assurance. That same evening I addressed about 200 delegates in the Madras tent of the Congress camp, especially for the purpose of removing the misapprehensions and there I not only assured them that the resolutions were all on the agenda paper, but also mentioned the exact verbal alterations that had been made. About 11 P.M. that night I met Babu Ashwani Kumar Dutt of Barisal at the President's residence, and I repeated to him what I had told the Madras delegates and he expressed himself satisfied. The next day, *i.e*, on the 26th, on going to the pandal as soon as I heard of the copies having arrived from the press, I procured and gave one to Mr. Tilak as I have mentioned in my last letter. The Hon. Pandit Madan Mohan Malaviya was sitting by Mr. Tilak at the time and I heard it afterwards from him that he asked Mr. Tilak if he was satisfied that the resolutions were all there and Mr. Tilak had to admit that it was so. Only the slight verbal alterations that had been made would have to be amended. And now as regards the wording of the four Resolutions :—

(*a*) Taking Self-Government first the Extremists' version says: "At the Calcutta Congress, under the Presidentship of Mr. Dadabhai Naoroji, it was resolved that the goal of the Congress should be *Swaraj* on the lines of self-governing British Colonies." This is not accurate. The word *Swaraj* was not used in any of the resolutions of the Congress last year though it was used by Mr. Dadhabhai in his own speech. Neither was there any mention of a goal in any of last year's resolutions. What last year's Congress had done was to prefix a preamble about Self-Government to certain specific proposals of reform and that preamble was in these words :—"This Congress is of opinion that the system of government obtaining in the Self-Governing Colonies should be extended to India and that, as steps leading to it, it urges that the following reforms should be immediately carried out." Now a reference to this year's draft resolutions will show that the whole of this resolution, preamble and all, was reproduced by the Reception Committee on the agenda paper with only a slight alteration in one of the clauses rendered necessary by the appointment of two Indians to the Secretary of State's Council. Mr. Tilak, however, compares last year's resolution on Self-Government, not with this year's draft resolution on the same subject, but with the preamble to another draft resolution—that on the constitution of the Congress, and he charges the Reception Committee with "a direct attempt to tamper with the ideal of Self-Government on the lines of the Self-Governing Colonies as settled at Calcutta." Now the portion of the preamble to the proposed constitution referring to Self-Government was as follows : "The Indian National Congress has, for its ultimate goal, the attainment by India of Self-Government similar to that enjoyed by other members of the British Empire and a participation by her in the privileges and responsibilities of the Empire on equal terms with the other members." This is interpreted by Mr. Tilak as meaning that "the goal of *Swaraj* on the lines of Self-Governing Colonies, as settled last year, was to be given up and in its stead Self-Government similar to that enjoyed by other members (not necessarily self-governing) of the British Empire was to set up as the ultimate goal." I should have thought it incredible that any one with any pretention to a knowledge of practical politics could put such an atrocious misconstruction on the preamble of the draft constitution, but for the fact that Mr. Tilak has actually done it.

Whoever talks of the form of Government obtaining in the Crown Colonies or Dependencies of the British Empire as Self-Government? Whoever talks of their partcipating in the privileges of the Empire? However, as soon as Mr. Tilak's construction was brought to my notice, I at once altered the expression, "Self-Government enjoyed by other members of the British Empire," to "Self-Government enjoyed by the Self-Governing members of the British Empire," so as to leave no room for his ludicrous objection and it will be seen that the Convention afterwards used this wording for its creed. In this connection, I would like to observe that it is most curious that Mr. Tilak should charge me with a desire to abandon the idea of Self-Government, as in the British Colonies, being the goal of our aspiration. Ever since I began to take an active interest in the national affairs this has been a part of my political faith. In the prospectus of the Servants of India Society which was started in June 1905, I have mentioned this goal in clear and explicit terms. "Self-Government on the lines of English Colonies," the prospectus says, "is our goal." From the Presidential Chair of the Congress at Benares in December 1905, I declared the same thing. "The goal of the Congress," I then stated, "is that India should be governed in the interests of the Indians themselves and that, in course of time, a form of Government should be attained in this country similar to what exists in the Self-Governing Colonies of the British Empire." In 1906, in a Paper read before the East India Association in London, on "Self Government for India" I elaborated the same idea. On the other hand, Mr. Tilak has not always known his own mind in this matter. After the Benares Congress, Mr. Shyamji Krishna-varma denounced me in his *Indian Sociologist* for my idea of Self-Government on Colonial lines and later on Mr. Tilak following Mr. Shyamji's lead joined in that denunication in his *Kesari*. Last year, however, Mr. Tilak veered round to the position that the goal of our political works was of equality for the Englishman and the Indian in the British Empire, but this year again at the Extremists' Conference he coquetted with the views of the Bengal School of Extremist politicians and yet it is Mr. Tilak who attributes to me a desire to alter the resolution of last year on this subject.

(*b*) As regards Swadeshi, there never was the least intention to alter a single word in last year's resolution and it was by a mere accident that the words, "even at some sacrifice," happened to be left out in the Reception Committee's drafts. It happened this way. The report of the Calcutta Congress was not out when the draft resolution were prepared. So far the text of last year's resolutions I had to rely on a newspaper file. Now, the only file I had with me containing those resolutions was of the journal *India* which had published all the resolutions of last year in its issue of 1st February 1907. As no change of even a word was contemplated in the resolution on *Swadeshi*, I had got one of my assistants merely to copy it from the *India* and include it among the drafts. Unfortunately the text as published in *India* was defective and did not contain the words, "even at some sacrifice," as a reference to the issue of that journal of 1st February, 1907, will show.

And the omission, perfectly unintentional, remained unnoticed till the meeting of the informal Conference which followed the Convention when the words which had been left out were at once restored. It is unnecessary to say that they would have been similarly restored if the Agenda paper had gone as usual to the Subjects Committee for consideration.

(*c*) In the resolution on Boycott, the only verbal alteration made was to substitute the words "the boycott of foreign goods resorted to in Bengal" for the words "the boycott movement inaugurated in Bengal" and the resolution was placed under Partition as the Boycott approved was "by way of protest against the Partition." The change in the wording had been rendered necessary by the unfair and unjustifiable attempt made by an Extremist leader from the Congress platform last year and by Mr. Tilak and others in the Press throughout the year to construe the phraseology employed last year as approving a universal boycott of all forms of association with the Government.

(*d*) In regard to National Education the slight alteration made was only with the object of improving the phraseology without altering the meaning in any way. It must be mentioned here that the wording adopted last year on this subject had not been considered in the Subjects Committee, there being no time for doing so. In last year's resolution, the word "National" appeared three times—national education on national lines and under national control. It appeared to me that the words, "a system of national education" suited to the requirements of the country and "independent of Government" really expressed all that had to be expressed and that this phraseology was more restrained and more in accord with what was being actually attempted in different parts of India. It will thus be seen that, in drawing up its draft resolutions on the four subjects, the Surat Committee had not intended or attempted any alteration in meaning, though verbal changes had been made here and there to remove ambiguity or to improve the phraseology. I have already pointed out that in making such changes, it was only following the practice of previous years. Moreover, as I have stated in my last letter, there were only drafts that bound nobody and the Subjects Committee would have determined the final form in which they were to be submitted to the Congress. All the storm raised in connection with them was really more to discredit the Surat Committee than for furthering any national interests, real or fancied.

The Extremist Statement speaks of certain attempts made by certain gentlemen to arrange "a compromise" and it mentions three gentlemen as having undertaken to speak to me—Lala Lajpat Rai, Mr. Surendra Nath Banerjee and Mr. Chunilal D. Suraya. Of these, Mr. Chunilal never saw me in any such connection. Lala Lajpat Rai had a brief talk with me—it was on the 25th December in the evening at the Railway Station when we had gone there to receive the President—about a proposal made by Mr. Tilak that five men on his side and five men on the other side should meet together and settle the wording of the different resolutions. I pointed out to Mr. Lajpat Rai that it was the business of the Subjects Committee to settle the wording and that a Committee such as Mr. Tilak suggested had never been appointed before. Moreover it was easy for Mr. Tilak, whose followers were meeting in a Conference day after day to nominate five men to represent his side, but amidst the excitement and bitterness of feeling then prevailing, what five men, I asked, could claim the authority or undertake the responsibility to act in the name of the other delegates? And I said to him, "let the Subjects Committee meet to-morrow and let us see if any differences remain to be adjusted. And, if any remain, you can make this proposal to the Subjects Committee." Lala Lajpat Rai saw the force of this and did not press the suggestion further. Mr. Surendra Nath Banerjee mentioned to me on the opening day of the Congress, only a few minutes before going to the Pandal, that he had had a conversation that morning with Mr. Tilak and that Mr. Tilak had said to him that if he (Mr. Banerjee) and myself guaranteed the passing of the four resolutions in the same form as last year, there would be no trouble in connection with the President's election. I pointed out to Mr. Banerjee how Mr. Tilak had shifted his ground—how, till the previous evening, the cry was for an assurance that the four resolutions would be on the agenda paper and how he now demanded a guarantee that they would be passed in the same form as last year and I said, "it is outrageous that Mr. Tilak should make such a demand and threaten now with trouble. How can any individual member with any sense of responsibility guarantee what would be done by Subjects Committee not yet appointed or by a Congress of sixteen hundred delegates? These men denounce us in one breath for autocracy and, in the next, they ask us to take upon ourselves such an impossible responsibility." The conversation then ended. Before passing away from this point, I would like to contradict here, in the most emphatic manner possible, the report to which such wide currency has been given, that Mr. Tilak tried three times at Surat to see me and that every time I declined to see him. There is not a word of truth in this report. Mr. Tilak never gave me to understand directly or indirectly that he wanted to meet me at Surat. He never wrote to me or sent me word with any one to express such a desire. He never came to my place and to my knowledge he never tried to meet me anywhere else.

Only one more matter in the Extremists' Statement concerns me personally. It is the version that it gives of what took place first between Mr. Malvi and Mr. Tilak and then between Dr. Ghosh and Mr. Tilak, when Mr. Tilak came to the platform to move the adjournment of the Congress. This version is in direct conflict with the official version issued immediately after the break-up of the Congress over the signatures of Dr. Ghosh, Mr. Malvi, Mr. Wacha and myself. Now, all four of us had heard every word of the conversation that took place between Mr. Tilak on one side and Mr. Malvi and Dr. Ghosh on the other. On the other hand, though the Extremist version is signed by five gentlemen, four of the five were not on the platform and could not have heard a syllable of what was said. The conflict between the two versions thus means the word of us four is against the word of Mr. Tilak and there I am content to let it stand. Here I must close and I would do so with one observation. The Reception Committee of Surat had not departed in a single particular from the established practice of the last twenty-two years. It had made its arrangements for the holding of the Congress and for the comfort of the delegates in the usual way. It had prepared the agenda paper for the Subjects Committee in the usual way. It had elected the President under a special rule adopted by the Congress itself last year. Having made these preparations in the course of single month, for which cities like Calcutta and Bombay have taken three to four months—having turned its nights into days for the purpose—it awaited for the Congress meeting and conducting its deliberations in the usual way. On the other hand, all the innovations were on Mr. Tilak's side. He set up a separate camp of his own followers. He harrangued them daily about the supposed intention of the Reception Committee and the high-handedness of imaginary bureaucracy in the Congress. He made from day to day wild and wreckless statements, some of which it is difficult to characterise properly in terms of due restraint.

He created a pledge-bound party to vote with him like a machine, whatever the personal views of individual delegates might be. He demanded guarantees from individual members on the other side unheard of in the history of the Congress. On the first day some of his followers by sheer rowdyism compelled the sitting to be suspended. On the second day when the sitting was resumed there was no expression of regret forthcoming for the discreditable occurrence of the previous day and though one day out of three had been already lost, Mr. Tilak himself came forward to interrupt the proceedings again by a motion of adjurnment. Under the mildest construction this was a move of obstruction, pure and simple, for as long as the rule under which the Reception Committee had elected Dr. Ghosh remained unrescinded, there was no possible way to get that election set aside. On the paltform, Mr. Tilak openly and persistently defied the authority of the Chair. Over the painful incidents that followed, it is perhaps best now to throw a pall. But in all this, I do not see where the responsibility of the Reception Committee comes in.

CALCUTTA,
13th January, 1908.

G. K. GOKHALE.

IV. EXTREMISTS' VERSION CONTRADICTED.

It is with great reluctance that I take up my pen to write on an event, the tragical nature of which cannot be felt more acutely by any one than by those who for the last twenty years and more have been devoting their best energies to the one great national institution, which gave hope of a better future, and who struck steadfastly to it when the leaders of the newly arisen new party were trying to stab it by ridicule, misrepresentation and calumny. Having been an eye-witness of all that happened on the two memorable days, the 26th and the 27th of December, I thought that deplorable, disgraceful and utterly unworthy of gentlemen as those occurrences were, even those who had so far forgotten what they owe to themselves, to the country and to posterity as to have indulged in rowdyism and open violence, would, despite party passions, admit the real facts and express their sorrow for the grievous mistakes committed by them. It is therefore humiliating—nay, disgusting to see that men of education and position, who must be regarded as representatives, have shown an open disregard for truth which augurs ill for the progress of our motherland. Whatever room for misapprehension there might have been as to the intentions and plans of the Bombay leaders and whatever scope one or two unintentional acts or omissions might have afforded for criticism there could be those who would not wilfully disregard the evidence of their senses. No doubt the whole rowdyism, unseemly squabbles and resort to sticks and physical violence, which disgraced the last session of the Congress, was due to the Extremists and that the responsibility for the *fracas* lies upon the leaders of that party. It appears that Mr. G. Subramania Iyer has written to the *Hindu* stating that he has modified the views which he had first expressed. I have not seen the latter, but, if the criticism which the *Indu Prakash* makes on it is well based, I must say, it is curious if Mr. Iyer throws on the Moderates any responsibility for the disorderly scenes on the 26th and the attack of the 27th. He was sitting next to me on the first day and when the din of cries, shouts and unparliamentary terms was raised against Mr. Surendranath Banerjee by some Nagpurians, Benarees and Madrasis, he became very angry and exclaimed excitedly: "This is most disgraceful, most shameful. This is all due to Tilak and Khaparde. They are responsible for all this." He further said to me "this is all the doing of your Central Provinces. Nagpur has brought troubles on the Congress." I felt that taunt and replied sharply "your rebuke is, I must admit, sorrowfully true so far as men of my province are concerned, but are there not 8 or 10 Madrasis, who are even wilder than they?" On the 27th, he was, again, not far from me and saw all the incidents and when we met again shortly afterwards he threw the whole blame on those same persons. On both occasions, the remarks were voluntarily made. On the following days, I remonstrated with several Berar Extremists and told them what Mr. G. Subramaniya Iyer had said, leader though he was till late of the Extremist party of the Madras Presidency.

Every one, who has the least regard for truth, will unhesitatingly say that every word in the statement issued under the signatures of Dr. Ghosh and Messrs. Malvi, Wacha and Gokhale is true. It is now well known from what quarter the shoe came and that it was aimed at Sir P. M. Mehta. It is a wicked lie to say that it was aimed at Mr. Tilak. It can be proved by the testimony of hundreds of eye-witnesses that signals were given by prominent Extremists and that thereon a number of persons from the Central Provinces and Berar, some of whom were delegates and some visitors, rushed to the platform wielding big long sticks. When Mr. Tilak was escorted, he was surrounded by more than 50 of his followers armed with these *lathies*. Is it usual for delegates or even visitors to carry about *lathies*? One fact throws a most lurid light on the affair. Among the Extremist delegates and visitors taken from Berar were gymnastic teachers, gymnastis, proclaimed touts, workmen from factories, fitters, oilmen, etc. There were, I am told, barber delegates from Nagpur, who for the money spent on them, made some small return by shaving the Nationalist delegates. These men are too poor to pay their travelling expenses, much less, their delegation fee. Who supplied the money and what was the object in taking such persons? For, most of them do not know English and have never taken part in public matters. With my own eyes, I saw Extremist delegates, holding two degrees, brandishing long and powerful sticks or rushing wildly and frantically at the occupants of the platform. I myself stopped the progress of a chair which was hurled at either the President or Sir Pherozeshah. The man picked up another and I snatched it away from him. He was then thrown down by some Gujarati gentlemen. He was a visitor from these provinces. Why did he rush on the platform? I rebuked sharply some C.P. graduates who were rushing towards Sir P. M. Mehta, who was being taken out by the hind entrance. They said, "we have no grievance against you, We want to punish these Parsee rascals." What again is the meaning of Mr. Khaparde rushing to the platform with a thick stick uplifted? Only half an hour previously he had like Mr. Tilak declined to take his seat in the chair reserved for him on the dais. Two Patels from the Akote Taluq who were staying in my quarters received on the 27th at about noon a warning from two men of their caste who lived in the Nationalist camp that day there would be enacted scenes far worse than those of the previous day and advised them either to stay away or to occupy back seats. These gentlemen tried to communicate the warning to me but they could not succeed. A well-known Extremist of these provinces has been taking credit that he sent me word "begging" me to leave the prominent seat I occupied on the platform. The word never reached me and even if it had I would not have left my place. All the same the fact is significant. Then again scan the list of Nagpur delegates and their occupations and literary qualifications. Not that the educated graduates were behind the uneducated rowdies in creating disturbance. But the extraordinary advent of the unruly element leaves little room for doubt that the whole disturbance had been planned, organised and deliberately brought about.

To me it is small comport that hooliganism was shown by Extremists and not by Moderates, and I would not have written a word for publication in regard to these disgraceful performances, but for the monstrous lies that are studiously being circulated by the foolish, misguided sinner and their culpable and designing leaders. Rowdyism and violence are bad enough but to add wicked untruthfulness to it is unfamous. The facts are all plain and lie on the surface and if people would only drive away the cloud of dust which the breakers of the peace purposely raise in order to conceal the real issues, there would be little room for doubt as to where the guilt lies.

The campaign of vilification of the Moderate party was commenced in the first fortnight of January last by Mr. Tilak at Allahabad where the people and especially the young men were exhorted to pull down their leaders and the high ideal was impressed upon them that morality had no place in politics. Mr. Khaparde followed in a few days by a most outragous speech at Nagpur in which the Moderate leaders were called "infamous," "the most debased of human kind," etc., and the fraternity of men who ventured to hold views different from those of the "New School" was questioned. In about 4 weeks more came the meeting at Nagpur for the formation of the working Committee when a respected old C. P. leader of 60 years of age was greeted with a shoe, burning powder was sent in a letter to the President of the meeting, Dr. Gour, and threatening letters were sent to some other prominent men. Simultaneously with this and four months after this, the *Kesari* at Poona and the *Deshasewak* at Nagpur carried on a regular crusade against those members of the Moderate party whose opposition to Mr. Tilak's Presidentship was feared by them. Week after week and month after month men like Mr. Gokhale became the subjects of the foulest calumnies and most wanton perversions of truth. It would be well if the articles in these papers and others of that school are translated word for word so that the whole Indian world might know how low have fallen those from whom much was expected. It is disspiriting to see the literary and moral garbage on which the new generation of Maharashtra is sought to be brought up.

The occurrences of 22nd September at Nagpur (which were the direct offspring of the spirit created and fed by these writings) are well known. The concerted rowdyism within the hall, the pre-arranged hooliganism outside and worse than all the shameless effrontery with which these proceedings are white washed and defended (which are the most distressing developments of the "*New Spirit*") need not be recounted.

Then came the All-India Congress Committee's meeting in which after refusal by Messrs. Tilak and Khaparde to adhere to the compromise which thay had accepted only three or four hours previously, the resolution was arrived at to transfer the venue of the Congress to Surat. And then followed the most vitriolic, venomous and bitter attacks on Sir P. M. Mehta, Mr, Gokhale and the Surat people, the language of which would put to shame even the street brawlers. It deservs to be noted that the *Deshasewak* and other Tilakite papers distinctly used the threat that no efforts would be spared to make a Congress at Surat impossible.

First, a difficulty is sought to be created by dragging in Mr. Lajpat Rai's name against his expressed wishes. Even when he definitely and openly puts his foot down, attempts to prevent Dr. Ghosh from taking the presidential chair is persevered in and carried out. Finding that Mr. Lajpat Rai would not allow himself to be made a catspaw the story is next invented and studiously spread that the Reception Committee wanted to go back on the propositions in regard to Self-Government, Swadeshi, Boycott in Bengal and National Education. On the evening of the 24th I told a number of delegates that there was no valid basis for this assertion and that propositions on the subjects substantially the same in spirit as those of last year would be put before the Subjects Committee. On the 25th at noon when Mr. N. C. Kelkar was at the place where I was putting up, I told him the same thing and begged that scenes and split be avoided. That day in the evening, Mr. Gokhale made a detailed statement to the delegates in the Congress Camp. About 150 attended and he told them the exact wording of the Resolution drafted by him as the draftsman of the Subjects Committee. Mr. R. P. Karandikar of Satara and other friends of Mr. Tilak were present on the occasion. In spite of this conclaves were held in the Nationalist Camp and the resolution arrived at to oppose the election of the President and other obstruction and organise rowdyism at every stage of the proceedings. On the 26th, when thousands were present in the Congress Pandal, Mr. Khare of Nasik went on shouting from block to block that Mr. Tilak had sent word that the election of the President was to be prevented. In the face of all these facts, can there be any doubt left that the rowdyism and voilence carried out had been deliberately planned and organised? It is admitted that before time for proposing the President came, Mr. Talik had in his possession a copy of the draft resolutions containing the ones on "Swaraj," "Swadeshi," "Boycott," and "National Education." And yet the row was made, carried on and persisted in and not the least efforts made to check it. It is sickening to see the ignoble tactics and dishonourable methods adopted by the leaders of the rowdies, and the lies that were invented and busily spread, even after contradiction, so as to create prejudice against the Moderates in general and Mr. Gokhale in particular.

One word and I shall conclude this already too long communication. What is said in the Manifesto issued by the Extremist leaders or by their very "impartial" friend and ally Babu Motilal Ghosh, is sufficient to prove the main charge that these people wanted to impose their will upon the Moderates who formed the majority and if that could not be done to create an uproar and to resort to the use of force. They only acted in obedience to a telegram which had been received from their headquarters at Calcutta : "Blow up if every thing else fails."

AMRAOTI,
January, 1912.

R. N. MUDHOLKAR.

V. BENGAL PROTEST.

After the rowdyism of the first day, the Bengal delegates met at Bose's Bungalow in the evening, when the following Resolution was passed on the motion of Mr. Didnarayan Singh of Bhagalpur:—

"We, the undersigned delegates of United Bengal, deeply regret the unseemly demonstration made at the Congress Pandal to-day, when Babu Surendranath Benerjee was seconding, the resolution proposing the election of the Honourable Dr. Rash Behari Ghosh, and say that we entirely dissociate ourselves from those that were guilty of such demonstration and irregular proceedings."